THE SEVEN AGES
OF THE BRITISH ARMY

THE SEVEN AGES
OF THE BRITISH ARMY

Field Marshal Lord Carver

Weidenfeld and Nicolson
London

It is true that the existence of the Soldier is (after the death penalty) the most painful relic of barbarism that remains among men; but also that nothing is more worthy of the interest and the affection of the Nation than this devoted family which sometimes brings it so much glory.

Alfred de Vigny, *Servitude et Grandeur Militaires* (1835)

George Weidenfeld and Nicolson Ltd
91 Clapham High Street London sw4 7TA

ISBN 0 297 78373 4

Printed in Great Britain by
Butler & Tanner Ltd, Frome and London

CONTENTS

ILLUSTRATIONS

vii

MAPS

ACKNOWLEDGEMENTS

The author wishes to express his thanks to Lord Weidenfeld for suggesting many years ago that he should write a book on this theme; to the staffs of the Prince Consort's Army Library, Aldershot, the Ministry of Defence's Central and Army Library and its Army Historical Branch, for their unfailing help and courtesy, and to Brigadier Ian Mackay, Commandant of the School of Infantry, for providing the information contained in Appendix A.

The author and publishers also wish to thank Michael Barthorp and the National Army Museum for permission to reproduce Appendix B from *The Armies of Britain 1485–1980*; Cassell Ltd, for permission to base the maps on pages 233, 245 and 248 on maps in *History of the Second World War* by Basil Liddell Hart; B.T. Batsford Ltd, for permission to base the map on page 107 on a map in *Wellington* by Michael Glover; and David Higham Ltd, for permission to base the map on page 128 on a map in *The Destruction of Lord Raglan* by Christopher Hibbert.

PREFACE

Britain has a Royal Navy and a Royal Air Force, but no Royal Army. The army consists of a large number of different regiments and corps, into which soldiers are enlisted and to which officers are commissioned and from which they will not normally be transferred to other corps and regiments. Most, but not all, of those corps and regiments enjoy the privilege of the prefix 'Royal' or have some other connection with the Royal Family in their title. The army's tribal organization, which is a source both of strength and weakness, stems from the circumstances of its origin and has its foundation in the struggle between King and Parliament for its control.

I have begun this history of the British army with the age of Cromwell, although purists may complain that the army, as a permanent national institution, did not come into being until 1660 or even 1685. I have started the story with the Civil War, which was fundamentally caused by the struggle between King and Parliament for control of soldiers and what they did, because it was in the armies of the two opposing sides that the form of the future standing army began to take shape.

All armed forces are by nature conservative, although they may cause or take part in revolutions. The British, with their long unbroken historical tradition, are fascinated by the pageantry of the past. It is little wonder, therefore, that the British army is almost obsessed by its traditions. Those who follow its story through the seven ages into which I have divided it will, I believe, be struck by the way in which the forms and attitudes into which the army was crystallized in the age of Marlborough have persisted through all the changes – organizational, technical and tactical – which have been imposed on them up to the age of Templer, the present day. In no sphere is this more true than in the preservation of the regiment, conceived as the basic family within which the soldier lives, fights and, if need be, dies.

The history of an army is, above all, that of its deeds; and the British army, although for most of its history very small, has been a very active one, fighting all over the world. It is the deeds of the past which inspire the soldiers of the present and the future. Most of the book is therefore taken up in describing those deeds, although space has limited the detailed descriptions of battles. I have been at pains to discover and record the strengths of the forces opposing each other in campaigns and battles, and the casualties which they suffered and inflicted. These are the basic factors in the military equation, which I have often found lacking in other histories and which bring a sense of proportion to the account. They seem to me to be of particular importance and interest when the army has been engaged, as it so often has, as part of an alliance. In popular national histories, the part played by allies is often neglected.

While giving action pride of place, I have found space also to describe the army's organization, its methods of recruitment, its weapons, tactics and general way of life, including its pay – or lack of it. I found no difficulty in selecting the general whose name should be given to the age, except in the nineteenth century, which is shared between Wolseley and Roberts, the latter an officer of the Indian Army which bore a large share of the minor campaigns which were a feature of that age. All eight were men of conservative mould, whose pragmatism led them – even Haig – to embrace and develop new methods in the light of their experience on the battlefield.

There are many aspects of the army's history about which the army itself and the nation have no reason to be proud. The combination of parsimony, neglect, indifference and conservatism have at various times, such as in the mid-nineteenth century, reduced it to a low ebb. But, when the challenge has come, both the army and the nation have risen to it, and there is much more in these Seven Ages of which to be justifiably proud than of which to be ashamed. It was a great honour and privilege for me to be, as Chief of the General Staff from 1971 to 1973, the army's professional head. This book has been written to give back to the army, in small part, what it gave to me.

M.C.
January 1984

I
THE AGE OF CROMWELL
1625–1685

Oliver Cromwell was born at Huntingdon in 1599, one of the ten children of Robert, a younger son of Sir Henry Cromwell, whose father had converted the nunnery of Hinchingbrooke into a magnificent mansion. Oliver was the only son to survive. His attendance at Sidney Sussex College at Cambridge, after education at Huntingdon Grammar School, was cut short by the death of his father in 1617, after which he read law at the Inns of Court in London. He returned to Huntingdon on his marriage in 1620, and became its Member of Parliament in 1628, the year of the Petition of Right. In the following year, he was one of those who took part in the protests, led by Sir John Eliot, against King Charles I's alleged sympathy with popery and his use of illegal subsidies that had not been granted by Parliament.

Much of the antagonism between King and Parliament arose out of the former's need for money to finance military expeditions overseas. When he came to the throne in 1625 there was no standing army in England, Scotland or Ireland. The King had to rely for his personal security on a bodyguard of 'Gentlemen Pensioners' and 'Yeomen of the Guard' whose duties were, as they are today, almost wholly ceremonial. If soldiers were needed for the security of the kingdom, recourse had to be made to the so-called 'trained bands' of militia, raised locally by the lords-lieutenant of counties. Trained bands was a misnomer, for trained was the one thing they were not, although those of London, drilled on the artillery ground where their successors, the Honourable Artillery Company, still drill today, were better trained than any other. This militia, as the bands were also called, did not expect to serve outside its own county. If soldiers were required for an expedition overseas, they were raised either by impressment, as the sailors largely were, or from volunteers, most of whom had gained their experience in foreign armies, notably with the French, the Dutch or the Swedes, all of whom maintained professional armies and were superior to England in all things military.

In the reigns of Elizabeth and James I, England had managed to keep herself free of direct involvement in the struggles raging on the Continent, which combined the conflict between Protestant and Catholic with the contest for power between Spain, France and the countries which formed the German Empire. English and Scottish soldiers, both as individuals and in formed bodies, fought in these wars in the service of the major powers – notably the Scots for the Swedes – but they were not British expeditions, financed and controlled from London. The only experienced soldiers in Britain, who could be called professional, were those who had served in this way, men such as Leicester and Sidney with the Dutch and Norreys, Williams and Essex with Henry IV of France. Charles, however, was drawn into the Thirty Years War by his relationship with his brother-in-law, Frederic, the Elector Palatine, who had been defeated at the Battle of the White Mountain in 1620 and forced to yield the imperial crown to Maximilian of Bavaria and take refuge in Holland. Parliament's support of the Protestant cause ensured that the King could not evade his obligations to his relative.

Buckingham's disastrous expedition to the Île de Ré, off La Rochelle on France's west coast, in 1627, following the failure of the one he had organized to Cadiz in 1625, was influential in aggravating relations between King and Parliament, and the nuisance caused by the presence of soldiers returning from the second expedition was reflected in an article of the Petition of Right. This demanded that billeting of soldiers on private citizens should cease and should, instead, be limited to inns, which should be paid for it. It was as he was about to embark for a further expedition, to La Rochelle, that Buckingham was murdered in 1628.

More trouble was caused when, in 1639, Charles raised a force of 15,000 men from the trained bands of the northern counties to suppress the Scottish Covenanters, led by Alexander Leslie, Earl of Leven, who had learnt his trade serving the Swedish King, Gustavus Adolphus, one of the foremost soldiers of the age. The force was lucky not to have to fight in this, the First Bishops' War, for it was far from fit to do so. 'Our men', wrote one who took part, 'are very raw, our arms of all sorts are naught, our victuals scarce, and provisions for horse worse . . . I daresay there was never so raw, so unskilful and so unwilling an army brought to fight'. When, after the recall of Strafford from Ireland (see below, p. 17), the Scots crossed the border in the following year, Charles raised a force from the trained bands of midland and southern counties, who had no heart for the fight. In the previous year, the bands of the north had at least faced their traditional enemies under the command of men they knew. These men were led by courtiers of no experience or by officers who had served abroad and were strangers to them. Many of the men were Puritans, and plunder and mutiny weakened the force before it faced Leven and was routed at Newburn, ending the Second Bishops' War and leaving the Scottish army on English soil at Charles's expense.

Cromwell was active in both the Short and the Long Parliaments which followed these events and culminated in the drawing up of the Grand Remonstrance in May 1641. This was followed at the end of the year by the Militia Bill, designed to deprive the King of command of the militia, which would have to be called up to crush the Irish rebellion, which had broken out in October. It was, therefore, over the question of who should control the army that the First Civil War broke out in January 1642, when Charles, accompanied by his 23-year-old nephew Prince Rupert, son of Frederic, tried to arrest Pym and his four fellow members of the House of Commons. Frustrated, the King left London for York, while Parliament claimed control of the militia, relying initially on the London trained bands.

Both sides spent the spring and summer of 1642 raising troops. Both had to improvise an army from men without any real training, although each had a nucleus of professional officers and soldiers on which to draw. On the Royalist side, Astley had served with Gustavus Adolphus, Hopton with Frederic of Bohemia, Prince Rupert and Goring with the Dutch, and Gage with the Spanish. Of the Parliamentary leaders, Fairfax, Skippon and Balfour had served with the Dutch, and Crawford, Ramsay and many other Scots with the Swedes. Monck, who fought initially for the King and later for Cromwell, had served with the Dutch. To fill the ranks, both sides called on the trained bands in counties where they had influence, the King using Commissioners of Array and Parliament its Militia Ordinance. Early objectives were the county magazines where powder and arms of the trained bands were stored. Cromwell's troop seized that of Cambridge in August. Charles used the trained bands of Yorkshire to lay siege to Hull in July and Hopton those of Cornwall to drive the Parliamentary commissioners out of the county but they would not follow him into Devon, any more than the Yorkshire trained bands would follow Charles to Edgehill. Faced with the refusal of many of the militia to leave their counties, particularly at harvest time, Charles was forced to turn to another method: disarming the trained bands and using their weapons to arm volunteers. Wherever possible this was done by persuasion. Parliament was not much more successful than the King with the trained bands, except those of London which were better trained and by 1643 were formed into 15 regiments, totalling 18,000 men. As late as the summer of 1644 the trained bands of Essex and Hertfordshire which, under the command of Major-General Brown, joined Sir William Waller, were described by the latter as 'so mutinous and uncommandable that there is no hope of their stay. They were like to have killed the Major-General and they hurt him in the face. Such men are only fit for the gallows here and hell hereafter.'

The trained bands having proved a broken reed, both sides had recourse to volunteers of which, at the start, there was no shortage. The method used by both sides was to appeal to 'gentlemen' to raise money, men and horses. The King relied on his supporters to equip the forces they raised, mostly from their own districts, at their own expense; Lord Paget, for instance, raised a regiment in Staffordshire and the Earl of Northampton raised one in North Oxfordshire, Oxford itself being a rich source of volunteers to the Royalist cause. However, there was no provision for wastage by casualty or any other cause, and, as time went by, the King kept up his numbers by granting more and more commissions to his supporters to raise troops of horse, companies or regiments from volunteers or by impressment, with the result that he had a large number of small poorly manned units.

Parliament was able to offer better terms. At first it also appealed for contributions at the expense of the contributor, although it promised to pay interest at 8 per cent of the value. Thereafter, like the King, it issued commissions to officers to raise regiments, those of foot being normally of 1,200 men and of horse 500. In the case of the latter, it paid 'mounting money' of £1,100 to any captain who undertook to raise a troop, the captain receiving £140 to equip himself, the lieutenant £60, the cornet £50, the quartermaster £30, and each NCO and trooper £5. The pay of the soldiers proved a constant problem to both sides, the question of arrears of pay dogging the army throughout the period and becoming one of the principal sources of difference between it and Parliament, with all the consequences that arose from that.

4

Cromwell was one of the 80 captains authorized to raise a troop of horse. He chose his men with care, rejecting drink-sodden veterans of foreign wars, and limiting his recruitment to sober, God-fearing Puritans like himself. He was reinforced in his confidence that this was the right policy by his experience in battle. After Edgehill, he said to his cousin Hampden:

Your troopers are most of them old decayed servingmen and tapsters and such kind of fellows; and their [the Royalists'] troopers are gentlemen's sons, younger sons and persons of quality; do you think that the spirits of such base and mean fellows will be ever able to encounter gentlemen that have honour and courage and resolution in them? You must get men of a spirit that is likely to go on as far as gentlemen will go, or else I am sure you will be beaten still.

By August 1642, having appointed Prince Rupert as his Lieutenant-General in command of the horse, Charles felt strong enough to raise his standard at Nottingham. He himself acted as Captain-General of the Royalist army. The Captain-General of the Parliamentary army was the Earl of Essex, son of Queen Elizabeth's favourite. He was at Northampton with 20,000 men, and the King decided to move further west and raise more men before attempting to march on London. Essex moved parallel to him. In October, Charles set off from Shrewsbury for London. Essex was at Worcester and moved south-east to intercept him, but was out-manoeuvred and on 22 October, when he was at Kineton, ten miles south of Warwick, Charles was at Edgecott about four miles to the south-east.

Charles could have continued south but, on the advice of Prince Rupert, he decided to give battle on the steep north-facing ridge at Edgehill next day. Essex moved forward slowly and drew up his line two miles north of the ridge astride a small stream. The two sides were almost equal, each with about 10,000 foot and 2,500 horse although the Royalists also had about 1,000 dragoons. Both were drawn up with the horse on either side of the foot. It was after midday before Essex had assembled his men, and the prospect of assaulting the ridge must have appeared daunting. However the Royalists, apparently eager for battle, came down from their commanding position and drew up a few hundred yards from Essex. Meanwhile a quarrel broke out between the Earl of Lindsay and Prince Rupert over whether the foot should be several ranks deep, on the Dutch model, or in the Swedish formation of only three, as Rupert favoured. After an ineffective artillery duel while the

5

NORTH SEA

IRISH SEA

- Inveraray
Perth
- Glasgow
Edinburgh • ✕ **Dunbar**
• Berwick
Philiphaugh ✕
- Londonderry
• Carlisle • Newcastle
Belfast •
Dundalk •
Drogheda ✕ **Marston Moor** ✕ • York
Trim • ✕ **Preston** Hull •
Dublin •
• Chester
• Newark
Wexford ✕
Waterford • • Shrewsbury
Cork • • Leicester
Worcester • ✕ **Naseby**
Tenby • • Cambridge
Pembroke • Gloucester • ✕ **Edgehill** • Saffron Walden
Chepstow • • Oxford
Bristol • **Newbury** London
Langport ✕ ✕
• Salisbury
Lostwithiel ✕ Plymouth Dover •

The battles of the English Civil War

Royalist dragoons cleared the bridges on the flanks of the battlefield, Prince Rupert charged on the right and quickly overwhelmed the Parliamentary cavalry, on the left of their line under Ramsay, as well as four regiments of their foot. Nothing could stop them and they carried on all the way to Kineton. Sir Jacob Astley led the Royalist foot across the stream to attack the centre, but when they came to 'push of pike', they do not seem to have pressed hard and both sides stood and fired at each other until darkness fell. On the left of their line, the other division of Royalist horse under Wilmot at first looked as if they also would carry all before them, but two successful counter-attacks by the Roundhead cavalry threw them back and at one stage captured the King's standard. Cromwell, who appears to have arrived late on the battlefield, probably took part in this action. By this time it was nearly dark, ammunition was running short and Prince Rupert and his horse returned to the battlefield. The two sides drew apart, and on the following day Essex withdrew to Warwick, leaving seven of his guns and many of his colours in Royalist hands.

Charles continued on his way to London and actually reached Turnham Green. But, faced by the London trained bands, he withdrew to Oxford, which remained his headquarters for the next three years, during which his army was never to get so close to the capital again. In 1643 the Royalists attempted to converge on London from three directions, the north, the west and from Oxford. The Earl of Newcastle was initially successful in the north, and confined Lord Fairfax and his son, Sir Thomas, in Hull; but when he moved south to Lincolnshire he came face to face with Cromwell, now a colonel. He had expanded his original troop of horse into a regiment numbering 1,000 men; this was to be the foundation of the 'Eastern Association' of similar regiments from East Anglia and became the basis of the 'New Model Army'. On 13 May, leading his regiment 'at a pretty round trot', Cromwell dispersed and routed a Royalist force of almost double his numbers at Grantham, and went on to relieve the sieges of Gainsborough and Hull. On 10 October, at Winceby, near Boston, he and Fairfax defeated another Royalist force in half an hour, although his horse was killed under him as he led the charge which brought the battle to an end. The Royalist thrust from the west was no more successful. Sir Ralph Hopton led his men of Cornwall and Devon as far as Devizes in Wiltshire, but the Parliamentary stronghold of Plymouth held out, supplied by sea from London, and Hopton's force turned back.

The thrust planned with the forces from Oxford followed the same pattern. A few skirmishes took place in the direction of London, in one of which, near Thame, John Hampden was mortally wounded. The city of Gloucester, in his rear, worried Charles, and he decided to lay siege to it. Essex marched from London and successfully relieved it, but on his return journey was intercepted by Charles at Newbury on 20 September. The King had reached the town the night before with about 12,000 men. Essex appears to have had about the same number, but was much weaker in cavalry. He was west of the town, south of the River Kennet, and the battle which followed consisted of attempts by each side to secure the high ground about a mile south of the western edge of the town, mostly by the action of horse assisted by artillery. The usual confrontation of two lines of foot does not seem to have taken place. The action went on until the Royalists began to run out of ammunition. When further supplies failed to arrive from Oxford, the King decided not to run the risk of facing Essex on the 21st and withdrew to Oxford, leaving the road to London free for a very much relieved Essex. The King's decision was one of the most fateful and ill-advised of the whole war.

In spite of the failure of the Royalists to implement their plan to reach London or to subdue Hull, Plymouth and Gloucester, their position at the end of 1643 was satisfactory – they held almost all of England, apart from East Anglia and the Home Counties – but 1644 was to see a bitter turn in their fortunes. Pym, who died shortly afterwards, had negotiated with the Scottish Covenanters that they should send an army of 20,000 men against the King in return for Parliament accepting 'the Solemn League and Covenant', agreeing that the Presbyterian church should be established in England. In January 1644, the Scots under Leven came south and combined with the forces of the Fairfaxes, father and son, to surround Newcastle's 5,000 horse and 6,000 foot at York. Rupert moved north with 14,000 to relieve him, fighting a successful battle at Newark on the way and joining with Goring, whose force of horse had escaped from York. Cromwell and Manchester also moved north from Lincolnshire to join Fairfax and Leven. The two armies met at Marston Moor late on 2 July and drew up facing each other on either side of a ditch about 500 yards north of the road between Long Marston and Tockwith. For the Royalists, Newcastle was in the centre with the foot, Rupert's horse was on the right and Goring's on the left. Facing them, from left to right, were Cromwell's horse, Manchester's, Fairfax's and the Scottish foot, with Sir Thomas Fairfax's horse on the right. Cromwell was, therefore, facing Rupert.

By 7 p.m. nothing had happened, and the Royalists decided that there would be no battle that day. Rupert went off for a meal and ordered food to come up from York for his soldiers, while Newcastle retired to his coach for a smoke. Suddenly the whole Roundhead line advanced, the principal action taking place on the eastern flank where Sir Thomas Fairfax's horse closed with Goring's. Fairfax's had been broken up as they crossed the ditch and found themselves among gorse-bushes. Goring counter-attacked and was brilliantly successful, routing not only the young Fairfax's horse, but much of the foot as well, except for some stubborn Scots who stood firm. Cromwell on the left was more successful – Rupert was still absent from the field and Byron was commanding the horse. However, Cromwell himself now left the field with a wound in his neck and David Leslie took over command of his horse. After a fierce struggle, Leslie and Manchester began to push the Royalist right flank round, and at about 8.30, as it was getting dark, Cromwell rejoined the battle and drew up his horse in line with Manchester, leaving Leslie to pursue the fleeing Royalist horse. Most of the generals seem to have left the battlefield by this time. The Scots were still holding out against repeated attacks by Goring, and it was at this stage that young Fairfax, who had been wounded, removing his 'field sign', made his way through the confused battlefield to Cromwell and persuaded him to move round Goring's rear and attack him, in order to relieve the Scots. This he did by moonlight, the whole battle having turned a full circle, and put Goring's horse to flight. The only part of the Royalist line left intact was Newcastle's own Whitecoat regiment. They were surrounded by the Roundhead foot and horse and, refusing to surrender, were shot to pieces; only 30–40 men survived. The total casualties were 4,000, and 1,500 were captured. Rupert managed to collect 6,000 horse together at York next day, but Newcastle, his infantry totally destroyed, gave up in despair and sailed to Hamburg. The north was lost to the King and Rupert made his way to Bristol by a roundabout route through Chester.

In spite of these losses the Royalists could count some successes to their credit. Montrose, who had served as Leven's commander of horse in both the Bishops' Wars, had now thrown in his lot with Charles and been appointed his Captain-General in Scotland, where the Covenanters had joined the Roundheads. Evading the Covenanters, he joined

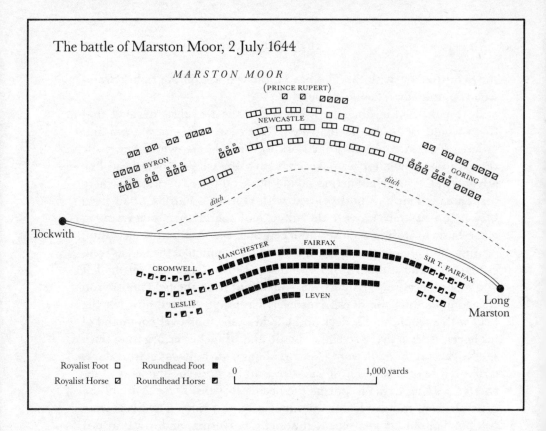

The battle of Marston Moor, 2 July 1644

MARSTON MOOR

(PRINCE RUPERT)

NEWCASTLE

BYRON

GORING

ditch

ditch

Tockwith

MANCHESTER   FAIRFAX

CROMWELL

SIR T. FAIRFAX

LESLIE   LEVEN

Long Marston

Royalist Foot ☐   Roundhead Foot ■
Royalist Horse ☒   Roundhead Horse ◪

0   1,000 yards

up with a force of Royalists from Ireland and with his own small force of Highlanders defeated the Covenanters, captured Perth and Aberdeen and succeeded in dominating the Highlands.

In the west of England a Royalist army, led by Charles himself, surrounded and defeated Essex at Lostwithiel in Cornwall. Essex had to escape by sea and most of his army surrendered. Clearly he could not continue as General of the Parliamentary armies, and the stage was set for Cromwell and his New Model.

The Parliamentary armies were suffering from the same ailment as the Royalists': to compensate for wastage, they had commissioned more and more gentlemen, many of them members of both Houses of Parliament, to raise regiments. By this time they had too few men in too many units, indifferently led, disciplined and trained. The first step was to get the command sorted out: this the Self-Denying Ordinance of December 1644 set out to do, calling on all Members of Parliament to lay down their commands. It had been instigated by Cromwell, principally as a means of getting rid of the weak-willed Earl of Manchester. As a member of the House of Commons, Cromwell himself should have resigned and indeed offered to do so, but the activities of the Royalists, notably Goring at Bristol, and later the need to prevent the King's forces at Oxford joining the Royalists in the West Midlands, kept him in the field as commander of the horse, first to Waller and then to Fairfax.

During these months the New Model Army was being formed from the remnants of the armies of Essex, Manchester and Waller, together with the Eastern Association and the men raised from London and the Home Counties. The target for Fairfax's army was set at 14,400 foot and it was necessary to raise about half their number by impressment, each county being given a quota to raise. However, they fell far short of the target, and Fairfax complained in June that he only had half the number of foot he should have.

Although, in the Second Civil War, the New Model was to absorb all the Parliamentary forces, at this stage it was outnumbered by others, notably the Scots under Leven with 21,000. Major-General Poyntz had an army of 10,000 men in the northern counties, Major-General Massey in the west probably as many, and there were forces in Wales, in the Midlands under Major-General Brown and in the east. Without the Scots, Parliament probably had over 60,000 men in all. Failure to pay them regularly had been one of the main causes of discontent and of desertion, of which Fairfax complained. The New Model Army was not only to be better trained and disciplined but Parliament had promised to pay it regularly. In the early years this word was kept and complaints of desertion faded away after a few months.

As the summer of 1645 advanced, the Parliamentary body which controlled the war, the 'Committee of Both Kingdoms', waited anxiously to see what Charles would do, particularly concerned lest he should move north and join with Montrose, but apparently equally worried that he might make another attempt to reach London. Fairfax shadowed the Royalist army as it moved between Oxford and the Midlands, anxious that Cromwell, further east, should join forces with him. The Committee was worried about the danger to the eastern counties if Cromwell moved too far north or west, and in May recalled him from Warwick just as Sir William Brereton had prepared a means of surrounding the Royalists by a concentration of the Scots, Cromwell and Fairfax.

It was Charles himself who provided the opportunity for an encounter in June after the Royalist capture and sack of Leicester, an ugly event which spurred the Committee into a more aggressive strategy. Charles wanted action, if only to bring his rival commanders of horse, Prince Rupert and Goring, to heel. The Royalists were on their way to Newark when the combined forces of Fairfax and Cromwell caught up with and surprised them south of Market Harborough. Faced with the alternatives of fleeing north or turning to fight, Charles chose the latter, and early in the morning of 14 June Prince Rupert with only 9,000 men, half of which were horse, faced Fairfax with 14,000, of whom 6,500 were horse under Cromwell.

Fairfax came up to look at a position from which they could be engaged, but Cromwell objected to it as the intervening ground was too boggy for cavalry and he feared that Rupert would not therefore attack them, but try an out-flanking movement. Fairfax agreed to move back to a ridge four miles to the south, two miles north of the village of Naseby. This was the first Rupert saw of the enemy and he decided to move forward, at the same time edging westwards to get the wind behind him. The two sides finally faced each other between two gentle ridges, the southern being the one chosen by Fairfax. His foot under Skippon was in the centre, at the last moment withdrawn slightly behind the rest. The horse on the left was under Ireton, just promoted Commissary-General of Horse and soon to become Cromwell's son-in-law. Lining the hedges forward of his position and facing east were Okey's dragoons. On the right, Cromwell, with his own and Whalley's horse, was higher up and slightly behind Skippon's right flank. The faithful Astley commanded the Royalist foot facing Skippon, with Rupert's horse on the right facing Ireton and Langdale's horse on the left. Charles, with a reserve of 900 horse and 700 foot, was behind the left centre of the line.

The action seems to have been begun with an attack across the valley by Astley's foot, while Rupert launched his attack east of the hedges lined by Okey's dragoons to coincide with the moment of contact. As usual his charge carried him through, disorganizing Skippon's left and then Ireton's right. Ireton himself was wounded and captured for a time. They charged on and came to the Roundhead baggage-train; but this was stoutly defended.

Langdale had not been successful and, as he charged up the slope, caught in bushes and rabbit warrens, he was put to flight by Whalley. Meanwhile things were not going well in the Roundhead centre, where Skippon had been wounded. But at this moment, egged on by the bare-headed Fairfax, Cromwell's well-disciplined horse came steadily in on the Royalist left flank, while Ireton recovered and came in on their right, supported by Okey's dragoons, now mounted and acting as horse. Charles ordered his reserve to intervene, but due either to the intervention of the Earl of Carnworth or to a misunderstanding of orders, they turned about and made off. Astley's foot was now totally surrounded and when Rupert returned from his sortie to the Round-head baggage-train he decided that it was too late to try and save them. When their ammunition ran out, they surrendered; the total Royalist casualties amounted to 4,000. Rupert and the King made off north while Cromwell pressed the pursuit to the gates of Leicester.

Naseby decided the outcome of the First Civil War: the rest was mopping up. Fairfax disposed of Goring at Langport in Somerset in July, and Montrose was surrounded and totally defeated by David Leslie at Philiphaugh near Selkirk in September. The war dragged on in a series of sieges of isolated Royalist garrisons until the middle of June 1646, until Charles, who left Oxford in May, surrendered to the Scots at Newark. In return for £400,000 to cover their expenses, they handed him over to Parliament, which incarcerated him at Hampton Court.

Parliament, flushed with victory, now made two serious mistakes in its handling of the army. First of all, in accordance with the Solemn League and Covenant with the Scots and relying on a Presbyterian majority in the House of Commons, it passed a bill to establish the Presbyterian church in England, in the process suppressing the Independents, Baptists and others who formed a large proportion of the New Model Army, particularly that part derived from the Eastern Association. Not content with this blow at the morale of many of its soldiers, it also decided to disband the army without arrears of pay, which by this time amounted to 18 weeks for the foot and 43 for the horse and dragoons, totalling about £300,000. The solution to the problem of the Independents was to form them into an army for Ireland, where the Earl of Ormonde, appointed Lord-Lieutenant by the King, had done his best to keep Catholics and Protestants at peace with each other since he had been forced to sign a truce with the rebels in 1643 in order that his troops, among them General Monck, could be withdrawn to England to serve against Parliament. In February 1647 he resigned his Lord-Lieutenancy and Parliament found itself fairly and squarely responsible for Ireland. In March, Fairfax was told that none of his soldiers must come within 25 miles of London, and many of them were

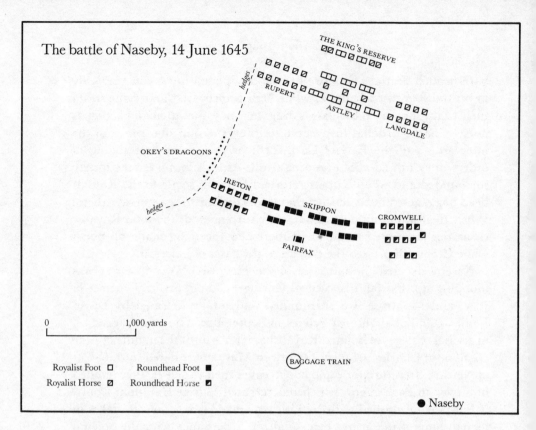

The battle of Naseby, 14 June 1645

THE KING'S RESERVE

hedges

RUPERT

ASTLEY

LANGDALE

OKEY'S DRAGOONS

IRETON

hedges

SKIPPON

CROMWELL

FAIRFAX

0   1,000 yards

Royalist Foot ☐   Roundhead Foot ■
Royalist Horse ▨   Roundhead Horse ▨

BAGGAGE TRAIN

● Naseby

concentrated at Saffron Walden where it was proposed to form the force for Ireland. When commissioners from Parliament went there to discuss their problems with the officers, they were presented with a petition asking a number of awkward questions about future pay, arrears and indemnity for past services. To this was added a petition from the lower ranks, covering arrears of pay, exemptions from impressment, indemnities and compensation for widows.

This led to a prolonged period of negotiation between Parliament and the army, in which Cromwell, who had been personally rewarded with lands worth £2,500 a year, took a leading part. To the dissatisfaction over conditions of service was added the disagreement between the Presbyterians, led by Denzil Holles, and the Independents, each suspecting the other of trying to make use of the King, who was himself intriguing with the Scots, as were the Presbyterians. The army's patience with Parliament wore thin, and in 1647, led by Fairfax and Cromwell, it moved on London and forced the withdrawal from Parliament of eleven of the leading Presbyterians.

The months following this victory for the army were spent in attempts by Cromwell and his son-in-law, Ireton, to come to an agreement with the King. But, at the same time, the 'Agitators' or 'Levellers' in the army reacted strongly against this, and in a series of extraordinary conferences in St Mary's Church at Putney, where the army's head-quarters was established, they argued for such things as universal suffrage, a general rendezvous of the whole army and no further dealings with the King. These discussions were still going on in November when, breaking his parole, Charles escaped from Hampton Court and threw himself on the mercy of Colonel Robert Hammond, Governor of the Isle of Wight, at Carisbrooke Castle. Hammond, who was in fact a cousin of Cromwell's, was horrified, treated him as a prisoner and reported his arrival to Parliament. Whether or not, as has been alleged, Cromwell connived at or even suggested this turn in events, he welcomed it as it removed the danger of the King falling into the hands of the Levellers and made it possible for Cromwell to align himself more closely with those in the army who wanted nothing to do with the King.

Charles's intrigues with the Scots continued, and one reaction to the weakness of Parliament in the face of the army was a resurgence of support for the Royalists. Cromwell was still arguing for some sort of return to the monarchy when, on 30 April 1648, the Royalists, helped by the Scots, seized Berwick and Carlisle, and a Royalist uprising in Wales coincided with one of disbanded and discontented ex-Parliamentary soldiers. Cromwell went off there, while Lambert went north and Waller to Cornwall. The Second Civil War had started.

Cromwell quickly subdued the castles of Chepstow and Tenby and controlled almost all of South Wales, but found no way to deal with the formidable Pembroke Castle other than the old-fashioned one of starving its garrison into surrender. This occurred on 11 July, three days after an 11,000-strong Scottish army, led by the Duke of Hamilton, crossed the border. It was not, however, of the calibre of the army that, led by the two Leslies, had taken part in the First Civil War and fought at Marston Moor. It was ill-equipped, its soldiers were inexperienced, its administration was non-existent and its leadership of doubtful ability. The Leslies and the more extreme Covenanters held themselves aloof, disapproving of an agreement with Charles which did not insist on him signing the Covenant. Even the weather, one of the wettest Julys on record, was against them.

Cromwell pressed his weary army northwards to join Lambert in Yorkshire and made contact with him on 12 August. By this time Hamilton was near Lancaster and Cromwell made the surprising decision to cross the Pennines and attack him. Cromwell, with 8,600 men, would face an army now of 21,000 (or 19,000 if Monro, who had been left at Kirkby Lonsdale, failed to join the main body before Cromwell reached them). Cromwell made another bold decision when he chose to come in to the north of Hamilton, now near Preston, and attack him from the rear. The Scots were surprised, and on the morning of 17 August Cromwell caught Hamilton in the act of crossing the Ribble with his cavalry sent on further south towards Wigan.

Of Cromwell's 8,600 men, 3,000 were horse. Hamilton himself had 14,000, his rearguard under Langdale another 3,000 foot and 600 horse. Further north there were 4,500 more. In spite of reports from Langdale in the morning of Cromwell's presence, Hamilton continued to pass his troops across the Ribble. The action started with skirmishes in muddy lanes on the edge of Ribbleton Moor and it was not until four in the afternoon that Cromwell was able to make an organized attack. It was not a neat well-drawn-up affair, but a shifting struggle of horse and foot combined. For four hours Langdale fought a gallant rearguard action, but was forced back into Preston, and a fierce struggle ensued which ended in the capture of the bridge by Cromwell's men, whom he drove on with great determination, while Hamilton kept changing his mind about sending his Scots back across the river from his position on Preston Moor – all this in darkness and rain after an exhausting march at speed across the Pennines. From then on, it became a pursuit all the way south into Cheshire, Hamilton finally surrendering at Uttoxeter.

While Cromwell was trouncing Hamilton at Preston, Fairfax had been subduing the Royalists at Colchester. After his victory, Cromwell returned to Yorkshire and headed north to recover Berwick and Carlisle, but the 'Engagers', as Hamilton and his sympathizers were called, were by this time out of favour and Scotland was in the hands of the hard-line Covenanters led by Argyll. Cromwell quickly came to terms with him and was welcomed in Edinburgh on 4 October 1648. Scottish intervention on behalf of Charles I was over. Having reported this to Parliament, Cromwell returned to Yorkshire to subdue the Royalist stronghold of Pontefract.

In his absence, the influence of the Levellers led to 'Pride's Purge' of Parliament, leaving only the 'Rump' of 100 members, and the decision to put the King on trial. The latter decision was taken by the Army Council on Christmas Day, Cromwell having joined the ranks of those determined on his execution. It took place, after the farce of his trial, on 30 January 1649, by which time the Rump had dwindled to 56, the Presbyterians having been purged and the Royalists abstaining. In February, the House of Lords was abolished and government lay in the hands of a Council of State of 41, 30 of whom were members of the Rump. In reality the army was in control. But who was in control of the army? Fairfax was still the General and Cromwell Lieutenant-General; but it seemed at times that the Leveller element, of which John Lilburne was the leader and Major Harrison one of the most outspoken and influential, held sway. Fairfax was to remain Commander-in-Chief of the army in England and Wales until 26 June 1650, when Cromwell assumed this post on his return from Ireland, of which he also remained nominally Commander-in-Chief, as he did of Scotland after the 1651 campaign, although Monck exercised actual command there.

Ireland had been a constant source of trouble. From 1634 until Charles had recalled him in 1641, Strafford (Sir Thomas Wentworth – 'Black Tom Tyrant') had kept the native Catholic Irish subdued by a policy of brutal repression. Their reaction to his departure was to turn on the Protestant settlers of Ulster, whom James I had imported from Scotland. They killed 4,000–5,000 of them and reduced many others to starvation. Wentworth's replacement as Lord-Lieutenant, the Earl of Ormonde, had been forced to come to terms with the rebels in 1643, when most of his soldiers, including Major-General Monck, had been withdrawn to fight for the King in the Civil War. Monck was captured by Fairfax in 1644 and consigned to the Tower, where he wrote his *Observations on Military and Political Affairs*, the equivalent of the twentieth century's *Field Service Regulations for the Army*. He also met there his future wife, Nan Clargess, who was his laundress. In 1646 he agreed to serve the Parliamentary army in Ireland under Lisle, and crossed over in 1647 to take command of the troops in Ulster fighting against Owen Roe O'Neill, relying largely on the support of a Scottish contingent. However, the King's execution changed the situation. The Scots changed sides, and both the Catholic and the Anglo-Irish Protestant landowners joined together under Ormonde in opposition to the Puritan Government of the Rump. Monck found himself in the same position as Ormonde in 1643, and came to an agreement with O'Neill, for which he was severely criticized. He was withdrawn to England, deprived of his regiment and retired to his estate in Devon.

In 1649, Cromwell was entrusted by the Council of State with the task of dealing with the rebels, and, after a great deal of trouble, he finally got his army together and landed near Dublin on 15 August, two weeks after the local commander, Colonel James, with only 5,000 men, had inflicted a severe defeat on Ormonde's 19,000, not far from the city. Cromwell arrived in confident mood, eager for action in a campaign intended to satisfy the Puritans' desire to impose their religion and take revenge on the Catholic natives for the horrors of 1641, and also to gain national benefits from extending the sort of colonization which had already been established in Ulster and in the Pale.

Ormonde had withdrawn northwards and the key position was clearly Drogheda on the Boyne, held by Sir Arthur Aston with 2,000 men (Ormonde having withdrawn further north). On 10 September Cromwell called on him to surrender, which he refused to do, thus, by the usage of war of the time, putting the lives of the civilian population, as well as those of the garrison, at risk. On the following day the assault took place and prevailed, the garrison fighting back fiercely. As so often happens in these circumstances, there were misunderstandings over negotiations to surrender in which both sides accused the other of failing to observe the conditions.

There is no doubt that Cromwell was in furious mood and showed no mercy. The death toll of Irish was between two and four thousand, and Cromwell's reputation in Ireland thereafter was to be blacker than that of any other Englishman who had set foot there. Dundalk and Trim were quickly dealt with, while Colonel Venables and Sir Charles Coote dealt with County Down and Antrim respectively. Cromwell then turned south to Wexford where the garrison commander, Colonel Sinnott, had been reinforced by Lord Castlehaven with 1,500 horse. Before he could lay siege to it, it was betrayed to him by a Captain Stafford. In spite of this, Cromwell's soldiers put the garrison to the sword and Cromwell himself estimated that 2,000 were killed. There is good evidence that 1,500 civilians also lost their lives. In this case there was no justification of a refusal to surrender to excuse the massacre. Cromwell continued on to Ross, Waterford and Cork. He spent the winter and spring subduing one rebel castle after another, until he was recalled to

England in May 1650 to deal with the serious situation that had arisen in Scotland.

Any hope that the young future Charles II might have had of basing support for his return on Ireland had clearly vanished, nor was there any realistic prospect of doing so with the support only of the Scottish Royalists under Montrose. It was only by allying himself with the Presbyterians, the Covenanters, that he could return. Sacrificing the gallant Montrose, Charles swore to uphold the Covenant and landed in Scotland on 10 June 1650. This was a serious threat to the Rump and to the Army Council. There was some argument as to who should lead an expedition to meet Charles's force, for which it was hoped to raise an army of 25,000 men. Fairfax was still officially Commander-in-Chief, but was not prepared to take command and was, indeed, opposed to the project. Cromwell was therefore the obvious choice and the command of troops in England in his absence was given to the Puritan, Thomas Harrison. Cromwell left London at the end of June and was at Newcastle by 10 July. The army assembled here consisted of 16,000 men, eight regiments each of horse and foot, one which was commanded by George Monck, summoned by Cromwell, not without protest from many of the hard-liners, from his retirement in Devon. His regiment was formed from five companies of Fenwick's regiment from Berwick and five from Hesilrege's from Newcastle and took its name from the town of Coldstream on the Tweed; it became one of the foundation pillars of the future regular army.

The Scots army, commanded by David Leslie, had 18,000 foot and 8,000 horse and the campaign opened with some indecisive manoeuvring round Edinburgh. The weather was wet and Cromwell's army, without tents, began to suffer severely from sickness. This and the fear of being cut off by Leslie's superior army, although he could always be supplied by sea, led to Cromwell's withdrawal southwards. Leslie moved to intercept him and by 2 September had got across the coast road south of Cromwell at Dunbar. Cromwell was in a serious position: he was outnumbered, the coast road was blocked and the enemy, in strength, was on the hills above it.

Crises brought the best out in Cromwell, and made him decisive and bold. In this, he had an advantage over Leslie, who was burdened with a political committee attached to his headquarters. Whether it was on their advice or by his own choice, Leslie made the mistake of over-insuring and moved the bulk of his force into a narrow front between the road and the coast itself. Cromwell, Lambert and Monck all claim credit for realizing that this opened up an opportunity for a bold attack. Monck is quoted as saying 'Sir, the Scots have numbers and the hills: these are their advantages. We have discipline and despair, two things that will make soldiers fight: these are ours. My advice therefore is to attack them immediately, which if you follow, I am ready to command the van.' It was a wet and stormy night and no easy task to make all the preliminary dispositions, if they were to be in position to cross the Broxburn and deliver a fierce concentrated attack on the left centre of the Scots, who were taken by surprise. At the crucial moment Cromwell sent in his own regiment of horse to exploit it. It was a quick and total victory, the Scots suffering 3,000 killed and 10,000 taken prisoner, and settled the campaign at one blow. Cromwell was in Edinburgh four days later, although the castle itself did not finally surrender until Christmas Eve.

The spring of 1651 found Cromwell an invalid, and it was not until June that operations to clear more of Scotland of Charles's supporters got under way, Stirling remaining their main stronghold. While Cromwell and Lambert moved northwards and were about to besiege Perth, Charles II and Leslie decided to move south into England by the west coast, and at Carlisle on 6 August Charles proclaimed himself King of England. Cromwell's reaction was swift. By 9 August Lambert with the horse was at Penrith and Harrison joined him from the south five days later, while Fleetwood prepared to defend London. Charles II did not find the enthusiasm for his cause that he had expected. The people were tired of war and they had no love for the Scots. By the time he had reached Worcester on 22 August his army was 16,000 strong. Meanwhile Cromwell pushed his men on by forced marches down the east coast, the daily march averaging double the normal at twenty miles a day, a pace which brought its own casualties. He passed Catterick on 16 August; by the time Charles had reached Worcester, he was at Mansfield, and on 27 August was at Stratford-on-Avon. From here he joined forces with Fleetwood at Evesham, their two armies together totalling 28,000 men, to which 3,000 of the local militia were added. With this two-to-one superiority Cromwell was in no hurry, and appears deliberately to have postponed his attack on Charles, surrounded in Worcester, until it could coincide with the anniversary of Dunbar, 3 September. Some of the delay was also due to the need to assemble enough boats to build bridges over both the Severn and the Teme.

The attack started at dawn and the whole morning was taken up in Fleetwood's crossing of the river. The battle began in earnest in the afternoon and fighting was fierce before it finally ended with Charles's largely Scottish army pinned helplessly inside the narrow streets of the city. Two thousand were killed and over 8,000 prisoners taken, including Leslie himself, while Cromwell's casualties were very light. Four thousand Scots escaped, as Charles also did, his adventures in doing so being well known.

After Worcester, the spotlight turned off the army and switched to the navy which, under Blake, was at war with the Dutch from 1652 to 1654 as a result of the passage of the Navigation Act in 1651. Monck, who had been left in Scotland to subdue and govern it, was made a 'general-at-sea' and did much to tighten up the navy's extremely loose discipline and at the same time improve the sailor's conditions of service, which were appalling. 'Honest' George Monck's reputation was always that of a highly professional officer who combined strict discipline and training with sympathetic concern for the welfare of his men and of their dependants. Monck returned to Scotland as Commander-in-Chief of the Commonwealth Army there in 1653 with very wide powers 'for the beating down and suppression of the rebellion within the said nation, and for the settling and maintaining of the public peace there'. The Scots were now fighting not so much to support the Royalist cause as to oppose the Commonwealth's proposal to unite the two countries and to suppress the Presbyterian church and its general assembly. Monck, with Morgan as his second-in-command, carried out a brilliant campaign in the Highlands, defeating John Middleton by a process of swift moves based on meticulous forward planning in the fields of intelligence and logistic support, making much use of dragoons. He drove his soldiers hard, but did not impose tiresome Puritan rules of behaviour on them, and treated the defeated Scots with generosity and understanding. The combination of respect and sympathy from both his soldiers and the Scots themselves was to provide Monck with the essential base of strength from which to play the vital part he did in the Restoration.

Monck's campaign in Scotland brought fighting in Britain to an end, but the country was still officially at war with Spain. Apart from an ill-fated expedition to the West Indies in 1652, hostilities had been limited to actions at sea. Money for them was hard to come by; but France was also at war with Spain, and, in spite of the religious differences between the two countries, in 1657 a treaty was signed with Louis xiv by which England would join France in attacking the Spanish Netherlands. An army of 6,000 men under Major-General Morgan was raised to serve under the command of the great French general Turenne, and their prize was the capture of Dunkirk after the Battle of the Dunes in 1658. The town became an English possession and most of Morgan's army remained there as a garrison. Charles ii was himself at this time in the Netherlands with a body of Royalist troops, serving with those of the Dutch Republic.

In 1658, on the anniversary of the Battle of Dunbar, 3 September, Oliver Cromwell died, to be succeeded as Protector by his weak son Richard. A struggle for power within the army and between the army and Parliament began immediately. It came to a head in April 1659 when, at a meeting of the Army Council, Fleetwood, Lambert and Desborough decided to petition Parliament to deprive Richard Cromwell of supreme control of the armed forces. Their efforts were frustrated by more junior officers who wanted control restored to the Rump Parliament. The outcome was that Parliament appointed Fleetwood as Commander-in-Chief, but at the same time appointed a commission to remodel the army. All officers' commissions, in future, instead of being signed by the Commander-in-Chief, were to be signed by the Speaker and handed to the officer personally, within the precincts of the Houses of Parliament. This order, directed clearly at the power of the generals, who were by now on the whole unpopular, was also greatly resented by Monck and his officers in Scotland, most of whom might lose their commissions.

Monck championed the cause of his army and drew it closer to him as a result. He now became a key figure. He made it clear that he supported Parliamentary control of the army, but at the same time he did not reject overtures from Charles ii, through intermediaries, to discuss the terms on which his return as sovereign would be acceptable. Matters had progressed fairly far when a Royalist insurrection, led by Sir George Booth, broke out in Cheshire. It was rapidly defeated by Lambert. Monck hurriedly suppressed a petition to Parliament in favour of negotiating with Charles, which he had already drafted. However, when Fleetwood and Lambert supported a revolt of fifty officers at Derby against Parliament, Monck publicly assured the latter of his support. The result of this was that Parliament transferred the supreme command from Fleetwood to a commission of seven officers – Fleetwood, March, Hesilrege, Morley, Ludlow, Overton and Walton.

In October 1659 the Army Council, led by Lambert, decided that henceforth it would undertake the business of government. When Monck heard of this, he said, 'I will reduce the military power in obedience to the civil' and assured the Speaker that he would support the liberty and authority of Parliament. 'Have I not been bred to arms in Holland,' he said, 'a commonwealth where soldiers received and observed commands, but gave none.' The die was cast and, while Monck took vigorous steps to bind the army in Scotland to his side, Lambert moved north to the border. They met in mid-winter at Coldstream, Monck with 6,000 foot and 1,800 horse, Lambert with 4,000 foot and 3,500 horse; but they never fought. Lambert was afraid that Fairfax in Yorkshire would raise a force in his rear and his soldiers showed no enthusiasm for the cause. He withdrew and, as general after general began to desert Fleetwood, Monck moved south.

On 26 December, after a meeting in London, the Rump was restored. Monck, meanwhile, had sounded out Fairfax on the subject of restoring Charles to the throne. At Parliament's request Monck began his march towards London, finding increasing support as he moved south. As he approached, he demanded the dismissal of the London garrison. In the last week of January 1660, he was made a member of the Council of State and confirmed as Commander-in-Chief, and on 3 February, with three regiments of horse and four of foot, he was ordered by the Rump to march into the City of London, arrest the members of the Common Council and remove their defences. Reluctantly Monck moved in, but, having done so, joined forces with the City and supported the demand for a return of the members of Parliament who had been excluded by Pride's Purge. He made four demands: to settle the command of the armies in England, Scotland and Ireland 'as might secure the common peace and safety of them'; to raise a tax to pay the arrears of the army and the navy and secure their future support; to issue writs for the election of a new Parliament to assemble on 20 April; and that Parliament agree to its dissolution.

All this was agreed, the composition of Parliament being by this means converted into one in favour of a restoration of the monarchy. Monck was made Captain-General of all its armies and set about 're-modelling' them to get rid of the Levellers, radical Puritans and the like.

There was considerable anxiety in the ranks that a restoration was intended. Monck countered it by appealing for support for the new Parliament, at the same time forbidding assemblies, saying that 'nothing was more injurious to discipline than their meeting in military councils to interpose in civil things'. He promptly entered into negotiations with Charles through Grenville, setting out his conditions for an acceptable return. At the same time, Parliament separately sent a delegation to Charles at Breda, demanding the acceptance of Presbyterianism as the state religion. Knowing that Monck's conditions only called for 'liberty of conscience to all subjects', Charles could afford to ignore this and his Declaration of Breda was the result.

The applecart was nearly upset by the escape of Lambert from the Tower. It looked as if a large part of the army might join him. But Monck acted quickly, and Lambert was caught and defeated at Daventry on Easter Day, 23 April 1660. Two days later, when the new Parliament assembled, Monck reviewed 14,000 troops in Hyde Park – the six London trained bands and some regiments of horse. On 8 May, Charles II was proclaimed King and landed at Dover on 29 May, his thirtieth birthday. Monck was rewarded by becoming Duke of Albemarle. To his detractors he seemed a turncoat, to his admirers a man who put duty to his country and his soldiers above quarrels about religion and politics. 'Honest George Monck' they called him, and when he died in 1670, Bishop Ward of Salisbury in his funeral sermon said: 'The soldiers looked upon him as their Father and were ready and ambitious to live and die with him.' Certainly he has good claim to be the founder of the regular army, now to rise out of the ashes of the Royalist and New Model armies.

Parliament and the King were united, both for political and financial reasons, in wishing to disband what was left of the New Model. The key to effecting this smoothly was payment of arrears. It cost £835,819 8s 10d, of which £560,000 was raised by Parliament through monthly assessment on counties and a Poll Bill; the rest had to be found by the King. In spite of the fact that, with the exception of Monck's own regiment of Coldstreamers, all officers of the New Model serving in England, Scotland and Ireland were discharged, there was little or no trouble. By the end of 1660, the only regiments left in existence in England were the King's Regiment of Life Guards, formed from the horse which had served with him in Holland (now the Life Guards) and Monck's regiment of foot.

A number of conspiracies in late 1660 and early 1661, however, persuaded Monck and the King that a standing force was needed to maintain order and guard the King. In January 1661 four permanent regiments were authorized at a cost of £122,407 15s 10d a year: the Life Guards; the Royal Horse Guards (or Blues), formed from Cromwell's Life Guard of Horse; the first Foot Guards (later the Grenadier Guards), largely formed from Wentworth's Guards withdrawn from Dunkirk; and the 2nd Foot Guards, Monck's Coldstreamers. In addition, 28 garrisons throughout the country were maintained, at a cost of £67,316 15s 6d a year.

Overseas, the garrison at Dunkirk was formed partly from the New Model garrison already there and partly from Royalist troops who had fought against them. Charles found Dunkirk an expensive luxury and sold it for £400,000 to Louis XIV, most of its garrison being transferred to Tangier, which had been acquired as part of the treaty with Portugal on Charles's marriage to Katherine of Braganza. Bombay came with it, and 400 luckless men were sent to garrison it. However, the Portuguese Governor refused to surrender and it was not until 1666 that the garrison, reduced by then to one officer and 97 men, entered it. Soon afterwards Charles sold it to the East India Company for a rental of £10 a year and the soldiers left there formed the basis of the Company's army.

The garrison of Tangier was initially about 3,000 strong, two-thirds ex-New Model and one-third Royalist. A special regiment of cavalry was raised in London as the Tangier Horse. By 1670, the garrison was reduced for reasons of economy to half this strength, and six years later to little over 1,000. However, the threat from the Moors in 1680 led to the restoration of its original size and two new regiments were formed; one by taking 600 men from each of the Guards regiments and one by forming a second battalion of the Earl of Dunbarton's Foot (later the Royal Scots). It was reduced again in 1681 when peace was signed with the Moors, and, when Tangier was abandoned in 1684, its garrison was withdrawn to England, adding two new regiments to the permanent establishment – the Royal Dragoons, as the Tangier Horse was renamed, and the Queen's Regiment of Foot.

Both English and Scottish soldiers had for many years been serving in an Anglo-Dutch brigade in the service of the Dutch Republic. When the Second Dutch War broke out in 1664, following the British seizure of New Amsterdam (renamed New York), Charles ordered its withdrawal. Most of the officers and soldiers formed the Holland Regiment and others joined the Admiralty Regiment, recently raised by Sir William Killigrew. Both became part of the permanent establishment. Some, however, remained in Dutch service. In 1674, after the Third Dutch War, they were joined by many professional officers and soldiers, left without employment in the disbandments which took place. The Anglo-Dutch brigade was then re-formed with three Scottish regiments, two English and one Irish.

There were also considerable numbers of soldiers from all three countries serving with the French. This was of constant concern to Parliament, who suspected the Anglo-French brigade of being a reserve of Royalist troops that could be used by the King for some infamous purpose such as supporting the Catholics. In the secret Treaty of Dover in 1670 Charles agreed to provide a force of 6,000 men to fight under French command against the Dutch. When England withdrew from the war in 1674, the brigade remained as mercenaries. It included the Royal English, commanded by John Churchill, the future Marlborough, and Monmouth's horse, Monmouth himself commanding the brigade for the six years it existed and being made a Lieutenant-General in the French army. When England joined the Dutch against the French in 1678, the brigade was withdrawn, although some of the regiment had returned to England four years earlier.

For this, the last occasion on which large levies were raised to provide an army for foreign service, Monmouth was made Commander-in-Chief. His force of 30,000 men was reviewed on Hounslow Heath on 22 June, after which it embarked for Ostend and moved on to Bruges. However by this time the war was over and the soldiers spent a miserable hard winter in what is now Belgium, suffering severely from disease, before they returned to England and were disbanded. Large reductions were also made in the regiments of the permanent establishment, which were then the Life Guards, Royal Horse Guards, 1st Foot Guards, 2nd Foot Guards (Coldstream), the Admiral's Regiment, the Holland Regiment, the Royal Dragoons and the Queen's Foot. 'The officers and soldiers are immediately to disperse to their own habitations and places of abode and behave themselves in all things as becomes dutiful subjects', read the general orders for disbandment.

At this time, there was trouble in Scotland, the Covenanters rebelling against the heavy hand of Lauderdale. In 1677 the Scottish establishment had been increased by a regiment of foot, two new formations of

Highlanders and three troops of dragoons. In 1681, these became a regiment, raised by Lieutenant-General Tam Dalyell (a patriarchically bearded figure who had fought with the Swedes in Russia), later to be known as the Royal Scots Greys. Matters came to a head in 1679 when the Covenanters under Robert Hamilton drove Claverhouse into Edinburgh and seized control of Glasgow. Reinforced by 5,500 men raised in England from soldiers returning from overseas, Monmouth was put in charge and, at the Battle of Bothwell Bridge on 19 June, totally defeated the 6,000 men under Hamilton, bringing the rebellion to an end.

Ireland, strangely enough, remained quiet in this period, apart from its endemic lawlessness. The large army of Cromwell's veterans that was there at the time of the Restoration changed sides without complaint, but many were disbanded or purged. A 7,500-strong army remained there, 30 troops of horse and 66 companies of foot scattered all over the island and not organized into regiments until 1672. It was a neglected and miserable army, more severely affected than most by arrears of pay. It lived in barracks and consisted largely of Protestants, the Catholics being recruited for foreign service.

By the end of Charles's reign in 1685 the existence of standing armies in England, Scotland and Ireland, small as they were, had come to be taken for granted, although the rivalry between Crown and Parliament for their allegiance and control remained close below the surface.

What was the army like to serve in this period? Apart from some of the senior officers, we know little about the officers and soldiers themselves, rather more about the former than the latter. Although the background of many of the officers in the Royalist and Parliamentary forces was very much the same – country gentlemen for the most part, with a sprinkling of professionals who had served overseas – the Royalists tended to include more aristocrats, courtiers, foreigners and the richer of the landowners. The Parliamentarians were not by any means all serious Puritans of low degree, but included more tradesmen, townspeople and professional men.

At the Restoration few of the officers of the New Model Army were able to retain their commissions, except in overseas garrisons; only in Monck's regiment of Coldstreamers did they do so without a break. In

England and Wales the officers of the Restoration army tended to be of three kinds: professionals, most of whom served almost continuously with foreign armies; well-to-do officers of the six regular regiments, many of whom were also Members of Parliament; and the officers of static garrisons scattered about the country, who were mostly ex-Royalist officers from the Civil War who lived in the country. They could be compared with the Territorial Army officer of the twentieth century.

The general organization of an army in the field was very much the same throughout the period, regardless of which side it was on. This stemmed from the fact that the pattern was derived from continental armies, from which the only professional experience came. The General (or Captain-General) was in overall command, the Lieutenant-General commanding the horse and accepted, as in Cromwell's case, as second-in-command. The Major-General (or Sergeant-Major-General) commanded the foot and could be likened to a glorified regimental sergeant-major: his task was to get the foot properly lined up on the battlefield. Within the horse there was a commissary-general who acted as second-in-command of the horse, two adjutant-generals, a markmaster-general, a muster-master general and a commissary-general of horse provisions. The Major-General had a quarter-master general and an adjutant-general of the foot. In addition there was a lieutenant-general of the Ordnance, who had a comptroller and an engineer-general under him. A most important figure was the Scoutmaster-General, responsible for reconnaissance and intelligence. On neither side in the Civil War did he appear to do his job very well, as both armies tended to be taken by surprise by the other, at Marston Moor, Naseby and Preston, for example.

On the administrative side, the Secretary at War was the Captain-General's permanent-under-secretary and carried out all his correspondence; the commissary-general of the musters, or muster-master general, presided over the whole system of musters. This was the procedure which checked that regiments had the men they were supposed to have and that they were properly clothed and armed. Every month each regiment would be mustered on parade to carry out this check and, only when it had been done and the report rendered to the treasurers, would the pay of everybody from the colonel to the private soldier be authorized, one of the contributory causes of all the troubles about arrears of pay.

Discipline and observance of the Articles of War, which included what is now incorporated into a combination of the Laws and Usages of War (i.e., internationally recognized), military law (e.g., the Army Act) and Queen's Regulations, were presided over by a judge advocate and provost-marshal generals for both horse and foot, who were represented in each regiment by provost-marshals, the military police of the day. There was a waggon-master general, a surgeon-general and a chaplain-general, all attached to the staff of the army to supervise their respective activities.

Within the army there were regiments of horse, some of whom might be dragoons, and of foot. Artillery, organized by the Ordnance, was just beginning to play a part in the battleline, although at none of the major battles in the Civil War was it significant. It was still regarded as principally a siege-weapon. Engineers also were principally concerned with sieges. They had very few skilled men to draw upon and had to rely on the labour of pioneers, who with scavengers were regarded as the dregs of the army. An illustration of the respective status of horse, foot and pioneers is that, for certain offences, a trooper of the horse could be reduced to serving with the foot or, even lower, to serve as a pioneer.

Regiments of horse normally consisted of six troops of a hundred men each. There was a colonel and a major, and each troop had as officers a captain, a lieutenant, a cornet, a quartermaster and three corporals - no sergeants, but corporals-of-horse, as in the household cavalry of today. The colonel and the major also, in theory, commanded troops and drew double pay both as field officers and as troop commanders, although the colonel's troop was actually commanded by the senior subaltern, a captain-lieutenant.

In the New Model Army in 1647, the colonel of a regiment of horse was paid 12s a day as colonel and 10s as a troop-commander or captain, a total of 22s. At that time the trooper was paid 2s 3d a day, although the dragoon received less - 1s 8d. Both these compared well with the foot, a private soldier in which received (or to be more correct, was entitled to) 9d a day. It must, however, be remembered that the trooper had to maintain his horse out of his pay, while the foot soldier only had to maintain himself. The major's pay (including his double pay) was 15s 8d, a captain's 10s, a lieutenant's 7s, a cornet's 5s 4d and a quartermaster 4s. This was raised at the Restoration to 26s for the colonel, 19s 6d for the lieutenant-colonel or major, 14s for the captain, 10s for the lieutenant, 9s[1] for the cornet, 6s for the quartermaster, 3s for the corporal, 2s 8d for the trumpeter, and 2s 6d for the trooper, from which 6d was deducted as 'off-reckonings', to pay for the soldier's clothing and equipment. He was therefore left with 2s on which to maintain himself and his horse. These rates of pay remained in force until 1685. Dragoons were paid less, although curiously their field officers[2] received slightly more than those of the horse. In Charles II's army the captain of dragoons received 11s, the cornet 5s, a sergeant 2s 6d and the private 1s 4d, losing $4\frac{1}{2}$d as off-reckonings.

A regiment of foot was normally 1,200 strong and consisted of ten companies, seven of 100, the major's of 140, the lieutenant-colonel's 160 and the colonel's 200. Few of them took the field more than 1,000 strong. The officers of a company were a captain, a lieutenant and an ensign, and in the normal company there were two sergeants, three corporals and, earlier on, a gentleman-at-arms, the equivalent of a company quartermaster-sergeant. As in the horse, the field officers drew pay both as such and as company commanders. In the New Model Army after the First Civil War the colonel's pay, including his captain's pay, was £1 a day, the lieutenant-colonel's 15s, the major's 13s, a captain's 8s, a lieutenant's 4s and an ensign's 3s. The private soldier was entitled to 8d in the earlier years and 9d a day for most of Cromwell's reign, 2d of which went in off-reckonings. At the Restoration, this went up to 10d. At that time the officers continued on the same rate of pay and a sergeant received 1s 6d, a corporal and a drummer 1s 2d.

Although the proportion of foot to horse was high, the ratio between the two was shifting throughout the period as the infantryman's weapons improved and he became more mobile and his use more flexible, the culmination of which was seen in the replacement of the pike by the bayonet fixed in the end of the musket. The arquebus and even the bow had been in use by English foot soldiers until just before the Stuarts came to the throne but by 1640 the English regiment of foot consisted of musketeers and pikemen only, the proportion between the two changing from one of the former to two of the latter to the reverse. The largest, strongest men were pikemen, who carried a 16-foot pike

[1] This should be compared with the 9s 10d which the author received as a 2nd lieutenant in 1935, although he did not have to maintain a horse on it. It has been estimated that, in terms of purchasing power, 9s in 1661 would have been equivalent to £3 15s in 1935 and £25 in 1983. In that light the pay in 1661 seems reasonable.

[2] The colonel, lieutenant-colonel and major.

and some heavy armour, an iron helmet called a combe-cap, a corslet to cover the breast and back, a gorget to protect the throat (the orgin of 'gorgettes' or red tabs) and tussets to cover the thighs. The pikeman also carried a sword, but it seems to have been little used. Gustavus Adolphus was largely responsible for setting the trend by which pikes were shortened and pikemen discarded their armour. In 1642 an experienced soldier called Lupton, who had served with the Swedes in Germany, wrote a treatise suggesting the total abolition of the pike, and there were several occasions in the Civil War when the pikemen were left behind in order to allow the army to move more quickly. But the pike was not finally abolished in the English army until 1705, one of the reasons given for its retention up to that time being, typically, that it was a more 'honourable' arm, as it was of greater antiquity than the musket.

At the beginning of the period the musket had a barrel four feet long, fired a bullet weighing about $1\frac{1}{4}$ oz and was so heavy it had to be supported on a rest made of ash with a fork at the top and an iron point at the bottom to stick into the ground. The soldier carried it either in his right hand or slung on his arm by a loop. By the end of the period barrel length had been reduced to three feet and the use of the rest discontinued. Bullets were usually kept in a pouch, but two or three were always kept in the soldier's mouth in battle as 'ready rounds'. He had two kinds of pouch, one for priming his piece and a coarser one for the main charge. He normally had twelve charges made up in little tubes of tin, leather or wood and carried in a leather bandolier over his left shoulder. They were notorious causes of noise on night-marches. Until the firelock (or flintlock) and the snaphouse (or fusil) replaced it, the musket was the matchlock, a piece of cord boiled in vinegar or the lees of wine acting as a permanent source from which to fire the primer. The soldier carried two or three yards of this cord on his belt and a two-foot length, lighted at both ends, in his left hand. This also was an obvious give-away at night, but on the other hand could be used for deception, several lighted bits of match being left about to deceive the enemy into thinking they were soldiers.

The matchlock finally disappeared at the same time as the pike, having by that time been surpassed both by the flintlock and the lighter fusil, originally used as a sporting weapon. In the early days of the musket, the files were drawn up as much as ten deep to allow each successive first rank to retire to the rear and get through all the complicated procedure of reloading and yet keep up a continuous fire. As the speed of reloading increased, the number of ranks could be decreased, the normal at the start of the Civil War on both sides being six. Gustavus Adolphus gradually introduced several ranks firing simultaneously, first three, front rank levelling, second stooping, and third upright, and then even six at a time, a method used in 1631 at the battle of Leipzig and also by Montrose in Scotland. The effective range of the musket against unarmoured men and horses was probably as much as 500 yards, but it was highly inaccurate and the normal range for opening fire seems to have been 100 to 150 yards. In many cases fire was held until the enemy were much nearer, even as close as 30 yards. When the enemy came to very close quarters, the musketeer had no defensive weapon himself, until the bayonet was introduced, although he was protected by the pikemen as long as they were there. He had to rely on using the butt of his musket, which he did with considerable effect, although it may not have done it much good.

The cavalry at this time was in a state of transition. In Elizabethan times there had been three types: heavily armoured cuirassiers, armed with large lances; light horsemen wearing coats of mail and carrying light lances and a single pistol; and 'petronels', carrying some form of carbine. By the time of the Civil War the cuirassiers had almost totally disappeared as had the light lancers, although the latter remained in the Scottish cavalry. There was considerable variety in the armament and the protection provided for the horsemen of both sides in the Civil War, and many changes and variations took place during the period. In general it can be said that the majority of the horse were equipped with either an arquebus or its more modern equivalent the carbine, essentially a shorter firelock musket, one or two pistols and a sword; but in the earlier years a considerable proportion of the Parliamentary horse carried pistols and sword only. During the period also armour protection gradually faded out.

This tendency in the horse meant that there was not a very great difference between them and dragoons, the latter becoming more and more popular during the period. The successors of both 'petronels' and light cavalry, they were regarded as mounted infantry and employed principally for reconnaissance, escort and what one might call gendarmerie or internal security duties. Their horses were inferior in size and stamina to those of the horse and they were not expected to take part in a charge, but were meant to fight on foot. Their task was very similar to that of the armoured reconnaissance regiment of today. They carried the same armament as the horse, except for the pistol.

At the start of the Civil War some of the cavalry leaders, trained in the Dutch army, followed the tactics introduced by the German *Reiters*. No longer charging at the gallop, they would trot up to the enemy in ranks five or six deep and then discharge their pistols rank by rank thus avoiding contact with the pikemen. But Gustavus Adolphus had diverged from this and trained his horse to charge in ranks three deep and hold their fire until they were among the enemy. Prince Rupert followed these tactics and they seem to have been adopted by Cromwell from his example. Eyewitness accounts of the latter's charge against Prince Rupert's horse at Marston Moor make this clear. 'They stood', wrote Cromwell's scout-master Watson, 'at swords point a pretty while, hacking one another, but at last it pleased God he broke through them, scattering them like a little dust.' Lord Saye in his account wrote: 'The enemy being many of them, if not the greatest part, gentlemen, stood very firm a long time, coming to a close fight with the sword, standing like an iron wall so that they were not easily broken'. 'The horse on both sides', wrote Edward Ludlow in his memoirs, 'behaved with the greatest bravery, for having discharged their pistols and flung them at each others heads they fell to it with the sword', an un-economic use of pistols it would seem. However, it appears to have been standard practice, as Major-General Morgan's orders to his troopers in Scotland in 1654 were 'that no man should fire [his carbine] until he came within a horse's length of the enemy and then [after firing] to throw pistols in their faces and so fall on with the sword'. The charge seems to have been made at 'a full trot' or 'a pretty sound trot', not at the gallop and the habit of reserving fire until close quarters made this possible. When the horse had carbines as well as pistols they had to stop and discharge them, which meant that the charge itself was then executed at a slow pace. Cromwell's principal contribution to tactics was the firm control he exercised of the horse. He waited to use it until its intervention could be decisive in turning the tide of battle. He then led it in a deliberate charge, ensuring that it did not turn into a wild mêlée, like that which he had witnessed at Edgehill.

In a typical battle, the first exchange of fire would be from the artillery, aimed at breaking up the enemy's battleline. However, it does not seem to have been very effective and in some cases, for instance the

Battle of Preston, neither side had any artillery as it had failed to keep up. The next step would be that a 'forlorn troope' of musketeers, static and in front of the battleline, would fire a volley in the hope of breaking up the enemy's attack, before retiring to the main position. As the foot drew near each other, the musketeers of each side would fire probably two volleys from all ranks and then close, the pikemen thrusting with their pikes while the musketeers laid about them with their butts. Monck, in his *Observations*, describes how the foot should meet a charge of horse. The pikemen would be drawn up two deep in the centre of the company with the musketeers on either side, front rank kneeling to fire and the first two ranks either firing together or in succession. They were to reserve their fire until the horse were within twenty yards and then to fire at their legs. If this did not stop them, it was up to the pikemen to do so, also by thrusting at the horses.

So much for the battle. One of the problems was to get there. The weapons and general equipment of the foot soldier, whether pikeman or musketeer, were heavy. In his knapsack he might carry up to seven days' provisions, and in Scotland and Ireland, where there was little or no billeting, he might also carry a bit of a tent. The weight of all this was certainly above the sixty pounds which the soldier of a hundred years later was expected to carry. It appears that a day's march was expected to be about ten miles, exceptionally extended to thirteen, and that they were expected to keep this up day after day for at least a week if necessary.

When they were halted or were not on the march, soldiers were billeted rather than encamped, except in Ireland and Scotland. This was a constant source of friction, trouble and complaint from those who had to accommodate them. One of the articles of the Petition of Right was to demand that there should be no billeting on private citizens – only in inns. It was of course impossible for either side to observe this during the Civil War, and there were constant complaints from those on whom soldiers were billeted about the behaviour of the soldiers or their failure to pay for their food and lodging, or that the cost of providing it was not met by the official sum. There also seem to have been many cases of people paying double the official rate in order to avoid having soldiers billeted on them. It is little wonder that this was a cause of trouble. Quite apart from the inevitable friction which the presence of rough and hungry soldiers in the house was bound to cause, it must be remembered that, after his off-reckonings had been deducted, the foot-soldier was left with only six or seven pence to pay for his food, drink and lodging and the horseman 2s for himself and his horse. As he was only in theory paid once a month, and that in arrears (for most of the period his pay was months behindhand), it is hardly surprising that he was unable to pay on the nail for his daily food, lodging and the beer he drank so much of.

If a soldier caused trouble, he was liable to be punished in various ways, of which riding the wooden horse seems to have been that most frequently imposed. The horse was made of two boards, nailed together at an angle, supported on four legs. The culprit would have to sit astride this for half an hour or more with his hands tied, one, two or three muskets tied to each leg and sometimes something round his neck as well. For more serious offences he might be given the lash, the number of strokes, usually up to 30, less than came to be inflicted in the next century; 60 appeared to be the maximum. Offences which called for more severe punishment might be dealt with by sentencing a man to run the gauntlet, a punishment adopted from the Swedish and German armies. Stripped naked to the waist the culprit would run through a lane formed from perhaps a whole regiment, each soldier hitting him with a stick as he ran past. For mutiny the penalty was death by hanging or firing squad, although not all those convicted suffered it. It was normal for a child to draw lots to determine which of the number convicted should be executed. For blasphemy the penalty in both the Royalist and Parliamentary armies was to have a hole bored in the tongue by a red-hot iron. The normal punishment for officers was cashiering.

While the Civil Wars were in progress and for most of the period of Cromwell's reign, the army dealt with offenders in its ranks by court-martial, but there were arguments, particularly in the City of London, about whether, for civil offences, the soldier should be tried by the civil courts. This became a major issue after the Restoration, when Parliament became very suspicious of any move by Charles II which might bring the Army outside the jurisdiction of the civil authorities. The state of the law was vague, resting principally on the Petition of Right. When Charles I had declared martial law for the levies raised for the expedition to La Rochelle in 1627, the Commons has passed a motion declaring that martial law was 'wholly and directly contrary to the said laws and statutes of this your realm . . . and hereafter no commission of like nature may issue forth to any person or persons whatsoever'. Charles II never dared introduce martial law in England, although he came near to doing so for the levies raised in 1673 and 1678.

Garrisons overseas, such as those in Tangier, Dunkirk and Bombay and the ill-fated expedition to Barbados, were subject to martial law, but in England all that officers could do was to arrest offenders and take them before the magistrates, which made it almost impossible to maintain discipline among the levies. After a number of test cases, a compromise was arrived at which has lasted to the present day. In overseas garrisons not under British jurisdiction, or on operations, the soldier would be tried for civil offences by a military court, but, when stationed in Britain (and this was later extended to British possessions overseas), primary jurisdiction would be with the civil court and it was only with their permission that a soldier could be tried by a military court for a civil offence; for purely military offences he would be tried by a military court acting under the 'Articles of War'.

Soldiers, whether they joined voluntarily or were impressed, were not enlisted for any specific period. In the Civil War and later in the levies for the wars in Charles II's reign, it was assumed that they would serve for the duration of hostilities; otherwise it was for life. Apart from these periods, a soldier met with little difficulty in obtaining a discharge. He normally had to find a substitute and there was a large pool of unemployed ex-soldiers on which to draw. For them, finding employment had been very difficult owing to the 'closed shop' practices of the guilds controlling entry into trades. Cromwell broke this in 1654 by an ordinance which laid down that any soldier who had served on the Parliamentary side, or in the campaigns in Ireland and Scotland that followed, for a period of not less than four years, would be free to practice his trade in spite of the legal restrictions, and at the Restoration this was extended to ex-soldiers of Monck's army, provided that they took the oaths of allegiance and supremacy.

Disabled ex-soldiers, according to a statute of 1600, virtually had to rely on their parishes to provide for them, and in 1643 Parliament ordered the constables and churchwardens of every parish to levy a rate for them and for the widows and orphans of those who died while serving. Later in that year a special tax of about £4,000 a month was levied in the counties for this purpose, the maximum allowance being fixed at 4s a week. In addition to these, sums of money were granted from time to time as compensation either for disablement or to widows. Money was also provided to almshouses and hospitals for the maintenance of wounded soldiers; but none of these remedial measures met the full demand, particularly since, in common with army pay, the actual disbursement of the money fell many months in arrears. At the Restoration these arrangements were cancelled, and the recipients were then thrown back on the charity of the parishes. This was not remedied until the establishment in 1680 of Kilmainham hospital for old soldiers in Dublin, followed by that of the Royal Hospital at Chelsea which opened its gates in 1684, financed by private donations, a deduction of 8d in the pound from army pay and a levy of 1s in the pound from the sale of army commissions.

One source of much hardship for ex-soldiers was the method of giving a soldier on discharge a debenture instead of arrears of pay due to him. This was a promissory note on the Treasury for the payment of his arrears in the future. The temptation to sell it quickly at much below its eventual value for the sake of ready cash was generally irresistible and a substantial market grew up trading in these debentures. Little wonder that there were many songs on the theme of the soldier turned beggar as well as widespread complaints that they swelled the ranks of robbers and highwaymen.

2
THE AGE OF MARLBOROUGH
1685-1763

John Churchill, son of Sir Winston Churchill, a country gentleman of Dorset, was born in 1650. He became a page to the Duke of York, later James II, and through his influence gained a commission in the 1st Foot Guards at the age of seventeen. In 1668 he joined the garrison of Tangier, and while there served at sea fighting the Barbary pirates of Algeria, and in the Third Dutch War, by the end of which he had been promoted captain in the Lord High Admiral's Regiment. His first experience of continental warfare came in 1673, serving in Monmouth's Royal English Regiment with the French under Turenne, who expressed his admiration for the courage and leadership the young English captain had shown at the Battle of Enzheim and the siege of Maastricht, where he was wounded. By the time the war ended in 1678, he had been appointed a brigadier of foot, but with the withdrawal of troops from the Continent and the subsequent reduction in numbers, he returned to the service of his royal patron, being rewarded with a peerage in 1682 and colonelcy of the Royal Dragoons in the following year. He was appointed second among the nine Gentlemen of the Bedchamber when James succeeded his brother Charles II as King in February 1685.

The accession of James II, a fervent Roman Catholic, threatened to disrupt the compromise arrived at between King and Parliament over the status of the army. In theory, the existence of a standing army was forbidden, the only permanently embodied troops recognized being 'Guards and Garrisons', that is the guards needed to protect King and Parliament, and the few old soldiers retained as caretakers of permanent fortifications. Any other military tasks, such as maintaining order and repelling invasion, were to be met by the militia, raised on a county basis, authority over which, when embodied, was a matter of dispute between Parliament and the Crown. This had become acute in the struggle between Charles II and the Earl of Shaftesbury over attempts by the latter and his Whig supporters to ban James from the succession on the grounds of religion. Charles had been forced to disband 10,000 soldiers, raised for the Third Dutch War, after the Treaty of Nymwegen in 1678 had brought it to an end. Parliament had refused to pay for them, and had demanded the raising of 60,000 militia instead, which the King refused.

There was, therefore, a very small standing force available to James II when his accession was challenged by Charles II's bastard son, James, Duke of Monmouth and Buccleuch. As Captain-General, Monmouth had commanded the army at the battle of Bothwell Bridge in 1679, where he had defeated Claverhouse and his Covenanters; but his pretensions to the succession, backed by Shaftesbury, had forced Charles to exile him to the Netherlands. On his father's death he rejected the advice of William of Orange to accept service under the Austrian Emperor to fight the Turks, and set sail with only 150 men, landing at Lyme Regis on 11 June 1685, hoping to raise support in the south-west. The Lords-Lieutenant were ordered to call out their militia, the six British regiments in the Dutch service were recalled from Holland and John Churchill, in the rank of brigadier, was entrusted with the command of the four troops of the Royal Horse Guards (the Blues), four of the King's Dragoons (the Royals) and five companies of the Queen Dowager's Regiment of Foot (the Queen's), a total of less than 2,000 men, his first independent command.

Before Churchill had brought Monmouth to battle, he was, much to his chagrin, superseded in overall command by the Earl of Feversham who, although Turenne's nephew, lacked any of his uncle's military qualities. After several lost opportunities, Feversham, who had reinforced Churchill with the regiments brought over from Holland, made contact with Monmouth's men on the evening of 5 July on Sedgemoor near Bridgwater. In desperation, Monmouth attempted a night march, and lost direction and control, so that Churchill had little difficulty in routing the whole force between dawn and mid-afternoon of the following day.

This threat to the Crown and the manifest ineffectiveness of the militia gave James the justification he desired to raise an effective standing army. Nine new regiments of foot, five of horse and two of dragoons were raised in that year and a number of garrisons were converted into regiments, a permanent encampment being established near London at Hounslow. Having been Lord High Admiral in his brother's reign, James was experienced in military administration and did much to improve the organization and administration of the army, paying for it by using money voted by Parliament for the militia. By 1688 its numbers had risen to 34,000, 10,000 of whom were in Ireland. These measures alone would have been enough to alarm Parliament. When they were accompanied by the appointment of Roman Catholics to key positions – in the army in Ireland by the almost total replacement of Protestant officers – fears of a Papist plot were intensified.

These fears, and the fact that James had no direct male heir until a son was born to his second wife, Mary of Modena, in 1688 after 15 years of childless marriage, were the factors which led to the approaches made to William of Orange to take James's place on the thrones of England, Scotland and Ireland. He was both James's nephew and his son-in-law. As a result of the political machinations which followed, William, having waited several weeks for a favourable easterly wind, and after one false start, set sail on 11 November 1688 with a fleet of 200 transports, escorted by 49 warships, and landed unopposed at Torbay four days later, James's fleet, inferior in numbers, having been beset by a combination of contrary winds and dead calm. William's army consisted of 11,000 foot and 4,000 horse, including 4,000 British in three English and three Scottish regiments. The rest were Swedes, Dutch and Germans from as far apart as Brandenburg and Würtemberg. As his force advanced methodically eastwards against little or no opposition, the grandees of the West Country rallied to his side, and encouraging news of similar support in the Midlands and the North came in. Even more telling were deserters from James's court and army, which by 29 November was at Salisbury. Churchill, still loyal to James, was in favour of a further westward move to seek battle, but James feared that London might turn against him and decided on withdrawal, at which Churchill, followed by Prince George of Denmark, husband of James's other daughter, Anne, deserted to William. Anne herself, escorted by the Bishop of London, escaped from the capital in disguise to join the rebels. James's cause was lost, and he played into William's hands by giving orders for his army to be disbanded without making provision for their inevitable arrears of pay. William promptly reassembled all but the Irish troops into his own army, the last regiment to change sides being Monck's old regiment, the Coldstream or 2nd Foot Guards. When

James finally left, after his first abortive attempt to sail away, he ordered them to let Dutch guards relieve them of their duty.

Once again, in the Declaration of Rights of 1689, it was declared illegal to maintain a standing army in time of peace. But, once again, this principle was frustrated by events. The first of these was James's attempt, with the support of France, to reverse the verdict of 1688 with the help of Catholics in Ireland. Initially the northern Protestants were reduced to the beleaguered towns of Derry and Enniskillen, and William was forced to deploy an army in Ireland which, by 1690, when his victory at the Battle of the Boyne turned the scales, had grown to 30,000. The soldiers were English, Dutch, and mercenaries from Denmark and some of the German principalities. They all suffered from the inexperience of many of their officers and from the chaotic administration. The rebellion, in which 7,000 French troops had taken part, came to an end with the fall of Limerick in 1691.

William was now free to turn his attention back to his main preoccupation: the war against France in the Low Countries (Flanders). This was the War of the Grand Alliance, a complex grouping of Holland, Denmark and Prussia with the Austrian Empire and Savoy, designed to contain the ambitions of Louis XIV of France to expand his power into the Spanish Netherlands (modern Belgium), east of the Rhine and into Spain itself, with an eye to the succession to the Spanish throne on the death of Charles II of Spain, who had no heir and clearly had not long to live. William's accession, with his wife Mary, to the English throne brought Britain into the coalition, with profound consequences for the army and for its place in the nation. Henceforth it became a permanent feature of the national scene, although almost all its activity was to be overseas.

Even while the war in Ireland had been in progress, 8,000 British troops were serving in Flanders, commanded by Churchill, who had been appointed Lieutenant-General in William's absence in Ireland. He was under the overall command of the Dutch Prince Waldeck. The key to operations in the area lay in the fortresses built at the crucial junctions or crossing places of the waterways which served as the principal transport routes. The French engineer Vauban and the less well-known Dutchman Cohorn were the acknowledged experts in the design and construction of these great star-like ramparts of earth, resistant to bombardment, extending beyond the stone walls which in earlier times had sufficed to hold the enemy at bay. The war in Flanders tended to take the form of prolonged sieges with the aim of extending the line of fortresses from one river line to another. Major battles were few and far between. They were expensive and could lead to serious losses in manpower, which could not easily be replaced or paid for.

When William returned from Ireland to the Netherlands, he faced a French army of 119,000, under Marshal de Luxembourg, with an army of his own of 71,000, of whom 17,000 were British. At this time Churchill, now Earl of Marlborough, was in disgrace. He had become the spokesman of those who, like himself, resented the appointment of Dutchmen to important posts and commands, and his close relations with Princess Anne's household, cemented by the friendship of Anne with his lively wife Sarah, led him to be suspected of treason. He was actually sent to the Tower for six weeks, while a forged letter was being investigated, and was not employed again while the war lasted. It came to an end in 1697 with the Treaty of Ryswick. By then the French army had been reduced, largely for financial reasons, to 84,000 men, while William's had risen to 89,000. He had recaptured the key fortress of Namur on the Meuse and forced the French, commanded by Villeroi after the death of Luxembourg, on to the defensive.

One of the least successful British actions of the war was a disastrous attempt in 1694 to land ten regiments at Brest under the command of Tollemache, who was killed. Marlborough was accused of having given the French prior information, which added to his unpopularity at court. But with the death of his Queen, Mary, in that year, William realized that he had to improve relations with her sister, now clearly heir to the throne, if the claims of James II or his young son were not to be revived; and Marlborough's gradual return to influence, if not to favour, began. He had already been made one of the Lords Justices in William's absence in Holland in 1700, when the death of Charles II of Spain in that year and Louis's support of his own grandson, Philip of Anjou, who had been nominated by Charles as his successor, resuscitated the spectre of French ambitions.

The Dutch formally requested the help of 10,000 troops from England under the terms of the Anglo-Dutch Treaty of 1678, and, in spite of initial Tory opposition, Parliament agreed in June 1701 to William's proposal to send twelve battalions from Ireland. Marlborough was not only appointed Commander-in-Chief, but also Ambassador to the Dutch United Provinces, with plenipotentiary powers. Conscious of his own failing powers, William had ensured that a strong team would carry on his policy; Sydney Godolphin as Treasurer worked in close cooperation with Marlborough, and both were favourites of Anne.

Marlborough's first task was to weld together the Grand Alliance of Britain, Holland and the Austrian Empire, the treaty being signed in September 1701, ten days before the death of James II, whose son, James Edward (the Old Pretender) was recognized by Louis as James III. The treaty fixed the British contribution of troops at 40,000, the Dutch at 10,000 and the Emperor's at 90,000. To find these, regiments that had been disbanded in 1697 were brought to life again, new ones were raised and existing ones brought up to strength. This force was still being raised when William died after a fall from his horse in March 1702. Anne confirmed Marlborough's appointments, adding that of Captain-General to Master-General of the Ordnance which he already held. Not since Monck had any British soldier, other than the sovereign, been entrusted with such power over the army, although Anne's husband, Prince George, held the nominally higher post of Generalissimo of All Land Forces in addition to that of Lord High Admiral. A dukedom was shortly to be added. Marlborough was now aged 52, six years older than both Wellington and Napoleon at Waterloo and three years younger than Montgomery at El Alamein.

Over on the Continent, however, his power was limited in two ways: first by the reluctance of the Dutch to give him command over their forces, and then, when persuaded to do so by their Veldt-Marshal Heinsius, by the attachment of two obstructive civilian deputies, de Heyd and Guildermalsen; secondly by the size of his army, which, at 60,000, was slightly inferior to that of his opponent, Boufflers, who in the interim had captured the Dutch 'barrier' fortresses in the Spanish Netherlands, controlled the Meuse, except at Maastricht, and occupied the Electorate of Cologne, thus threatening communications between Holland and Austria. The British contingent numbered some 12,000, seven regiments of cavalry and 14 battalions of foot, organized into three brigades. The 38 guns in its artillery-train accounted for half of the artillery at Marlborough's disposal.

The campaigns of 1702 and 1703 were inconclusive, largely due to the obstruction of the Dutch deputies. Whenever Marlborough, by a combination of deception and rapid marching, created the opportunity for a successful battle against Boufller's successor, Villeroi, they refused to let him take the risk. Meanwhile the French, under Villars, had joined hands with Bavaria and had inflicted a defeat on the Emperor's troops at Hochstadt on the Danube; and Tallard had improved the French position on the Rhine with the capture of Landau and Breisach. Two additions to the Grand Alliance offset these setbacks: that of Portugal, which provided a base for operations in Spain and in the Mediterranean, and that of Savoy, whose Prince Eugène was to prove a valuable companion in arms.

Both the dangers and the opportunities arising from these developments prompted Marlborough's bold strategy for the campaigning season of 1704. He proposed to exploit the addition of Portugal and Savoy by despatching an expedition to the Mediterranean under Rooke. Depositing the Habsburg claimant to the Spanish throne, the Archduke Charles, in Portugal, and seizing Gibraltar en route, Rooke was to join hands with Savoy and capture the French naval base of Toulon. Marlborough himself, leaving only the minimum force needed to guard the Netherlands, would march right across Germany to join forces with the Margrave Louis of Baden, the Emperor and Prince Eugène of Savoy on the Danube to defeat the combined forces of the Elector of Bavaria and the French under Marsin, who had replaced Villars. The success of this bold stroke depended on secrecy, not merely to mislead the French, so that the forces of Villeroi in the Netherlands and of Tallard on the Rhine could not be brought to bear against him, but also to prevent Tory opposition in England and Dutch fears from obstructing his aim. Assured of the support of the faithful Godolphin in raising the money and the 10,000 additional troops he needed, he put it about that the main feature of the year's campaigning season was to be an advance up the Moselle from its confluence with the Rhine at Koblenz. Concentration in that area and logistic preparations, such as the provisions of shoes, served both his actual and his deception plans.

He crossed the Channel in late April and by mid-May his force of 40,000 (90 cavalry squadrons and 51 infantry battalions)[1] was concentrated at Bedburg, 20 miles north-west of Cologne. The British contingent, 14,000 strong, was commanded by his brother Charles and consisted of 19 cavalry squadrons[2] and 14 infantry battalions. On 20 May this army set off on its remarkable 250-mile march. Not until 8 June, when Marlborough turned east from Heidelberg, where his troops had rested for four days and been supplied with new shoes, ordered in

[1] Sources differ about this figure. I have followed Atkinson's *Marlborough and the Rise of the British Army*.

[2] A squadron normally consisted of three troops.

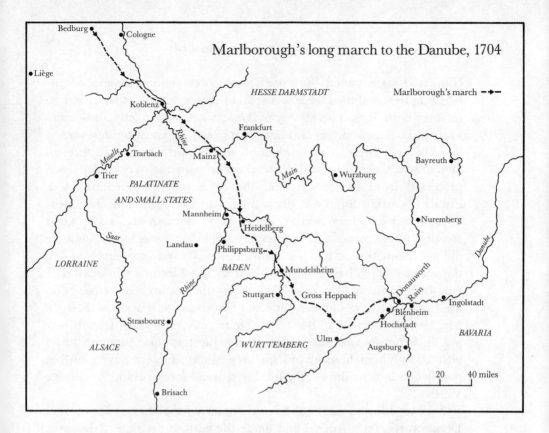

Marlborough's long march to the Danube, 1704

advance through his faithful Jewish contractor Medina, did it become clear to the French that he was not intending to cross the Rhine. Once he had passed Koblenz, his threat of an advance up the Moselle was seen to be a feint, and Villeroi, who had detached a force from the Netherlands to meet it at Trier, continued to move east to join Tallard, expecting Marlborough to cross the Rhine at Philipsburg and threaten Alsace and Lorraine.

It was now clearly a race for Marlborough to join the 7,000 men under the Margrave of Baden and the 30,000 of the Emperor's forces under Eugène before Marsin and the Elector of Bavaria's force, already augmented to 57,000 by a reinforcement sent by Tallard, could attack them. It was not until 1 July that Tallard's army crossed the Rhine and hurried east to join forces with Marsin. On 10 June Marlborough and the 41-year-old Eugène had met for the first time at Mundelsheim, south-east of Stuttgart. Three days later, at Gross Heppach, they were joined by Louis of Baden and agreement was reached that, while Eugène held off Tallard, Marlborough should deal with Marsin and the Bavarians. On 22 June their forces linked up at Lauensheim, north-west of

Ulm, and were joined by more Dutch forces under General Goor, bringing the combined force to a total of 177 cavalry squadrons and 76 infantry battalions. The Elector of Bavaria's army was only a few miles away at Dillingen. Before he engaged it in battle, Marlborough wished to secure his line of communication to the north by the capture of Donauworth, the junction of the Danube with the Wörmitz. It was protected by a prominent hill, the Schellenberg, defended by a Franco-Bavarian force of 15,000 men. Marlborough laid on a swift direct attack on 2 July, overwhelming the garrison, of whom only 3,000 escaped, at the cost of 4,500 casualties to his own force. Surprisingly he did not follow this up by an advance to the Bavarian capital, Munich, the way to which had been laid open by the Elector's withdrawal to Augsburg. Instead, he spent July laying the countryside to waste in the hope that it would persuade the Bavarians to desert the French. Meanwhile Eugène had not been able to prevent Tallard from bringing his army to join Marsin's with the Elector, their junction being effected at Biberach, south of Ulm, on 5 August, Eugène having moved parallel to him to the north, leaving a small force behind to deceive Villeroi.

Eugène, Marlborough and Louis conferred together at Rain, near Donauworth, on 7 August and made the curious decision to despatch the Margrave with 20,000 men to besiege Ingolstadt, 30 miles further downstream on the Danube. In the evening of the day after he had set off, 10 August, Marlborough received an urgent message from Eugène that the whole Franco-Bavarian army had crossed to the north side of the Danube at Lauingen, only a few miles west of Eugène's small force of only 18 battalions at Hochstadt. Sending his brother Charles off only three hours later with 20 battalions, Marlborough himself followed at 3 am on 11 August, crossing to the north of the river at Donauworth and moving west to join Eugène. By 11 pm the whole army was north of the river and united west of the town. Early next day, protected by 40 squadrons of cavalry, Marlborough and Eugène rode west and climbed the church tower at Tapfheim. Four miles away, between the small village of Blenheim, at a bend in the Danube, and the low wooded hills three miles to the north of it lay the Franco-Bavarian army of 60,000 men, 147 cavalry squadrons and 84 infantry battalions with 120 guns. Without the Margrave's force, Marlborough and Eugène could muster 56,000 in 160 squadrons and 66 battalions, supported by 66 guns, 9,000 of these men being English or Scots. In spite both of his inferiority in numbers and of the natural strength of the enemy's position, not only protected by the river on one flank and wooded hills on the other, but also by a stream, the Nebel, running across its front, Marlborough and Eugène decided to attack the following day, 13 August.

From the disposition of the enemy's tents, they had deduced his plan of battle. Tallard, on the southern flank, had concentrated his infantry to defend the village of Blenheim, placing his cavalry on slightly higher ground north-west of the village, a thousand yards west of the marshy Nebel stream, covering the two miles of open ground between Blenheim and the village of Oberglau. The latter formed the right flank of the forces of Marsin and the Elector, their infantry concentrated in defence of Oberglau and of the village of Lutzingen, on the edge of the woods a mile and a half further west, and most of their cavalry on their right. The centre of the position was therefore filled principally by cavalry, the arm in which Marlborough and Eugène were superior, and the stream itself was not closely defended. It appears that Tallard, who was in overall command, was not expecting attack; a letter he wrote to Louis XIV on the very morning of the battle gives no indication that he thought it likely. Once he did realize it, it has been suggested that his plan was to lure Marlborough across the stream in the centre, where, with both flanks resting on the village defences, he could destroy the troops that had crossed before they could be reinforced from the far side.

Marlborough's plan was to launch such fierce attacks on the enemy's extreme flank positions – Cutts on Blenheim and Eugène on Lutzingen – that he would be forced to commit his reserves there for fear of his flanks being turned. Meanwhile crossings of the stream in the centre would be prepared and his main force, under his brother Charles, would be ready to cross in an unorthodox formation of four lines, the first of 17 battalions of infantry, the next two of 36 and 35 squadrons respectively of cavalry, the final one a reserve of 11 battalions of infantry to be held east of the stream to cover a possible withdrawal and re-formation of the cavalry. This force included British, Dutch, Hanoverians and Hessians, although most of the British were with Cutts, who also had some Hanoverians and Hessians under his command. But the attack in the centre, including that on Oberglau, would not be launched until Eugène on the right and Cutts on the left had played their part, Eugène, with his Danish and Prussian infantry and Austrian cavalry, having a much longer approach march to his objective at Lutzingen.

Dawn saw Marlborough's and Eugène's men on the move, and the first French gun opened fire at 8 am. However, Tallard made no attempt, other than by artillery fire, to contest Churchill's approach to the stream and the preparations of his engineers to build six bridges over it. At 10 am Cutts's column advanced across the stream, led by Rowe's British brigade of five battalions, the First Guards and the 10th, 21st, 23rd and 24th Foot[3] but, once across, it had an uncomfortable two hours subjected to artillery fire, before the order was given to launch the attack on Blenheim, Eugène having reported that he was ready to start his attack on Lutzingen. The attack was launched with great gallantry and served its purpose well, forcing the Marquis de Clérambault to reinforce the nine defending battalions with a further seven, with the result that the village was so congested that none of them could move.

While Eugène's men fought fiercely at the other end of the line, Churchill launched ten battalions under the Prince of Holstein-Beck against Oberglau. They were thrown back by a counter-attack, led by the Irish brigade in French service, which Marsin's cavalry attempted to exploit; but the situation was saved by Marlborough's prompt action and by Eugène, who sent a cavalry brigade to help him. By 4 pm, with this crisis over and Eugène's attacks on Lutzingen showing progress, Marlborough decided that the time had come to prepare his main blow in the centre; but it was 5.30 before he had assembled the whole force west of the stream. By that time he had concentrated 90 cavalry squadrons, 23 infantry battalions and most of his guns against the 60 squadrons and 9 battalions that Tallard now had between Blenheim and Oberglau. As this force advanced, the cavalry at a steady trot, sabre in hand, Tallard's and Marsin's cavalry made ineffectual charges, culminating in the discharge of their fusils, until they saw that nothing they could do would stop its inexorable advance. Marsin's horse pulled back to protect his infantry, while Tallard's recoiled in the opposite direction or galloped westward in confusion, and Marlborough's infantry, under Lord Orkney, wheeled to encircle Blenheim from the rear. Clérambault threw himself into the Danube and was drowned and the 9,000 still unwounded defenders of the village surrendered. Tallard's army had collapsed and he himself was captured. Marsin managed to avoid encirclement, and by 7 pm had begun to withdraw, taking some 20,000 men with him.

[3] See Appendix A for subsequent nomenclature of numbered regiments.

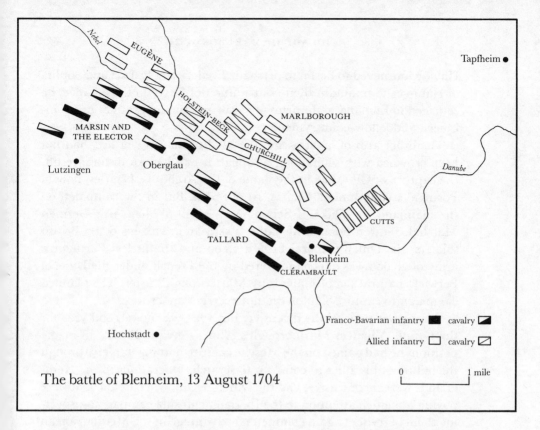

The battle of Blenheim, 13 August 1704

The Franco-Bavarian casualties are thought to have been about 38,000, including 14,000 prisoners, while those of Marlborough and Eugène were put at 4,542 killed and 7,942 wounded, British casualties within that total amounting to 2,234. On the back of a receipt from an innkeeper Marlborough scribbled a note to Sarah, preserved to this day at Blenheim Palace, which ends: 'I have not time to say more, but to beg you will give my duty to the Queen, and let her know Her Army has had a Glorious Victory.' If the army was not entirely, nor even mainly, hers, but that of the Grand Alliance, her soldiers and her Commander-in-Chief and Captain-General had played a decisive and rightly renowned part after their epic march across Germany.

Marlborough's victory had saved the alliance and dealt a severe blow to France. It was followed up by a return to the Rhine, the Margrave of Baden crossing it to attack Landau, while Marlborough turned the original feint into a reality by thrusting up the Moselle to Trier and laying siege to Trarbach, between there and Koblenz. With the capture of Landau in mid-November and Trarbach a month later, Marlborough had laid the foundations of the following year's campaign.

Having journeyed to Berlin to persuade Frederick of Prussia and Sophia of Hanover to maintain their contribution of forces to the alliance, he returned to England to the arms of Sarah and the congratulations of his Queen and fellow-countrymen.

The other arm of his strategy, the Mediterranean venture, had not been crowned with such glory, although it had had an historic result, the capture of Gibraltar in the name of the Archduke Charles, now in Portugal styling himself Charles III of Spain. But in the campaign on the mainland the Duke of Schomberg, son of William III's German Marshal, showed none of his father's skill and, with his 6,500 British soldiers, the Dutch General Fegel's 2,000 and the useless Portuguese army of 28,000 was out-manoeuvred by the French under the Duke of Berwick, natural son of James II by Marlborough's sister. The planned campaign to capture Toulon did not even get under way.

France was now on the defensive, but 1705 was not a good year for the Grand Alliance. Marlborough's plan to invade France from the positions he had gained on the Moselle came to nothing, largely through the failure of his allies to come up to scratch. Operations in the Netherlands were inconclusive, and the Dutch began to accuse the British of paying too much attention to the Iberian peninsula campaign, suspecting them of trying to gain commercial advantage in the Mediterranean at their expense. The garrison of Gibraltar successfully survived Spanish attempts to recapture it, and an expedition under the command of the Earl of Peterborough captured Barcelona and established Charles III there. His force, after he had picked up more troops from Portugal, where Galway had succeeded Schomberg, and from Gibraltar, consisted of twelve British and four Dutch battalions and two regiments of British dragoons. These operations, although successful, placed a severe strain on the army, as the incidence of sickness among men and horses, both at sea and on arrival in the peninsula, was exceptionally high, and the general administrative arrangements were chaotic. One of Marlborough's main concerns during the winter was, therefore, to recruit both more men and more horses, not only to bring existing units up to strength, but to raise another regiment of dragoons and twelve new infantry battalions.

Malborough, disillusioned with both the Austrians, whose Emperor Leopold had died in 1705 and been succeeded by the more vigorous Joseph, and with the Margrave of Baden, conceived the ambitious project of taking his army across the Alps to join Eugène in Savoy, from

where he would launch a campaign into France. He had almost persuaded the Dutch to agree, when Villars delivered a sharp attack on the
Margrave, and the Dutch took fright. Marlborough had to resign
himself to yet another campaign in the Netherlands. By mid-May 1706
he had concentrated his English and Dutch troops north of Liège and
was still awaiting Danish, Hanoverian and Hessian contingents, when
he decided to open the campaign with a threat to Namur. He hoped to
provoke Villeroi into action but the latter needed no provocation – as
Louis XIV had decided to return to the offensive – and had crossed the
River Dyle, heading for Tirlemont. This threatened the rear of an
advance to Namur, and Marlborough decided to seek battle.

Early in the morning of 22 May his advanced guard, under Cadogan,
found Villeroi's army deployed in a position remarkably reminiscent of
Blenheim. Its right flank rested on the villages of Francqnée and Taviers,
bordering the River Mehaigne. A mile and a half north of it was the
larger village of Ramillies, from which the Petite Gette stream ran in
front of the villages of Offus and Autre Eglise, two miles further north.
Cavalry would have difficulty negotiating this stream, while there was
no such obstacle between Taviers and Ramillies. The opposing armies
were of much the same size, some 60,000 men in 130 cavalry squadrons
and 76 battalions, but Marlborough had 120 guns to Villeroi's 80. The
latter had no intention of repeating Tallard's fatal error at Blenheim
and kept his infantry and cavalry together, although the latter predominated between Ramillies, held by 20 battalions, and the two villages
on his right flank.

Marlborough's plan was to draw Villeroi's reserves to the north by
an attack across the Petite Gette, led by Lord Orkney with English and
Scottish troops, while Overkirk led his Dutchmen against Francqnée and
Taviers. These attacks did not get under way until 1 pm, but they had
the desired effect. Villeroi became increasingly anxious about his left
flank, where he had positioned his least reliable troops, and began to
move reserves from south of Ramillies to strengthen the defences round
Offus, now closely threatened by Orkney. To the latter's chagrin, just
as success seemed to be in his grasp after some intense fighting, he was
ordered to withdraw behind the Petite Gette, Marlborough sending five
aides-de-camp in succession to ensure that, not having been privy to
the Commander-in-Chief's main plan, he would conform. Villeroi remained anxious that a second assault across the stream was intended,
because he was unable to see that Marlborough was moving Lumley's

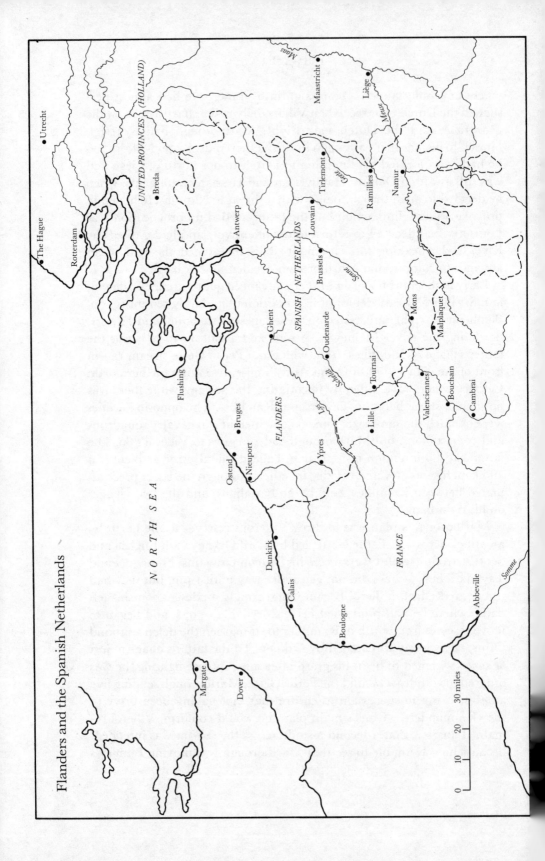

Flanders and the Spanish Netherlands

cavalry, which had supported Orkney, from his right to his centre, where Overkirk's horse had suffered a temporary reverse at the hands of the French south of Ramillies. The Dutch General Schultz, with Scottish and English battalions, was attacking Ramillies, and Overkirk, with Dutch, German and Swiss battalions and the allied cavalry, was engaged in a fierce battle, which swayed this way and that, south of the village.

Marlborough, who fed in every reinforcement he could switch from his right, was in the thick of the fighting, and at one stage was thrown from his horse and nearly captured by French cavalry. He escaped on an aide-de-camp's, and, as he mounted a second horse of his own, Colonel Bingfield, his equerry who was holding the stirrup, had his head removed by a cannon-ball. Marlborough rallied his troops once more, and made his final effort about 4 pm. An hour later Ramillies fell and the French cavalry south of it gave way. '*Sauve qui peut*' was the general cry; their horse deserted the foot and all the guns, 50 of which fell into Marlborough's hands. Villeroi and the Bavarian Elector only narrowly escaped capture, their coach stuck in a traffic jam of fleeing carriages. The French lost 15,000 men, while Marlborough's casualties came to 4,000, few of which were British. Only the troops attacking Ramillies, the Buffs and Scots Fusiliers and the Scots in Dutch service, suffered severely.

It was an exhilarating start to the year's campaigning. The French abandoned Louvain, Brussels and Antwerp without a fight. Ostend held out for three weeks, after which Marlborough turned south towards France itself, as Villeroi was replaced by the Duke de Vendôme. When the campaigning season was over, practically the whole of the Spanish Netherlands was clear of the French and Marlborough's reputation was at its height. His former companion-in-arms, Eugène, had had an equally significant success in northern Italy, trouncing the French at Turin in July and forcing them to evacuate Piedmont. However, the Duke's very success brought trouble in its train. The Dutch were talking of peace and claiming the Spanish Netherlands for themselves, while Marlborough was careful to insist that he had liberated them in the name of Charles III of Spain. At home, Whig demands for participation in the Government, strongly resisted by Queen Anne, threatened to produce cracks in the unity of the team that had supported him.

Marlborough's plans for 1707 were affected by the startling success of Charles XII of Sweden in eastern Europe. Fears were aroused that he might ally himself with France, and the Grand Alliance be crushed between them. Marlborough was despatched to sound him out, and was reassured to find his attitude friendly, although cool towards Vienna. Marlborough had initially toyed with the idea of another try at the Moselle, but abandoned that in favour of encouraging Eugène to thrust to Toulon and a renewal of activity in Spain, where Galway had reached Madrid in 1706 only to be forced back to Valencia and where Barcelona had successfully resisted attacks. Unfortunately the year started with a rebuff there, when Berwick defeated Galway at Almanza in April. This led to a prolonged enquiry into why the strength of the British forces was only 8,660, when Parliament had voted estimates for 29,395 in the peninsula. Marlborough's hopes that the main effort for the year should be in Spain and southern France were dashed, and it was in an uncertain mood that he took the field in the Netherlands in May 1707 with 80,000 men – 164 cavalry squadrons, 97 infantry battalions and 112 guns – to face Vendôme's 100,000, concentrated near Mons. Discouraged by the Dutch deputies from risking a general action and dubious himself, he waited until Eugène was launched against Toulon in July before he attempted to seize the initiative. It was an exceptionally wet August, and Vendôme succeeded in avoiding battle, until October brought the frustrating campaigning season to an end. Nor was it relieved by any good news from the Mediterranean. The Emperor Joseph had insisted on detaching troops from Eugène for a fruitless attack on Naples. Berwick's victory at Almanza had freed him to move north, and Eugène was forced to abandon his thrust to Toulon and withdraw.

Marlborough was in poor health and depressed. Sarah's relations with Queen Anne had deteriorated as a result partly of her constant nagging at her royal mistress, partly of the sinister influence of Abigail Hill. The Whigs were even more troublesome, but the combination of Marlborough and Godolphin still predominated, the revival of a Jacobite plot, backed by France, tending to bring the warring factions together. Marlborough's grand strategy for 1708 was to rouse Emperor Leopold to greater efforts to support the claims of his brother Charles to the Spanish throne. He managed to persuade him to send 7,000 troops from Italy to Catalonia, on condition that Britain and Holland paid for all the German and Austrian troops in Spain, to keep 12,000 in Italy and to provide 20,000 as half the troops available to Eugène on the Rhine, ostensibly for another thrust up the Moselle.

Marlborough and Eugène, however, agreed that the latter's army would be regarded as a potential reinforcement to Marlborough's in the Netherlands, increased to 180 cavalry squadrons and 112 battalions. South of Eugène, the Elector of Hanover, with another 30,000 men, would occupy the attention of Berwick and the Elector of Bavaria. The French had 100,000 in the Netherlands – 205 cavalry squadrons and 135 battalions – under the nominal command of Louis xiv's grandson, the Duke of Burgundy, with Vendôme at his side. It was a wet spring and campaigning started late, with a French move towards Louvain. Marlborough did not wish to risk an engagement until Eugène had joined him, but his opportunity came when Burgundy and Vendôme decided to take advantage of discontent with Dutch rule in western Flanders. They moved towards Ghent and Bruges, hoping to regain Ostend and cut Marlborough's communications with England, and then regain Antwerp and Brussels. Marlborough followed them. By 6 July, when the French had captured Ghent, Eugène personally had joined him, although his army was still on the move a long way behind. Berwick, realizing that he had left the Moselle, was also moving north to join Vendôme, whose next objective was Oudenarde on the Scheldt. Leaving Orkney to cover Brussels, Marlborough moved to place his army between the French and France. By forced marches – 30 miles in 36 hours – the advanced guard under Cadogan forestalled the French at Oudenarde, bridging the river and seizing the high ground north of the town on the far side in the morning of 11 July. Vendôme and Burgundy, at odds with each other, were only a few miles to the north, having crossed the river at Gavère. Vendôme, judging correctly that he was faced only by an advanced guard, urged immediate attack, but Burgundy over-ruled him in favour of assembling his whole army.

Marlborough and Eugène joined Cadogan at midday, and at 3 pm, when the main body of their troops was still crossing the pontoon bridges over the river, Marlborough told Cadogan to attack an isolated brigade of seven Swiss battalions which had been thrust forward of the main French position. This prompted Burgundy to change his mind and order his troops forward, which Vendôme opposed. Through a misunderstanding between them, the whole left wing of the French stayed where it was. The advancing right hit Cadogan at 5 pm, and a fierce and confused infantry battle raged among the hedgerows south of the Norken stream, hopeless ground for cavalry. Marlborough fed in reinforcements as his troops became available, but it was a close-run thing. Vendôme, in the thick of the fight, asked Burgundy to move the left wing to help him, but the message went astray and no help came. Giving Eugène responsibility for his right wing, largely with British troops, holding the centre himself with Dutch infantry, Marlborough sent the trusty old Dutch General Overkirk, who had borne the brunt of the battle at Ramillies, with all the rest of the Dutch infantry and cavalry on an out-flanking move on open high ground round Vendôme's western flank. It was between 7 and 8 pm, with not much more than an hour of daylight left, when Overkirk's attack, synchronized with one by Eugène on the right, encircled and overwhelmed the French, who fled in all directions under cover of darkness. Although their left wing had hardly been engaged at all, watched by the British cavalry, their losses totalled 20,000, of whom 9,000 were taken prisoner, while Marlborough's came to 3,000, of whom only 230 were British, and of those only 53 killed.

His elation at such a brilliant victory in his fifty-ninth year was tempered by concern at the result of the general election in the same month, which returned a Parliament in which the Whigs increased their strength. His anxiety over the growing squabbles between his strong-willed 50-year-old wife and the Queen aggravated the ill health from which he was suffering. In spite of these worries, he proposed a bold strategy to exploit his victory: an amphibious assault on Abbeville at the mouth of the Somme, to which he would advance, ignoring the French frontier fortresses. With that as a base, he would march on Paris. But this was ruled out as too risky both by the Dutch, once more seeking peace, and by the experienced Eugène. Instead they decided to lay siege to Lille, Eugène's army, now arrived from the Moselle, protecting the huge siege-train as 16,000 horses pulled its 94 guns, 64 mortars and 3,000 ammunition wagons the 70 miles from Brussels. On 27 August these guns began to fire, Marlborough fending off the superior numbers of Vendôme's and Berwick's combined armies, as they manoeuvred around him; but it was not until 8 December that, after repeated assaults, which had cost the attackers 15,600 casualties – 1,000 British – that the fortress commander, Boufflers, was forced to capitulate. Before that, Marlborough had made a personal approach to Berwick, suggesting negotiations for peace, fearing that the Dutch might do so behind his back. It proved fruitless. By that time he had recaptured Ghent and Bruges, and one of the coldest winters on record held Europe in its icy grip.

The severe winter of 1708–9 encouraged Louis xiv to approach the Dutch for peace. He was prepared to concede a great deal, even the claim of Charles iii to the Spanish Empire, but stuck at the demand that his grandson, Philip v, must hand over its crown within two months, for he knew that he did not have the power to enforce that on the proud Spaniards. Marlborough and Eugène urged that this demand be dropped, but the Whig ministers, encouraged by the death of Queen Anne's Tory husband, Prince George, insisted. Marlborough was not prepared to fight against them. Increasingly he felt that his political position, at Court and in Westminster generally, was being undermined. His judgement was affected, and he made a cardinal error in asking Queen Anne to appoint him Captain-General for life, which she refused.

The peace talks having broken down, Marlborough took the field late in June 1709 with an army of 120,000 men, opposing Villars, ensconced behind his frontier fortresses, linked by water obstacles. After a feint move, he laid siege to Tournai, another prolonged and bloody affair which lasted until 3 September, whereupon he made for Mons. Villars moved to meet him, and, after a feint approach to Mons from the west, turned south and took up a position among some woods by the village of Malplaquet, ten miles to the south of the fortress. On 9 September Marlborough and Eugène found him posted there, his flanks resting firmly on the woods, the ground between sodden from an exceptionally wet summer. The bulk of their troops were still some way away, all but twenty battalions arriving next day. That evening they decided to attack, believing that only another major defeat could force the French to make peace. There was little subtlety about their plan, a direct attack, launched at dawn on 11 September, against an enemy who had had several days in which to prepare a naturally strong position, with little or no opportunity to exploit the use of cavalry which had played such a significant part in their previous victories. It was a bloody slogging match, in which the determination of Marlborough's men finally prevailed by breaking the French centre, after which Villars retreated in good order. The battle cost Marlborough 18,000 casualties, of whom half were Dutch, a fifth of the whole force. The British came off more lightly: of their 14,000 men, 575 were killed and 1,286 wounded, most of them from only four regiments. The French lost 12,000. The lack of imagination in the plan may have owed something to Marlborough's illness. He was running a fever and had to take to his bed after the battle, and from then on his affairs went downhill.

His political position was crumbling, as was that of his supporters, including Godolphin, who was dismissed the following year while Marlborough and Eugène were once more in the field in Flanders, facing Villars. Having considered resignation earlier in the year, he made no move to follow his faithful ally into retirement, nor did he do so when Sarah was dismissed from her position at Court in January 1711. It was to be his last year on campaign, and he showed all his old brilliance in deceiving the enemy by unexpected moves, made possible by the efficiency of his staff arrangements and the willing endurance of his soldiers. Its result was the forcing of the Ne Plus Ultra lines in August, leading to the successful siege of Bouchain, which surrendered on 14 September, while Villars with his larger army was held at bay. But while he was defeating the French on the battlefields of Flanders, he was losing the battle at Westminster.

The Tory Harley, who had replaced Godolphin, had been negotiating with Louis xiv behind his back, and on 17 December 1711 the Queen announced the fact, 'notwithstanding the arts of those who delight in war'. On New Year's Day 1712 Marlborough was accused of misappropriating public funds, and ten days later 'that the matter might have impartial examination' the Queen dismissed him in a letter 'so very offensive that the Duke flung it into the fire'. So one who must rank with Wellington as among Britain's greatest soldiers – some would say higher than the Iron Duke, because of his wider responsibility in welding and holding together a delicate alliance, operating its forces right across Europe – was sacrificed to political intrigue and domestic quarrels. He had done more than any other man to create the British regular army and endow it with the traditions and attitudes which were to see it through bad times and good, disappointments and victories, for centuries to come.

The defeat of the allies in Spain had contributed to the pressure for peace. The garrison of Gibraltar had held out against a long siege with staunch gallantry, enduring great hardship; but the tide of war had turned decisively with Louis's despatch of Vendôme to Spain in 1710. Fifteen thousand Portuguese, with 3,000 British under Galway, had been defeated by an inferior Spanish force under Bay at the Cayac river in 1709; but in 1710 the Austrian General Stahremberg, with 25,000 men, including 4,200 British under Stanhope, had advanced from Catalonia and installed Charles iii in Madrid, having defeated Bay at Saragoza. This setback to the Spanish prompted Louis to send Vendôme with a French army, which, having forced Stahremberg to withdraw from Madrid, defeated Stanhope's isolated force of 2,000 at Brihuega on 9 December 1710. After a gallant fight, in which 600 fell, the rest surrendered to Vendôme's 20,000. On the following day, Stahremberg's 13,000 were defeated at Villa Vicosia. He had to abandon his artillery and withdraw to the isolated garrisons of Barcelona, Tarragona and Balaguer, yielding the whole of Spain to Philip v. The War of the Spanish Succession, brought to an end by the Treaty of Utrecht in 1713, had therefore failed in its nominal objective. But it had contained France from expanding her power eastwards in Europe, and Britain in particular gained by the cession of Spanish and French territories and claims – Gibraltar and Minorca in the Mediterranean, and Newfoundland and other areas of what was later to become Canada.

Looked at from the point of view of a twentieth-century soldier, the most remarkable feature of Marlborough's campaigns is how he persuaded his soldiers to perform the feats of endurance involved in the length of some and the speed of other marches – Blenheim an example of the first; Oudenarde and the forcing of the Ne Plus Ultra lines of the second – and of courage and resolution in his battles, such as Cutts's attack on Blenheim and all aspects of Ramillies and Malplaquet. What were the motives that impelled them not just to obey their orders, but, as contemporary accounts bear witness, to do so with enthusiasm and genuine affection, as well as respect for their Commander-in-Chief, colloquially known as Corporal John? It was not fear of the lash. That was sparingly used in comparison with later years. It could hardly have been patriotic fervour, as it cannot have been evident to many of the soldiers, either under Marlborough or in Spain, that Britain's interests or defence were much involved. Pride perhaps: to show both the traditional enemy, France, as well as the Dutch and other soldiers of the Grand Alliance, that the British soldier was as good or better than those who regarded themselves as more professional soldiers. Not loot, as opportunities for that were few and far between, and unauthorized pillage was severely punished. Not pay either, as the meagre sum officially due to the soldier, from which off-reckonings and various other deductions were made before he could lay his hands on it, was not even generally sufficient to cover his daily needs (and that of his horse, if he were a cavalryman), and was often weeks, months or even years in arrears.

The strongest motive seems to have been, as it has remained within the British army ever since, the feeling of being a member of a family, in which the opinion of his fellow soldiers, of a community based on sharing common dangers and hardships, exercising mutual responsibility for the lives of comrades-in-arms, mattered more than any consideration of national, moral or personal factors. For the cavalry and the infantry, this centred on a soldier's regiment – of horse, dragoons or foot. Marlborough's campaigns, eleven years of continuous active service in company with other professional European armies, laid the firm foundation, based on the regiment as an entity, which, in spite of obvious disadvantages, has endured as the basic organization of the British army. Its psychological advantages have to be weighed against its administrative cost and inflexibility. That was as true in the eighteenth century as it is in the twentieth.

The reasons for the development of the regimental system, and its perpetuation, lie fundamentally in the contest between Parliament and the Crown over the control both of finance and of the army, the latter being intimately linked with the former. Parliament was constantly trying to ensure that the Crown did not have at its beck and call a permanent monolithic body of armed men which could be used to flout Parliament's wishes, either at home or abroad. It therefore encouraged a financial system which operated through several channels, each of which was subject to its own control, and an organization which was not wholly dependent on the Crown. It favoured a system by which men of standing, often Members of Parliament themselves, were authorized to raise a regiment, provided with a sum of money with which to do so, and given a considerable degree of freedom as to how they set about it. Patronage and financial commissions for services rendered played their part, as they did in every other walk of life at that time. Having been given authority and a grant to raise a regiment, a colonel regarded it as a business, to be conducted on commercial lines, his officers filling the dual capacity of shareholders, by their purchase of commissions and promotion, and managers. The soldiers formed the workforce, expected to remain with the firm for life, unless they could find a replacement for themselves, or died in battle or, as was more likely, of sickness. The provision of weapons and ammunition was not his responsibility: they were supplied by the Master-General of the

Ordnance, who also provided the manpower of siege-trains – artillery and engineers – and was responsible direct to the Treasury and not to the Captain-General or Commander-in-Chief and his Secretary at War. The colonel was, however, responsible for clothing, feeding and housing his regiment, no permanent accommodation being provided except in Ireland; but the money for this was deducted from the soldier's pay, either as off-reckonings to cover clothing and 'necessaries', or to pay the innkeeper or householder on whom he was billeted, who also normally provided food and drink.

If the regiment suffered casualties during a season's campaigning, the officers were sent back to Britain in the winter to go round the country recruiting replacements; they were given a sum of money partly to cover expenses and partly as an initial payment to the recruit. If the latter deserted, died or was otherwise incapacitated before he joined the regiment – a frequent occurrence – no further money was available to provide a replacement, and the officer was out of pocket. This was a source of much discontent. The colonel expected to make his profit out of the off-reckonings from the soldier's pay, once the latter had served for two years. By that time, the off-reckonings should have covered the cost of his initial clothing and equipment, the replacement of which, unless the regiments was heavily involved in campaigning, should not cost as much as the initial issue. A regiment which suffered casualties could be a dead loss, due to the cost both of recruiting and of new clothing and equipment for the recruit.

It must be remembered that the Government's own administrative machinery, and control of finance generally, was primitive and chaotic by modern standards, with various agents taking their commissions here and there. It is not surprising that this applied to the army, and that opportunities for fraud and corruption were widespread, owing not a little to the complicated system designed to prevent them. As one author put it: 'The whole system of military finance in the seventeenth century was one vast entanglement of fraud. Not only did officers defraud the soldiers, but they defrauded the government also, while the government in turn defrauded the soldiers.'[4] The system in at least the early part of the eighteenth century was no different. One aspect of it, which was clearly open to abuse, was that by which regiments were allowed to count as 'mustered' men who were not there at all, and not expected to be. It was inevitable that new requirements arose involving expendi-

[4] Colonel Clifford Walton, *History of the British Standing Army 1660-1700* (1894), p. 671.

ture, which were not covered by items provided from Ordnance. Rather than go through the cumbrous procedure of attempting to alter the warrant under which the regiment was raised, authority would be given by the Secretary at War to allow a certain number of non-existent soldiers' pay to be used to meet this expenditure – pensions for widows was one case.

Overseas, however, the Commander-in-Chief could exercise a closer control over the administration of his army. This Marlborough did with significant effect both on the efficiency of his army and on its morale. He was able to do so because he was strongly supported by his friend and colleague, Sydney Godolphin, as Lord High Treasurer, who ensured that he received the money he needed. Marlborough, through his Commissary-General, placed his own contracts, many of them with the invaluable and reliable Jewish brothers, Moses and Solomon Medina, who began to suffer severe financial embarrassment when first Godolphin and then Marlborough himself fell from power.

Marlborough also benefitted from being both Captain-General and Master-General of the Ordnance. The provision of new shoes for all his soldiers, when they reached Heidelberg on their way to Blenheim, is the best-known example of the efficiency of Marlborough's administration. The march itself, and the fact that both horse and foot reached the Danube in excellent condition, was proof of his concern for administration and the welfare of his soldiers, reflected in their affection for him and their readiness to respond to his demands. The two previous years of the campaign in the Netherlands, disappointing as the operational results may have been, gave Marlborough the opportunity to weld his army together, improve its administration and training, and build up its morale, thus forging the weapon which he wielded to such effect at Blenheim and thereafter. It was in that army that the tradition was established that men must care for their horses before they considered their own needs, and that officers must see that the needs of horses and men were met before they themselves were refreshed or rested. Leadership in Marlborough's army, taking its example from the top, was of a high standard, not maintained in the peace which followed the Treaty of Utrecht. The army in Spain was not so fortunate. Dependence on the Portuguese army, which had no administration worth the name, the paucity of local supplies and the lack of money were a constant handicap to Galway and, notably, to Peterborough in Catalonia, who found himself having to meet his army's needs out of his own pocket.

Neither the general organization of the army nor the constitutional methods of its control differed fundamentally in Marlborough's day from that described in Chapter 1, although a Board of General Officers was established in 1706, its original purpose being to inquire into and, acting as a general court-martial, deal with:

Great Abuses and Disorders that have been committed by Several Officers and Soldiers of Our Army as well as of Disputes that have happened between officer and officer, and more especially of the ill-practices of some officers Employed in Recruiting Our Forces pursuant to the Recruiting Act and the Act for Discharge of Insolvent Debtors[5] contrary to the true intent and meaning of the Said Acts and to the great prejudice of Our Service.[6]

The Board became involved in other matters, most of them those which later became the responsibility of the Adjutant-General (who at that time was the Commander-in-Chief's chief-of-staff), among them the details of correct uniform. The legal basis on which military discipline – and, in the view of some, the very existence of the standing army – rested was the Mutiny Act, requiring annual renewal in Parliament. It originated in 1689, when some soldiers of the Royal Scots, sympathetic to the cause of James II, tried to make their way to Scotland, although they had been ordered to embark at Ipswich for service in Holland. It authorized punishment for mutiny and desertion, was valid only for six months and was not renewed again until 1702. Thereafter it became the annual act to authorize the army's discipline until 1879, when it was replaced by the annual Army Act, in the 1920s to be transformed into the Army and Air Force Annual Act, and in more recent years into the quinquennial Armed Forces (Discipline) Act.

One important organizational change, for which Marlborough's influence was responsible, but which came after his time, was the formation of the Royal Regiment of Artillery in 1727, two permanent companies of artillery having been formed in 1716. Before that, artillery was provided by the Board of Ordnance and manned as required. Artillery and engineer officers did not have to purchase their commissions nor their promotion, which was supposed to be determined by merit, but in practice was more often dependent on seniority. The development of

---

[5] 'Insolvent Debtors' referred to the practice of allowing imprisoned debtors to enlist. This did not cancel their debt, but their creditors then often found it difficult to trace them.

[6] *Register of Court Martial Warrants* WO30/18.

artillery for use in battle, and not just primarily as part of a siege-train, had been one of Marlborough's principal contributions to the conduct of the battle, perhaps following the example set by his contemporary, Charles XII of Sweden, like Gustavus Adolphus a tactical innovator. Marlborough cannot be ranked among these, although his use of cavalry differed from that of many of both his predecessors and his contemporaries. Whereas they tended to train their horsemen to use firearms, Marlborough favoured the sword, employed by cavalry moving forward not in a mad gallop but at a steady, gradually increasing pace, forming a great wedge which he pushed into the battle line at the crucial moment. The principal difference between the form which battles took in Marlborough's day from those of Cromwell's were the greater size of the armies and the increasing use and effectiveness of artillery to try and break up the cohesion of the enemy's battleline before foot or horse were launched against it. The gradual improvement in the foot-soldier's firearm did not fundamentally affect the way in which the musket was used nor, significantly, the effect it produced. The principal change was to lighten the infantryman's burden, simplify the complicated business of preparing to fire, and with the replacement of the pike and reduction in the number of ranks necessary to maintain a continuous fusillade, to increase the effectiveness of a given number of men.

As had happened before, and was to happen again with monotonous regularity, the army was drastically reduced once the war was over. At its height in 1709, it had numbered nearly 70,000, excluding the separate Irish establishment, generally of 12,000. When peace negotiations started in 1713, its establishment was 47,400, of which 16,600 were in the Netherlands, 4,700 in Minorca, 3,000 in Gibraltar, 8,300 in Dunkirk, 2,750 in the West Indies and the remainder, some 12,000, in England, Scotland and the Channel Islands. In 1714 this was reduced to 26,000 (2,200 cavalry and 23,800 infantry) of which 8,000 were authorized for England and Scotland. Discontent at this drastic reduction was intensified by the selection of regiments for disbandment not by the date on which they had been raised but by the Government's view of their tendency to Jacobite sympathies, a factor which had become urgent with the death of Queen Anne in 1714. Sixty-nine new regiments of horse and foot had been raised during the war, 35 had been disbanded before the end of 1712, and many more went when the

Treaty of Utrecht was signed, including such senior ones as the 6th and 14th of Foot, later to be resurrected and known as the Royal Warwickshire and West Yorkshire Regiments.

In the prolonged period of peace that followed, interrupted only by the Jacobite rebellions of 1715 and 1745, the army's size dwindled further, its total establishment falling to 12,400 in 1721. With no active employment and no permanent accommodation, its own efficiency and the attitudes of both the public and the politicians towards it deteriorated. Billeted mostly in inns, the soldiers had little to do but drink, and officers spent a great deal of time away from their units. After the death of Louis XIV in 1715, the Earl of Mar's rising in Scotland caused great alarm. Twenty-six regiments were raised again, bringing the army's strength to 36,000, which, with 6,000 troops lent by Holland, enabled Stanhope to crush the rebellion by April 1716, after Forster had advanced down the west coast of England as far as Preston and Mar himself had been defeated at Sheriffmuir.

The next challenge arose in 1742, when the royal link with Hanover involved the army in the War of the Austrian Succession, although the country was not officially at war with France. Parliament voted money to increase the army to a strength of 62,000, of whom 16,000 were intended as an expeditionary force for the Netherlands. New regiments were raised, and the aged Earl of Stair appointed Commander-in-Chief. After an inconclusive campaign in the Netherlands in 1742, in which his army suffered from the absence on leave of a great many of its officers, Stair in 1743 led his 16,000 men to join an equal number of Hanoverians and 12,000 Austrians at Aschaffenburg on the River Main, 30 miles upstream of Frankfurt. Here on 19 June, George II, who, like Stair, had fought under Marlborough at Oudenarde, took over command of the army, the last British monarch to do so in the field, and paid more attention to advice from the Hanoverians than that given by the experienced and prudent Stair.

A French army of 70,000, under the Duke de Noailles, was advancing towards Aschaffenburg from Frankfurt, and by 26 June George II was in danger of being surrounded, pinned between the river and the wooded Spessart Hills to the north. He was already cut off from supply. In desperation he decided to march downstream to Hanau, whence he could escape northwards. But Noailles forestalled him, having sent 28,000 men under Marshal Grammont to cross the river at Seligenstadt and block King George's escape route at the village of Dettingen.

Grammont was outnumbered, and, after a fierce ding-dong battle, in which British fire discipline and sheer dogged determination played a significant part, and the 16-year-old James Wolfe, adjutant of the 12th Foot, received his baptism of fire, the French gave way. Their casualties were 5,000, double those of King George's army, in which the British lost 265 killed and 561 wounded. At one stage the King's horse bolted and carried him off to the rear, while the opposite happened to his 22-year-old son, the Duke of Cumberland, who had difficulty in controlling his mount when he led a gallant cavalry charge, in which the 3rd Dragoons suffered heavily. Meanwhile the rest of Noailles's army had remained south of the river, taking no part in the battle, apart from contributing artillery fire. Escaping Noailles's clutches, the King's army continued its march to Hanau, having failed to sever the link between France and Bavaria.

War was officially declared next year, 1744, and in 1745 Cumberland, in command of the allied army in Flanders, the British contribution to which had been raised to 25,000 (reducing numbers in Britain to 15,000), found himself opposed by the experienced Marshal Saxe, the Dutch at first being unwilling to do more than man their fortresses. The two armies met on 11 May at Fontenoy, east of the Scheldt south of Tournai, Cumberland's 50,000 against Saxe's 56,000. Given his inferiority and the strength of the French position, which they had occupied for several days, it was imprudent of Cumberland and his colleagues, Königsegg and Waldeck, to decide on an attack. Things went wrong from the start, with the failure of the Dutch attack. Cumberland made the mistake, common among inexperienced commanders, of becoming too involved in one particular action, and he lost general control. In spite of some very gallant fighting by both Hanoverians and British, he was defeated and had to withdraw, having suffered heavy casualties, the Hanoverians losing 6,000, the twenty British infantry battalions 4,000 and the cavalry 300 men and 600 horses. The French are thought to have suffered equally, but remained masters of the field.

They had by this time also provided a major diversion to draw troops away from Flanders by their support of another Jacobite rebellion, led by the Young Pretender, Charles Edward, generally known as Bonnie Prince Charlie. He landed in Scotland in July 1745, rallying the Macdonalds and the Camerons to his cause, and capturing a company of the Royal Scots on their way to Fort William. There were 3,750 troops in Scotland under Sir John Cope, but they were scattered about in small garrisons. In the process of gathering them together, Cope let the Pretender, who had now received the support of Stewarts and Frasers also, occupy Edinburgh in September. By then he had assembled 4,500 infantry and 400 horse. The 72-year-old Field-Marshal Wade was at Newcastle with 18,000 troops, many of them withdrawn from Flanders and including Dutch, Hanoverians and Hessians. Charles therefore followed the pattern of the 1715 rebellion and moved south down the west coast, reaching Derby on 4 December and causing panic in London. Cumberland was by then at Lichfield with another army, and the Jacobites decided to withdraw, looting on the way, but skilfully holding the English at bay. Cumberland followed up closely and bided his time, while inter-clan quarrels and problems of supply began to weaken the Young Pretender's support. On 15 April 1746 Cumberland's army of 9,000 found Charles's 5,000 half-starving and ill-clad Highlanders, worn out after a night march, on Culloden Moor near Nairn. It did not take him long to crush them, killing 1,000 and capturing the same number at the cost of 310 casualties to his men. This, and the ruthlessness with which this 25-year-old pursued and punished the rebels, were to earn him the nickname of 'Butcher'. The Jacobite cause was finally lost.

Before the Peace of Aix-la-Chapelle brought the war with France to an end in 1748, fighting had spread both to India and America, in both of which it continued. In the former, Clive, after the successful defence of Arcot in 1751, defeated the French at Covelang in the following year, his rival Dupleix being recalled to France in 1755. In America Braddock's attempt to prevent the French from linking up her colonies in Canada and Louisiana by extending her power along the Mississippi and its tributaries met with disaster at Turtle Creek in 1755, the colonial officer, George Washington, taking over command when Braddock died of his wounds. He was lucky to be among the 16 out of 86 officers and 459 out of 1,373 soldiers to survive.

These imperial clashes were the prelude to the Seven Years' War. In spite of preparations for war against France, the estimates for 1756 only allowed for an army of 34,000 in Great Britain and 13,000 in the colonies, ten new regiments being raised and others increased in strength, another four also to be raised in America. The principal concern of both the Government and the public was an invasion from France, and a fierce political battle began over whether to bring troops from Hanover and Hesse to defend the shores or to raise militia. It was not until Minorca was lost (for which Admiral Byng was court-martialled and shot) and Pitt had replaced Newcastle as head of the Government that a firm grip was taken. Hanoverians and Hessians were sent home, the militia reorganized, and estimates submitted for an army of 30,000 in Great Britain and 19,000 in the colonies. This was to be achieved by forming second battalions for every regiment of the line and the formation of two regiments of Highlanders – Fraser's and Montgomery's – each 1,100 strong. Two thousand men for the artillery and engineers were also authorized, the Royal Regiment being increased to 24 companies of guns and incorporating a company of Miners. The Marines were increased from 100 to 130 companies, and the whole military machine invigorated. For the militia, every county was to provide 1,600 men, chosen by lot by the parish authorities under the control of the lords-lieutenant. Those thus chosen would serve for three years and then be exempt until all others eligible had served.

The war started badly, Cumberland being forced to seek terms when the French invaded Hanover. British arms fared no better in America, where the late arrival of reinforcements prevented Loudoun from attacking Louisburg and lost him Fort William Henry to Montcalm. Only Clive in India brought any relief to this depressing start to the war. At Plassey, with only 3,500 men against 50,000, he had defeated Surajah Dowlah, bringing Bengal under British influence. Had it not been for the victories of Frederick the Great at Rossbach and Leuthen, George II might have lost Hanover and been forced to make general peace with France.

The tide turned in 1758, largely thanks to the efforts of Prince Ferdinand of Brunswick in clearing the French from Hanover during the winter, his army, which had included British mercenaries, being joined in September by a regular contingent of five infantry regiments and 14 cavalry squadrons.

Meanwhile in America, Pitt planned a double thrust. Under Abercromby's overall command, Amherst, with 11,000 British regulars, was to capture Louisburg and move up the St Lawrence to Quebec, while Abercromby and Howe, with 10,000 regulars and 20,000 colonial militia, moved up the Hudson from New York, directed on Montreal, recapturing Fort William Henry on the way. A third thrust of 1,900 regulars and 5,000 militia was to revenge Braddock and capture Fort Duquesne. Amherst had taken Louisburg by 27 July, but Admiral Boscawen refused to sail up the river to Quebec. Before then, Aber-

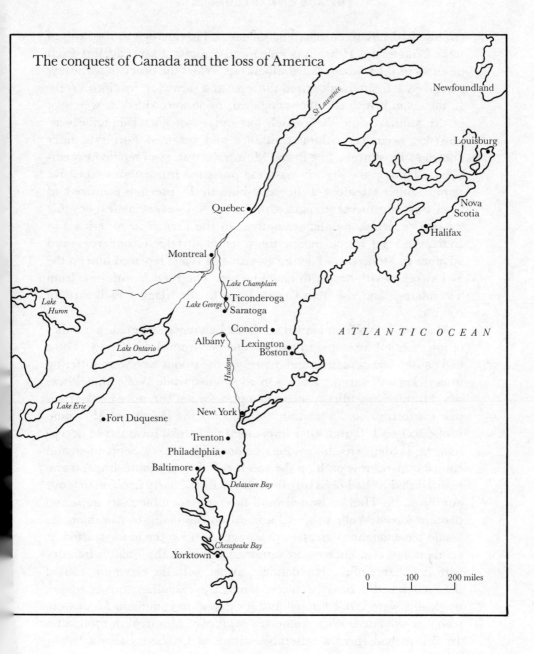

The conquest of Canada and the loss of America

Newfoundland

Louisburg

St Lawrence

Nova Scotia

Quebec

Halifax

Montreal

Lake Huron

Lake Champlain

Ticonderoga

Lake George

Saratoga

Concord

Albany

Lexington

Lake Ontario

Boston

ATLANTIC OCEAN

Hudson

Lake Erie

Fort Duquesne

New York

Trenton

Philadelphia

Baltimore

Delaware Bay

Chesapeake Bay

Yorktown

0   100   200 miles

cromby had suffered a crippling defeat at Ticonderoga at the head of Lake Champlain. Howe was killed and a direct assault against fixed defences in thick woods failed miserably. When the order to withdraw was given at 6 pm, panic seized the force and turned retreat into a rout. In the seven British battalions engaged, 1,600 were killed, as were 334 of the militia, while the French lost only 350. Fort Duquesne was, however, occupied without resistance and renamed Fort Pitt, later known as Pittsburgh. The Prime Minister's strategy of sending expeditions to land on the French coast had proved as fruitless and expensive as most other attempts of the same kind in the previous century had been, but the growing strength of the Royal Navy at sea made it possible for him to deploy greater strength than the French in America and India. Amherst was to renew the attempt to take Ticonderoga and advance to Montreal, while the 32-year-old Wolfe replaced him on the St Lawrence with orders to take Quebec. The French withdrew from Ticonderoga and also from Crown Point by the Niagara Falls early in August.

Meanwhile Wolfe had sailed up the St Lawrence and made a number of unsuccessful attempts to assault Quebec from downstream. These had caused 800 casualties and depressed the troops who were suffering from sickness of varying kinds. On 20 August, while Wolfe himself was sick, his three brigadiers concocted a plan for a silent move up the river past the fortress, and a landing at the foot of the Heights of Abraham. Wolfe accepted it, and, after implementing careful measures of deception, he landed with his soldiers before dawn on 13 September and climbed the narrow path up the 200-ft cliff. When Montcalm, at 6 am, realized that he had been surprised, he made the hasty decision to move out for battle. Had he waited until he could assemble more guns and perhaps forced Wolfe to spend a night on the Plains of Abraham, he would have fought at greater advantage. At 9 am the battle started. A combination of accurate and sustained fire from the English infantry with the charge of the Highlanders, armed with the claymore, routed the French within hours, at a cost of only 630 casualties, among whom, tragically, were Wolfe himself and his second-in-command Monckton, who was wounded. With Amherst's capture of Montreal in 1760, after the British had spent a miserable winter in Quebec, Canada fell to Britain.

1759 had also been a bright year for British arms in Europe. Twelve thousand men under Lords Sackville and Granby had been sent to join

Brunswick, who was facing a French army of 80,000 under de Contades. At the end of July the latter was in a strong position at Minden, where the River Weser passes through a narrow gap in a range of hills. Brunswick sent a corps under Wagenheim to face him, keeping the rest of his army, including the British contingent, in reserve. When, on 1 August, de Contades attacked Wangenheim, Brunswick, who had been waiting for such an opportunity, quickly brought the rest of his army up on Wangenheim's right, the British cavalry, under Sackville, being slow to move off. In an astonishing and unintended feat of disciplined courage, the British infantry, closely supported by the Hanoverians and their own artillery, but not by their cavalry, advanced in the teeth of cavalry charges and artillery fire and routed the French by 10 am, at a cost to themselves of 78 officers and 1,252 men out of a total strength of 4,434. The total allied loss was 2,600 out of 45,000, while the French lost at least 7,000, perhaps as many as 10,000, out of a probable 60,000, 43 of their guns being left on the battlefield.

The only further battle of note in which the British took part in Germany before the end of the war was that of Warburg on 31 July 1760, when 22 squadrons of British cavalry, under the Marquis of Granby, redeemed the failure of Sackville at Minden. When the infantry were almost overcome by the extreme heat, a brilliant charge, led by Granby himself, who, losing his wig, went 'bald-headed at it', routed the French cavalry and brought victory at a cost of 1,200 casualties, very few of which were from the cavalry. The French lost about 7,000, leaving 12 guns behind, but were not removed from Germany.

The death of Frederick the Great's enemy, Elizabeth of Russia, and general war weariness on all sides, particularly at the cost, led all the participants to consider bringing the war to an end. The estimates for 1760, the year of George II's death, allowed for 100,000 men on the British establishment in addition to Ireland's 12,000, 20,000 embodied militia and 55,000 German troops in British pay. British infantry regiments had been increased to 96, and dragoons to 21. But with the resignation of Pitt in October 1761, enthusiasm for continuation of the war waned. When 1763 brought it to an end with the Treaty of Paris, Britain had significantly extended her empire in America and the West Indies, and had practically eliminated French power from India. From Spain she regained Minorca and gained Florida. All this had been done without engaging a large force on the continent, although British subsidies had been essential to help her allies to restrain the French, while

Frederick of Prussia dealt with the Russians and the Austrians, now once more threatened by the Turks. The age of Marlborough, who had died forty-one years before, was now at an end, six years before the birth of Arthur Wellesley, whose fame was to equal his.

3
THE AGE OF WELLINGTON
1769-1815

Arthur Wellesley (or Wesley, as the family spelt their name at the time) was born in Dublin on 1 May 1769, the third son of the first Earl of Mornington, a member of the Anglo-Irish Protestant ascendancy, remembered only for the psalm chants he composed as Professor of Music at Trinity College. All his five surviving sons were to gain distinction in public life, Arthur most of all. In his youth he showed little promise of this and appeared to share the interests of his father who died in 1781, the year in which Arthur entered Eton, from which, having shown no academic inclination, he was removed in 1784 to make room for his younger brothers. The decision to send him in 1786 to the French Royal Academy of Equitation at Angers, in preparation for a career in the army, appears to have been taken by his strong-willed mother and elder brother Richard, both financially embarrassed at the time. Arthur accepted the decision with no apparent enthusiasm. The year he spent there did more to improve his command of French than his expertise on horseback, and three months after his return, on 17 March 1787, six weeks short of his 18th birthday, Richard bought him a commission in the 73rd Highland Regiment as an ensign.

This method of entry into the army as an officer was normal at that time. Britain's only military academy was at Woolwich and had been founded in 1741 for the instruction of cadets who aspired to commissions in the artillery and engineers under the Master-General of the Ordnance. Purchase was the normal method of obtaining a commission and subsequent promotion in the infantry and cavalry, although there were other ways of obtaining both, and, when the army expanded rapidly during the Napoleonic wars, these became the norm. One method was by filling the vacancy caused by the death of an officer on service. This was often used to provide a commission for a deserving sergeant from

73

the ranks. Another was 'recruiting for rank'. This only occurred when the army was expanding in wartime. It was a device by which commissions (or promotion) could be granted to men who could raise recruits to form a new company for an existing battalion, or for a newly raised one. It was open to abuse, as the recipients were often unsuitable as officers and, having received their commission, sometimes absented themselves.

From a twentieth-century point of view, it would appear that the system for commissioning and promotion of officers for the artillery and engineers was greatly preferable to that for the infantry and the cavalry. Cadets underwent a rigorous course of instruction, principally in mathematics and science, and, after commissioning, their promotion was, in theory, based on merit. In fact it was almost entirely regulated by seniority. As there were no pensions and no fixed ages for promotion or retirement, the senior ranks of the officers of the artillery and engineers tended to be the equivalent of the 'Invalids', who acted as caretakers of the ancient fortifications round Britain's coasts. Seniority and senility became synonymous. Purchase, open to abuse and criticism as it undoubtedly was, worked in the opposite direction. In the absence of pensions, the officer's commission and subsequent promotions were the equivalent of buying into a practice in another profession, such as medicine or the law. It made it possible for officers to retire on the proceeds of selling their final rank, and it opened up the possibility of rapid promotion for keen officers who, by one means or another, could raise the money for an initial commission and subsequent promotions. It provided a degree of flexibility within the infantry and cavalry, introducing an element of cross-fertilization into strict adherence to the regimental system.

Arthur Wellesley's career provides the clearest possible justification for the prevalent system, just as, in the nineteenth century, that of the Earl of Cardigan does for its condemnation. On Christmas Day 1787, only nine months after being commissioned into the 73rd, Wellesley was transferred to the 76th as a lieutenant in order to be aide-de-camp to the Viceroy of Ireland, who would pay him 10s a day on top of his pay of nearly the same amount and his private income, provided by Mornington, of £125 a year. A month later he transferred again to the 41st, as the 76th had been ordered to the West Indies, and he transferred in June of the same year to the 12th Light Dragoons, a regiment which had the advantage of being stationed in Ireland, where it had been for

74

the past 70 years. Three years later he acquired a captaincy, nominally in command of a company, in the 58th Foot, also on the Irish establishment. He did not have to pay for this promotion, perhaps through the good offices of his patron, the Viceroy. He transferred again on 31 October 1792 to the 18th Light Dragoons, also stationed in Ireland. He does not appear actually to have served with any of these regiments, his duties as ADC on the staff of the Viceroy in Dublin Castle being added to by his election as Member of the Irish Parliament for Trim in 1790.

Wellesley's first years in the army coincided with a low point in its fortunes, following the War of American Independence. After the end of the Seven Years' War, it had been reduced in 1764 to 17,500 men at home, including 3,000 'Invalids', 10,000 for the colonies to meet the commitments which had been increased by that war, 4,000 for the garrisons of Minorca and Gibraltar, 1,800 for the artillery and 12,000 for Ireland, a total of 45,300. But trouble in America, arising out of the dissatisfaction of the colonists, soon demonstrated that 10,000 men would not meet all colonial commitments. By 1775, when the War of Independence began with the affair at Lexington, General Howe commanded that number of men in North America, 2,500 of them facing Washington's 1,700 militia at Boston and defeating them at the bloody battle of Bunker's Hill on 17 June, at a cost of 1,054 casualties, 226 of whom were killed. Howe hung on to Boston, until he was attacked there by Washington in March 1776, when he decided to evacuate it.

During this time Washington's colleague, Benedict Arnold, had led a successful thrust into Canada, capturing Montreal, but was defeated by Carleton when he attempted to attack Quebec in a snowstorm on the last day of the year. By July, reinforced by Clinton, who had carried out an unsuccessful raid on Charleston in South Carolina, Howe had concentrated 30,000 men at New York, and Washington could only raise 10,000 to oppose his advance towards Philadelphia. A lengthy exchange of views between Germain, Secretary of State for America,[1] Howe and Burgoyne, who had taken over command in Canada but was in England during the winter, led to a plan by which Howe, reinforced by 2,500 men instead of the 20,000 he had asked for, would advance north up the Hudson to Albany, where he would meet Burgoyne, who would bring his 8,000 men south by Lakes Champlain and George. Howe changed his mind as a result of the defeat of Cornwallis at Trenton on 3 January 1777, after which Washington reoccupied almost

[1] Sackville, who had led the cavalry at Minden, inherited this title in 1770.

all of New Jersey. Howe therefore decided that he must throw Washington back at least as far as Philadelphia before he could risk an advance up the Hudson to Albany. Unfortunately Burgoyne had left for Canada before Germain received and approved Howe's change of plan, and his subsequent orders did not make it clear to Howe that his move on Philadelphia must not prejudice the coordination of his advance to Albany with Burgoyne's. Ignorant of Howe's intention, Burgoyne set off on Lake Champlain on 17 June, by which time Howe was engaged in operations against Washington. These took a long time to develop, and it was not until 23 September that he entered Philadelphia after defeating Washington at Brandywine Creek. It took him until 15 November to clear Washington's troops away from Delaware Bay so that he could use it to bring supplies from New York. A month before that Burgoyne had surrendered at Saratoga, his troops exhausted by a long land advance, chosen by Burgoyne in place of the more traditional use of lake and river transport, surrounded and cut off from supply by the American Gates's superior force. An attempt by Clinton to join him with 3,000 men had got no further than Fort Montgomery, 50 miles north of New York, from which he had set out.

Burgoyne's surrender was instrumental in bringing France into the contest on the side of the rebels, who now styled themselves the United States of America, and an alliance between them was signed in March 1778, which Spain and Holland joined the following year, the former laying siege to Gibraltar. The whole character of the war had changed, and the possibility of crushing the rebels by a land campaign – which it was estimated would need 80,000 men – was remote. Instead the decision was taken to concentrate on securing the southern colonies, linking this to the security of the West Indies.

Clinton succeeded Howe as Commander-in-Chief, but left operations in South Carolina to Cornwallis, who was encouraged by Germain to over-commit himself by extending operations further north, exploiting the situation produced by the defection of Benedict Arnold, who was leading a force of 1,700 men in raids up the rivers of Virginia. Clinton reinforced him with a further 2,000 and Cornwallis moved north to join him and face the Frenchman La Fayette, whom Washington had detached to deal with the threat to Virginia. Cornwallis chose to concentrate his force of 7,000 at Yorktown, between the York and James Rivers near the mouth of the Chesapeake. There he hoped to establish a base in which to spend the winter and build up an effective force. But, as

Washington marched south to attack him, the French sent a fleet under Admiral de Grasse to prevent Clinton moving his force of 7,000 by sea to join Cornwallis.

The British fleet under Hood was greatly outnumbered and, after the indecisive action of Chesapeake Bay on 5 September, returned to New York. Cornwallis, cut off from supply and reinforcement, was left to face 8,000 French and 5,000 Americans. He held out until 19 October, when, with a large proportion of his force disabled by wounds or sickness and with hardly a gun able to fire, he surrendered only five days before Clinton with 5,000 men in a fleet of 26 under Admiral Digby arrived off the mouth of the Chesapeake. Of the 6,630 men who surrendered, 2,500 were German and 2,000 of them were sick or wounded. It was the virtual end of the war, although peace was not signed until Britain recognized American independence in 1783.

Once more the army was reduced to its peacetime level, which was fixed at 52,000: 17,500 for Great Britain, 9,400 for 'Plantations', 2,800 for Gibraltar, 6,400 for India, 3,300 for the artillery and 12,000 for the Irish establishment. However the actual strength of the army in Britain sank well below that, and, with the post of Commander-in-Chief left vacant, its general state fell to one of the lowest ever, the soldier's pay remaining at its 1660 level of 6d a day, from which off-reckonings and the cost of his daily keep were deducted.

This was the army which Arthur Wellesley joined in 1787; but, while he was leading an idle life in Ireland, revolution had broken out in France, and its impact began to spread beyond her borders. In 1792 Austria and Prussia had invaded France and been rebuffed, while France in return had occupied Austrian possessions on her borders, including the Austrian Netherlands, from which she threatened Holland. William Pitt (the younger), who had been Prime Minister since 1784, was determined to keep Britain out of war, but was drawn into it by the threat to the Low Countries and reaction to the execution of Louis xvi in January 1793. France declared war on Britain and Holland in February, and George iii's second son, Frederick Duke of York, was sent to Holland with three battalions of Guards to help defend it against a French invasion, which was defeated by Austrian intervention in April. By the end of August, Pitt had agreed that Britain would finance an alliance of Austria, Prussia, Hesse-Cassel, Sardinia and Spain in a war against France, although he refused to commit Britain to the demand for restoration of the French monarchy. Pitt hoped to limit

Britain's direct military involvement to his favourite one of acquiring French possessions overseas, but had to accept that she must make some contribution to a force, which would primarily be drawn from Hanover and Holland, and include the usual element of Hessian mercenaries, to cooperate with the Austrians under Prince Frederick of Saxe-Coburg.

The army was in no state to provide an effective force. In spite of the measures he had taken to improve matters when he took office in 1784, Pitt had reduced the establishment of the army at home to 13,000 as a sop to those who argued that the best defence against revolution was to placate the discontented masses. Steps were immediately taken to increase its numbers, the principal one being to call up the militia for home defence in order to free the regulars for service overseas. This was combined with a scheme by which those chosen by ballot for the militia could evade service by paying men to take their place; these substitutes were just those men who would have provided the material for regular recruitment. The army was forced to fall back on the discredited method of accepting criminals and debtors, who volunteered to serve in the ranks as an alternative to remaining in prison. The Government was not prepared to apply any form of conscription, not even of the unemployed and destitute, as had been imposed in Marlborough's day. With the traditional division of responsibility for the affairs of the army between the Secretary of State, the Secretary at War and the Master-General of the Ordnance made worse by the absence of any Commander-in-Chief, and the years of neglect since the end of the war in America, the army was in no state to face a Continental war. In any case, with the defeat of the French in the Netherlands in April, the politicians were inclined to think the war already over.

It was in this atmosphere that Arthur Wellesley decided to take his military profession seriously. Having asked his brother Richard to use his influence to have him posted to the force the Duke of York took to Holland, a request that produced no result, he begged him in March 1793 to lend him the money to buy a majority in the 33rd Foot. Richard, in spite of his debts and personal extravagance, obliged and never asked for repayment. Having become a major on 30 April, he somehow managed to acquire command of the regiment on 30 September. Thus, at the age of 24, having seen no real military service, he assumed all the duties, military and financial, of regimental command. He had hoped to lead his regiment on an expedition under Lord Moira to raid the Normandy coast. In anticipation of seeing active service, he resigned his parliamentary seat and arranged for a linen-draper to service his debts, but nothing came of it and he returned to the business of trying to sort out the regimental accounts, which he had found in a typical eighteenth-century mess.

Meanwhile the Duke of York, with 6,500 British, 13,000 Hanoverians, 8,000 Hessians and 15,000 Dutch, had been ordered by Pitt to capture Dunkirk, but had been forced to withdraw to Ostend when the Austrians were defeated by the French further south. Things went no better in 1794, the Austrians deliberately leaving the Duke of York alone to face the French, having decided that they wished to withdraw from the Netherlands to concentrate their forces elsewhere. Pitt decided to reinforce the Duke with 10,000 men under Lord Moira: one of the 11 battalions chosen was Wellesley's 33rd, which sailed from Cork on 21 June. On arrival he was given command of a brigade, a command which in those days was usually held by a major-general.

Soon after Moira's force had arrived, the Austrians finally withdrew, and the Duke of York took his 40,000 men, 25,000 of whom were British, back into Holland. Here at Boxtel on 15 September Wellesley fought his first action, nearly a year after his exact contemporary, Napoleon Bonaparte, had gained fame for his handling of the revolutionary artillery against the royalists, supported by British, at Toulon. The Duke's army was greatly outnumbered by the French and totally unprepared to spend a winter in the open. Losing men constantly from sickness, some even from starvation, he was forced to withdraw into northern Germany, and by the time he had reached the River Ems at the beginning of February 1795, its state was described by the Hanoverian general, Walmoden, in a letter to the Duke of York in these words: 'Your army is destroyed: the officers, their carriages, and a large train are safe, but the men are destroyed. The army has now no more than six thousand fighting men, but it has all the drawbacks of thirty-three battalions, and consumes a vast quantity of forage.' When the force was withdrawn to Britain in April, 15,000 were embarked, leaving part of the artillery and all the cavalry to support the Hanoverians. The losses, few of them incurred in action, although great and clear evidence of the disgraceful lack of adequate administration, were not therefore, perhaps, as extensive as Walmoden stated.

The experience of this disastrous campaign made a deep impression on two young men whose influence on the British army in the following two decades, one at the Horse Guards in Whitehall, the other on the battlefields of India and the Iberian Peninsula, was to be profound. The first was the 32-year-old Duke of York, who was appointed Commander-in-Chief and a field-marshal in February of that year, the other the 26-year-old Lieutenant-Colonel Arthur Wellesley. In a panic fear of French invasion, both of Britain and of her overseas possessions, the Government had ordered the raising of new units by all and every means. The army's strength of rank and file had been expanded from 40,000 in 1793 to 125,000 in 1795. In addition the government decided to make a major increase in the size of the navy. The result was total chaos, as units were produced in which no officer had any qualification for the post, and all and sundry competed to enlist any man they could persuade, trick or force into the ranks, usually under the influence of drink. Little wonder that Wellesley once described his soldiers as 'the scum of the earth'. It is not generally realized that he was referring to the recruits when they were enlisted, and that he added: 'It is really wonderful that we should have made them the fine fellows they are.'

The Duke of York immediately set about trying to bring some order out of the chaos: to prevent the commissioning and promotion of un-suitable officers (even infants had been commissioned); to bring some order into the field of recruitment in spite of the plethora of Acts of Parliament on the matter, which, following each other in rapid succession, added to the confusion; to institute some regular training for officers, both at regimental duty and on the staff, resulting in the formation of the Royal Military College in 1801, from which both the Camberley Staff College and Sandhurst were derived[2]; and to improve and produce some form of standardization in the training of the rank and file, making use of such publications as David Dundas's *Principles of Military Movements* and Le Marchant's works on fortifications and the use of swords by the cavalry. By these means he sought to bring the training of the infantry and cavalry more into line with that of the artillery and engineers, on which the influence of the able Duke of Richmond, who had been Master-General of the Ordnance since 1782 and was succeeded by Cornwallis in 1795, had been beneficial.

The capable and sensible Duke of York had to compete against every type of obstruction, not least from those with political interest, both those who were merely concerned with feathering the nests of them-

[2] Their common predecessor was a private tutorial establishment at High Wycombe, run by an émigré French General Jarry.

selves, their friends, relations and supporters, but also those who instinc-
tively opposed any extension of the power and influence of a royal
prince over the army. Division of political responsibility for the control
of the army and the conduct of its affairs and operations remained, but
was at least simplified by the appointment by Pitt in 1794 of Henry
Dundas as Secretary of State *for* War, who however retained his other
ministerial responsibilities as Treasurer of the Navy and President of the
Indian Board of Control. The Secretary *at* War (William Windham
from 1794 to 1801) remained separately responsible for the army's
administration and finance. The division of responsibility for operations
overseas between the Foreign Secretary and the Secretary of State for
the Colonies was thus eliminated, although it did not stop them from
interfering, and the latter post was combined with that of Secretary of
State for War in 1798. It was ironic that, when the Duke of York had
done so much to clean up the Augean stables of the traffic in commissions
and promotions, it should have been a scandal concerning the involvement in it of his mistress, Mrs Clarke, that forced his resignation in
1809. He was reappointed in 1811.

In his task of recruiting and organizing an efficient army, the strength
of which had risen by 1807 to 205,000, the Duke of York was greatly
assisted by one of the most effective Secretaries of State for War the
country ever had, Lord Castlereagh, another exact contemporary of
Arthur Wellesley. In the two years, 1807-9, that he held the post, he
brought order and sound sense into the field of recruitment and organization both for the regular army and for the militia and the volunteers.
He made the militia a source of recruitment for the regular army, and
the volunteers, who, with 'Fencibles', provided an ill-organized and ill-
trained reinforcement to the militia for home defence, a source for filling
the ranks, thus emptied, of the militia. Although Arthur Wellesley, as
Wellington in the Peninsula, had some differences of opinion with the
Duke of York over matters concerning their respective powers over
promotion and appointment of officers, he paid eloquent tribute to him,
when he gave evidence to the inquiry arising out of the Mrs Clarke
scandal, in the following words:

I know that, since HRH has had the command of the army, the regulations
framed by him for managing the promotion of the army have been strictly
adhered to, and that the mode in which the promotion is conducted has given
general satisfaction ... the officers are improved in knowledge; that the staff of
the army is much better than it was ... and everything that relates to military

discipline of the soldiers and the military efficiency of the army has been greatly improved since HRH was appointed C-in-C.[3]

To the Duke of York, in forging the weapon, and to Castlereagh, for keeping the ranks filled, Wellington was to owe much when he assumed command in the Iberian peninsula. Between 1795 and 1807 his own experience and natural ability were to teach him how to make use of what they provided.

Arthur Wellesley arrived back in Ireland in March 1795, and immediately resumed his duties as ADC at Dublin Castle and MP for Trim. His first thought was to seek more remunerative employment, and he even aspired to the post of Secretary at War, but his attempts to find political preferment came to nought and he resigned himself to continuing his career as a soldier. The 33rd embarked for that cemetery of soldiers, the West Indies, in September, but their commanding officer already had a fever and was lucky not to accompany them, as the ships were driven back, several being wrecked near Portland Bill. They tried again in December, Wellesley on this occasion with them, but, after seven weeks at sea, they were driven back again. Such were the hazards of what in later years came to be known as trooping.

One must wonder what Wellington's[4] career would have been if he had sailed to the West Indies and survived the hazards of the climate there. As it was, he was ill when the 33rd sailed in April 1796 for India, catching them up, now a colonel, at the Cape and landing with them at Calcutta in February 1797. His first military task was to prepare for an expedition to capture Manila in the Philippines and Batavia in what is now Indonesia, in the preparations for which he displayed a mastery of detail and concern for the personal needs of his soldiers, which had been evident since, as a newly joined ensign, he had carefully weighed all that the soldier was expected to carry. He had hoped to be in command, but seniority dictated otherwise, and General Braithwaite was chosen. The expedition was recalled when it was off Malaya, the naval mutinies at the Nore and Spithead and the threat of revolution in Ireland

[3] Stratford's Authentic Edition of the Investigation of the Charges Brought against HRH. the Duke of York by Gwyllym Lloyd Wardle Esq. (London n.d.), II, pp. 352–3, quoted in R. Glover, *Peninsular Preparation*, p. 161.

[4] He was not created Viscount Wellington until 1809, but will be referred to here as Wellington to distinguish him from his elder brother.

making the British Government feel that it was no time to be sending an expedition into the Pacific.

The Irish troubles had another important effect on Wellington's career. His brother Richard had been appointed Governor-General in India and arrived in Calcutta in May 1798, bringing another brother, Henry (later Lord Cowley), as his secretary, just as Napoleon was embarking on his expedition to Egypt. Mornington was immediately faced with the problem of what to do about the activities of the aggressive ruler of Mysore, Tipoo Sultan. Tipoo had recovered from his defeat by Cornwallis in 1792 and had intervened in a war between the Mahratta Confederacy and Hyderabad with the aim of substituting his own influence for that of the British in the latter, whose Nizam was on the point of death, and had also made approaches to the French for support. In spite of the discouragement to military operations enshrined in Pitt's India Act of 1784, the Wellesley brothers were all for action against Tipoo, which they saw in the light of Napoleon's oriental ambitions.

From the moment of his arrival in India, Wellington studied the possibility of a campaign against Mysore in detail. Mornington was for immediate action, and Wellington tried to restrain him until diplomatic and military preparations had been made to secure the support and practical help of Hyderabad and the Mahratta Scindia of Gwalior. In August 1798 Wellington and his 33rd sailed from Calcutta to Madras, running aground on a reef on the way. There, although General Harris was in command under the direction of the Governor, Lord Clive, and the troops for the intended expedition were being concentrated under the direction of Major-General Floyd, Wellington played an important part as a general agent for his brother in pressing forward preparations against the obstruction, idleness and confusion which characterized the bureaucratic administration in Madras.

There were three other major-generals in the force, and the brigade in which the 33rd was placed was commanded by a colonel senior to Wellington. The overall plan for the force of some 21,000, concentrated at Vellore, 90 miles west of Madras (of which the British element consisted of 900 cavalry and 4,400 infantry), was to advance under General Harris's command to capture Seringapatam, 180 miles away. They were to be joined by a force of 16,000 provided by the Nizam of Hyderabad. The officer selected to command this contingent was killed in a duel, and Wellington was chosen to take his place, much to the chagrin of Major-General Baird who had expected to receive the appointment. The 33rd joined the Hyderabad force as its only British element. At the same time a force of 6,000, of whom 1,600 were British, was to sail under General Stuart from Bombay, land at Cannanore on the Malabar coast, 100 miles as the crow flies west of Seringapatam, and advance on it from the opposite direction. These forces were accompanied by a huge train, that of Harris's and Wellington's combined amounting to 150,000 followers and 120,000 bullocks and other assorted transport animals, varying in size from elephants to donkeys. Against this total force of 43,000, Tipoo was expected to be able to muster 50,000, 15,000 of them cavalry.

Mornington gave the order for the advance on 3 February 1799, and the ponderous expedition set off, following a zigzag course to find forage for its huge menagerie. By 2 March Stuart was at Peripatan, fifty miles west of Tipoo's capital, while Harris was still double that distance to the east. Putting it about that he was moving his main force to the east to deal with the latter, Tipoo led 12,000 of his men to deal with Stuart first. His presence was detected and, in a skilfully fought action in difficult country, Stuart routed him. By 5 April Harris had closed up to Seringapatam, and it was here that Wellington led his 33rd in a night attack to clear a grove of trees, the Sultanpettah Tope. It ended in failure and confusion, which was redeemed by a successful attack next day; but it prejudiced Wellington against night attacks. 'I have come to a determination', he wrote to his brother, 'never to suffer an attack to be made by night upon an enemy who is prepared and strongly posted, and whose posts have not been reconnoitred in daylight.' On 26 April the assault on the city began, led by Baird, and ended on 4 May, Tipoo being killed in the fighting, as were, it was estimated, 10,000 of his troops and their supporters. Harris's men plundered and pillaged the city without restraint. Wellington was placed in command of the city to restore order, which he did by hanging and flogging those caught in the act. Ever thereafter he was to take the sternest measures against indiscipline of this nature and to ensure that the lives and property of non-combatants were respected.

In August Harris led his army back to Madras, leaving Wellington in Mysore with full military and civil powers over the country, once more to the chagrin of Baird, who regarded the appointment as his by right both of seniority and of having led the assault with undoubted courage and skill. He was compensated with Tipoo's sword, while

Oliver Cromwell, painted by Robert Walker in 1649. Cromwell's main contribution to tactics was his firm and careful control of the cavalry.

Prince Rupert in 1641 aged twenty-one, a brilliant but reckless cavalry commander in the Civil War.

Musketeers and a dragoon, 1650. Note the bandolier carrying the individual powder charges, the forked rest for the musket and the pieces of cord for firing the primer.

Cromwell at the battle of Marston Moor, 1644. During the battle Cromwell was wounded but he returned to lead a decisive cavalry charge.

Civil War trooper's helmet, breast and back plates.

George Monck, 1st Duke of Albemarle, by Sir Peter Lely. A highly professional soldier who combined strict discipline with concern for his men, Monck was a key figure in the foundation of a regular standing army in Britain.

John Churchill, 1st Duke of
Marlborough, a soldier of genius who
was able to inspire enthusiasm and
real affection.

The battle of Blenheim, 13 August
1704, a great victory for Marlborough
and the Grand Alliance, won deep
into Europe.

George II's son, the Duke of Cumberland, in 1760. Known as 'Butcher Cumberland' after the battle of Culloden in 1746.

James Wolfe, who died aged thirty-two of wounds received in the battle which captured the town of Quebec in 1759.

The west front of the Horse Guards building in Whitehall in the 1750s. Designed by William Kent, construction started in 1750. Infantry are being drilled on the right.

A private and a grenadier of the 48th Foot in 1742 and, on the right, a grenadier of the 58th Foot in 1769.

3 Shillings a Day. 2 Shillings a Day. 1 Shilling a Day.   SIX-PENCE A DAY.   Yankees. Fire and Water. Sword and Famine.

'Exposed to the Horrors of War, Pestilence and Famine for a Farthing an Hour.' A cartoon of 1775 depicts the miserable pay of the private infantryman of 6d a day when a coachman would receive 2s and even a child chimneysweep 1s. It was not raised until 1794, when it was still only half that of a farm labourer.

Frederick, Duke of York, George III's second son, after Lawrence. A capable and energetic reformer of recruitment, promotion and training, to whom Wellington owed much.

Sir Arthur Wellesley (later 1st Duke of Wellington) in 1804, by Robert Home.

Sir John Moore by Lawrence.

The battle of Talavera, 28 July 1809, where Anglo-Spanish troops under Wellington defeated the French in one of the toughest battles in the history of the British army.

The battle of Waterloo, 18 June 1815. The British met the massed cavalry charges of the French by forming squares, taking a wheel from each gun inside the square.

The Royal Military College, Sandhurst, in 1824. The College had been founded in 1801 as part of the Duke of York's reforms.

An elephant being used to pull a six-pounder, *c.* 1830. Napier's Abyssinian campaign of 1867–8 was accompanied by 27,000 animals, including elephants.

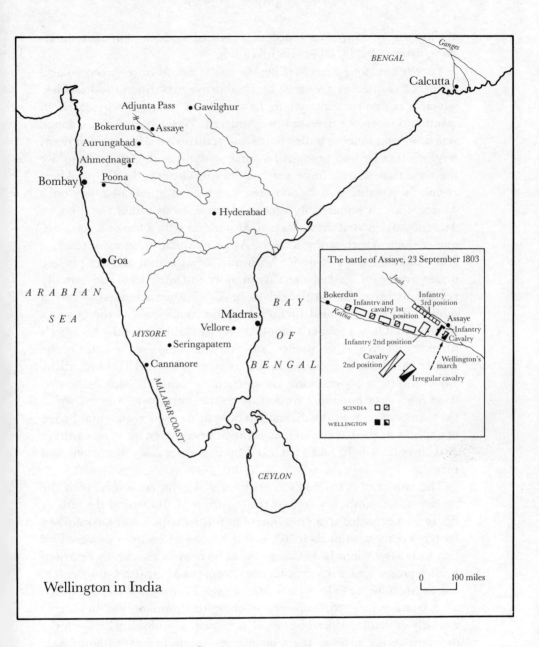

BENGAL

Ganges

Calcutta

Adjunta Pass •Gawilghur

Bokerdun• •Assaye

Aurungabad•

Ahmednagar•

Bombay•   Poona
            •

           •Hyderabad

A R B I A N

S E A

•Goa

MYSORE

                    B A Y
Madras•
Vellore•
            O F

•Seringapatem   B E N G A L

•Cannanore

MALABAR COAST

CEYLON

The battle of Assaye, 23 September 1803

Juah

Bokerdun

Kaitna

Infantry and
cavalry 1st
position

Infantry
3rd position

Assaye

•Infantry

Cavalry

Infantry 2nd position

Cavalry
2nd position

Wellington's
march

Irregular cavalry

SCINDIA

WELLINGTON

Wellington in India

0   100 miles

85

Wellington, in a rapid and successful campaign, dealt with the remaining resistance led by Dhoondiah Waugh.

For the next four years Wellington was to rule Mysore, his command being interrupted at one stage by an abortive expedition to Mauritius, which was diverted instead to Egypt, Baird having been placed in command when the diversion was ordered. Wellington, still a colonel, was unwilling to serve under Baird and returned to Mysore from Bombay, whither he had brought his force without authority to do so. By the time that Baird's force reached Egypt, General Sir Ralph Abercromby's expedition of 15,000 men had landed at Aboukir Bay on 8 March 1801, a remarkably successful amphibious assault, and on 21 March had defeated the French at Alexandria with a loss of 1,500 men, one of them Abercromby himself. As he was placed on a stretcher, a folded blanket was put under his head. 'What is that you are placing under my head?', asked the Commander-in-Chief, who had initially refused to leave the battlefield to have his wound tended. 'Only a soldier's blanket', replied Lieutenant John Macdonald of the Queen's Regiment. 'Only a soldier's blanket!', retorted the General: 'A soldier's blanket is of great consequence, and you must send me the name of the soldier to whom it belongs, that it may be returned to him'. Little wonder that, as he was borne dying from the field, his soldiers shouted 'God bless your honour.'[5] In that battle the 28th Foot (later known as the Gloucesters) won the distinction of wearing their regimental badge of a sphinx at the back as well as at the front of their caps in recognition of their gallant fight when attacked by French cavalry from front and rear.

The failure of Napoleon's expedition to Egypt, combined with the success of his campaign against the Austrians in Italy, and the latter's desire for peace, led to a cessation of hostilities with France, confirmed by the Treaty of Amiens in 1802, Pitt having fallen from power. This had its repercussions in India, as one of its provisions was the return of French possessions. French influence within the Mahratta Confederacy, which Mornington, elevated to the rank of Marquess Wellesley in the Irish peerage in 1779, had been working to eliminate, was in danger not only of being restored but even increased, as jealousies between the different states forming the Confederacy intensified. Wellington was himself promoted major-general on 29 April 1802 at the age of 33.

[5] Fortescue, Vol. IV, p. 843.

Wellesley (as the Marquess will henceforth be referred to) now embarked on a tortuous round of negotiations in the course of which Scindia of Gwalior persuaded Holkar of Indore and Bhonsla of Nagpur to join him in resistance to Wellesley's demands, concentrating their forces near the Ajunta Pass, 200 miles north-east of Poona. When the negotiations finally broke down on 6 August 1803, Wellington moved swiftly to attack the fortress of Ahmednagar, where he wished to establish a forward base, 80 miles north-east of Poona, which was 500 miles from his main base at Seringapatam. He seized it at a cost of 120 casualties, provoking the comment of a Mahratta chief: 'These Englishmen are strange people, and their general a wonderful man. They came here in the morning, looked at the pettah wall, walked over it, killed all the garrison, and returned to breakfast.'[6]

Wellington had 11,000 men, of whom 1,600 were British. He was to be joined by Stevenson, who had 9,500, of whom 900 were British, at Aurungabad in the extreme north of Hyderabad, and who would come under his command. Together they faced 50,000 men, under Scindia and the Rajah of Berar, of whom 38,000 were cavalry, with 190 guns. By the end of August, Wellington had advanced 80 miles to Aurungabad, while Scindia kept the nervous Stevenson marching to and fro in fear of being cut off.

By 20 September Wellington and Stevenson had joined forces to face Scindia and the Rajah, whom they expected to find south of Ajunta. They advanced north independently on two routes, Stevenson's column separated from Wellington's by some 12 miles of rugged country, intending to join forces again when they reached the River Kaitna near Bokerdun. Wellington had almost reached it on 23 September, when he discovered that the whole of Scindia's and the Rajah's force was drawn up beyond the river, while there was no sign of Stevenson, who had been delayed, some say by losing his way. He was faced with a difficult decision. If he waited for Stevenson, or even attempted to withdraw, he was liable to be attacked by a greatly superior force. Although he had stated as a firm principle that the Mahrattas should not be attacked when they were drawn up in a position they had chosen to defend, that was the only alternative, and he chose it, in spite of the gross disparity in numbers between his force – about 7,000 men actually available – and that of the enemy.

He noticed that the left of their line lay on a narrow neck of land

[6] Fortescue, Vol. V, p. 17.

between the Kaitna and Juah rivers. He also saw that, although the Kaitna's banks were steep and the river deep, two villages lay opposite each other beyond Scindia's left. If he could cross there and swing left, he could bring all his force to bear on the enemy's extreme left flank, where they could not concentrate all their cavalry. It was a bold, perhaps a foolhardy plan; but, in spite of some aspects of it going awry, such as the gallant Colonel Ottock's assault on the village of Assaye; the unexpected skill with which the Mahratta infantry, under their German commander Pohlmann, changed front to meet his attack; and the diversion of his cavalry's charge by the death of their equally gallant commander, Colonel Maxwell, it succeeded.

In the face of intense artillery fire Wellington, who was always cool and collected in the thick of the fray and had three horses killed under him and his orderly's head shot off, inspired his British and Indian soldiers to unequalled heights of gallantry. By the end of the day his opponents had abandoned the battlefield, leaving 6,000 casualties and 98 guns behind. His own losses had been 428 killed, half of them British, and 1,156 wounded and missing, 442 British. His men, having marched 24 miles that day, were too exhausted to pursue, and slept, as did Wellington himself, among their own dead. Assaye was, in Wellington's own eyes, his greatest victory. Operations against Scindia and Bhonsla continued until the end of the year, when Wellington and Stevenson finally overwhelmed their forces in an assault on the rugged fortress at Gawilgur on 15 December, but it was not until 24 December 1805, two years after Gawilgur had fallen, that the war with Holkar was finally brought to an end.

By that time both the Wellesleys had left India, Wellington in March 1805 and the Marquess in August, to be succeeded by Cornwallis who died a few months later. While they had been fighting the Mahrattas, Britain had faced the threat of invasion. The precarious peace established by the Treaty of Amiens broke down in 1803, when Pitt returned to power, and, with nothing to fear from Britain's former Continental allies, Napoleon concentrated his Grande Armée of 120,000 on the Channel coast, while he tried in vain to draw the Royal Navy elsewhere. The threat produced a burgeoning in the forces intended for home defence.

The militia was increased by the creation of a Supplementary Militia in addition to Volunteers and Fencibles, and the ranks of the regular army increased by the passage of the Army of Reserve Act. These measures brought the total of men under arms to 380,000 in Great Britain and 70,000 in Ireland, a force for which there was great difficulty in providing weapons, but which gave the tailors a field day in providing uniforms – and the cartoonists in making fun of them! Not until Nelson's victory at Trafalgar on 21 October 1805 was the danger of invasion finally removed. By then the threat from Austria had drawn the Grande Armée away to inflict a crushing defeat on most of the Austrians at Ulm on 20 October and on the rest of their forces and the Russians at Austerlitz in December. In 1806 it was the turn of Prussia, crushed at Jena and Auerstadt on 14 October.

The only British intervention on the Continent in all this time had been the despatch to the River Weser of 25,000 men under Lord Cathcart in the hope of cooperating with a Russian and a Swedish force, operating on Napoleon's northern flank, to free Holland and Hanover from Napoleon's grip and draw Prussia into the alliance. Austerlitz put paid to this last of Pitt's impractical military adventures, and Cathcart's force was withdrawn in January 1806, the month Pitt died. Wellington commanded a brigade in this abortive expedition. With Austria and Prussia crushed, Napoleon made peace with Tsar Alexander on the raft at Tilsit in 1807, and Britain was once more left alone to face France and her ally Spain. Her first fear was that the Danish fleet would fall into Napoleon's hands, and an expedition under Lord Cathcart was sent to Copenhagen with 20,000 men to capture the fleet in August. This was accomplished without difficulty, Wellington leaving his duties as Chief Secretary of Ireland to command the reserve brigade, which had a brief and successful encounter with the Danes.

The opportunity to do something effective came when Napoleon invaded Spain in February 1808. In 1807 he had forced his unwilling ally to promise to join in an attack on Britain's oldest ally, Portugal. It was on the pretext of this, but with the real intent of getting rid of the Bourbon dynasty in Spain, that his troops crossed the Pyrenees and advanced to Madrid. Charles iv abdicated in favour of his son Ferdinand, whom Napoleon refused to recognize, installing his own brother Joseph on the throne instead, a humiliation which no Spaniard could tolerate. The Spanish rose in revolt and called on Britain to help. It so happened that a force of 5,000 men, part of an expedition sent to the Mediterranean under General Spencer to reinforce resistance to Napoleon in the Kingdom of Naples and Sicily, was in Gibraltar. As the French invaded the southern provinces of Spain, and Portugal joined in to oppose them, Spencer's force sailed up and down the coast between Gibraltar and Lisbon to encourage them. Wellington, who had been promoted lieutenant-general at the age of 39 in April, had been placed in command of a force of 9,000 men, assembled at Cork for an expedition to South America. He was quick to recommend that it should be sent instead to exploit the situation in the Iberian peninsula. His advice was accepted, and on 12 July he sailed with it to Corunna, where he was to be joined by Spencer's force.

News at Corunna was hard to come by and there was no sign of Spencer; so he sailed on, eventually landing on 1 August at Figueira, about 100 miles north of Lisbon, where the navy had already put some marines ashore. He had meanwhile made arrangements with the Bishop of Oporto to provide mules and horses, of which he was desperately in need. Good and bad news reached him at this stage. The good was that the French had suffered a severe defeat at the hands of the Spanish at Baylen and that the British Government had decided to reinforce its army in Portugal with a further 15,000 men, 10,000 being Sir John Moore's corps, which had been sent on a wild goose chase to Sweden. The bad news was that the French under Junot had, perhaps, up to 20,000 men in Portugal; Spencer had still not turned up, and the Government had decided to superimpose a galaxy of senior generals over his head. The last news reached him from yet another Wellesley brother, William (later Lord Maryborough), who was Secretary to the Admiralty. The object of this was clearly to prevent either Moore or Wellington being in command of such a major expeditionary force. Both were unpopular with the politicians, the former because of his outspoken realism, the latter because he was one of the Wellesley brothers who were thought to be getting too big for their boots. Cobbett called them 'that damned infernal family'.

Wellington estimated that, by the time Junot had made provision for guarding various fortresses and Lisbon itself, he could not put more than 12,000 men into the field against the 17,000 he himself would have when all were ashore, although he would be short of cavalry. In a letter to the Duke of Richmond, his former chief in Ireland, he wrote: 'I hope I shall have beat Junot before any of them arrive, and then they may do with me as they please'; and that is almost exactly what he did. He marched south, defeating a French delaying force at Rolica, until he reached Vimiero, a village two miles inland from the mouth of the Maceira River, where the first elements of the reinforcements from England were intending to land. With them was General Burrard, the old Guardee buffer sent out to be second-in-command to Dalrymple, the Governor of Gibraltar, who had been appointed Commander-in-Chief. Wellington went aboard his frigate to explain his plan to bring Junot to battle. Burrard was horrified, and told him to hold hard until the whole force was ashore. Wellington returned disgusted, but was delighted when a Hessian sergeant reported that Junot was on his way to attack him. Wellington's troops had not been drawn up for defence, but were in fact well disposed on two ridges astride the river, with a forward post covering Vimiero village south of it, to deal with an attack, which came next day, 21 August.

Junot had 13,000 men and launched them from the east. Wellington, with his quicksilver mind, divined his intention and rapidly transferred battalions from right to left to frustrate him. The French attack was ill-coordinated, and by midday they were streaming away to the east. Wellington saw his opportunity and wished to press forward to Lisbon and get behind Junot; but the cautious Burrard would have none of it. Dalrymple arrived at this point and agreed to a proposal by the French that they should evacuate Portugal and be sent back to France in British ships. Wellington, always the realist, accepted the task of signing the document that sealed this agreement – known as the Convention of Cintra – as all that could be achieved in the light of the caution of his superiors. Shrugging his shoulders, as he spent most of his life doing, Wellington returned to Ireland to face the accusation that, by signing the Convention, he had betrayed Britain's cause.

Before leaving, Wellington had tried to persuade Moore, under whom he said he would be happy to serve, to bring pressure to bear to have Dalrymple and Burrard removed and to take over as Commander-in-Chief himself; but Moore refused, reading Wellington a lecture on loyalty to the superiors appointed by his political masters. However public dissatisfaction at the turn of events led to their dismissal and Moore's assumption of command on 6 October 1808, under orders to join the Spanish in resistance to a renewed French invasion, led by Napoleon himself, who had made peace with Prussia and transferred the bulk of his army to the Peninsula. Moore was to leave 12,000 of his 32,000 men under Craddock at Lisbon and be reinforced with 10,000, a high proportion cavalry of which he was deficient, under Baird, who would sail from England to Corunna. The campaign was embarked upon under the mistaken impression not only that the Spanish army would remain intact, but also that the Spanish authorities would meet most of Moore's administrative and logistic needs. The first assumption was rapidly dispelled by Napoleon's vigorous dispersion of the Spanish forces; the second had never been on the cards. Dogged by difficulties of every kind, including the refusal of the local authorities to allow Baird to land at Corunna – he was diverted to Vigo; his force being split into three, the main body at Salamanca, Baird between there and Vigo, Hope with the artillery well to the east – Moore had decided to withdraw to Lisbon, but, when he received information that Napoleon's main body was moving south, leaving Soult's corps isolated in the north, he decided instead to take the offensive against him. It proved to be a major error, and he was left with no alternative but to withdraw his troops to Corunna, a move for which he had made no preparation. Through mountainous country in the depths of winter, so harried by the French that he had constantly to press the pace, the retreat almost turned into a rout, redeemed only by the stout defence of the port of embarkation itself, in which Moore died of his wounds. Twenty-four thousand men were embarked.

The Government was inclined to cut its losses, but Wellington assured his friend Castlereagh, the Secretary of State for War, that with a force of 30,000 British and a reorganization of the Portuguese army with British leadership and administration, Portugal could be defended, and the tide of events in Spain eventually reversed. There was some discussion as to whether a force should be sent to Portugal or to Cadiz in Spain itself, the argument being decided by the Spanish who refused to allow it to land there. In April 1809 Wellington was appointed to command and given his orders. They were:

To prepare and equip the British army (in Portugal) for the field [and to] bring forward the Portuguese army, and render it capable of co-operating with His Majesty's troops ... The defence of Portugal you will consider as the first and immediate object of your attention. But as the security of Portugal can only be effectively provided for in connexion with the defence of the Peninsula in the larger sense, His Majesty leaves it to your judgement to decide, when your army shall be advanced on the frontier of Portugal, how your efforts can best be combined with the Spanish as well as the Portuguese troops in support of the common cause ... It is not His Majesty's intention, in authorizing you to co-operate with the Spanish armies in the defence of Portugal and the

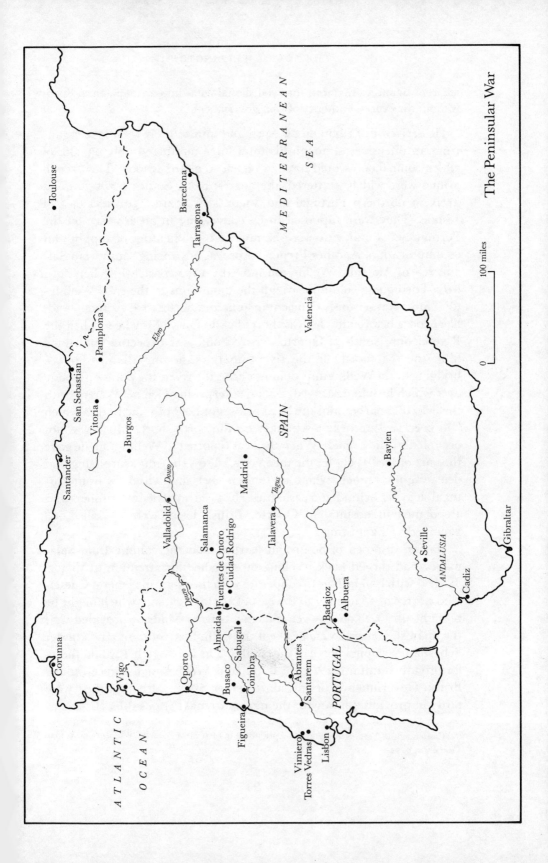

The Peninsular War

adjacent Spanish provinces, that you should enter into a campaign in Spain without the express authority of your government.[7]

He arrived in Lisbon on 22 April and immediately set about organizing an offensive, although his total force numbered only 23,200, of which some 6,000 would have to be left to guard Lisbon. The French armies were widely scattered, the nearest being Soult's corps 70 miles away in northern Portugal and Victor's in Spain, 150 miles east of Lisbon. They were supposed to be converging in an advance on the Portuguese capital, but were hampered by difficulties of supply and communication. Another French corps was advancing south from Salamanca to Almeida. Wellington moved up the coast, while Beresford led a Portuguese column through the mountains to the east. Wellington's force was seriously deficient in guns and horses to draw them, and, like Moore before him, he was short of cash. On 12 May he reached the River Douro south of Oporto, where Soult was expecting an attack from the sea, north of the river mouth, assuming that without a bridging-train Wellington could not cross the river, the pontoon bridge over which he had destroyed. But an enterprising Colonel Waters, with the help of a barber and the local prior, got hold of some barges which had been tied up near a seminary on the north shore, which was not occupied by the French. When this was reported to Wellington, he gave the curt order: 'Well, let the men cross.' Cross they did, surprising and defeating the French, who took to their heels and withdrew from Portugal, leaving behind 300 casualties, the same number of prisoners and 1,000 men in hospital in Oporto. British losses were 23 killed, 98 wounded and 2 missing.

Having disposed of Soult and learned that the column from Salamanca had turned back, Wellington switched his attention to Victor. To deal with him he had to cooperate with the Spanish General Cuesta, whose force of 30,000 lay to the east of Victor's 23,000, which might be brought up to 28,000 by reinforcements from Madrid, provided that the Spanish General Venegas kept the main body of the French under Sebastiani occupied north of the capital. The two together would therefore greatly outnumber Victor. By 11 June Wellington had received the British Government's permission to enter Spain, although they were tardy in providing him with the money to make it possible. His troops

[7] Castlereagh to Wellington, 2 and 3 April 1809, quoted in M. Glover, *Wellington as Military Commander*, p. 74.

were unpaid, and therefore took to looting, their boots were worn out and his medical service was grossly inadequate. Coordination with Cuesta also proved difficult. On 27 June sufficient cash arrived to make the move into Spain from his base at Abrantes.

Victor, meanwhile, had moved back up the Tagus valley towards Madrid, and Cuesta was hesitant to attack him. Moreover Victor was reinforced and Venegas repulsed by the French. Cuesta missed an opportunity to attack Victor while he was isolated, and on 26 July found himself facing the combined forces of Joseph, Victor and Sebastiani, some 46,000 men. Fortunately Wellington was nearby and had already chosen a suitable defensive position at Talavera on the Tagus, resting on a slight ridge behind a stream between Talavera and the mountains of the Sierra de Seguilla. Cuesta joined him there, but the burden of the defence was borne by Wellington's 20,000 men, who, in a fierce battle over two days, held their ground, inflicting 7,268 casualties on the French (761 killed) for the loss of 5,363 themselves (801 killed), of whom nearly half were from the King's German Legion. The Spaniards lost 1,200.

Talavera was one of the toughest battles in the annals of the British army. The French withdrew, but, in spite of receiving reinforcements, Wellington, abandoned by Cuesta and threatened by Soult advancing south from Salamanca, was forced to withdraw also. At the end of August he was back on the Portuguese frontier at Badajoz determined, as he told his brother the Marquess, now ambassador to Spain, never to try and work with the Spanish again. He therefore strongly opposed renewed pressure that his force should be withdrawn from Portugal and moved to Cadiz. For his victory at Talavera he was created Viscount Wellington.

The French continued to push the Spanish army back in the south. By the beginning of 1810 they had 300,000 troops in Spain, and in February they were at the gates of Cadiz, the garrison of which Wellington had reinforced. In March the number of British troops there was brought up to 8,000 under the command of General Graham. By then the threat to Portugal had increased by the pressure of Massena's Army of Portugal on its north-east frontier. Wellington had been busy all winter constructing the lines of Torres Vedras, a comprehensive continuous fortification between the Tagus and the sea, 25 miles north of Lisbon. His army, now 60,000, of whom about half were British, was concentrated over a hundred miles north of the lines in the upper

Mondego valley, covered by Craufurd's Light Division between there and the frontier near Almeida. Hill's 2nd Division was detached at Abrantes on the Tagus.

On 15 June Massena laid siege to the fortress of Ciudad Rodrigo. After a gallant resistance, the Spanish garrison surrendered on 10 July and Craufurd's patrols were forced back, so that Almeida was in turn invested. An explosion in its magazine forced its surrender, and, after a pause of three weeks to collect supplies, Massena began his advance down what Wellington called 'the worst road in Portugal', following the north bank of the Mondego to Coimbra. Bringing in Hill to join the main body, Wellington withdrew south of the river and forestalled Massena on the ridge of Busaco, ten miles north of Coimbra, on 26 September, his force consisting of 26,000 British and 25,000 Portuguese. Next day, urged on by the impetuous Ney and with insufficient reconnaissance, Massena hurried his mostly inexperienced troops into a direct attack. Their columns, panting up the hillside, received a severe shock both from the intensity of the musket fire and from the ferocity of the bayonet charges delivered by the British, notably the 45th and 88th Foot. By 2 pm Massena had abandoned the attack, having lost some 4,000 men, while the British casualties were only 631 and the Portuguese 620.

Instead of renewing his attack, Massena decided to move by mountain tracks round Wellington's left flank. The latter carried out an orderly withdrawal to the lines of Torres Vedras, the existence of which came as a shock to Massena when he reached them on 10 October. Prudently he declined to attack, and, finding himself after a month in difficulty in supplying his forces there, he drew them back 25 miles to Santarem, where he spent the winter, while Wellington's officers enjoyed themselves fox-hunting behind the lines.

In January 1811 a potential threat to the east had been posed by Soult's capture of the Spanish fortress of Badajoz; but he then had to turn back to deal with the situation in Andalusia, where the Spanish were developing a threat to Seville and another force under the Spanish General Lapeña, which included 5,000 British under Graham extracted from Cadiz, was threatening the rear of Victor's army investing the port. Lapeña moved slowly and was surprised by the French at Barrosa on 5 March. Graham's men were not supported by the Spanish and fought a gallant action which repulsed the French, inflicting 2,062 casualties on the 7,000 men opposed to them and losing 1,238 out of their 5,200, the three battalions of the Guards suffering particularly heavily. The expedition had failed in its immediate purpose, but its failure assisted the general strategy of the campaign by persuading the French to maintain their siege of Cadiz, which continued to tie their troops down to no good purpose.

On the day of the battle at Barrosa, Massena surprised Wellington by withdrawing from Santarem, intending to place his army north of the Mondego, where he could obtain supplies and await reinforcements. Wellington was quick to pursue him and, the bridge at Coimbra having been destroyed by Portuguese irregulars under Colonel Trant, Massena withdrew up the south side of the river towards Almeida, his supply position becoming more desperate every day. Wellington manoeuvred him out of one position after another in a series of skilful actions, the most notable being that at Sabugal on 3 April, when Reynier's corps was caught isolated and defeated in a battle fought in the fog. Massena withdrew to Salamanca, leaving a garrison in Almeida, having lost 25,000 men, his strength reduced to 40,000. Wellington could keep only 25,000 in the field and had outrun his own supplies. He did not, therefore, attempt to pursue Massena into Spain, but settled down to invest Almeida, and detached Beresford, whose Portuguese, owing to their inadequate supply arrangements, had been unable to keep up with him, to restore the situation at Badajoz, taking 19,000 men with him. Wellington set off to see him on 16 April and got back twelve days later, just in time to deal with an attempt by Massena to raise the siege of Almeida.

The latter waited for Bessières to join him from the north, which gave Wellington time to occupy a position in the village of Fuentes de Oñoro, and on the ridge which marks the frontier two miles west of it, with 21,450 British and 2,500 Portuguese troops. Massena had some 46,000 men with him. As at Busaco, he launched his attack with hardly any previous reconnaissance. Fighting in the village, held by 2,500 men under Colonel Wilson of the 60th, was fierce, and Wellington reinforced it with three more battalions. The defence held until nightfall when Massena withdrew his 14 battalions, having lost 650 men. He spent the next day reconnoitring and regrouping, and decided to turn Wellington's right flank, moving his troops south for this purpose during the night. Sensing this, Wellington moved Houston's inexperienced division of only two brigades to extend his right to the village of Poco Velho. When daylight came, he could clearly see that the force Massena had sent in that direction was much larger than he had suspected and

97

dangerously strong in cavalry. He took immediate steps to readjust his dispositions on the right, covering the moves with repeated cavalry charges, most gallantly executed by the Royals, the 14th and 16th Light Dragoons and the 1st Hussars of the King's German Legion.

The French assault on the village was renewed, and at one stage its position appeared to be lost; but it was restored with a bayonet charge by the 74th Highlanders and 88th Foot. The right flank also held, and by the end of the day Massena gave up, having lost 2,260 men to Wellington's 1,550. On 10 May he withdrew to Ciudad Rodrigo. A day later the French garrison of 1,400 blew up their stores and abandoned Almeida, succeeding in making their way through both the investing force and the troops ordered to intercept them, although they lost 400 men and all their baggage before they rejoined Massena. Fuentes de Oñoro left the British confident that they could always stop the French, but Wellington realized that it had been a 'close run thing' and told his brother Richard, now Foreign Secretary, that 'If Boney had been there, we should have been beaten.'

Wellington himself set off to join Beresford, reinforcing him with 10,000 men, hoping that this, together with 10,000 Spanish under Blake, would suffice to deal with Soult who was threatening Beresford's besieging force. He found that Soult had already got there, and had been engaged by Beresford at Albuera on 16 May. The French were repulsed, but at heavy cost. The British lost 4,000 out of 10,000, the Portuguese 400 out of the same number and Blake's Spanish 1,400 out of 14,000. Out of Soult's 24,000 men, he reported a loss of 6,000, although it is generally accepted to have been nearer 8,000. Wellington realized that he had only about two weeks to take Badajoz before Marmont could join Soult. Two attempts with a totally inadequate Portuguese siege-train failed, and on 18 June Marmont and Soult had joined forces, so that Wellington had to move away, realizing that, although Soult withdrew at the end of June, the French could always concentrate a superior force round Badajoz, if he attempted to renew the siege.

He, therefore, turned his attention back to the north and began to invest Ciudad Rodrigo in August; but before long faced the same problem there. His army was suffering badly from sickness; 14,000 were ill, reducing the force he could keep there to 46,000, whereas the French could produce 60,000 to raise the siege. He was short of money and he complained that the Government gave him no clear objective other than to preserve his army. The answer he received was: 'You know our means, both military and financial, are limited; but such as they are, we are determined not to be diverted from the Peninsula to other objects. If we can strike a blow, we will strike it there.'[8] Before the end of September, when the garrison's supplies would run out, Marmont came with 58,000 men and drove Wellington away.

The frustration which this state of affairs imposed on Wellington in 1811 was relieved in 1812 by two decisions taken by Napoleon: the first to invade Russia; the second, which had a more immediate and direct effect, to complete his conquest of Spain by the occupation of Valencia, for which troops were to be moved from the north-west. Believing that the British had been reduced by sickness to only 20,000 (in fact they had 34,000), Marmont, at the end of December 1811, moved two divisions and all his light cavalry to Valencia. Wellington, whose siege-train was conveniently at Almeida, was quick to seize his opportunity – to capture Ciudad Rodrigo.

Invested on 8 January, the town fell to the 3rd and Light Divisions on 19 January at a cost of 1,100 casualties, among whom was the Light Division's gallant commander Craufurd. The assaulting troops gave vent to their feelings by running riot, the voice of the 3rd Division's General, Picton, being heard above the noise 'with the power of twenty trumpets, proclaiming damnation to everybody'.[9] Leaving a Spanish garrison for the fortress and his Portuguese troops to look after the area, Wellington moved south in February to deliver a similar blow to Badajoz, hoping to forestall any intervention by Marmont and trusting Graham to keep Soult at bay. Napoleon played into his hands by refusing to allow Marmont to move south, but insisting that he should concentrate at Salamanca, recapture Ciudad Rodrigo and Almeida and drive to Lisbon, while Wellington was in the south, disregarding Marmont's protests that he could not keep his forces supplied there. Marmont made a feeble attempt to obey his orders in March, but without a siege-train made no impression on the Spanish and Portuguese defenders, and withdrew to Salamanca in mid-April.

Wellington, meanwhile, had laid siege to Badajoz. This began on 17 March, hampered, as Wellington constantly was, by a lack of trained

[8] Liverpool to Wellington, 11 April 1811, quoted in Glover, p. 98.
[9] Fortescue, Vol. VIII, p. 363.

sappers and miners and of mortars. The final assault, in which the 3rd Division played a prominent part, took place on the night of 6 April, and was successful. The scenes of indiscipline were even worse than those at Ciudad Rodrigo. In Fortescue's words 'It is undeniable that for a time the British army in Badajoz was dissolved into a mob of intoxicated robbers'.[10] The siege cost Wellington nearly 5,000 casualties, of which 1,000 were Portuguese. Most were incurred in the final assault, the conduct of which has been much criticized. Six generals, including Picton, were wounded and four battalion commanders killed. The 4th, 43rd and 52nd and the Rifle Brigade suffered most heavily.

With the key fortresses dominating the routes into Portugal in his hands, Wellington felt free to turn to the offensive. He rejected an advance into Andalusia as likely to bring Marmont down on his rear and join forces with Soult, while the latter, tied to Cadiz, was not free to join Marmont in the north. He decided therefore to seek battle with Marmont, confident in the generally superior state of his army over that of the French, in spite of a sick list of 13,000, a shortage of doctors and continued problems over finance. On 13 June, with 50,000 men, of whom 18,000 were Portuguese and 3,500 Spanish, he advanced from Ciudad Rodrigo, reaching Salamanca four days later, concerned to find from a captured document that Marmont was stronger than he had expected, also having some 50,000 men. Here he was delayed by the forts protecting the town, which were not reduced until 27 June. Marmont had now gathered his force together, and Wellington appreciated that Joseph Bonaparte would send his reserve of 15,000 men to reinforce him. Having moved north of Salamanca to the River Douro, he was vulnerable to an advance by Marmont against his communications, and began to plan a withdrawal to Portugal. Marmont attacked across the river on 16 July and forced Wellington to start his withdrawal. On 21 July he was back at Salamanca and preparing to continue towards Ciudad Rodrigo, when Marmont made a false move. In his eagerness to cut Wellington off, he had overextended himself.

On the morning of 22 July, most of Wellington's troops were in position on some low hills south-east of Salamanca, while the main body of Marmont's army was the other side of a small stream to the east of them. The skirmishers of both sides began jockeying for position on a hill called the Greater Arapile. Marmont, who could see little of Wellington's main body, not yet joined by the 3rd Division which was still

[10] Fortescue, VIII, p. 403.

moving through Salamanca, assumed that he was faced only by a rearguard position covering the British withdrawal to Rodrigo, and that they could be manoeuvred out of it, as they had been from successive positions north of Salamanca. In the afternoon he began moving round Wellington's right flank. The latter was watching his movements with an eagle eye, and had just been persuaded to have something to eat, when he saw that an opportunity had been presented to him, as Marmont's move had separated his divisions. Flinging away the chicken-leg he was gnawing, he galloped off to set his army into action. ('I knew that something *very serious* was about to happen when an article so precious as the leg of a roast fowl was thus thrown away', recounted his Spanish liaison officer.[11]) Bringing in 3rd Division to head off the French, he galvanized his other four divisions and two cavalry brigades into action on their flank, bringing 32,000 infantry and 2,000 cavalry into the battle against 14,000 French infantry and 1,700 cavalry. The French were surprised, thrown into confusion and routed, the British cavalry coming into its own in an action where the enemy was not drawn up to receive them. Wellington hoped to cut off the enemy's retreat across the River Tormes, but the Spanish, who were supposed to be holding the bridge at Alba de Tormes, were not there. Clausel, who had taken over command from the wounded Marmont, escaped that way, leaving behind over 12,000 casualties, some 1,200 horses, dead and alive, and 12 guns. Wellington's losses had not been light – 5,220, of which 3,176 were British. It was the decisive battle of the whole campaign and established a moral superiority for Wellington's army over the French, wherever they were again to meet. The immediate consequence was Wellington's triumphal entry into Madrid on 12 August.

Euphoria was not to reign for long. The French realized that they must abandon Andalusia and concentrate in the north. Wellington was forced to withdraw from Burgos, which, in pursuit of Clausel, he was besieging in October. Madrid was abandoned, and by 19 November Wellington's whole army was back behind Ciudad Rodrigo, having lost 9,000 men in the retreat, the last stage of which, south of Salamanca, had seen a breakdown both of administration and of discipline, the latter largely a consequence of the former. Disappointing as it had been to have to withdraw to Portugal for the winter, Wellington faced 1813 with confidence. Napoleon's campaign in Russia had ended in disaster,

[11] The Croker Papers, Vol. II, London, 1884, p. 120.

and his army in Spain, although considerably outnumbering Wellington's, was tied down and harassed by the increasingly widespread activity of the Spanish guerrilla bands. Wellington could put into the field a total of 106,000 men, including 28,000 Portuguese and 25,000 Spaniards, while the whole French army in Spain amounted to about double that number, but it was doubtful if they could concentrate more than 60,000 men to oppose him.

Wellington planned to concentrate his force on the Douro north of Salamanca when the spring rains had produced enough forage for his horses, Graham bringing 42,000 men up a separate route which crossed the river in its lower reaches. Wellington was back at Salamanca on 26 May and joined forces with Graham at Toro on 2 June. The French had assembled 57,000 men at Valladolid, but were manoeuvred out of their position, as they were out of Burgos also. Wellington had achieved his aim of occupying Castile and now saw nothing to prevent him from throwing the French out of Spain altogether. He therefore decided to continue to press Joseph back towards the Pyrenees, switching his line of communication, as he had planned to do, to Santander on the north coast of Spain. Out-manoeuvred again, the French fell back behind the Ebro, but at last stood at Vitoria on 21 June, 58,000 men facing Wellington's 70,000. They attempted to hold the ridge west of Vitoria, through which flowed the River Zadorra, along the valley of which they were trying to get their baggage away. Wellington planned to outflank them to the north, coming in to cross the bridges over the river in the rear of their positions. It was a complicated manoeuvre which, although in the end successful, did not go entirely according to plan, partly because the action of the cavalry, for which the terrain was unsuitable in any case, was ill-coordinated.

Although the French were defeated and dispersed in disorder, leaving 7,000 casualties behind, most of them got away. The baggage-train, including King Joseph's possessions, distracted the attention of Wellington's victorious soldiers on that day and for some time after. Wellington had lost 5,000 men, of whom 3,500 were British, and it was some days before he could restore complete order among his suddenly enriched soldiers, some 5,000 of whom appear to have deserted the ranks for loot. Supply problems also held him up, as the navy had failed to bring his supply ships to Santander from Lisbon, where they had been ready loaded since 12 May. The French under Soult took advantage of this pause to concentrate their forces to relieve the investment of the fortresses of Pamplona and San Sebastian, but failed in the attempt and retired to the Pyrenees at the end of July to lick their wounds.

San Sebastian proved a hard nut for the British to crack. After a siege lasting 51 days, it fell to Graham on 31 August at a cost to him of 3,700 casualties, 2,400 British. The French lost 3,000 and the town was totally destroyed, mostly by fire caused by the assaulting soldiers, who, as at Ciudad Rodrigo and Badajoz, ran riot. As at those previous sieges, there was considerable criticism of the lack of expertise in carrying out the siege and the final assault, although none of the gallantry of the soldiers who took part in it. Pamplona surrendered on 31 October, and by the end of the year, after a series of sharp actions, which had taken British troops onto the soil of France, both sides settled down for the winter on the line of the Pyrenees.

Events elsewhere were now affecting affairs in the Peninsula. One had only a marginal effect: the war which erupted on 18 June 1812 with the United States of America, the origin of which lay in their frustration both over interference with their maritime trade with France and over their westward expansion, which caused disputes with Canada. The war, which continued until the end of 1814 and is remembered principally because the British in that year set fire to the President's house in Washington, so that it had to be whitewashed afterwards to hide traces of the fire, affected Wellington by the diversion of the navy from his support. Far more relevant were events elsewhere in Europe.

Having forced Napoleon to leave their country, the Russians exerted pressure on Prussia to join them in alliance against him. In February 1813 they did so. Austria intervened as a mediator between them and France, but at Dresden in August Napoleon rejected the terms offered and Austria joined the alliance to oppose him. The operations which followed culminated in the Battle of Leipzig, where Napoleon's 177,000 men faced 257, 000 of his opponents' on 16 October. The 'Battle of the Nations' lasted for four days, and, having lost 73,000 men and inflicted 54,000 casualties on the allies, Napoleon withdrew to the Rhine, his fate sealed. When Wellington faced Soult across the Pyrenees at the beginning of 1814, Napoleon was threatened by a far larger army, led by the veteran Prussian Blücher, across the Rhine. He was hoping to forestall these threats by exploiting differences between the allies over possible terms of a peace treaty, including the withdrawal of Suchet's corps, still in Catalonia, where it had been ineffectively threatened by a combined British and Spanish force based on Tarragona. Until the future of

Suchet's force was known, Wellington thought it prudent to limit his operations beyond the Pyrenees to enlarging a bridgehead into France on the west so that he could base his force on Bordeaux, which he occupied in March 1814, after a battle with Soult at Orthez, in which the French lost 4,000 and inflicted casualties of half that number on their opponents. Soult then moved east to Toulouse, where, in an unnecessary and unsatisfactory battle on 10 April, in which the ratio of casualties was the reverse of that at Orthez, the war came to an end with the news that Napoleon had abdicated.

While Wellington, made a Duke, represented Britain in Paris and at the Congress of Vienna, which was attempting to settle the affairs of Europe, his army was dispersed, some being sent to join the war in America, some disbanded and a small element stationed in the Netherlands to support the Dutch, whose king, by the peace settlement, had acquired sovereignty over the Belgians, who had become accustomed to French rule and many of whom had served in Napoleon's armies. All the usual steps were taken to reduce the British army, while, with the threat removed, the militia and other home defence forces were stood down.

Wellington was at Vienna on 7 March 1815, when the news broke that Napoleon had escaped from Elba and was calling his old soldiers to arms. He immediately recommended to the Prime Minister, Lord Liverpool, that the army in England should be despatched to the Netherlands, while he set about organizing action by the allied powers assembled at the Congress. When he himself reached Brussels on 29 March, he was taken aback by the meagreness of Liverpool's response. Six weak regiments of cavalry and 25 battalions of infantry were all he had provided, and 15 of the latter were the weak and inefficient units which had been there since 1814. Only six of the others had served in the Peninsula, and many of their experienced soldiers had since left the ranks. Two were almost entirely composed of very young raw recruits. Instead of the 150 guns he had asked for, only 42 were available for lack of crews, and there were no drivers for their horses. In all, the British troops amounted to 800 cavalry and 11,000 infantry. In addition there was the King's German Legion and 25 battalions of Hanoverian militia, the former providing 3,000 horse and an equal number of foot, the latter 1,000 and 12,000 of each. The Dutch, commanded by the young Prince of Orange, with the able General Constant de Rebeque to help him, could provide only 7,250.

The overall allied plan was for a concentric movement to engage Napoleon's army, wherever he might concentrate it. It was not a war against France, which could not be invaded until the allegedly rebel army had been located. The allies were therefore to assemble around France's frontiers, Wellington on the extreme right, with the Prussians, who could put 100,000 men into the field under the 71-year-old Field-Marshal Blücher, on his left.

Napoleon's plan was to try and deal with his opponents one by one. The Dutch were an obvious target, exploiting the dislike of the Belgians at being placed under their rule. An attack on them would involve the British also. If successful, it might bring down the Tory Government, and a Whig one might not be prepared to subsidize the other allies, who, without that support, would not be able to provide effective opposition. Frustrated at not being able to seize the initiative by a move into France, Wellington could only dispose his force to cover the routes leading towards Brussels and his line of communication to Ostend. However, he agreed with Blücher, whose supply-line naturally ran in the opposite direction, that, if Napoleon tried to drive a wedge between them, he would abandon his link with the Channel ports and join the Prussians.

On 15 June 1815 Napoleon crossed the Sambre at Charleroi and Marchienne and drove the Prussians back. By nightfall he had 120,000 men north of the river, his leading cavalry having reached Quatre Bras, only 20 miles from Brussels, before withdrawing a few miles for the night. He had taken both Wellington and Blücher by surprise. The former had his eyes mainly on the road leading from Maubeuge through Mons, and his troops were strung out over an area of 40 miles covering that approach. It was not until 10 pm on 15 June that he knew that Napoleon had chosen to advance by Charleroi, and he still did not know that he had crossed the Sambre and driven the Prussians back. He then ordered his army to move eastward and Picton to take his 3rd Division south from Brussels to Mont St Jean, south of the Forêt de Soigny, before himself going off to the Duchess of Richmond's ball.

Blücher's forces were equally dispersed east of Brussels, and had not finished their concentration. Fortunately Constant de Rebeque, on his own initiative, had posted some of his troops forward of Quatre Bras when he heard that French cavalry had reached the crossroads there. It was a message from him to this effect which reached the Duke during the ball and caused him to summon his senior officers and send them off to rouse their men, while he snatched a few hours' sleep. By 9 am on 16 June he was at Quatre Bras himself, and spent the day bringing up all the troops he could lay his hands on to hold it against Ney, commanding the left wing of Napoleon's army, the main body of which, under Soult, was attacking the Prussians at Ligny, five miles away to the south-east. Ney had 42,000 men and 92 guns at his disposal, while at that stage Wellington had only 6,500 infantry, eight guns and no cavalry; but Ney was in no hurry, and thought that he had only a light rearguard to deal with before he secured the area as the place at which Napoleon intended to concentrate his force that evening for the advance to Brussels. He did not attack until the afternoon, and then only with 8,000 men and six guns, to which Wellington by then could oppose 7,000 and 16. Not surprisingly he failed, and a mass cavalry charge later was no more successful against the squares of British infantry.

Soult, with 65,000 men, had been more successful against the 82,000 under Blücher, who had been unhorsed and trampled on in a cavalry charge, but remained as robust as ever. Some of his staff, advised Blücher to withdraw towards Liège, which would have taken his army away to the east, but he decided to go north towards Wavre, where Bülow's corps, which had not been engaged, could join him. Wavre was 13 miles south-east of Brussels and nine east of Waterloo. It was not until early on 17 June that Wellington realized that the Prussians had withdrawn, and not until 9 am that he received word from Blücher of his intentions, at the same time asking what the Duke intended to do. By then the latter had 42,000 men at Quatre Bras. An hour later he began to withdraw them to Mont St Jean, the French making no move against them until the afternoon, when the heavens opened and turned the fields of rye into bog.

By nightfall, Wellington had his army back in the position he had chosen and his own headquarters in the nearby village of Waterloo, where he received a message at 1 am on Sunday 18 June from Blücher that he would march to join the British during the day. Under his own command Wellington had about 67,000 men and 154 guns, but he could only confidently rely on the 24,000 British and the King's German Legion; and some of the former were raw recruits, while others had been badly knocked about at Quatre Bras. Unknown to Wellington, Napoleon had detached 33,000 men under Grouchy to follow up the Prussians: without them he could deploy also 67,000 men, but had 266 guns. The Duke drew up his battleline on a slight ridge south of Mont

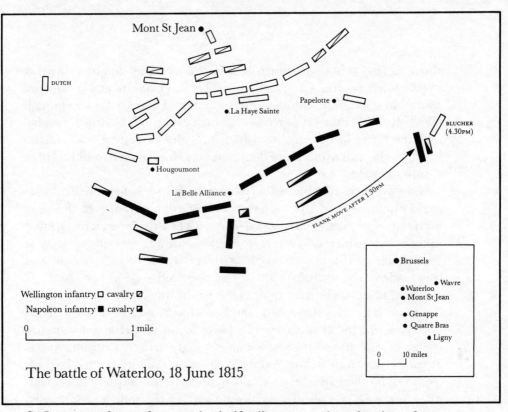

Mont St Jean ●

◻ DUTCH

Papelotte ●

●La Haye Sainte

BLUCHER
(4.30PM)

● Hougoumont

La Belle Alliance ●

FLANK MOVE AFTER 1.30PM

Wellington infantry ◻ cavalry ☒
Napoleon infantry ■ cavalry ◪

0   1 mile

● Brussels

● Wavre
● Waterloo
● Mont St Jean

● Genappe
● Quatre Bras
● Ligny

0   10 miles

The battle of Waterloo, 18 June 1815

St Jean on a front of two and a half miles, occupying also three farms just in front of it, Hougoumont on the right, La Haye Sainte in the centre and Papelotte on the left. He was still worried about his open right flank, fearing that instead of a direct assault, which, after their experiences in the Peninsula, the French would probably avoid, they might try and march round that flank. He therefore posted 18,000 men, mostly Dutch, with 20 guns ten miles away to the west, where they took no part in the battle.

Napoleon had decided to wait until 1 pm before launching his attack, perhaps in order to allow the ground to dry, and he intended to make his main effort to break the centre of Wellington's position astride the main road between La Belle Alliance, from which he would direct the battle, and La Haye Sainte, behind which, beside a prominent elm tree, Wellington was to do the same. In the hope of drawing reserves away from the centre Napoleon ordered preliminary demonstrations on the flanks at 11 am. His brother Jerome turned that on Hougoumont into a full-scale attack and suffered heavy casualties in doing so. At the hour chosen for his assault, the Prussians could be seen approaching some five miles away, and 11,000 men and 32 guns were detached to face them, as 16,000 in four dense columns, supported by 80 guns, drove at Wellington's centre. They surrounded La Haye Sainte and pressed on to the ridge beyond, but a counter-attack by Picton, who was himself killed, drove them back, pursued with such vigour by the British cavalry that the latter lost control and had difficulty in getting back to the ridge, having lost a quarter of their number. Hougoumont and La Haye Sainte still held.

Napoleon was determined to trounce the British before the Prussians could intervene, and, after a pause, the assault was renewed, this time with a massive cavalry charge, led by Ney. The British met it by forming squares, into which one wheel from each gun was brought to prevent the French from taking away the artillery which their horsemen had surrounded. The British infantry and their allies stood firm until, at 4.30 pm, Blücher's leading troops entered the fray on the left of the line. An hour later Ney launched another attack, having massed 9,000 horsemen into the area between La Haye Sainte and Hougoumont, less than a mile wide and the sector most strongly held by British infantry. It was a disastrous failure. While Wellington skilfully reorganized his troops to fill the gaps these assaults had made and mustered his dwindling reserves, Napoleon, anxiously awaiting the return of Grouchy, who had been slow to act on the order for his recall, decided to play his last card, his beloved Imperial Guard. The withering fire of Wellington's musketry halted them as they surged up and over the ridge, until, with the horrified cry of '*La Garde recule*', they faltered and staggered back. The Duke raised his hat as the sign for his infantry to press forward with the bayonet and the cavalry to drive victory home with their sabres. As his Guards retreated in confusion, Napoleon tried in vain to hold the Prussians off his right flank, but failed in that also.

At 9.15 pm Blücher and Wellington met at La Belle Alliance, while Napoleon, struggling to get his coach through the mêlée in Genappe, took to his horse and galloped off. In Wellington's words, it had been 'a damned nice thing, the nearest run thing that you ever saw in your life'. His soldiers would have agreed with the remark he added: 'By God, I don't think it would have done if I had not been there.' As he dismounted and patted the neck of his faithful charger Copenhagen (who lashed out) at 11 pm that night, he was in sober mood at the thought of the narrow margin between defeat and victory and of the cost, 15,000 of his own men, 7,000 of Blücher's and 25,000 of Napoleon's lying dead or wounded in the mud of that small area of not much more than two square miles. For Napoleon and Wellington, both 46 years old, masters of war of their age, it was their last battle.

In fundamentals, there was little difference between the army of Wellington and that of Marlborough: the same divided responsibility for its overall control, leading to an almost total absence of coherence and efficiency in its administration both at home and in the field; the same basic reliance, except for the artillery and engineers, on the regimental system, which was the foundation of the morale which carried it through the dangers, hardships and privations of the campaign. Pay had remained the same until 1794, when that of the private in the infantry was raised to 1s a day at a time when a farm labourer could earn twice that amount and a bricklayer five times. By the time deductions had been made for his food and towards the upkeep and cleaning of his uncomfortable and inappropriate clothing, there was little or nothing left. The ensign received 5s 6d, but by the time he had paid for his daily needs and the customary deductions had been made, he was left as penniless as the soldiers he commanded. In 1804 Sir John Moore wrote that few subalterns lived on their pay: 'It requires a degree of attention which few young men, at starting, are equal to.'

If there was little change in its administration, there was not much either in the way it fought. The rigid battle drill, designed to produce concentrated volleys of musket fire, their result exploited by the charge of infantry with the bayonet and cavalry with the sabre, although still effective in the close-quarter battle, had not always been applicable in the rough wooded terrain of America. The campaign there had led to the use both of specialized marksmen, using rifles, and light infantry. In Britain shooting as a sport was based on the shotgun, but in Germany, where deer and wild boar were the quarry, the rifle had been developed and their forest huntsmen, or *Jäger*, were first recruited into a special unit to be employed as snipers in America – the 6oth Rifles or Royal American Regiment. This was later expanded into several battalions, into which foreigners, other than Hanoverians and Hessians, could be recruited. The last two, when Napoleon cut Britain off from direct contact with their states, were formed into the King's German Legion, which contributed three cavalry regiments and five infantry battalions, two of them light, in the Peninsula, all of high quality. In 1802 the 95th Regiment of Foot was formed as a regular regiment of riflemen, expanded to three battalions and in 1816 known as the Rifle Brigade. These were the only units equipped with rifles, as opposed to muskets. Ramming the bullet down the rifled barrel to load it took much longer than ramming one down the smooth bore of the musket. It was not therefore considered suitable for the battleline, quite apart from the problems of producing it in large numbers.

Light infantry, for which the American war created a great demand, were first raised as light companies within battalions to act as skirmishers, partly for reconnaissance and partly to harass the enemy on the march in his approach to battle, on the flanks while it was in process, and in pursuit. A great impetus to their development was the Duke of York's appointment of Sir John Moore in 1803, when England was threatened with invasion and had no major expeditionary force overseas, to establish a training camp at Shorncliffe to give specialized training to light infantry companies and four complete battalions of such, of which the 43rd and 52nd Foot were the first to be converted. The fifth battalion of the 60th and all of the 95th were dressed in green uniform, as the *Jägers* had been, and were known as the Green Jackets, to be joined in recent years by the 43rd and 52nd. In the Peninsula Craufurd's Light Division was to cover itself in glory.

There had been, nonetheless, a reaction against too much emphasis on light infantry, led by David Dundas, author of the army's 1803 *Rules and Regulations for the Formations, Field Exercise and Movements of His Majesty's Forces*. Only strict close-order battle drill, based on a regulation pace and step, could keep the ranks firm enough to bring concentrated fire to bear and stand up to the onslaught of Napoleon's massive infantry columns, cavalry charges and artillery fire. He laid down that the line should consist of three ranks, the men touching each other, occupying 22 inches.

Wellington's significant modification to the standard tactics was to accept two ranks and to keep his men as far as possible out of sight behind a crest, so that they escaped the effects of artillery fire before the enemy infantry closed. The standard method of attack was to advance in column and deploy into line as late as possible, the French often hoping to carry the day by a charge while still in column. Most of Wellington's defensive victories in the Peninsula were based on meeting these tactics by a 'thin red line' which, concealed as far as possible, held its fire until the enemy was within a hundred yards. As he reeled under these concentrated volleys, the infantry would charge forward with the bayonet and the cavalry be let loose to slash with their sabres. The latter was most effective if it could charge the enemy while he was executing a manoeuvre. A cavalry charge against infantry drawn up in line, or forming squares as Wellington's did at Waterloo, was seldom effective.

In Wellington's day all the cavalry regiments, other than the two of Horse Guards, were known as Dragoons of some sort, although none of them conformed to the original idea of a dragoon as a mounted infantryman, armed with a carbine. The original regiments of horse had been renamed Dragoon Guards in order to preserve their social superiority, and most of the other cavalry regiments were styled Light Dragoons. In theory Dragoon Guards and Dragoons were meant to charge in battle, and the Light Dragoons to carry out all the other tasks of cavalry, such as scouting, skirmishing and the pursuit. In practice, because it was impossible to reserve regiments for special tasks, they were all liable to do both. They had discarded firearms and relied on the sword, or sabre – the *arme blanche*. Three regiments changed their name from Light Dragoons to Hussars in the Peninsula in imitation of the cavalry of Central Europe, especially that of the Hungarians, from whom the name was derived, and the Poles – possibly as an excuse to wear more splendid uniform. This fashion was followed later in the nineteenth century, when all the Light Dragoons became either Hussars or Lancers, the latter adopting the weapon, a mobile form of pike, from which they derived their name. Wellington was sceptical of the value of British cavalry in battle, owing to their inability to maintain control once they had been launched into the charge, although they served him well at Salamanca.

Artillery was employed in two forms, field and siege. The former, brass guns firing 6 or 12lb shot, was employed to batter the enemy's ranks before the infantry closed, using either a solid round ball or a canister, full of small balls. Another round was known as common shell, a hollow sphere filled with explosive, detonated by a fuse lit before the gun was fired. It was seldom effective and often burst prematurely, but a development by Colonel Henry Shrapnell, combining common and canister shell, gave British artillery a distinct advantage. Shrapnell's shell exploded the canister at a range determined by a pre-set fuse and was effective up to 1,200 yards. Use was also made of rockets, Congreve's rocket troop being employed at Waterloo, but they were very inaccurate. Siege artillery consisted of heavy iron guns firing 18 or 24 lb solid shot, used traditionally to batter down fortress walls, and of howitzers to lob projectiles over them. Moving siege artillery was a major problem.

Leadership was, as always, a vital element. There can be no doubt that Wellington's leadership was critical in welding the British army in the Peninsula into the weapon which played a significant part in the downfall of Napoleon. No aspect of the life of his army or of the battlefield escaped his eagle eye or was unaffected by his pragmatic, cynical common-sense. He never expected too much, but never accepted a standard lower than he knew could be achieved, if men could be brought, by one means or another, to do their best. If encouragement was needed, he was there in person, cool, calm and collected, to give it; if a rebuke, it was scathing. He was not a lovable personality, but he was a great commander: he knew his business, he won battles, and he did his best to care for the needs of his men. They recognized all this, and were confident that they could always beat the French if 'Old Nosey' was there to lead them.

4
THE AGE OF WOLSELEY AND ROBERTS

1816–1902

It is not possible to describe the British army's Victorian age – from the Battle of Waterloo to the end of the Boer War – as that of one man. Until the death of the Duke of Wellington in 1852, there was no significant military figure. Indeed, there were no significant campaigns, and the Duke himself, increasingly conservative in outlook as the years passed, overshadowed all others. His rôle as *laudator temporis acti* was to be taken over by Queen Victoria's cousin, the Duke of Cambridge, who succeeded Wellington as Commander-in-Chief at the Horse Guards in 1856, a post he was to hold for 36 years. He had been made a major-general at the age of 26 and commanded the 1st Division in the Crimean War. Chief among the military figures who were to rise to prominence in his time were Garnet Wolseley and Frederick Roberts, the former in the British and the latter in the Indian army. Almost the same age, Roberts born in September 1832 and Wolseley in June 1833, both were sons of army officers and products of that fertile breeding ground of field-marshals – the Anglo-Irish Protestant ascendancy. Roberts's father had reached the rank of colonel in the East India Company's army, Wolseley's that of lieutenant-colonel in the British. After a year at Eton, Roberts entered the Royal Military College at Sandhurst at the age of 15, moving on to the East India Company's school for officers at Addiscombe two years later, to be commissioned in the Bengal artillery in 1851. He did not therefore have to purchase his commission; neither did Wolseley.

The Commander-in-Chief[1] could grant commissions without purchase to young men who had successfully qualified at Sandhurst or whose fathers had distinguished themselves in the service of the nation.

---

[1] 1811–27 the Duke of York; 1827 and 1842–52 the Duke of Wellington; 1828–42 Lord Hill; 1852–6 Lord Hardinge; 1856–95 the Duke of Cambridge; 1895–1904 Lord Wolseley.

Wolseley's widowed mother had first applied for a commission for him when he was 14, and continued to press her case without success until, when Garnet Wolseley had almost abandoned hope, the Duke of Wellington gave way and he was appointed an ensign in the 12th Foot in July 1852.

Although the two men were in action very close to each other at the relief of Lucknow in 1857 and were to succeed each other in a staff appointment in India thereafter, they were not actually to meet until they were 60 years old. Their respective careers were to illustrate the two different areas of the British army's experience in the Victorian age: that of Roberts, the many campaigns in or based on India; that of Wolseley, the Crimean War and the many colonial campaigns all over the world. Before following their careers and those of their companions in arms, mention must be made of the campaigns in which the army had been involved between Waterloo and the commissioning of the two future field-marshals.

In 1816 the army's total establishment was reduced to 225,000 men, half of its strength in 1814. In the subsequent five years it was further reduced to a total of 100,000, half of whom were in Britain, including Ireland, 20,000 in India (in addition to the East India Company's army) and 30,000 scattered about the world in colonial garrisons. The latter two were fully employed but the former only faced action again in the middle of the century in the Crimea.

India was the main scene of activity. Wellesley's extension of British power brought further trouble in its train, partly by letting loose in Central India a host of unemployed fighting men, known as Pindaris, whose depredations received the tacit support of their former Mahratta employers, partly because the extension of the East India Company's borders brought it up against other rulers and races, who resisted the spread of its power and influence. Among these were the Gurkhas of Nepal, who had for some time indulged in raids into the northern plains from their Himalayan strongholds, and had begun to occupy part of the territory permanently. Soon after his appointment as Governor-General in 1813, Lord Moira sent them an ultimatum to withdraw. When this was rejected, he prepared to invade their homeland, not an easy task. A force of 34,000, the British army element of which consisted of the 17th, 24th and 53rd Foot, a dismounted detachment, 100 strong, of the 8th Light Dragoons, and a battery of horse artillery, was assembled to invade Nepal in four widely separated columns. Only the westernmost, commanded by Colonel Ochterlony, was successful, trapping the main Gurkha force between the River Sutlej and Simla. The other three columns, commanded by major-generals, failed, one with heavy loss at Dehra Dun. Ochterlony was then transferred to the easternmost column, and, in the brilliant forcing of the Churaghati Pass, 30 miles south of Katmandu, brought the campaign to an end in February 1816. His action acquired at one and the same time the desirable hill-stations round Simla, in which to take refuge from the sultry heat of the Indian summer, and the lasting friendship and alliance of the hill people of Nepal, whose Gurkha soldiers were to serve so faithfully in both the Indian and, after independence, the British army.

While engaged in these operations at the extreme north of its territory, the East India Company was also involved in extending its control over the extreme south. In 1815 a force of 4,000 men under the Governor, Sir Robert Browning, which included the 19th and 73rd Foot, attempted to extend the Company's control in Ceylon, which since 1803 had been limited to a small area, over the whole rugged, forested island. It took him three years to complete the task, by which time the troops, who had been joined by the 83rd Foot, had suffered far more from disease than they had from casualties in action. By that time the activity of the Pindaris in Central India had reached such a pitch that Moira could tolerate them no longer. Between 1817 and 1819 he assembled a force of 100,000 men, which, split up into a large number of columns, operated throughout the whole of Central India, from Delhi in the north to as far south as Dhaswar, 200 miles south of Poona. Using infantry to deal with fortresses, while mobile columns, principally of cavalry, among whom the 17th Light Dragoons were prominent, relentelssly hunted the bandits until they were rounded up, Moira defeated Wellington's old enemies of the Mahratta Confederacy and laid the foundations of a permanent peace.

Five years later, the attention of Moira's successor, Lord Amherst, was switched to the east, where the Burmese kingdom of Ava had been encroaching on the eastern area of the Bengali Presidency, the area of India east of modern Bangladesh. In February 1824 war was declared and an expedition, found mainly from the Madras Presidency, the Bengalis being unwilling to go to sea, prepared to capture Rangoon and advance up the Irawaddy to Ava, near Mandalay, 500 miles upstream, while another force drove the enemy out of Assam. To undertake the former formidable task, the practical difficulties of which, stemming

from the nature of the country and its climate, were grossly underesti-
mated, Major-General Sir Archibald Campbell had 10,600 men, of
which the British army element consisted of the 13th, 38th, 41st and
89th Foot and some artillery.

The campaign was notable for a lack of realism on the part of the
higher command and the failure to provide adequate logistic support
for the unfortunate soldiers who took part. It ended in February 1826
when the Burmese surrendered their claim to Assam, Cachon, Manipur
and the coastal provinces of Chittagong and Arakan. Disease had been
the principal enemy. Of the 3,586 British soldiers who had set out from
Madras in 1824, 3,115 died, over 95 per cent from disease: of their 150
officers, 61 died, 16 only from wounds in action. In Fortescue's words:

Few British soldiers can have spent a more miserable year than those who
landed at Rangoon in May 1824. Unsuitably clothed, vilely fed, imperfectly
tended, drenched with rain when they were not bathed in sweat, eaten up by
mosquitoes, leeches and the manifold plagues of a tropical delta, they had
literally nothing but misery and death before them.[2]

Fourteen years later, the Governor-General, Lord Auckland, looked
in the opposite direction, where the fear that was to dominate military
thinking in India for the rest of the century and longer – Russian
ambitions – led to one of the most notorious disasters in Britain's military
history. These fears were aroused by a Persian attack, which it was
believed had been instigated by Russia, on Herat on the north-west of
Afghanistan. That country was in its customary state of chaos, and it
was feared that Russia would exploit this. Auckland tried to persuade
Dost Mahomed, the ruling Amir in Kabul, to accept an alliance. When
he declined, Auckland decided to oust him and install in his place one
of his predecessors, Shah Sooja, who had made some unsuccessful
attempts to restore himself. The original intention had been to provide
Shah Sooja with arms, money and British officers to train and lead his
troops. But there had been justifiable doubt about whether Shah Sooja
could succeed and, having obtained Sikh support, Auckland decided
on a full-scale invasion.

The plan was to concentrate a force of 20,000 men, 5,000 from the
Bombay army and 15,000 from Bengal and Sooja's men, on the lower
reaches of the Indus, whence they would advance over the Bolan Pass
to Quetta and capture Kandahar, a 300-mile march. Having estab-

[2] Fortescue, Vol. XI, p. 350.

lished a base there, the force would then move north-east another 200 miles to Ghazni and then another 100 to Kabul, towards which the Sikhs would advance separately through the Khyber pass. Once Sooja was on his throne in Kabul and the Persians had been driven from Herat, the British and Indians would return to India, leaving Sooja on his own. The British army element of the Bengal contribution, commanded by Major-General Cotton, consisted of the 16th Lancers and the 13th Light Infantry, and of the Bombay contingent, two squadrons of the 4th Light Dragoons, the 2nd (Queen's) and the 17th Foot. The whole force was under General Sir John Keane of the Bombay army.

Difficulties of many kinds dogged and delayed the assembly of the force, the principal one being the objection of the rulers of Sind to having a large force imposed on their country, a breach of their treaty with the Company. In September 1838, thanks largely to the effective diplomacy of Mr McNeill, the British Resident at Teheran, the Persians withdrew from Herat. The ostensible reason for the expedition was thus removed, but Auckland decided that he was already too far committed. He went ahead with the expedition, but reduced the number of troops committed to it, keeping some in reserve in case of trouble with the Sikhs or the Amirs of Sind.

By the end of 1838, Cotton's force had concentrated at Shikarpur on the Indus, but, although the Bombay contingent had landed at Karachi, 400 miles to the south, lack of transport and supplies had prevented them from moving north. They had still not moved by February 1839 and Keane decided that Cotton should start without them. Although he met no opposition, the lack of transport and supplies prevented him from reaching Kandahar until May. Keane waited there for two months while the Bombay contingent caught up and supplies were built up for the next phase. When he did then resume the advance, he had insufficient transport to move his siege-train, and was fortunate that Ghazni was secured without it. Dost Mahomed's soldiers lost heart, and he fled to take refuge in the Hindu Kush mountains, the main body of his army having been concentrated to face the Sikhs at the Khyber. They melted away into the mountains when Keane entered Kabul in August, with Sooja in his train. There was no need to continue to Herat but, appreciating that if Sooja were left without support he would not stay there long, Keane left 5,000 men at Kabul under Cotton, who assumed overall command, and another 5,000 at Kandahar under Nott. Keane himself returned with the rest of the army to India.

Cotton's position was subordinate to that of Sir William Macnaghten, the political representative of the Governor-General and very particular in insisting on the superiority of his standing. Sooja's position was precarious. Dost Mahomed stirred up trouble all over the country, including Baluchistan, threatening the long line of communication back through Quetta. Cotton's forces were kept busy suppressing trouble throughout 1840. By mid-1841 the situation seemed more peaceful: economies were enforced, subsidies to the tribal chiefs among them, and reliefs were put in hand for some of the troops who had been in the original force, including Sale's 1st Brigade in which the 13th Light Infantry served. In April Cotton had himself been relieved by Major-General Elphinstone, an able soldier experienced in European warfare, but crippled with gout and generally in poor health. He had been appointed by Auckland because he was senior to Nott, who had made it clear that he would refuse to take orders from Macnaghten.

In October 1841, while Sale's brigade was on its way back from Kabul via the Khyber Pass, the whole country rose in revolt, Sale having to take refuge in the fort of Jellalabad. The garrison of Ghazni was surrounded, Nott besieged in Kandahar, and the supply route through Quetta cut. Elphinstone, under the influence of Macnaghten, reacted feebly at Kabul. He failed to secure the dominating fortress of Bala Hissar and allowed his garrison to be shut up in their cantonment, which was impossible to defend, and cut off from their supplies. In this hopeless position, the voice of good sense was that of the one-armed Colonel Shelton, whose brigade had relieved Sale's. He urged a fighting withdrawal to Jellalabad, less than a hundred miles away, before the winter snows made it impossible. But Macnaghten would have none of it. He could not see Auckland's policy collapse and abandon Sooja, although the latter had refused to let Elphinstone occupy the Bala Hissar. Vain hopes were held that Sale would march to their relief. After a series of shameful incidents and unsuccessful clashes with the forces of Akbar, Dost Mahomed's son, Macnaghten accepted the latter's proposal that the British, taking Sooja with them, should leave the country. Haggling about conditions, including that of leaving some British officers and families as hostages and handing over the artillery, was protracted, as Akbar raised the stakes. On 23 December, at a meeting to discuss terms, Macnaghten and the three officers with him were murdered, and on 6 January 1842, on Akbar's promise of safe conduct, Elphinstone led his 4,500 soldiers, of which Shelton's 44th

Foot formed the majority of the 690-strong British element, out on the snow-covered road towards the Khyber. He was accompanied by 12,000 followers, including Lady Sale.

Whether or not Akbar meant to keep his word – and his conduct in the days following tends to show that perhaps he did – he could not control the Ghilzai tribesmen on the route, who closed in mercilessly as, in the bitter cold, the column straggled through the Khoord-Kabul Pass. A week later none was left, save Doctor William Brydon, who with two native followers arrived wounded on horseback at Jellalabad on 12 January. This disaster was followed by the massacre of the garrison of Ghazni, the 27th Native Infantry, when they were forced to surrender on 6 March 1842. The garrison of Jellalabad might have suffered the same fate, had Sale and his political officer, Macgregor, had their way; but the refusal of his subordinates to approve their plan to treat with the Afghans for a safe conduct to Peshawar prevented it.

The new Governor-General, Lord Ellenborough, who succeeded Auckland at the end of February, having initially considered a renewed invasion of Afghanistan to be followed by a withdrawal, changed his mind and opted for the latter without the former. But the robust attitude of Major-General George Pollock, commanding the forces at Peshawar, prevailed. In April he had relieved Akbar's siege of Jellalabad, and, after a pause of four months, he was allowed by Ellenborough to 'withdraw' via Kabul, where he collected the surviving British prisoners, including Shelton,[3] and Kandahar, where Nott joined him as they marched out through Quetta. Shah Sooja had meanwhile been assassinated, and Dost Mahomed was restored to his throne. Thus ended the First Afghan War, probably the worst conceived and executed of all Britain's politico-military ventures.

It was immediately followed by campaigns which brought under British control the areas immediately adjacent to Afghanistan. In a swift campaign, launched in February 1843, Sir Charles Napier subdued the Amirs of Sind by June, punningly announcing his victory in a single Latin word *Peccavi*, which translated means 'I have sinned'. After that, it was the turn of their neighbours, the Sikhs. Their enlightened ruler, Ranjit Singh, who had cooperated with the Company, had died in 1839 and a struggle for succession ensued. Britain's humiliation in Afghanistan, followed by Napier's high-handed subjugation of Sind,

---

[3] He was not to live long, dying from a fall from his horse in a Dublin barracks in 1845. Elphinstone had died of dysentery before Pollock reached Kabul.

persuaded the Sikhs that they should strike before they were struck. In December 1845 they crossed the Sutlej with 50,000 men and 100 guns. The war that followed had two brief phases, broken by a peaceful period of nearly two years. The first phase was ended by the successful Battle of Sobraon on 10 February 1846, following that of Major-General Sir Harry Smith at Aliwal, where the 16th Light Dragoons distinguished themselves.

Peace reigned for the next three years and the Company's army was greatly reduced; but trouble flared up again at Multan in April 1848. It was not until November that General Sir Hugh Gough could assemble a force, 16,000-strong, sufficient to deal with the Sikhs. By that time the whole Punjab was aflame. The first engagement, at Chillianwala on 13 January 1849, was inconclusive. Finding the Sikh army already in position covering the area in which he was assembling his force, Gough launched an attack without reconnaissance late in the day over ground largely covered with jungle. The battle had already reached a stage of almost utter confusion when the incompetent commander of one of the cavalry brigades, Pope, gave an order which was interpreted to mean retreat, whereupon his brigade, which included the 9th Lancers and 14th Light Dragoons, galloped back through the lines of their own infantry. Gough lost 2,300 men, casualties being high in the British battalions, particularly in the 24th and 29th Foot. The next major engagement, at Gujerat exactly a month later, was a very different affair. Gough's attack was carefully prepared and methodically executed, and his 20,000 men routed the Sikh army of three times that number, bringing the campaign to an end two years before Frederick Roberts was commissioned into the Bengal artillery.

India was not the only area in which British soldiers had fought since Waterloo; Africa and China also saw them in action. For some time the trading posts on the Gold Coast in West Africa had been troubled by the Ashanti tribe in the hinterland, and in January 1824 Sir Charles Macarthy, whom the Government had appointed as Governor-in-Chief of all the settlements on the West Coast, led an expedition to deal with them. On 21 January his small force, totally dependent on unreliable native porters, was surrounded and exterminated by a greatly superior Ashanti army. An inconclusive campaign of raids and counter-raids followed, until a battle on 7 August 1826 at Dowdah, 24 miles north-east of Accra, in which 300 British and 500 African troops, assisted by 5,000 native levies, defeated 10,000 Ashantis. The British soldiers were all from the Royal African Corps, and were men who had volunteered rather than serve the terms of imprisonment to which they had been sentenced.

Not long after this, there was trouble further south in Africa, where the acquisition of Cape Colony from the Dutch in the Napoleonic wars led to clashes with the Kaffirs to the east. In December 1834 they suddenly crossed the Great Fish River, spreading panic among the settlements to the west. Harry Smith, then a colonel and chief-of-staff to the Governor, Sir Benjamin d'Urban, set off on horseback and rode the 600 miles in midsummer heat in six days to take command at Grahamstown. The force on the frontier totalled 755 men, less than a quarter mounted, the majority being the 482 men of the 75th Foot. The 72nd had been ordered up from Cape Town, half by sea and half by waggon-train. The Kaffirs were thought to number between 12,000 and 15,000. With his small force Smith restored the situation until d'Urban had assembled 3,000 men. With these, Smith crossed into the Kaffirs' own territory and, in a series of skilfully directed and executed operations by flying columns, exploiting Kaffir dependence on their huge herds of cattle, brought them to the negotiating table in September. A treaty was signed which ceded to Cape Colony all the land between the Great Fish and the Kei, 100 miles further east. This was repudiated by Lord Glenelg, Secretary of State for the Colonies, the frontier being fixed at the Keishamma, only 20 miles east of the Great Fish. Harry Smith was much criticized in liberal circles for his treatment of the Kaffirs and was removed from command of the troops.

These events made many of the Boer settlers, who had contributed significant numbers of mounted men to Smith's force, feel that the British Government was not prepared to defend them effectively against the natives. In the next seven years 10,000 of them moved out of Cape Colony, some east to Natal, others to the area between the Orange and Vaal Rivers, and some north of the Vaal. However, the Government of the Cape Colony still claimed authority over them; and in 1843 Natal was declared a British colony, whereupon most of the Boers trekked north over the Drakensberg mountains.

In 1846 there was more trouble with the Kaffirs after an incident in March near Grahamstown. A force of 2,600 British soldiers, including the 7th Dragoon Guards, the 27th, 1/45th, 90th and 91st Foot, and 624

Cape Mounted Rifles was assembled in June, reinforced by four more battalions before the end of the year, by which time most of the tribes had sued for peace. However, operations on a lower scale lasted for another year, when Harry Smith returned, this time as Governor. His arrival was greeted with enthusiasm by the settlers who expected him to pursue a tough policy. Having settled affairs with the Kaffirs, he turned his attention to the Boers. He first tried to persuade them not to leave Natal, and had some success; but, when he set about establishing his authority over the area between the Orange and the Vaal, he met armed opposition. He dealt with it effectively at Boomplatz on 29 August 1848, thereafter installing a British garrison at Bloemfontein. More Kaffir trouble raised its head in 1850, when the troops available to Smith had been reduced to four weak battalions (6th, 45th, 73rd and 91st Foot). With the Cape Mounted Rifles and 400 native police, he could only muster 2,000 men for operations. He was nearing success in these when he was superseded by Major-General Sir George Cathcart, who brought the campaign to an end in December 1852, the last resistance to be dealt with being that of the Basuto under their famous leader Mosheshe.

Five months before the end of Cathcart's Orange River campaign, Garnet Wolseley had received his commission in the 12th Foot. He immediately applied for and was granted a transfer to the 80th, which was serving in Burma, where war had broken out again in February 1852. By the time he joined them, the main phase of the campaign had been concluded with the capture of Rangoon in April, followed several months later by an almost unopposed move up the Irawaddy to Prome by a force of 5,700 men, drawn partly from the Bengal and partly from the Madras army, under Major-General Godwin. The Court of Ava, although it would not accept the cession of the southern province of Pegu, agreed that it would not interfere with Britain's occupation of it, and it was annexed to British India in December 1852. Fighting however did not stop. Bands of Burmese ex-soldiers, joined by bandits, known as dacoits, roamed the country under dacoit leaders, the principal of whom was Myat Toon. Operations against them were known as the Subalterns' War, Wolseley being one of the subalterns who led columns in their pursuit. He was severely wounded in the thigh in an attack on Myat Toon's base near Donubyu after the 800-strong force under Sir John Cheape had lost many of its men from cholera. He had the satisfaction of being both mentioned in despatches and promoted lieutenant for his gallantry, and also of knowing that the attack was the last major action of the campaign.

Wolseley was invalided back to Ireland, where he transferred to the 90th Light Infantry in Dublin. He was fit to join them in March 1854, by which time the situation was threatening war.

A combination of factors, which included Britain's fear of the expansion of Russian influence in the Near East and Napoleon III's personal ambitions, led to British and French support of Turkey in resisting Russian pressure. Turkey declared war on Russia in October 1853, and, when its fleet in the Black Sea had been totally destroyed, Britain and France sent their fleets through the Bosphorus with orders to bottle up the Russian fleet in its base at Sebastopol in the Crimea, and delivered an ultimatum to the Tsar to withdraw his forces from the Danubian principalities of Moldavia and Wallachia (modern Romania). When no answer was received, war was declared in March 1854, Britain and France having decided to send an expeditionary force to help Turkey force the Russians to meet their demands and ensure that they did not move any nearer to the Bosphorus.

The British army in 1854 was totally unprepared for any such expedition. Under the stiflingly conservative influence of the Duke of Wellington, who had died in 1852, it had not only not improved its efficiency, it had slipped back into its old ways. Successive Governments had starved it of money; its administration was still chaotic, its soldiers ill-paid, ill-fed, inadequately and unsuitably clothed, still armed with the weapons of the Napoleonic wars, and, if trained at all, only in the tactics of that time. Its function had been seen as that of keeping Ireland in order and helping the newly-formed police in Britain to do the same when needed, but primarily to supply men for service in India and the colonies. In 1854 30,000 men were serving in India, 40,000 in the colonies and there were 65,000 at home, including Ireland.

The first troops sailed for Malta in February, the 66-year-old Master-General of the Ordnance, Lord Raglan, having been appointed Commander-in-Chief of the expedition. He had seen no action since he had lost an arm at Waterloo, where he had been an ADC to the Duke, whose niece he had married. He had served on the Duke's staff almost continuously thereafter, and had never commanded anything. He was an able and respected man of strong character and great charm, but not one accustomed to making hard decisions and executing them ruthlessly. The French had appointed as his colleague an excitable, ill-tempered political general, St Arnaud, who was a sick man. It was far from clear what the troops were to do. Having established bases, the French at Gallipoli, the British at Scutari, it was decided to move the joint force to the Bulgarian coast at Varna to force the Russians away from the Danube. It had been assumed that the expedition would land from the sea and, as in previous ages, somehow find its means of transport locally. There was no hope of this, and by the time the force of 26,000 British with 66 guns and 30,000 French with 70 had been transported to the area of Varna, Austrian pressure had persuaded the Russians to leave the principalities. By this time British blood was up and Louis Napoleon was in no mood to back down. Meanwhile, men and horses were dying of disease at an alarming rate, and the brothers-in-law, the Earls of Lucan and Cardigan, the former aged 54 commanding the cavalry division, the latter, three years older, the Light Cavalry Brigade, bickered endlessly. Something had to be done – anything was better than staying and dying of cholera or dysentery where they were: the answer was to attack Sebastopol and destroy the Russian fleet.

On 24 August an extraordinary armada of sailing ships, towed by steamers, set off across the Black Sea, men and horses crowded into the transports like sardines. Nobody knew how many men General Menschikoff had in the Crimea or where they were. In fact he had 80,000. St Arnaud was nervous and wanted to land on the east coast of the Crimea and spend the winter getting ready to attack Sebastopol, but Raglan persuaded him that the whole force, which also included 5,000 Turks, should land at Eupatoria 45 miles from Sebastopol on the northern side of the unfortunately named Kalamita Bay. No opposition was met, and, suffering severely from lack of water and inadequacy of other supplies, the combined force moved south, the French on the right near the coast, as they had little cavalry to protect their flanks.

Menschikoff had drawn up 46,000 men supported by 100 guns on the top of a steep escarpment overlooking the southern bank of the River Alma. Making no use of his cavalry to attempt an out-flanking move, Raglan launched his whole force in a direct assault on this seemingly impregnable position. The French, having found an unguarded route up the western end, and then apparently lost it, urged Raglan to greater efforts to save them. In an attack, the sheer gallantry

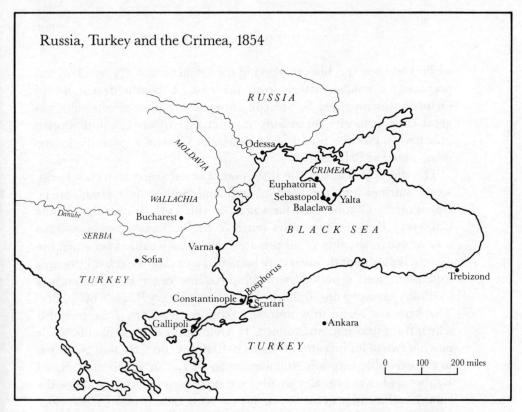

Russia, Turkey and the Crimea, 1854

of which has probably had no equal, the Great Redoubt was captured and the Russians withdrew. Raglan, who had lost 2,000 men, wished to pursue them into Sebastopol, but St Arnaud refused, and thereby lost an opportunity which could have brought the campaign to an end and saved many lives.

They could not stay where they were, as the exposed beaches, on which they had landed, could not be used to supply them. It was therefore decided to move round to the south of Sebastopol and base the British force on the small sheltered port of Balaclava and the French on two smaller ones further west. Menschikoff meanwhile had decided that he did not want to be shut up inside Sebastopol. Blocking the harbour entrance with sunken ships, he moved his force away to the east, leaving the remainder under the able Colonel Todleben, reinforced by sailors from the fleet, to defend the fortress. In doing so, he nearly captured Raglan and his staff, who were leading the British cavalry on their flanking move. It was a long time before Raglan and Canrobert (successor to St Arnaud who had died) were ready to launch an attack from the south. Landing stores at Balaclava and moving them by pack-animal up on to the bare plateau was a laborious affair. Meanwhile Todleben was busy improving the defences, and Menschikoff was preparing a counter-attack from the east. A bombardment on 17 October was intended to precede an assault, but its effects were not great enough to give an assault much chance of success, and Raglan now had to face the threat of an attack by General Liprandi's 27,000 men, aimed at Balaclava.

The direct defence of the little port was entrusted to 3,000 Turks, 1,000 marines and the 93rd (Argyll and Sutherland) Highlanders. Dawn on 25 October saw an attack on the Turkish redoubts on the Causeway Heights, two miles north of the harbour where Cardigan was, as usual, sleeping in his private yacht. The Russians occupied the eastern redoubts and, when they launched a cavalry attack southwards from them, were repulsed by the 'thin red line' of the Highlanders and a skilfully executed uphill charge by Scarlett's Heavy Brigade of cavalry. The Russians began to withdraw, taking the guns from the redoubts which the Turks had abandoned. In an attempt to prevent this, while moving two of his infantry divisions in that direction, Raglan entrusted to the excitable Captain Nolan an order to Lucan which read: 'Lord Raglan wishes the cavalry to advance rapidly to the front – follow the enemy and try to prevent the enemy carrying away the guns.' Previous orders to counter-attack the redoubts for that purpose had been interpreted by Lucan to mean that he should wait for the infantry, which still had not arrived, partly because of the reluctance to move of Sir George Cathcart, who thought that he, not Raglan, should have been appointed Commander-in-Chief.

To Lucan the order made no sense. From where he was, he could see no guns but those a mile and a half away, where the Russians had drawn up their force at the end of a valley between the Causeway Heights to the south and the Fedioukine Heights to the north, which they also occupied. To attack these with cavalry would be suicidal. But Nolan insisted that Raglan had demanded an immediate attack. Lucan, who had been constantly angered by Raglan's habit of issuing orders direct to Cardigan, felt that he could not disobey a direct order, and rode over to Cardigan, showed him the order and told him to advance down the valley, while he, Lucan, would follow with the Heavy Brigade. Cardigan pointed out that the Russians had 'a battery in the valley on our front and batteries and riflemen on both sides', to which Lucan replied, 'I know it, but Lord Raglan will have it. We have no choice but to obey.' With the comment to Lord George Paget, his second-in-command, 'Here goes the last of the Brudenells', Cardigan drew his brigade up in two lines, the 13th Light Dragoons, 11th Hussars and 17th Lancers in the first, the 4th Light Dragoons and the 8th Hussars in the second, placed himself five horses' length ahead and gave the order to advance.

As the Russian guns poured shell into the mass of horses, the pace quickened to a gallop, until only 50 horsemen were left to charge the guns. Miraculously Cardigan himself survived, and trotted slowly back up the valley through the shattered remnants of his brigade to a violent altercation with Lucan, whom he accused of failing to support him, when he had halted the Heavy Brigade, sensibly seeing no point in adding to the slaughter. Of the 700 horses and men who had charged, only 195 returned. The 13th Light Dragoons were reduced to two officers and eight mounted men, the 17th Lancers to 37 troopers. The Russians continued their withdrawal, but to a position which covered the only metalled road, a spur from which could have been built to Balaclava. On 5 November, having received reinforcements from Odessa, they renewed the attack with 70,000 men on the extreme right of the British position investing Sebastopol, on the heights of Inkerman. After a confused and fierce battle, which started in the early morning mist and developed into a series of ill-coordinated actions on both sides, the Russians were beaten off. They lost 12,000 men to the British 2,573 (653 killed) and the French 929 (143 killed), and the Russians never again attempted an attack to raise the siege.

The 90th Light Infantry had been ordered to India, but were diverted to the Crimea to replace these losses. Wolseley, promoted captain at the age of 21, was with them, but on arrival transferred to the Royal Engineers, who were short-handed. He therefore shared the privations which the army endured that winter in the bitter cold on the top of the windswept plateau between Sebastopol and Balaclava. No provision had been made for supply and transport services to cater for the climate and the absence of a road, and the medical services to deal with the casualties and high rate of sickness were totally inadequate. In January and February 1855 there were nearly 14,000 men in hospital, and many of the raw recruits sent to fill the ranks fell sick before they reached the front line. Florence Nightingale had arrived at the main base hospital at Scutari in October 1854; but it was a long time before any significant improvement was seen anywhere else. It was not until September 1855 that the final assault on Sebastopol brought victory, six months after

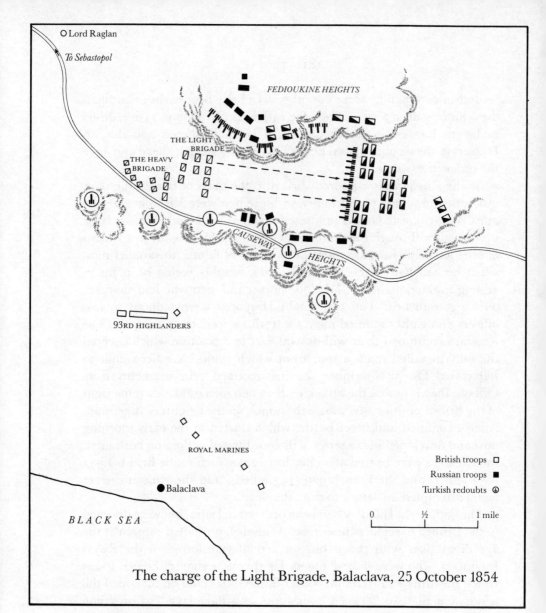

O Lord Raglan

To Sebastopol

FEDIOUKINE HEIGHTS

THE LIGHT
BRIGADE

THE HEAVY
BRIGADE

CAUSEWAY   HEIGHTS

93RD HIGHLANDERS

ROYAL MARINES

British troops □
Russian troops ■
Turkish redoubts ◉

Balaclava

BLACK SEA

0   ½   1 mile

The charge of the Light Brigade, Balaclava, 25 October 1854

Tsar Nicholas had died, and not until March 1856 that the war was finally brought to an end by the Treaty of Paris, Russia being removed from the Danube, conventions covering navigation of the Danube and transit of the Dardanelles signed, and the neutralization of the Black Sea established, only to be repudiated by Russia in 1870.

By the time the war ended, the British force had been built up to a strength of 90,000 men, commanded by General Sir William Codrington. He had succeeded the tough 64-year-old Scot, Sir James Simpson, who had stepped into Raglan's shoes after the latter's death in June

1855, attributed to disappointment at the failure on the anniversary of Waterloo of an assault on Sebastopol, in which his troops had lost 1,500 men and the French 3,500. By the end of the campaign the French forces outnumbered the British three to one. They had despatched a total of 300,000 men to the war and lost 11,000 dead in action and 21,000 from disease. Comparable figures for the British were 111,300 despatched, 4,774 dead in action and 16,323 from disease. Turkish losses from all causes were thought to be over 30,000 and Russian over 110,000.

The war had been the first in which the influence of the press was significant. The development of education, the expansion of the press itself, and the introduction of both the electric telegraph and the camera, made it possible for the British public to appreciate soon after the event what its soldiers experienced on the battlefield. It was the age of reform in every field, and William Howard Russell, the famous correspondent of *The Times*, was foremost among those who were intent on its application to the army. The army had not woken up to the implications of having in the field newspaper correspondents, who could almost instantly report what went on and what they thought about it to the Great British Public. There was no censorship. It would have been strongly resisted, if only because other civilians, like Cardigan's friend Mrs Duberly, were allowed to accompany the forces in the field and write freely about their experiences. Russell's reports, combined with Florence Nightingale's activities, were instrumental in forcing the Horse Guards and the Government to take action to redress the disgraceful conditions which the soldiers endured in the first winter of the war. In the second, after the fall of Sebastopol, they had huts to live in, better food and clothing, and improved medical services, all easier to provide as there were no active operations. The scandalous state of affairs in the first winter led to the resignation of Aberdeen as Prime Minister and his succession by Palmerston. More fundamental reforms of army organization were to take longer to effect, but the inadequacies and absurdities, the conditions which could allow Cardigan and Lucan to reach their respective positions of responsibility and act as they did, had been clearly revealed.

Captain Wolseley left the Crimea in July 1856, one of the last to go. He had been wounded in the face during the preparations for the final attack on Sebastopol, which he had therefore missed. He recovered, although he lost the sight of one eye permanently, and was appointed a Deputy Assistant Quartermaster-General (DAQMG). In that capacity he was much involved in making the arrangements to see that the conditions under which the troops spent the winter were as good as he could make them. When he left, he returned to the 90th, and in April 1857 sailed with them for service in China. However, just after their ship had been wrecked in the narrow waters between Sumatra and Java, they were diverted to Calcutta to deal with the mutiny that had broken out in the Indian Army.

The causes of the Indian Mutiny were numerous. A significant one was the weakness of the European element in the army – only 34,000 out of 290,000 – and a high proportion was involved either on expeditions outside India or in the Punjab. There were fewer than 11 full battalions in the whole vast area south and east of the Sutlej. A number of measures had recently been taken which offended the caste or other sensibilities of the different racial elements, culminating in the allegation that cartridges for the new Enfield rifle, which had to be bitten before use, were smeared with either beef or pig fat, one abhorrent to the Hindu, the other to the Muslim troops. There were also local rulers, such as the Rani of Shansi, who harboured grievances and were ready to exploit disaffection in the ranks. Trouble had started at Barrackpore near Calcutta in January 1857, and had become general after mutineers at Meerut in May were sentenced to the barbarous method of execution of being blown from the muzzle of guns in front of their comrades. British officers were murdered and the mutineers moved to Delhi, where all the Europeans of both sexes that they could lay their hands on suffered the same fate.

The reactions of the Governor-General in Calcutta, Canning, and the aged Commander-in-Chief, General Anson, who was at Simla, were hesitant and ineffective. Cawnpore and Lucknow were besieged. A force was assembled to recapture Delhi, but was not strong enough to do so, and remained throughout the summer, almost besieged itself, on the bare ridge outside the city covering the route to the Punjab. Before the force under Havelock, sent from Allahabad to relieve the garrison of Cawnpore, reached its destination, the whole garrison and all the women and children, to whom safe conduct had been given, were murdered. Havelock had to wait for reinforcements under Outram before he could continue to the relief of Lucknow, where a garrison of less than 1,000 British troops and 700 loyal Indian soldiers, with 150 civilians and 600 women and children, was holding out in the Residency against 60,000 rebels. On 27 September Outram and Havelock joined forces there with Inglis, who had succeeded the dead Henry Lawrence, but, having left their transport behind, they merely became an addition to the number besieged.

A few days before, General Archdale Wilson's force outside Delhi, reinforced by John Lawrence from the Punjab, had recaptured the city, the 25-year-old Frederick Roberts distinguishing himself in command of a battery of the 1st Bengal Artillery. A column was immediately despatched to Cawnpore, and Roberts was appointed a DAQMG on its staff, clearing the route between the two cities through Agra. Cawnpore, Roberts's birthplace, was reached on 26 October. The 90th Light Infantry, with Wolseley commanding the rearguard company, had left there on 10 October escorting a convoy of provisions for the force which Sir Colin Campbell was moving up for the relief of Lucknow. His attack began on 14 November and lasted three days, Wolseley playing a prominent part in the final stages in which the 90th joined hands with one of their own companies that had been detached with Outram's force. He had shown great courage and initiative in capturing a building called the Mess House, on top of which Roberts, who had now joined Campbell's staff, placed the regimental colour of the 2nd Punjab Infantry to show the defenders of the Residency how close their rescuers were. The garrison was evacuated and Campbell had to return to Cawnpore to deal with rebels led by Tanlia Topi, who had reoccupied it. Operations against Topi continued for several months, in the course of which Roberts gained the Victoria Cross for rescuing a standard which two rebellious sepoys were making away with, as well as for his conduct from the relief of Delhi onward. Wolseley had also expected a VC, but had temporarily offended Campbell by initiating the final attack which relieved the Lucknow Residency. This preempted the General's intention to give the honour to his beloved 93rd Highlanders. Although Topi was not finally run to earth until April 1859, the spring of 1858 saw the virtual end of the campaign to restore the authority of Britain in Central India, resulting in the final extinction of the East India Company and the assumption of sovereignty *de jure* as well as *de facto* by the British Crown in the person of Queen Victoria. Roberts returned to Ireland on sick leave with £500 prize money, handing over his appointment on the staff of Sir Hope Grant, commander of the

Lucknow Field Force, to Major Garnet Wolseley, who, on his twenty-sixth birthday in June 1859 was promoted brevet lieutenant-colonel.

Wolseley's next active service arose out of the consequences of the East India Company's trade with China, of which, until 1833, it had enjoyed a monopoly. After that date, the British Government found itself directly involved in the disputes which arose out of the high-handed manner with which both the Chinese treated foreigners and the traders attempted to deal with the Chinese authorities, especially when the latter tried to clamp down on the smuggling of opium. This had led to the Opium War in 1839, in which Canton was bombarded. At its conclusion in 1842 China agreed to open Shanghai, Canton and three other 'treaty' ports to foreign trade and to cede the island of Hong Kong to Britain. This did not, however, satisfy the traders who exploited the weakness of the Chinese Government during the Taiping rebellion in the early 1850s to demand greater concessions. This led to further incidents, including another bombardment of Canton, as a result of which Palmerston despatched Lord Elgin with a list of demands, including one for diplomatic representation in Peking, a demand supported by the United States, Russia and France. After a naval bombardment of the Taku forts at the mouth of the Peiko River, the Chinese submitted and signed the Treaty of Tientsin in 1858; but then obstructed every effort to implement it. When the prospective British and French envoys appeared off the Taku forts in June 1859, ready to proceed upriver, their arrival was opposed, and, when Admiral Hope tried to land a force of 1,100 men to seize the forts, he lost 434 of them and four of his ships.

A Franco-British force was thereupon despatched to avenge this insult and enforce the treaty. General Hope Grant was chosen to command the 11,000 British, and Wolseley went with him as the DAQMG in charge of the topographical side – what today would be known as the general staff officer responsible for intelligence. The 7,000 French were under the command of General Montauban. They consisted almost solely of infantry and were ill-prepared for the expedition, being as dependent for everything on the British as they were determined to act independently, if they wished. The British were well prepared and equipped, notably with the new Armstrong breech-loading rifled field-gun.

The force arrived off the Taku forts at the end of July 1860, and, having landed at Pei-tang, made its way with some difficulty round to the rear of the forts. These were successfully assaulted on 21 August, and the advance up the Peiko River began, partly by land and partly in boats. Tientsin was entered unopposed on 5 September and the advance resumed on the 8th. At this stage Lord Elgin, who was accompanying the force, was in principle negotiating with the Chinese. However, as the force, ostensibly no more than an escort to the British envoy whom the Chinese had agreed to receive, was 20 miles from Peking on 18 September with only 4,000 men, Hope Grant found himself face to face with an army of 20,000. While discussions were taking place, the Chinese opened fire, having already abducted the negotiating party, and Hope Grant and Montauban attacked, forcing the enemy to withdraw, abandoning 80 guns. After an unsuccessful attempt to establish a truce in the hope of saving the lives of the negotiating party, the attack was resumed, and, after further similar attempts, Peking was attacked on 13 October, and 11 days later the Summer Palace was deliberately burnt down. It had already been extensively plundered by the French, the British being let in later to pick up what was left. The Chinese submitted and ratified the 1858 treaty; the troops were withdrawn, and Wolseley returned to England on leave, after having paid a visit, in the company of his friend Charles Gordon, to the area in which the Taiping rebels were active.

Instead of returning to the east, 1861 was to see him sailing west. The American Civil War had led to incidents which strained the relations between the North and Britain, with potential repercussions in Canada, where there was only one British battalion. Colonel Graham, who had been Hope Grant's chief-of-staff (or Quartermaster-General as it was then known), was appointed to the same post in Canada, and obtained the services of his able assistant once more. Wolseley was still there in 1870, as Deputy Quartermaster-General, when the settlers of the Red River valley in Manitoba, which had been under the sovereignty of the Hudson's Bay Company, revolted against the decision to incorporate them in the newly-formed Dominion of Canada. Many of them were descendants of the French who had intermarried with, or had children by, Red Indians. The revolt was led by one of them, Louis Riel, and there were fears that he would receive support from Irish Fenians over the border in the United States.

Wolseley was placed in command of an expedition of 1,200 men, 373 of the 60th Rifles, a battery of four 7-pounder guns, some Royal Engineers and men of the newly-formed Army Service and Army Medical

Corps, with two battalions of Canadian militia, of the same strength as the 60th. Of the 1,200 miles from Toronto to their destination at Winnipeg's Fort Garry, the first 100 were by rail, the next 500 by steamer across the lakes, followed by 50 miles overland, where Wolseley had to build his own 'corduroy' road of felled tree-trunks, and the final 550 by boat, carrying all his supplies with him. It was a remarkable feat of detailed planning, physical endurance and leadership on Wolseley's part that brought his force, after a journey which had lasted from 6 May until 24 August 1870, in an excellent state of morale and health to its destination. The rebels fled, and his soldiers, with the 'voyageurs' who had so faithfully rowed their boats and Red Indians who had guided them, went berserk under the influence of the first alcohol they had tasted since they had left Toronto. For his service in this bloodless campaign he was created a Knight Commander of the Bath, but placed on half-pay on his return to England, and he occupied himself by writing articles about Canada, highly critical of its politicians.

These and the success of his *Soldier's Pocketbook for Field Service*, published a few years before – a comprehensive *vade-mecum*, later to be transformed into the invaluable official *Field Service Pocket Book* – brought him to the notice of Gladstone's reforming Secretary of State for War, Edward Cardwell. In spite of some very reactionary views, Wolseley was regarded as a progressive officer, keen on army reform. At Cardwell's insistence he was appointed as Assistant Adjutant-General (AAG) in the rank of colonel in the discipline branch of the Commander-in-Chief's headquarters in the Horse Guards, and became one of the Secretary of State's advisers on such contentious measures as terms of service and abolition of the purchase of commissions. There he found himself frequently in opposition to the highly conservative views of the Commander-in-Chief himself, the Duke of Cambridge, and over no subject more so than that of the abolition of purchase, which, having been rejected by the House of Lords, was finally effected by Royal Warrant in the summer of 1871.

As a reward for his support of Cardwell's reforms, Wolseley was given command of the punitive expedition which it was decided, in August 1873, was to be organized to deal with the activities of the Ashanti. Under their king, Coffee Calcalli, they were causing trouble in the West African colony of the Gold Coast, which had developed out of British, Danish and Dutch trading posts in that area. The Ashanti had crossed the River Prah and attacked the tribes who were under British protection, near the coast west of Cape Coast Castle. Wolseley's plan was to take a force of 1,400 men from England and move up the river, following the pattern of his Red River campaign. However the Duke of Cambridge did not favour the use of white troops, and Wolseley, promoted Major-General, set sail in September with 34 officer volunteers to raise native levies from other colonies of the West Coast on his way. Among the 34 were those who became known as the 'Ashanti Ring', favourites of Wolseley's who were to hitch their wagon to his star and become the object of jealousy among others. Several of them had served with him in Canada, and others had attracted his notice through particularly gallant exploits or through their writings, Brackenbury preeminent among the latter.

Wolseley landed at Cape Coast Castle, a former embarkation point for the slave trade, on 2 October and immediately despatched an ultimatum to Coffee to withdraw behind the Prah. At the same time he wrote to Cardwell asking for three battalions of British troops to be sent to reinforce him, as he could not be expected to achieve his objective with the motley collection of some 500 Africans soldiers that he had been able to recruit. He promised to ensure that meticulous arrangements would be made for their health, well-being and supply, and that they would be sent back as soon as he had reached Coffee's capital of Kumasi, over 100 miles inland. Cardwell acted promptly and promised that they would arrive by the end of the year. Meanwhile Wolseley, with his small native force reinforced by the local warriors of the Elmina tribe, defeated a force of 4,000 Ashanti, who then withdrew behind the Prah. His experience of native levies in the confused battles in thick bush reinforced Wolseley in his conviction that he must have British troops. They arrived in early December, but Wolseley's administrative preparations to support an advance beyond the Prah were not completed. They were therefore kept cruising about the sea to avoid the dangers of disease on land until 15 January 1874.

Wolseley's plan was to invade Ashanti territory in four columns, the principal one, which he would accompany, following the main direct route, crossing the Prah at Prahsu, where a large camp had been constructed, one of eight between there and Cape Coast Castle. Coffee protested at the intended invasion, and was presented with a further ultimatum demanding the release of all prisoners, the payment of 50,000 ounces of gold (worth £20,000 at the time) and the handing over of six named important personages as hostages until a peace treaty had been signed. After Wolseley's troops had advanced 30 miles beyond the Prah, three European prisoners were produced with a promise from Coffee to pay the indemnity, if he halted his advance. Wolseley demanded the release also of African prisoners and the delivery of half the indemnity by hostages who had to include the Queen Mother and heir-apparent. Meanwhile he continued his advance.

Sickness was already reducing his numbers and he would brook no delay. On 30 January he came up against the main Ashanti army at Amoaful, 20 miles south of Kumasi. Wolseley's force formed square and the 42nd Highlanders (Black Watch) led the attack. A fierce and confused battle lasted for five hours before the enemy were finally driven off, having suffered heavy casualties from the superior firepower of Wolseley's force. His casualties were 4 killed and 194 wounded, of whom 2 and 113 were from the Black Watch, while those of the Ashanti were estimated at 800 to 1,200 killed and an equal number wounded. Wolseley now took a risk. He had only four days' rations for his force and it would be five or six days before more supplies would be available. He decided on a rapid advance to Kumasi in the hope that he could get there and back in that time, dealing with the rest of Coffee's army on the way. His gamble paid off. While part of the force, led by the Rifle Brigade, battled with Coffee himself at the village of Ordahsu on 4 February, Wolseley slipped the remainder, led by the Black Watch, round them into Kumasi, which they entered unopposed that evening, fulfilling to the day Wolseley's forecast of how long it would take him to get there. The following day the rains broke, and Wolseley set off back to the coast, having reduced Kumasi, from which the population of 30,000–40,000 had fled, to a heap of rubble.

On 13 February Coffee submitted and signed a treaty, although he could not produce more than 1,000 ounces of gold in various forms. Wolseley reached the coast on 19 February, by which time Brackenbury alone of his staff had not succumbed to fever. The European troops were re-embarked, the native levies disbanded, and an unfortunate Colonel Maxwell was persuaded to remain behind as Governor, when Wolseley himself left on 4 March. Six weeks later Maxwell died, while Wolseley was enjoying a hero's welcome in England, personally invested with the Grand Cross of the Order of St Michael and St George by Queen Victoria at Windsor and received by both Houses of Parliament. He was now 'our only general', the 'very model of a modern major-general' of Gilbert and Sullivan's *Pirates of Penzance*, and 'All Sir Garnet' became an expression for affairs that were neatly and methodically organized.

Roberts was lagging behind, having spent the whole period on the Indian army staff. This had included some active service. In 1863, having been promoted to the appointment of Assistant Quartermaster-General (AQMG) in the rank of major on the Commander-in-Chief India's staff, he was sent to report on the prospects of a punitive expedition which the Lieutenant-Governor of the Punjab had ordered north of Peshawar, and became involved in a short sharp action lasting a few days. 1865 found him on sick leave again, his ill-health attributed to overwork. After his return to India in 1866, he went as AQMG to the Bengal brigade which formed part of General Sir Robert Napier's Bombay-based expedition to Abyssinia. Its purpose was to rescue 60 Europeans who were being held prisoner by the temperamental, if not actually mad, Emperor Theodore.

As was the case in Wolseley's Red River and Ashanti campaigns, the problem was not that of defeating the enemy's army so much as overcoming the difficulties imposed by the terrain and the climate, including the lack of any local sources of supply or transport. A force of 12,000 men was assembled, of which the British army element included the 3rd Dragoon Guards, the 4th, 26th, 33rd and 45th Foot, four batteries of the Royal Artillery and one company of Royal Engineers – nearly a third of the force. They were accompanied by 27,000 animals[4] – elephants, camels, mules, ponies and bullocks – of which 7,000 died. Not surprisingly there were the usual muddles and misunderstandings in the despatch, landing, movement and support of the force. The first advanced parties began making preparations for the arrival of the main body in Annesly Bay, just south of Massawa in Eritrea, in September 1867, and the first troops landed in October. It was not until January 1868 that Napier began his march through the rugged mountain country towards the fortress of Magdala, 379 miles away and 9,000 feet above sea level, where the prisoners were held. When he finally reached it four months later, he overcame the resistance of Theodore's feeble army, occupying what appeared to be an almost impregnable position, at a cost of 15 casualties, so lightly wounded that they refused to leave their units. It took another two months for the ponderous expedition to make its way back to the coast and embark for India. In contrast to so

[4] According to Fortescue, Vol. XIII, p. 473, that number was landed. Other accounts state that 55,000 were despatched from India with 51,000 civilian personnel.

many other expeditions, the casualty list from disease was low, 46 British and 284 Indians having died of disease or natural causes.

Roberts had arrived at the coastal base at the end of 1867 and had spent four months helping to organize and run it, not an exciting task in an unpleasant climate. His frustration at not being more actively engaged was to a certain degree compensated for by being entrusted with the task of conveying Napier's final despatch to the Duke of Cambridge. This honour was traditionally regarded as a sign of special favour, carrying with it expectation of promotion. In 1869 he returned to India as AQMG on the staff of the Commander-in-Chief, Napier succeeding Mansfield in that post in 1870. In 1871 he acted as chief-of-staff to a punitive expedition of 10,000 men under General Bouchier, sent to rescue an English girl abducted by the Lushai tribe, who had been making a nuisance of themselves raiding the plantations near Chittagong, near the border with Burma. There was no fighting, the girl was released and good relations were established with the Lushai. As usual the problems were the terrain, the climate, the lack of local resources and the dreaded scourge of cholera. Roberts was rewarded by being made a Companion of the Order of the Bath and promoted from Assistant to Deputy QMG, gaining further promotion on 1 January 1875 to the rank of colonel and the post of Quartermaster-General of the Indian army.

His chance to catch up with Wolseley was soon to come. In 1863 the Emir of Afghanistan, Dost Mahomed, had died and been succeeded by his son, Sher Ali, who did not have the same hold over the country. In addition he was threatened with encroachment by Persia from the west and the spread of Russian power and influence in Turkestan to the north. His appeals for help to successive Viceroys, Lords Mayo and Northbrook, met with no response, the British Liberal Government favouring the 'Masterly Inactivity' policy advocated by John Lawrence of the Punjab. This was to treat the Indus as the frontier and not to get involved in the troublesome affairs of the area west of it. Sher Ali was therefore inclined to look north towards the Russians, who had annexed the Khanate of Khiva in 1873 and that of Khokand in 1875. In 1878 a Russian mission under General Stoletov had been established in Kabul. The Viceroy, Lord Lytton, appointed by Disraeli's Conservative administration to pursue a Forward Policy, demanded that a British mission should also be established, and despatched Sir Neville Chamberlain to head it. When it was turned back at the frontier, an

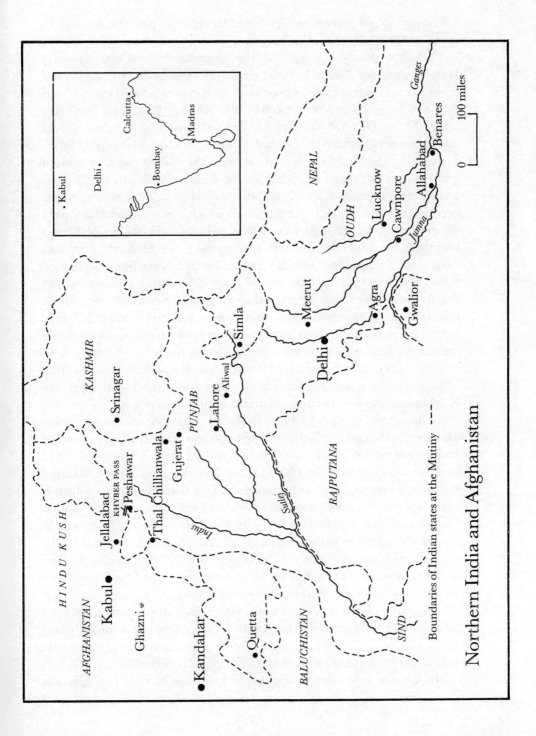

Northern India and Afghanistan

Boundaries of Indian states at the Mutiny ---

ultimatum was delivered, which Sher Ali ignored, and the decision to invade Afghanistan again was taken.

The plan finally adopted by the Commander-in-Chief, General Haines, provided for three separate forces. The northern one, under Lieutenant-General Sam Browne with 15,800 men and 48 guns, would advance from Peshawar to occupy the Khyber Pass. The southern, under Major-General Stewart with 12,600 men and 78 guns, would advance from Quetta to Kandahar. Forty miles south of Browne's force, Roberts, in the acting rank of major-general with 6,500 men and 18 guns, was to advance from Thal up the Kurram valley to the Shutar-gadan Pass, 60 miles from Kabul, driving away any enemy forces and occupying the fertile valley of Khost, on which it was thought they were dependent for supplies. His force originally included only one British battalion, the 8th Foot, but at his request the 72nd (Seaforth) Highlanders were added. The advance began in mid-November 1878, and Roberts's force was the only one to meet opposition. This was at the precipitous Peiwar Kotal Pass at the head of the Kurram valley. In an imaginatively conceived night movement, Roberts himself led four battalions through the mountains in an outflanking move, which drove off the Afghan defenders, who outnumbered them by at least two to one, at a cost of 20 killed and 78 wounded. He advanced to his final objective without meeting further opposition. Browne had reached the Khyber and Stewart occupied Kandahar in January 1879.

By that time Sher Ali had fled to Russia, where he died a few weeks afterwards. He had handed over rule to his son, Yakub Khan, whom he had kept in prison for the previous five years. Lytton immediately tried to come to an agreement with the latter, but five months were to elapse before a treaty was signed by which Yakub Khan accepted a British ambassador, Sir Louis Cavagnari, Stewart's force was to be withdrawn from Kandahar and Browne's much reduced. Roberts's force was to stay in the Kurram valley, although he himself, promoted to the substantive rank of major-general and created a KCB, returned to the staff of the C.-in-C. at Simla. Not for long, however. On 5 September news was received that the Afghan army had risen in revolt and murdered Cavagnari and his escort. Yakub Khan had apparently made no attempt to restrain them. The Kurram valley force was the only one ready and available for action, and Roberts returned to it immediately, with orders to advance to Kabul and demand retribution.

His force of 2,750 British and 3,870 Indian soldiers in two brigades

included a squadron of the 9th Lancers, three Royal Artillery batteries
the 67th Foot and the 72nd and 92nd Highlanders. He began his
advance on 27 September, and, after an unsatisfactory meeting with
Yakub Khan, met the Afghan army holding a strong position at Char-
asia, covering Kabul, on 6 October. He was greatly outnumbered and
realized that his best chance lay in an immediate attack. Putting all his
available effort into attacks on their flanks, he put them to flight in a
three-hour battle, the first in which the heliograph was used for communication. A week later, Roberts made his formal entry into the city,
while Yakub tried to evade the responsibility of remaining ruler. His
resignation was eventually accepted, and he was sent off to India under
escort, so that he could not become the focus of anti-British feeling.
Roberts was in the unenviable position of having to try and impose
British rule on the unruly Afghans himself. They naturally resisted, and
at the end of the year he found himself besieged in his camp at Sherpur
outside Kabul. However he had made better preparations than Elphinstone in his day. His besiegers were driven off and a relief column sent
from Kandahar to which Stewart had by then returned. Stewart arrived
with this reinforcement in May 1880 and, being the senior, assumed
overall command.

By that time the British Government had decided to evacuate northern Afghanistan, hoping to install one of Sher Ali's nephews, Abdul
Rahman, as ruler. The evacuation was on the point of starting when, at
the end of July, bad news was received from Kandahar. Yakub Khan's
brother, Ayub Khan, had no love for his cousin and had gathered a
band of soldiers at Herat and advanced towards Kandahar. Brigadier
Burrows led a force of 2,500 men of the Bombay army from Kandahar
to support local Afghan troops on the Helmand River 80 miles away;
but the latter deserted to Ayub Khan. Burrows was surrounded at
Maiwand and nearly half his force was killed. The survivors, starved
and dying of thirst, struggled back to Kandahar, which was soon
besieged by Ayub.

Roberts immediately suggested that he should lead a force to its
relief, while Stewart supervised the withdrawal of the remainder of the
troops at Kabul by the Khyber Pass and the Kurram valley. Stewart
agreed, as did the Viceroy, Lord Ripon. On 8 August, only 11 days
after the disaster at Maiwand, Roberts set off southwards with 10,600
men, 6,000 camp followers and a large number of animals, carrying all
his supplies with him. Forage for the animals and water for all were the

main problems. It was the height of summer, when the shade temperature reached 110°F, so Roberts made his men start early in the morning. The average daily stint was 13 miles, although it varied from as little as 7 to one day of 22½, and there were 2 days in the 24, which it took him to complete the 320 miles, when the force halted for a complete day. No opposition was met, morale was high and everybody seems to have enjoyed the experience, gruelling as it was.

When he reached Kandahar on 31 August, Roberts was suffering from fever, but, reinforced by the Kandahar garrison, he immediately organized an attack on Ayub's force, which was holding a strong position at the pass of Baba Wali Kotal nearby. After a careful reconnaissance, he once more committed his main strength, two brigades and the cavalry, to a wide flanking attack, and yet again it brought swift success, the 72nd and 92nd Highlanders playing a prominent part and Ayub's army melting away into the desert. A personal message from Queen Victoria, the award of the GCB and the promise of appointment as C.-in-C. at Madras were Roberts's immediate rewards. However, his exertions had proved too much for him, and for the third time he returned to England on sick leave, to be welcomed as a national hero on a scale not seen since that given to the Duke of Wellington after Waterloo. Some thought it bad luck on Stewart.

While Roberts had been gaining glory in India, the British army had been involved in a series of little wars in South Africa. Clashes with the Kaffirs had been almost continuous since the end of Cathcart's campaign in 1852. These had reached a climax in 1877 in the area east of the Kei River against the Galeka and Gaiko tribes. The result was the extension of British authority over the whole area between Cape Colony and Natal. This left the Zulus further east as the only major unconquered and hostile tribe. In the same year Britain's assumption of authority over the Boer settlements in the Transvaal, which were involved in continuous clashes with the Zulus, was announced.

In December 1878 the aggressive High Commissioner, Sir Bartle Frere, without authority from London, sent an ultimatum to Cetewayo, the Zulu chief, which he knew he could not accept. It was promptly followed by an invasion, commanded by Lord Chelmsford. His force was split into three columns, each 3,000-strong, which were intended to converge on Cetewayo's capital of Ulundi. The right, under Pearson, was to land at the mouth of the Tugela, the left under Evelyn Wood to enter Zululand from the Transvaal, while Chelmsford himself would lead the centre column of 1,600 British and 2,500 native troops across the Buffalo River at Rorke's Drift. Soon after he had moved beyond it, Chelmsford split his column, under-estimating the Zulu force opposed to him. At Isandlhwana on 22 January 1879 some 13,000 of their fierce and highly disciplined warriors attacked and surprised his camp, defended by seven companies of the 24th Foot, four of Natal natives and two guns. They were not prepared to meet an attack and were overwhelmed and annihilated. On the same day a detachment of 3,000 Zulus attacked the isolated company of the 24th which had been left to guard stores and the crossing at Rorke's Drift. The garrison consisted of only 139 men, 20 of whom were sick, under the command of two subalterns, Lieutenants Bromhead of the 24th and Chard of the Royal Engineers. From 4.30 p.m. on the 22nd to 4 a.m. next day this gallant little band of men repulsed six attacks, some at bayonet point, until the Zulus finally withdrew leaving 350 of their warriors dead. The British casualties were 17 killed and 10 wounded. Pearson was already hemmed in at Etshowe, and Wood, who had reached Mount Kambula on the Umwolosi, was told to stay where he was until Chelmsford, who had withdrawn the rest of his force behind the Buffalo, had sorted himself out.

Little happened for the next four months. Chelmsford led a force to extricate Pearson, and Wood found himself facing the bulk of Cetewayo's army, on which he inflicted heavy casualties when they attacked his mountain stronghold. In June Chelmsford advanced again with 4,000 British and 1,100 native troops, this time taking careful precautions against surprise. On 4 July he met the Zulu army at Ulundi and drew up his force in a tight square, which Cetewayo was foolish enough to attack. It was all over in half an hour, the Zulus having lost about 1,000 men killed, while Chelmsford's casualties were no more than 18 killed and 85 wounded.

The most frustrated man was Wolseley. He had been languishing away as Governor of Cyprus since Britain had occupied it as a '*place d'armes*' in July 1878, as part of a convention with Turkey which was incorporated in the series of agreements ratified by the Congress of Berlin. When the news of the disaster at Isandlhwana reached London on 11 February 1879, Disraeli's instant reaction was to send for 'our only general' and despatch him to replace Chelmsford. The Duke of

Cambridge and Queen Victoria opposed the move. They did not like Wolseley's support of army reform, his cocksureness and self-publicizing. The attitude of the 'establishment' to him was much the same as it was to be in the twentieth century towards Montgomery, with whom he had much in common. Disraeli prevailed and, having been recalled from Cyprus, Wolseley was despatched on 29 May amid scenes of remarkable public enthusiasm to assume overall military command, with Chelmsford as deputy, as well as civil authority outside Cape Colony, where Bartle Frere would continue to hold sway. It was only when he reached Cape Town on 1 June that Wolseley discovered that Chelmsford had renewed his invasion of Zululand. Hurrying eastwards in the hope of being able to assume direct command of operations, he was defeated by the surf which prevented him landing at the optimistically named Port Durnford to which he had set sail from Durban on 1 July. He had to return to Durban, and, while attempting to catch up with Chelmsford overland, he received the news of his victory at Ulundi. He had to pretend to be pleased.

Wolseley spent the next year establishing firm control of the Transvaal, which involved him in a series of skirmishes with the Bapedi. The Boer settlers welcomed his success in these, but they were openly showing their discontent at British rule by the time he left in April 1880. This broke out in open rebellion in December. Wolseley's former staff officer, Colley, was in command. Advancing from Natal with a force of only 1,500 men, he was checked by the Boers under Joubert at Laing's Nek in January 1881. He tried again a month later, but met with disaster when his small force of 359 men was overwhelmed on Majuba Hill, he himself being killed. Meanwhile Wolseley, first as Quartermaster-General and then as Adjutant-General at the Horse Guards, was engaged in fierce battles with the Duke of Cambridge over army reform. He was to escape from these in the following year to add to his laurels at the opposite end of Africa – Egypt.

The Suez Canal had been opened in 1869. Eight years later Egypt's finances were in such a chaotic state that a Franco-British condominium to protect the interests of foreign bondholders was imposed on the Khedive Ismail. Ismail's resistance to this led to his deposition and the succession of his son Tewfik, which aroused national resentment, not least among the officers of the army, large numbers of whom were dismissed as an economy measure. Colonel Ahmed Arabi exploited this, and in May 1882 became virtual dictator. The French refused to join in military action, and, after a naval bombardment of Alexandria had produced no change in Arabi's defiance, Gladstone decided in July to despatch a military force to bring him to heel. The 'Ashanti Ring', without poor Colley, was once more called together. A large force, by the standards of the British army of the day, was assembled: 40,560 men, of whom 7,000 came from India, 61 steamships ferrying the army and its supplies from England.

Wolseley's objective was Cairo. He realized that, if he landed at Alexandria, he was liable to get bogged down in the Nile delta. He therefore decided to sail down the canal and land at Ismailia, which was 96 miles from Cairo and nearer still to Arabi's main camp in the desert at Tel-el-Kebir, while keeping up the pretence that he would reinforce the troops already at Alexandria. On 20 August the first troops went ashore at Ismailia and were immediately faced with a problem of water supply, which Arabi, 30 miles away, had cut off. Wolseley acted quickly and took the risk of pushing forward an advanced guard of 2,000 men under Graham to capture the dam on the Sweet Water Canal and what railway rolling stock he could at Kassassin, 20 miles away. His gamble paid off. At a cost of only five killed and 25 wounded on 26 August, he secured his water supply, 75 railway trucks full of stores, seven new Krupp guns and large quantities of rifles and ammunition. After Arabi had made two unsuccessful attempts to regain Kassassin, Wolseley, having made a careful personal reconnaissance, attacked Arabi's main position at Tel-el-Kebir on 13 September.

Arabi was thought to have 20,000 regular infantry, supported by 6,000 Bedouin irregulars, 2,500 cavalry and 60 guns. Wolseley could muster 11,000 infantry, 2,000 cavalry, 61 guns and 6 machine-guns. After a silent approach march by night, a manoeuvre in which the army had had little or no training, Wolseley launched his two divisions, Hamley's 2nd on the left, Willis's 1st on the right, straight at the Egyptian defences as dawn broke, the former led by Alison's brigade of Highlanders (Black Watch, Gordons, Camerons and Highland Light Infantry), the latter by Graham's brigade of Royal Irish, Royal Marines, York and Lancaster and Royal Irish Fusiliers. The battle lasted for 35 minutes, in which 2,000 Egyptians died and thousands fled. Wolseley lost 480, 243 from the Highland Brigade. The way to Cairo was open and the cavalry rode into the city next day. Arabi was captured there, tried and exiled to Ceylon. Wolseley returned to England on 28 October in a blaze of glory, which eclipsed that with which

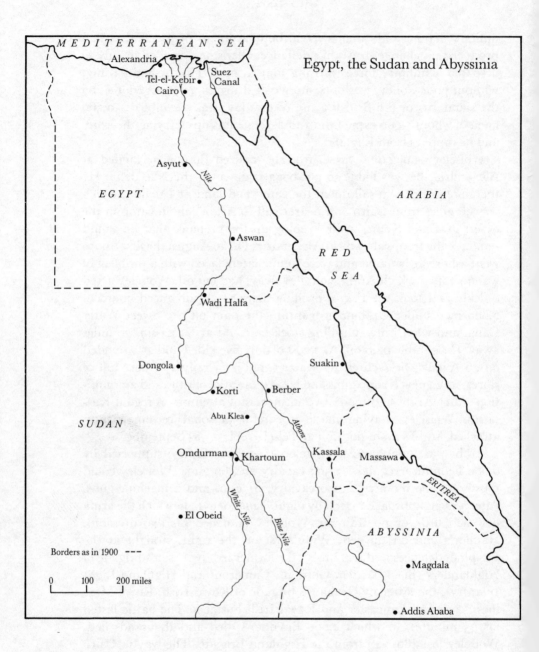

MEDITERRANEAN SEA

Alexandria

Tel-el-Kebir

Cairo

Suez
Canal

Egypt, the Sudan and Abyssinia

Asyut

EGYPT

ARABIA

Nile

Aswan

RED

SEA

Wadi Halfa

Dongola

Suakin

Korti

Berber

Abu Klea

SUDAN

Atbara

Omdurman

Khartoum

Kassala

Massawa

ERITREA

White Nile

Blue Nile

El Obeid

ABYSSINIA

Borders as in 1900 - - -

Magdala

0   100   200 miles

Addis Ababa

Roberts had been received two years before. He had been made a GCB after the Zulu War, annoyed that Chelmsford had also received the honour. He was now made a peer, and, after a haggle with Gladstone over a grant of cash to go with it, settled for £30,000 and promotion to full general. Cambridge had to congratulate him warmly, and Queen Victoria was mollified by his having agreed to take her favourite son, Arthur, Duke of Connaught, on the campaign with him, as well as the Household Cavalry, on whom he lavished fulsome praise.

Those who have drunk of the waters of the Nile (if they survive the experience) are said to be bound to return, and so it was with Wolseley. At the same time as Arabi had been causing trouble in Egypt, one Mohammed Ahmed declared himself to be the 'Mahdi' or guide, destined to regenerate Islam and make it a universal faith. He soon gained control of almost the whole of the Sudan, defeating a Turco-Egyptian army under Hicks at El Obeid in November 1883. This swung to his side Osman Digna, leader of the Arabs who lived between Khartoum and the Red Sea port of Suakim. He slaughtered the Egyptian garrisons in the area and defeated a relief expedition under Baker. The Egyptian Government appealed for help and for the services of General Gordon, who had served in the Sudan from 1873 to 1880, engaged in suppressing the slave trade. He had made his mark leading a Chinese army to suppress the Taiping rebels from 1863 to 1865, after taking part in the expedition to Peking in 1860, where he and Wolseley had become friends.

Gordon left London on 18 January 1884, originally to join a force of 4,000 Egyptians sent under Graham to Suakim. The situation in the Nile valley had persuaded Gladstone's Government that the only sensible course was to withdraw all the remaining garrisons from the Sudan, and Gordon, sent as Governor-General, was given secret instructions to that effect. Sir Evelyn Baring, the British Government's representative in Egypt, opposed the plan on the grounds that, if a British Governor-General found himself in difficulties in the Sudan, there would be a demand to use British troops to extricate him, and that Gordon, whose fanatical courage was notorious, was likely to get himself into just such a scrape. He was unfortunately overruled. Equally unfortunately Gordon revealed the secret of his orders on his way through Berber, and, on arrival in Khartoum in February, ignored them by concocting a plan by which Zobeir, an ex-slave trader whom he had fought and whose son he had killed, should be made Governor-General and helped to suppress the Mahdi. Whether or not his plan would have succeeded, it was vetoed in London.

Meanwhile, precious time had been lost. In May, Berber was in the hands of the Mahdi's men and Gordon was cut off in Khartoum. Both Baring and Wolseley urged Gladstone to take immediate steps to plan a relief expedition, but Gladstone's mind was on other things, and it was not until the beginning of August that permission was given to start making preparations and Wolseley appointed to command. On 9 September he was in Cairo with as many of the 'Ashanti Ring' as he could muster, supervising every aspect of the detailed preparations for the move of 6,000 men and 8,000 animals the 1,650 miles up the Nile, river steamers towing boats which Wolseley, harking back to his Red River expedition, had had specially constructed. He had even enlisted some Canadian 'voyageurs'.

Wolseley left Cairo by train for Assiut on 27 September, expecting to reach Khartoum on 31 January 1885, and established his headquarters on the Khedive's royal yacht at Wadi Halfa. There he learned that a party of Europeans under Colonel Stewart, whom Gordon had sent down the Nile to make contact with Major Kitchener, Wolseley's intelligence officer at Dongola, had been murdered after their steamer had struck a rock. Recognizing the urgency of establishing communication with Gordon, Wolseley rode on to Dongola by camel, and then back again to Wadi Halfa to try and hurry on the forward move of his troops, delayed by a host of administrative difficulties, chief of which was shortage of camels. On 17 November he received a message from Gordon, dated the 4th, which made it clear that he doubted if he could hold out beyond 14 December. In spite of all his efforts to galvanize the move up the Nile, it became clear to Wolseley that there was no hope of getting the whole force to Khartoum by that date. He therefore decided to send a 'flying column' of 2,000 men 196 miles across the desert from Korti, where a forward base was being established 300 miles upriver from Wadi Halfa, to Metereme 96 miles downriver from Khartoum, where two of Gordon's steamers would meet them and take them to Khartoum. The rest of the force would make its methodical way upriver round the great bend past Berber.

Not even the flying column, under Sir Herbert Stuart, could start until 30 December. On the 31st a message from Gordon, dated the 14th, reached Korti, saying 'Khartoum all right'. However, it was accompanied by a more urgent verbal one: 'We want you to come quickly.'

A plough being used in the Crimean War to lay telegraph cables. Picture from the
Illustrated London News, 1855.

The battle of the Alma, 20 September 1854. Raglan's direct attack across the river
Alma and up the other side was, thanks to great gallantry, successful. Had this battle
been exploited it might have ended the Crimean War.

The famous charge of the Light Brigade led by Lord Cardigan at the battle of
Balaclava, 25 October 1854, painted by Caton Woodville.

The Indian Mutiny: in 1857 mutinous sepoys at Meerut were blown from the guns in front of
their comrades, a barbarous method of execution which helped to spread the Mutiny.

Major-General Sir Garnet (later Field Marshal Viscount) Wolseley in 1873, at the time of the Ashanti wars.

Field Marshal Earl Roberts in 1904, by Sargent.

The Gordon Highlanders go into the attack at the battle of Kandahar in August 1880, which followed Roberts' famous march from Kabul.

General (later Field Marshal Earl) Kitchener in 1899, by C.M. Horsfall.

A Maxim gun detachment of the King's Royal Rifle Corps, 1896. The Maxim gun, the first fully automatic machine-gun, was introduced into the British army in 1889.

British dead at Spion Kop, where Buller's attempt to relieve Ladysmith in January 1900 was stopped by the Boers.

General (later Field Marshal) Sir William Robertson, Chief of the Imperial General Staff 1915–18.

Field Marshal Sir Douglas (later Earl) Haig, Commander-in-Chief of British armies in France 1915–18.

Cape Helles, Gallipoli, 1915. Troops resting on the beach watch a Turkish shell burst in the sea.

British troops advance through barbed wire during the battle of the Somme in 1916.

A front-line trench at Ovillers, the Somme, July 1916.

Jacking and hauling a field gun out of the never-ending mud, Pilckem Ridge, north of Ypres, August 1917.

11 November 1918 at Cambrai: Field Marshal Sir Douglas Haig is flanked by (front step, from left) Generals Plumer and Rawlinson, and (on second step) Byng, Birdwood and Horne.

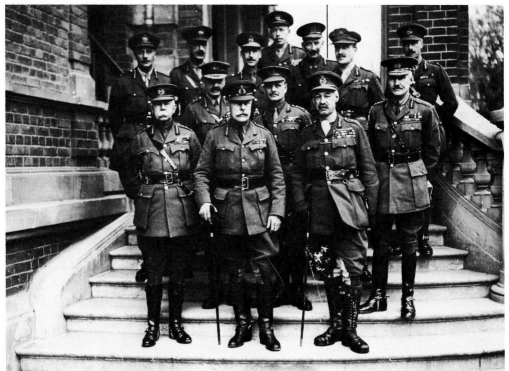

The flying column had a desperate battle at the wells of Abu Klea and another at Gulat, where Stuart was killed, before reaching the river on 21 January, where the steamers were awaiting them. Three whole days were then spent in preparing for the move by river, and when Wilson, who had assumed command, reached Khartoum on 28 January, he found that the Mahdists had overwhelmed the garrison and killed Gordon two days earlier. Although Wolseley was created a Viscount and later a Field-Marshal, and became Commander-in-Chief on the retirement of the Duke of Cambridge in 1895, the course of his star had set in decline.

That of Roberts was to continue to rise. In November 1885 he became C.-in-C. India as an acting general, a post he was to hold for eight years, which included the conquest of Upper Burma and almost continuous minor skirmishes on India's north-west frontier. The Burma campaign lasted from 1 January 1886 until 1889, although minor operations continued until 1891. He was made a peer in 1892 and a Field-Marshal in 1895, when he succeeded Wolseley as C.-in-C. in Ireland. That was the year of the Jameson Raid, a warning sign of events which were to mark the climax of his career. Before that, Wolseley's failure to rescue Gordon had been avenged by Kitchener in a campaign, the origin of which was to relieve pressure on the Italians, who had been defeated by the Abyssinians at Adowa in 1896 and were being assailed at Kassala by Sudanese. Kitchener was then the Sirdar, that is C.-in-C. of the Egyptian army. Against the advice of Lord Cromer (as Evelyn Baring had become), he managed to persuade the Prime Minister, Lord Salisbury, that he should conduct a methodical advance up the Nile, building a railway as he went, with 15,000 men, the great majority Egyptian. After a brief brush with the enemy in June, Kitchener was delayed by a series of mishaps, including an outbreak of cholera, until September, when he captured Dongola. There he remained for nearly a year, pacifying the Dongola province and building the railway across the desert from Wadi Halfa in preparation for the advance of his army, reinforced to 26,000, one third of whom were British, to Khartoum. At Omdurman on 2 September 1897 the Khalifa's army of 60,000 threw itself against the superior firepower of Kitchener's 20,000 and was destroyed, over a third being killed. The unnecessary charge of the 21st Lancers, in which the 22-year-old Winston Churchill took part, is the best known feature of the battle.

In that year Alfred Milner was appointed High Commissioner in

South Africa, determined to bring matters to a head with President Krüger of the Boer Republic of the Transvaal, the independence of which Gladstone had recognized in 1881 after Colley's defeat at Majuba. Relations had become tense and Krüger spent increasing sums on the purchase of arms, as the Uitlanders protested more strongly for recognition of their rights and appealed for British intervention to assert them. After prolonged negotiations, in which Krüger kept increasing his demands, the Orange Free State threw in its lot with the Transvaal, giving the Boers a potential strength of 50,000 mounted men. On 9 October 1899 Krüger presented Milner with an ultimatum which he could clearly not accept, certainly not with Britain in the bellicose mood which Omdurman had encouraged. Milner had only 10,000 British troops in Cape Colony and Natal. A further 10,000 from India and the Mediterranean were due to land at Durban on 8 October under the command of the 64-year-old Sir George White, one of Roberts's favourites. Reinforcements from Britain had not been authorized until 29 September, when an expeditionary force of 47,000 men was approved. It was to be under the command of the 60-year-old Sir Redvers Buller, a veteran of the Ashanti Ring, who knew South Africa well. Fortunately for him the Boers made a major strategic error in wasting time and effort in sieges of Kimberley and Ladysmith and in concentrating their effort in Natal in the hope of securing Durban as a link to the world outside. Had they concentrated their effort on an immediate invasion of Cape Colony, they could perhaps have added to their strength 30,000 mounted men, for whom they had the rifles and ammunition, and radically altered the course of the war. As it was, it did not start well for the British.

By the end of October, White in Natal found himself besieged in Ladysmith, having advanced beyond the Tugela River, contrary to the plan of Buller, who arrived at the Cape at that very moment. Kimberley, 600 miles away on the western border of the Orange Free State, which contained Cecil Rhodes and his diamond mines, and Mafeking, 200 miles further north, defended by the irrepressible Baden-Powell, were already surrounded. Buller had originally intended to concentrate his force in an advance to Bloemfontein, capital of the Free State; but the situation in Natal appeared to have priority. Ordering Methuen to take 10,000 men to relieve Kimberley, and Gatacre, with a smaller force, to remain on the defensive south of the Orange River, covering the approaches to the Cape from Bloemfontein, Buller decided to take

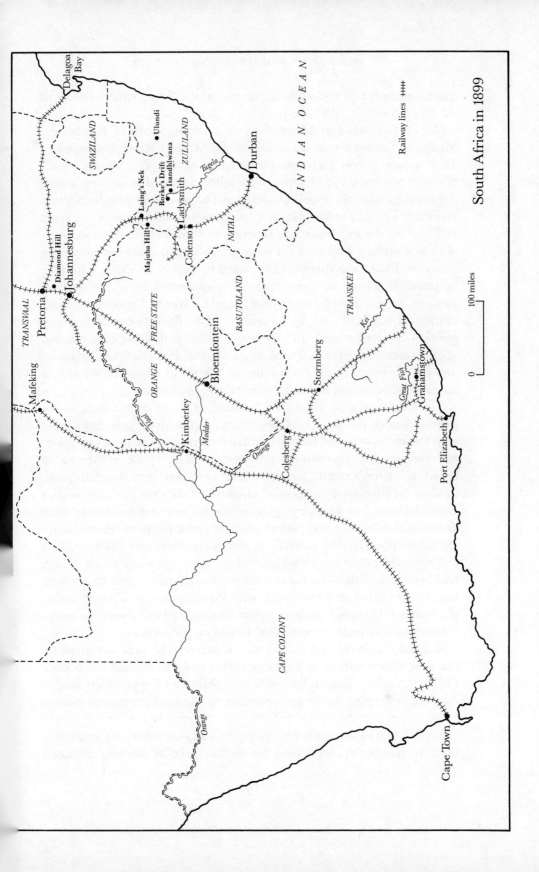

South Africa in 1899

Railway lines ┼┼┼┼

INDIAN OCEAN

Delagoa Bay

SWAZILAND

Ulundi

ZULULAND

Durban

Laing's Nek
Rorke's Drift
Isandhlwana
Ladysmith
Majuba Hill
Colenso

Tugela

Pretoria
Diamond Hill
Johannesburg

TRANSVAAL

NATAL

BASUTOLAND

100 miles

0

Mafeking

ORANGE FREE STATE

Bloemfontein

Stormberg

TRANSKEI

Kei

Kimberley

Vaal

Modder

Orange

Colesberg

Great Fish

Grahamstown

Port Elizabeth

CAPE COLONY

Orange

Cape Town

command in Natal himself with the rest of the force, some 20,000. All these projects met with failure.

On 11 December at Magersfontein, 10 miles south of Kimberley, Methuen, having forced a crossing of the Modder River, attempted a dawn attack after a night march. It failed against Piet Cronje's well-placed 6,000 men, 236 of whom were killed, while Methuen lost 902 of the 3,500 men involved in that attack. All hopes of relieving Kimberley vanished. The day before, Gatacre, thinking he could surprise the Boers and capture the important rail junction of Stormberg in the north-east of Cape Province, had tried the same tactics with the same result, losing 700 men. Buller was therefore oppressed by bad news when, with four brigades of infantry and one of cavalry, supported by six batteries of artillery, he attempted to cross the Tugela River at Colenso, 20 miles south of Ladysmith, on 15 December. The Boers were in a strong position and well armed, and the attack failed with a loss of 143 killed, among them Roberts's only son, 755 wounded and 240 taken prisoner, dashing all hopes of an early relief of White, to whom Buller sent a message advising surrender. Fortunately he ignored it.

The events of this 'Black Week' came as a profound shock to the jingoist British public. The Government's immediate reaction was to send for the 68-year-old Roberts, still in Ireland and thirsting for action. He received the appointment on the same day, 17 December, as he heard of his son's death. Six days later he sailed from Southampton, picking up Kitchener as his chief-of-staff at Gibraltar, and arriving at Cape Town on 10 January 1900, where he received a message from Buller, saying that he was planning a renewed attempt to relieve Lady-smith, the Boers having failed in an attack on White on 6 January. This was contrary to the advice which Roberts had sent while at sea, which had been that Buller should remain on the defensive until he arrived; but, not yet being in direct touch with the situation, he allowed Buller to go ahead. He failed again at Spion Kop on 24 January with a loss of 1,700 men, and once more at Vaal Kranz on 5 February.

Roberts was intent on seizing the initiative. The plan favoured by the War Office had been a double thrust towards Bloemfontein from Colesberg, which French had held with skill, and Burgersdorp further east. While keeping up the pretence that he intended to threaten Bloem-fontein from that direction, Roberts concentrated all the force he could muster – 37,000 men, 12,000 horses and 22,000 transport animals – south of Kimberley, increasing his mobile force by forming mounted infantry to add to French's cavalry. Undeterred by the capture of most of his transport by Christian de Wet, he executed a bold out-flanking move, which relieved Kimberley and threatened Cronje's communications with Bloemfontein. Cronje began to move east and was brought to battle at Paardeberg on 18 February; Kitchener came in for criticism for the way in which he directed the battle in the absence of Roberts, who was sick. His casualties amounted to 320 killed and 924 wounded. Cronje had been halted and surrounded, but not defeated. On 26 February, however, he surrendered with 4,000 men. It was the turning point of the war. On 1 March Buller at last relieved Ladysmith, and, after a brush with de Wet at Poplar Grove on 6 March, Roberts entered Bloemfontein on the 13th. He remained there until 1 May, organizing his line of communication back by rail to the Cape and making preparations for an advance to Pretoria, while reinforcements poured out from England and his army was swept by an outbreak of enteric fever. Since the war had started 85,000 men had been sent from Britain.

De Wet continued to be a nuisance, harrying his communications, but did not deflect Roberts from his resolve to make certain that, once his advance to Pretoria had begun, it could be carried through to its conclusion without a setback. His move reduced pressure on Mafeking, which, after a siege lasting 217 days, was relieved on 17 May, to the delight of the British public. On 28 May the annexation of the Orange Free State was announced; on the last day of the month Johannesburg was reached, and five days later Pretoria, where 3,000 British prisoners of war were liberated. Krüger and the main Boer force under Louis Botha had moved east down the railway leading to Delagoa Bay (modern Maputo) in Portuguese East Africa. Botha's force was defeated and dispersed at Diamond Hill on 9 June. Operations against the remaining Boer forces in both the Transvaal and the Free State continued until the last remaining organized force under Botha was defeated at Bergendal on 27 August. The British prisoners were freed three days later, and on 11 September Krüger crossed the frontier into Portuguese territory. On 25 October the Transvaal was formally annexed: on 29 November Roberts handed over command to Kitchener, and on 11 December sailed from the Cape in the hospital ship *Canada*, from which he went ashore at Cowes on 2 January 1901 to be ushered into the presence of Queen Victoria at Osborne, who conferred on him an earldom and the Order of the Garter.

Everyone assumed that the war was over, but they had reckoned without de Wet and others like him. The war changed its nature into that of a guerrilla campaign, and Kitchener found himself forced into the pattern which became familiar to those faced with similar campaigns later in the century – a laborious process of attempting to cut the guerrillas off from their sources of information and supply, which, in the case of the Boers, were their farms scattered over the length and breadth of the country. By criss-crossing the whole vast area with barbed-wire fences and interning the Boers' families in concentration camps, Kitchener finally brought the war to an end by signing the Treaty of Vereeniging on 31 May 1902. By that time Queen Victoria had died, and, although Wolseley lived on until 1913 and Roberts a year longer, when he died while visiting his beloved Indian troops in France, their age was also dead.

It had been an age which saw major reforms in the army, provoked by the Crimean War, most of them brought about by Edward Cardwell in the teeth of opposition from the Duke of Cambridge. Nevertheless there were certain fundamental elements of its basic organization which were never to change, however much they might be modified. The principal one was the devotion of cavalry and infantry to the concept that the individual regiment was the fundamental entity, a private family which had the first claim on a man's loyalty, linking it to allegiance to the sovereign, preferably through a personal connection between the regiment and a member of the royal family. Higher military formations were temporary wartime arrangements of no lasting significance. The artillery and engineers were a class apart, superior in their own estimation by reason of their higher intelligence and skill, while struggling for equal recognition in the social scale, the heights of which were occupied by the Household troops and the cavalry. Struggling behind them were the administrative services, only recently in history having escaped from their civilian status. The Land Transport Corps, formed in the Crimean War, was one such service.

From Waterloo until the death of Queen Victoria there were three major problem areas: the organization at the summit for command and control of the army; the commissioning and promotion of officers; and the conditions of service of the soldier, with which the recruiting problem was intimately linked. The chaotic division of political and administrative control, which was reflected lower down in the division of responsibility in the field for such matters as finance, transport and supply, from which Marlborough and Wellington had suffered so keenly, was not changed until after the scandals of the Crimea. For that Wellington must bear a heavy load of blame. After Waterloo he was in a unique position to cure those ills, but, conservative by nature and upbringing and with an aristocratic disdain for getting too worked up about anything, he lent his great authority not just to a lack of reform but to a positive emphasis on maintaining the existing structure. Not until Gladstone made Cardwell his Secretary of State for War in 1868 was a fundamental change made, and even then the relative responsibilities of the Secretary of State and the Commander-in-Chief remained ill-defined.

The Crimean War forced a number of significant changes. The post of Secretary of State *for* War had once more been separated from that of Secretary of State for the Colonies, and in 1855 he absorbed the responsibilities of the Secretary *at* War, to whom responsibility for supply and transport had been transferred from the Treasury. He acquired responsibility from the Home Office for the militia and yeomanry and assumed it also for the army medical department, as well as depriving regimental colonels of their task – and financial perk – of clothing soldiers. In the same year the Master-General of the Ordance handed over his command of the artillery and engineers to the Commander-in-Chief, who remained responsible for the discipline and training of the army and the selection and promotion of officers.

There was a change of relationship between the Secretary of State and the Commander-in-Chief, greater power passing to the former, when Wolseley took over the latter post from the Duke of Cambridge in 1895. He complained that he then had nothing to do, and the relationship remained ill-defined until the abolition of the post in 1904 as part of the Esher reforms. Cardwell had helped pave the way for this by moving the Commander-in-Chief from his traditional office in the Horse Guards[5] into the War Office. He had also made the Adjutant-General subservient to the Quartermaster-General, the nearest he could get to the formation of a unified staff. This was modified when Wolseley became Commander-in-Chief; but it was not until the Esher reforms of 1904 that the recommendations of the 1890 Hartington Commission were put into effect.

[5] Now occupied by the Major-General commanding the Household Division and London District.

These included the formation of a general staff, responsible for operations, intelligence, training and organization, the chief of which replaced the Commander-in-Chief and was the senior military member of the Army Council. The other military members were the Adjutant-General, responsible for all personnel matters, the Quartermaster-General for transport and supply, and the Master-General of the Ordance for weapon procurement. The Council was presided over by the Secretary of State for War and included the Permanent Under-Secretary, with primary responsibility for finance, and two junior ministers, an organization that was to prove effective through two world wars and has lasted to the present day.

Of all the reforms, the abolition of purchase as a method of obtaining commissions and promotion was to arouse the greatest controversy. The method was indefensible that allowed men like Cardigan and Lucan with no military experience to rise to high command, because they were ready to spend large sums on buying their way up the military ladder for reasons of social prestige. But it was not until 1871 that it was done away with, Gladstone overcoming the opposition of the House of Lords by persuading Queen Victoria to abolish it by the same method as it had been introduced – Royal Warrant. Attempts to regulate its abuse by establishing the sums to be paid for initial commissions and subsequent promotions, and by requiring educational qualifications for entry, had been consistently evaded. The strongest argument in its favour was that it meant that officers had a stake in maintaining the status quo, and that it avoided the danger of creating a class of professional officers who would look only to the army for their careers. They could become a threat to the established order and to the constitution. The example of the professionals in the Prussian army in the Franco-Prussian war was a major factor in persuading the House of Commons of the need to make the British army professional, both by the abolition of purchase and by the creation and training of a general staff. It did not have as great an effect on the type of officer commissioned into the army as its sponsors had hoped. A high proportion continued to be sons of the aristocracy, of landed gentry and of former army officers, products of the burgeoning public schools with their concentration on a classical education, their emphasis on the importance of character rather than knowledge, and their neglect of the sciences.

The major reforms were concerned with the conditions under which the soldier served. Some were prompted by shame at the primitive life he had to endure both in barracks and in the field, highlighted by the publicity given to it during the Crimean War; but the primary motive was the need to attract recruits and to create reserves of trained military manpower. Those in favour of the introduction of these reforms had to fight against the emphasis given by all governments to economy in expenditure on the army, and also the conservative outlook of its senior officers, notably the Dukes of Wellington and Cambridge. In 1858 it was revealed that the rate of mortality of troops stationed in England was far higher than in the population as a whole, and this was attributed to the crowded and unhygienic barracks in which they lived. The death rate from tuberculosis was five times that of civilians. In foreign stations, particularly in the West Indies, mortality was even higher. The stimulus given by Florence Nightingale to the army's medical service, allied to the major advances in medicine generally in the second half of the nineteenth century, revolutionized the army's health. Improvements in clothing and food, and the introduction of positive measures to improve health, such as physical training and the promotion of games and sports, all contributed.

The same sort of process, influenced by reforms in the civilian field, affected discipline and punishment for military offences. There was a significant reduction in courts-martial and in civil offences by soldiers after the Crimean War, undoubtedly linked to improvements in the conditions of service which lessened the temptation for soldiers to drown their sorrows in drink; but it was not until Cardwell's time, in 1868, that flogging was abolished in peacetime, and not until 1900 that it was abandoned on active service also. Branding, or tattooing, for desertion and other serious offences was also abolished by Cardwell. Improvement in pay contributed to improvement in health and behaviour. At the time of the Crimea, the soldier was still in the position he had occupied since Cromwell's time: that, after deductions had been made for this, that and the other, he had virtually nothing left to spend on himself; what little he had went on drink. However, even in 1890 he was not a great deal better off: stoppages imposed by the War Office had taken the place of the colonel's off-reckonings. A survey carried out in Aldershot in that year showed that, out of an average annual private soldier's pay of £18 0s 5d, £7 3s 3d was deducted. The only wage-earner worse off in real terms was the Irish farm labourer. At least there was a better chance that the soldier would be paid regularly the correct sum due to him, as a result of the establishment by Cardwell in 1878 of the

Army Pay Department, from which the Army Pay Corps was evolved in 1893. But the soldier's pay account was still compiled by regimental officers of his unit, and the system broke down in the field in the Boer War. It was not until 1913 that a new system was adopted, by which the soldier's account was kept at a fixed pay centre for each regiment and corps, the responsibility of the regimental officer being reduced to handing out each Friday the sum which the pay office determined was due to him.

The fundamental problem of how to maintain an army of the strength the country needed was brought home to the Government first by the Crimean War, and then by Britain's helplessness in the face of Bismarck's forceful unification of Germany which followed that war. The expansion of imperial responsibilities, which included the need to station a larger proportion of British forces in India after the Mutiny, had greatly increased the requirement to base troops overseas. Bismarck's absorption of the Duchies of Schleswig and Holstein, linked to the Danish crown, in the face of Palmerston's protests, and the subsequent chain of events which culminated in the defeat of France in the 1870-1 war, underlined the awkward fact that a maritime strategy, without the ability to provide and maintain an expeditionary force on the mainland of Europe, was of no avail in influencing events on Britain's doorstep; and that the sort of army that Britain had fielded against France under Marlborough and Wellington would not suffice against the massive modern military machine which Prussia had developed. The Crimea had shown up the two major deficiencies in the army's composition and organization: that too high a proportion of its strength was stationed overseas and that there was virtually no reserve to call upon. Of the 144,000 men on the army's establishment, only 27,000 could be provided for the expedition, and, after they had left, reinforcements depended on raising new recruits. A factor contributing to the difficulty in doing this was the dramatic fall in that traditional reservoir of military manpower - Ireland. The combination of the potato famine and emigration reduced its population from 8 million in 1840 to less than half that 20 years later.

Up till 1847 enlistment had been for 21 years or life. With the demand for men overseas, a large number of soldiers spent many years on end in India or the colonies, where they were lucky if they survived. Their lot was similar to that of deported convicts. In 1847 enlistment had been reduced to 10 years for infantry and 14 for cavalry, with an option to serve on to 21 for pension. This had made little fundamental difference. Cardwell's radical reform was designed to achieve two objects: to balance home and overseas service, and to create a reserve of trained men who could be called up, if an expeditionary force was required. His method was to change the 12 years, all with the colours, to six with the colours and six with the reserve (later changed to seven and five), and to link two regular battalions of infantry together and give them a territorial affiliation and association with the militia and volunteers in that area, in which would be established a training depot for them all. Both aspects of his reform met with strong opposition from the traditionalists. He was accused of undermining both the traditional regimental system and the precious experience of the tough, trained veteran soldier. Wolseley was a strong supporter of the reforms, but Roberts opposed the introduction of shorter service on the latter ground. The 'Cardwell System', based on the principle that one battalion of a regiment would be serving at home and the other overseas, exchanging personnel until the battalions themselves changed over, provided a more or less satisfactory basis for the organization of the infantry until the outbreak of the Second World War. It was also applied unofficially to the cavalry, although there were no formal links between cavalry regiments which changed places in this way.

Major changes in the conduct of campaigns and battles had been brought about by the industrial revolution of the nineteenth century. The development of the railway network in Europe, and of the electric telegraph as a means of communication, combined with universal conscription for military service, meant that huge armies could be mobilized, moved into the field and maintained there in a fraction of the time taken in previous ages and at all times of the year. The telegraph, carried overseas by cables laid on the bed of the sea, meant that news of events and orders to the commanders could be instantly conveyed, limiting the freedom of action the latter had enjoyed in far distant theatres of war.

There had been a revolution also in the weapons with which the soldiers fought. In the Crimea, most infantrymen had still been equipped with muskets, although some carried the Minié rifle. That was succeeded in 1866 by the Sneider, the army's first breech-loader and in 1871 by the Martini-Henry, the first hammerless rifle. It gave way to the Lee-Metford, forerunner of the Lee-Enfield, which was to see the British army through the First and Second World Wars. In 1884

Maxim's water-cooled, automatically loaded machine-gun, which could fire 600 rounds per minute, had replaced Gatling's 200 rpm model. Artillery had improved almost out of recognition. The development of breech-loading rifled guns, improved explosives, mobile carriages, optical sights and mechanical fuzes, and the ability to mass-produce shells, all made artillery infinitely more effective against men and horses in the open. The casualties that it had inflicted at short range in the American Civil War in the middle of the century had been appalling, and the Russo-Japanese War of 1904–5 demonstrated that artillery was forcing infantry to seek protection by digging into the ground and making cavalry hopelessly vulnerable. The machine-gun intensified the process. The British army, having been solely concerned with colonial campaigns after the Crimea, was largely unaffected by these developments, until the shock of the Boer War forced it to realize that new methods had to be devised for fighting battles. No longer could infantry face the enemy and advance towards him in dense lines, nor could cavalry charge *en masse*, as they had in the Crimea. Neither had found the answer before the Boer War had come to an end.

At least by that time the army had some land of its own on which to train. The years after the Crimean War had seen a gradual change in the way that soldiers in Britain had been housed and trained. Until then they had been scattered about the country either as garrisons, largely to protect ports, or in the major county towns, originally to act as a reserve to maintain order before police forces came into existence. There had seldom been a sufficient concentration of troops in one place for more than one regiment to exercise by itself. Exceptions had been periodic concentrations at Hounslow and, in Wellington's day, Moore's training camp for the Light Infantry at Shorncliffe. The introduction of rifles and guns of longer range, as well as the requirement to put an end to billeting and build hygienic barracks, led to the concentration of the army in three main areas: Colchester, which had always had a garrison, Aldershot and, towards the end of the century, Salisbury Plain. A summer camp had been established on heathland of no agricultural value at Aldershot in 1853. Huts were built there for militia raised in the Crimean War, and they were used after the war for troops making use of the surrounding heathland for rifle ranges and manoeuvres. Permanent barracks were built between 1880 and 1890, at which time the bare downland of Salisbury Plain was purchased as a training area for cavalry and artillery.

5
THE AGE OF HAIG

1902–1919

Douglas Haig was born in Edinburgh in 1861, five years after the end of the Crimean War, the son of a whisky distiller who came from a long line of Border landed gentry. He was as typical a product of the new system of obtaining commissions, after purchase had been abolished, as his fellow cavalryman, who rose to equal heights, 'Wully' Robertson, was not. Haig was untypical in that, after leaving that cradle of army officers, Clifton College, he went up to Oxford, where he spent three years at Brasenose College without taking a degree, before he went to Sandhurst. Illness, not idleness, prevented him from graduating. He made up for it by passing out first from Sandhurst, from which he was commissioned into the 7th Hussars in 1885.

Robertson, the son of a village tailor, joined the 16th Lancers and made his way through the ranks to a commission. He was the first who had done so to attend the Camberley staff college, having passed the entrance examination, which Haig failed, mathematics, as well as colour blindness, proving the stumbling block. Haig, however, managed to gain entry through the influence of the Quartermaster-General, Sir Evelyn Wood, on whom his report on the German army, which he had visited in 1895, had made a strong impression. The staff college was by then regarded as a much more important step to a successful army career than it had been earlier in the century. Of the 216 officers who had graduated from it between 1836 and 1854, only 15 ever served on the staff. It had been separated from the Royal Military College at Sandhurst in 1857, and its status improved, but few of the senior officers in the Boer War had attended it.

After leaving the staff college Haig commanded a squadron of Egyptian cavalry in Kitchener's campaign in the Sudan, and in the Boer War gained a high reputation as an efficient staff officer, first to French, commanding the cavalry, and later to Kitchener. In the final phase of the war, in 1901, he took over command of the 17th Lancers shortly before they suffered a defeat at the Battle of Eland's River at the hands of Smuts. After the war he went to India as Inspector-General of cavalry, where, in 1903, he opposed the abolition of the lance. In spite of his experience in South Africa, he could not bring himself to abandon the concept of a cavalry charge as the ultimate aim of cavalry training. He had been scathing about the introduction of mounted infantry, a hark-back to the original dragoons, in South Africa; but, when he came to supervise the production of *Field Service Regulations* as Director of Military Training in 1907, and was regarded as the army's greatest expert on cavalry, he did not make it at all clear what the cavalry trooper was meant to do with his carbine, the shortened version of the Lee-Enfield rifle, with which he was then equipped.

The Boer War had revealed that the arrangements for providing an expeditionary force were far from satisfactory, particularly in respect of the organization and training of reserves. The major and fundamental reform in this field was brought about by Haldane, when he became Secretary of State for War in Campbell-Bannerman's Liberal administration in 1906. A shrewd, canny and highly intelligent Scot, who knew Germany well, he put into effect the reforms which had been recommended by the Esher Committee's report in 1904, and he was instrumental in bringing Haig into the War Office, as Director of Military Training and later Director of Staff Duties, to implement his decisions. The most important of these was to abolish the militia and merge the yeomanry and volunteers into one territorial army, and to link its training and organization to that of the regular army at home. The latter, in addition to its task of acting as the base for the provision of garrisons overseas, was to be formed into the nucleus of an expeditionary force of one cavalry and six infantry divisions. The Territorial Army would provide 14 infantry divisions and the same number of cavalry brigades. Also from the experience of the Boer War, in which volunteers from all the Dominions overseas had participated, this organization was extended to cover an association with Dominion forces, the newly created General Staff being considered as part of an Imperial General Staff, whose head would hold the title of Chief of the Imperial General Staff, until it became an anachronism in 1965.

Haig was, therefore, not only intimately involved in the organization of the army which he was to lead in the field, but also in its training, particularly the production in 1909 of its *Field Service Regulations* in two volumes, the first truly comprehensive training manuals which the army ever had. In compiling them, he had to take account of the revolutions that had occurred in equipment, transport and communications (see above, Chapter 4).

After this important spell at the War Office, he spent three years as Chief of the General Staff to the Commander-in-Chief India before taking over, in 1912, Aldershot Command, a post which it was assumed entailed command of a corps in any expeditionary force which might be sent to the continent of Europe. There he was in command of part of an army which had changed in a great many ways since the Boer War had ended only ten years before. It was far better equipped, trained and organized than any army in Britain had ever been before in peacetime; but, at heart and in fundamentals, it was still the army it had been since Cromwell's day, particularly in its devotion to the traditions of the past, and it had not evolved a strategy or tactics to meet the conditions of the battlefield which technical advances since the Crimean War had brought about.

Before it faced that challenge, the age-old problem of Ireland became acute, and caused a major crisis among the army's officers. Early in 1914 Asquith's Liberal Government was proposing to grant Home Rule to Ireland. Ulster Protestant resistance to this, led by Edward Carson, had produced an illegal force of Ulster Volunteers, in which many retired army officers held high positions, supported by the 81-year-old Field-Marshal Roberts. In March the Government suspected that this force was intent on seizing British Army weapons and ammunition in Ulster. The Secretary of State for War, Colonel Seely, told the Commander-in-Chief in Ireland, Major-General Paget, to move troops from the main garrison area, The Curragh, not far from Dublin, into Ulster to prevent this. Paget was appalled, knowing that a large number of officers, especially in Hubert Gough's cavalry brigade, came from the Irish Protestant ascendancy, and might interpret the order as a move to suppress the Ulster Volunteers and therefore might refuse to obey. He hurried to London and persuaded Seely to agree that any officers whose homes were in Ulster should be allowed to 'disappear'; but that other officers, who were not prepared to undertake the operation, should be called upon to resign their commissions.

Gough headed the list of 58 out of 70 officers of the 3rd Cavalry Brigade who proffered their resignations, encouraged by that arch-intriguer and rifleman, Major-General Henry Wilson, who held the key post of Director of Military Operations in the War Office and was in constant communication with the Unionist (as the Tory or Conservative party was then called) opposition. Gough and his three commanding officers were summoned to the War Office, where they succeeded in forcing Seely, the Chief of the Imperial General Staff (CIGS), Sir John French, and the Quartermaster-General to sign a document, stating that they would not be called upon 'to enforce the present Home Rule Bill on Ulster.' Haig was indirectly involved, as his chief-of-staff at Aldershot was Hubert Gough's brother, John, who also proffered his resignation. Haig refused to accept it and rushed up to London to see Haldane, then Lord Chancellor, to urge upon him the need for a definite statement of the Government's intentions. Haldane gave it in the House of Lords, when he said: 'No orders were issued, no orders are likely to be issued, and no orders will be issued for the coercion of Ulster.'

The nation's, and the army's, eyes were therefore still on Ireland when the Archduke Francis Ferdinand, nephew of the Emperor Francis-Joseph of Austria, and his wife were assassinated by a Serbian student, Gavrilo Princip, on 28 June 1914. To the British, at least, it would have seemed absurd that such an incident, so typical of Balkan politics, could lead to the most extensive and expensive (in terms of both casualties and economic effects) war that the world had hitherto ever seen – so much so that, until the 1939–45 war occurred, it was known as the Great War. But it was a spark that ignited a fire of very combustible material, which had been laid all ready for somebody to touch off.

German ambitions had drawn Britain and France together in the 'Entente' of 1904, as a result of which, in 1906, Sir Edward Grey, the Foreign Secretary, with the authority of the Prime Minister, Campbell-Bannerman, authorized staff talks between the general staffs of Britain and France. These were entered into with enthusiasm by Henry Wilson, and resulted in a plan for Britain's expeditionary force of one cavalry and six infantry divisions to be transported across the Channel, if France were attacked, and moved by rail to Maubeuge, a few miles from the Belgian border south of Mons, where they would be on the left flank of the French army. Not only were these plans not approved by the Cabinet, the latter was not even informed of the existence of the talks.

When Austria delivered an ultimatum to Serbia on 23 July 1914, demanding an answer within 48 hours, and, as a result, a week later the

European powers began to mobilize their implacable war machines, Britain was not formally committed, in spite of her inclination, on grounds both of moral commitment and self-interest, to side with France. Grey had made it clear to both Germany and France that preservation of the neutrality and independence of Belgium, guaranteed by the treaty of 1839, was the critical factor for Britain. As late as 31 July two-thirds of Asquith's Cabinet favoured Britain's neutrality; but, when, on 2 August, the Germans attacked Luxemburg and presented an ultimatum to Belgium demanding free use of her territory for their forces, and King Albert had appealed to King George V for support, it became clear that Britain had no choice. Belgium's rejection of the German ultimatum and the latter's invasion on 4 August clinched the matter, and at midnight Britain, and her Empire with her, was at war.

The strength of the regular army in 1914 was 250,000, but the only part of it ready to cross the Channel was the expeditionary force which Haldane, with Haig's help, had created. Behind it stood the Territorial Army, also of 250,000 men, organized in 14 divisions for home defence, and 200,000 reservists. Asquith had assumed the office of Secretary of State for War when Seely had resigned over the Curragh incident, but Haldane was in fact deputizing for him at the War Office. On 5 August a meeting was held to decide what to do. Asquith, Grey, Haldane and Churchill, First Lord of the Admiralty, were joined by the First Sea Lord, Prince Louis of Battenberg, the military members of the Army Council, Sir John French, who was to command the British Expeditionary Force (BEF), Sir Archibald Murray, his chief-of-staff, and Haig and Grierson, his corps commanders. Sir Ian Hamilton and the veteran Field-Marshals, Roberts (82) and Kitchener (64), were also present.

Antwerp and Amiens were mooted as destinations for the force or part of it; but Wilson explained that the only practical plan was to implement what had been agreed in detail with the French: the train time-tables were inexorable. The meeting agreed, but next day the Cabinet, which Kitchener had reluctantly joined as Secretary of State for War, insisted that two of the infantry divisions should stay behind and the destination of the force be switched to Amiens, in the hope that Britain could exercise some choice as to how its force should be used. The French protested that so small a force could not act independently, and pressure from them forced Kitchener and the Cabinet to agree to send over the other two divisions and to Maubeuge as the concentration area. Haig shared Kitchener's initial doubts. He would have liked to see the BEF concentrate near Amiens, to be joined there by the Territorial Army. Like Kitchener, he foresaw a long war and believed that, if Britain was to influence its results, she would have to build up a significant army of her own, capable of acting independently.

Their fears were soon seen to have been justified. The plans of the French and German armies dovetailed into each other. The former, based on belief in the importance of taking the offensive and on a desire to regain Alsace and Lorraine as soon as possible, involved an immediate advance into Lorraine. The German plan, devised by Schlieffen, head of their general staff from 1891 to 1906, entailed swinging five of their seven armies – 1,140,000 men out of 1,485,000 – like a door hinged on Metz, sweeping through Belgium, round behind Paris, to seal off the rear of France's five armies, 1,071,000-strong. Beside these, the Belgian army of 117,000 and the BEF's 110,000 were hardly taken into account. The former imposed little delay on the Germans and fell back to Antwerp and the Channel coast. The French attacks failed, and their Fifth Army on the left was defeated at Charleroi on 21 August, while the BEF, with Haig's 1st Corps (1st and 2nd Divisions) on the right, was marching north from Maubeuge to man the line of the Mons–Condé canal.

On 23 August the 2nd Corps (3rd and 5th Divisions), now commanded by Smith-Dorrien,[1] held the canal for 15 miles west from Mons and was attacked by five German corps, totalling 44 divisions, while Haig's corps, extending south-east from Mons for the same distance to link up with the French on the Sambre, faced one corps of 17 divisions and a corps of cavalry. The Germans were surprised to find the British there, having expected to surround them in their concentration area. Haig's corps was not seriously attacked, and he was able to send help to Smith-Dorrien, whose front was assaulted by five German divisions attacking shoulder to shoulder. They suffered heavily from the rapid and accurate rifle fire of the regular British infantry, giving rise to the legend that the Germans believed it had to come from machine-guns, of which each British infantry battalion at that time had only two. Smith-Dorrien's line held, but Sir John French had at last realized that his army was in grave danger of being enveloped, with the French

[1]Grierson had died on 17 August.

falling back on his right flank. Orders for withdrawal were given, and the retreat from Mons began, Smith-Dorrien having lost 1,600 men and Haig 40. In the heat of the summer, it was an exhausting and bewildering experience. After continuous clashes with von Klück's First Army, which Allenby's cavalry division was not able to keep off the retreating infantry, Smith-Dorrien decided on 26 August that his troops were too exhausted to continue and must stand and face the enemy, although Haig's corps on his right was separated from him by a forest. This rearguard action at Le Cateau cost him 7,800 casualties on top of the 4,000 he had suffered since leaving Mons.

The retreat continued towards Paris, a distance of 200 miles in 13 days, and, while the spirit of the weary troops remained resilient, that of their Commander-in-Chief did not. French signalled to Kitchener on 31 August that he had told Joffre, the French C.-in-C., that his troops could not 'remain in the front line' and that, as Joffre had 'begun his retirement', he was going to withdraw across the Seine, west of Paris, having decided to take the BEF off to recuperate in Brittany and transfer his base from Le Havre to St Nazaire on the Loire. This message brought Kitchener hot foot to France in order to reverse his decision and alter the BEF's withdrawal route to the east of Paris.

On that very day aircraft of the Royal Flying Corps, of which 63 had accompanied the BEF, saw that von Klück, on the outer wing of the German armies, had turned south-east, so that his advance would bring him east of Paris. This change from Schlieffen's plan had been caused by the anxiety of von Moltke that his armies, delayed by unexpected resistance at Mons and subsequently, were getting too strung out, in particular that a wide gap was being opened up between von Klück's First and von Bülow's Second armies. Joffre, who had started forming a new Sixth Army in Paris two weeks before, saw his opportunity to attack von Klück's right flank, and gave orders for this to take place on 6 September, counting on the BEF to play a major part. French was reluctant to oblige. He was still intent on retreating even further south from the BEF's position 20 miles east-south-east of Paris. Under pressure he gave way to the extent of issuing a lukewarm order at 5.15 pm on 5 September: 'The Army will advance eastward with a view to attacking. Its left will be covered by the Sixth French Army and its right will be linked to the Fifth French Army marching north.' Fortunately for the BEF, this led them into a gap between the two halves of von Klück's army, and their part in the Battle of the Marne, which marked the turning of the German army's tide, was an easy one. They advanced against only light opposition, crossing the Marne unopposed on 9 September and suffering only 1,700 casualties in the five days of the battle.

Haig was critical of the cautious handling of the battle by the higher command, and felt that a more vigorous drive to the north could have inflicted severe casualties on von Klück's army. By 14 September the German withdrawal had come to a halt, and the Kaiser replaced von Moltke by von Falkenhayn. There then began what has been called the 'race to the sea', in which both sides tried to out-flank each other and obtain control of the Channel ports. The climax of this for the British was the First Battle of Ypres, which began on 20 October. By that time the BEF had expanded to form four infantry and one cavalry corps and numbered nearly 250,000 men. French's attempts to advance came to a grinding halt against strong German resistance on the semi-circular ridge which ringed the town of Ypres from the east. On 30 October the Germans counter-attacked, and fierce fighting continued until 11 November, when the last of a series of German attacks was held by what was left of the old regular army, reinforced by its reservists and some territorials. Haig's 1st Corps had played a major part, and, in recognition of this, he was promoted to the rank of general on 20 November. The 1st Division had been reduced from its nominal establishment of 18,000 to 68 officers and 2,776 other ranks, and the losses in other divisions were on the same scale. The intensity of the German artillery and machine-gun fire, the rain and mud were to become only too familiar to the British army on and around that ridge for the next four years.

Schlieffen's plan had failed. A rapid victory over France was to have been followed by a major redeployment of troops to inflict a crushing defeat on Russia. The map of Europe could then be redrawn, providing a strategic base for imperial expansion. A major switch to the east was now ruled out, unless all the territorial gains in France and Belgium were to be abandoned. As it was, Hindenburg and Ludendorff, with only minor reinforcement, had inflicted a severe defeat on the Russians at Tannenberg in East Prussia at the end of August, balanced by a Russian victory over the Austrians at Lemberg (the modern L'vov in the Ukraine), which lost the latter the province of Galicia. Italy had remained neutral; but a major source of hope, one to which von Falkenhayn attached much importance, was the adherence of Turkey to Germany's side. Paradoxically this offered a ray of hope also to the Entente. Italy, Greece and Bulgaria were sitting on the fence, and the latter had claims against Turkey, arising from the Balkan War of 1912–13.

Kitchener could see no prospect of decisive action on the Western Front until he had created a large new army, planned at a strength of 70 divisions. This could not be fully trained and equipped to make a significant contribution in France until 1916. Meanwhile action against Turkey could strike an indirect blow against the Central Powers, rally to the allied side the southern neighbours of the Austro-Hungarian empire, and perhaps its non-German or Magyar peoples also; and, if the Dardanelles and Bosphorus were secured, provide a warm water link with Russia. Further east the navy's oil supplies from the Persian Gulf, at the extremity of the Ottoman Empire, could be secured by an expedition from India. Admiral Sir John Fisher, who, at the age of 73, had returned to his post as First Sea Lord to replace Prince Louis of Battenberg, had other ideas. He wished to land a force on Germany's Baltic coast, the least realistic of all the schemes to find an alternative to battering away at the Germans in France and Belgium. Kitchener had proposed a landing at Alexandretta to cut the Turkish communications through Syria to Egypt, which Britain had announced was no longer part of the Ottoman Empire, but under her protection. The 29th Division had been sent to the Near East to join the contingents from Australia and New Zealand in the Army Corps (ANZAC), assembling there with no very clear purpose other than to secure the Suez Canal.

At a meeting of the War Council on 13 January 1915, at which Sir John French pressed hard for a renewed offensive on the Western Front, which Joffre was advocating, Winston Churchill used all his powers of persuasion to gain agreement to a proposal to force a passage of the Dardanelles. The result was a compromise. French was promised two more Territorial divisions with provisional approval for a renewed offensive, and authority was given for 'the Admiralty to prepare for a naval expedition in February to bombard and take the Gallipoli Peninsula with Constantinople as its object'. Kitchener was determined that the army should not get involved and Fisher that it should not affect the navy's strength in the North Sea. But the navy's attempts to force a passage on its own failed, and in March Kitchener agreed to the

29th Division and ANZAC being used to help them. Ian Hamilton was placed in command, his orders from Kitchener being limited to the words: 'We are sending a military force to support the Fleet now at the Dardanelles and you are to have command.' It soon became clear that supporting the fleet entailed an opposed landing on the peninsula, for which no plans had been made.

After delays due to the need to reorganize the force and improvise methods of landing, the troops were put ashore at the southern end of the peninsula on 25 April. They suffered heavy casualties from determined Turkish resistance and succeeded only in capturing two small enclaves, each of about four square miles, at Cape Helles and Anzac Cove. From the latter the Australians were on the point of capturing the dominating heights, when they were flung back by a counter-attack commanded by the young Mustafa Kemal, as Ataturk to become the first President of the Turkish Republic after the war. For the next two months casualties mounted from fruitless attempts to recapture the heights and from disease, while arguments developed between Fisher, Kitchener and Churchill about whether the navy should make another attempt to force their way through. The upshot of all this was the dramatic resignation of Fisher, the formation of a coalition Government, the replacement of Churchill at the Admiralty by Balfour and the formation of the 'Dardanelles Committee' as a small inner Cabinet to run the war.

Hamilton, meanwhile, had launched a further unsuccessful attempt to break out, which brought the total Gallipoli casualty list to 60,000, a third of whom were French. Churchill, as Chancellor of the Duchy of Lancaster, urged a further vigorous effort, and Kitchener agreed to reinforce Hamilton with two Territorial Army divisions, the 53rd (Welsh) and 54th (East Anglian), and three newly raised divisions of 'Kitchener's Army', the 10th (Irish), 11th and 12th. These were used in a landing on 6 August at Suvla Bay, further up the peninsula, but also further away from its critical neck. The landings were successful, but the elderly corps commander, Stopford, lent no urgency to the need to exploit them and link up with the ANZAC Corps. The impetus petered out and the Turks remained in possession of the high ground dominating the straits. The first of the 'sideshows' had failed in all its aims.

No more promise was to be seen in the BEF's operations. In December 1914 it had been formed into two armies, Haig commanding the First, which consisted of Monro's 1st Corps, Rawlinson's 4th and Willcocks's

Indian Corps, Smith-Dorrien the Second, with the 2nd and 3rd Corps, Allenby's Cavalry and Rimington's Indian Cavalry Corps. At the same time Sir Archibald Murray was replaced as Sir John French's chief-of-staff by Sir William Robertson, who had been his Quartermaster-General. In March 1915, as part of a general offensive designed to exploit the transfer of 32 German divisions to the Russian front, Haig's army was ordered to launch a limited offensive to capture the village of Neuve Chapelle, north of La Bassée, and exploit it to secure the low Aubers ridge, a mile further east, which overlooked the waterlogged British trenches. He launched the attack by the Indian and 4th Corps on 9 March. They captured Neuve Chapelle, but a German counter-attack prevented exploitation, and three days later Haig called it off, having suffered 12,892 casualties and expended 60,000 rounds of artillery ammunition, almost exhausting available stocks and forcing French to postpone further offensive action for at least two months.

The Germans took advantage of this situation to attack the Ypres salient in April 1915, using gas for the first time. This caused near panic in the northern sector, held by two French divisions, one Algerian, leaving Smith-Dorrien's army in an even more vulnerable salient. Plumer took his place in command, and a week later, on 6 May, withdrew to a line conforming to that of the French. A few days later Haig renewed his attempt to gain the Aubers ridge and failed again at a cost of 11,629 casualties in one day from the three divisions taking part. A week later he tried again at Festubert and lost a further 16,648, once more exhausting all available stocks of artillery ammunition, which French and Haig now saw as the key to making any progress: to silence the enemy's machine-guns, cut the barbed-wire entanglements and counter, as far as possible, the effects of the enemy's longer-range and higher-calibre artillery.

The Gallipoli expedition was doing nothing to help the Russians, who were now being hard pressed by the German divisions which von Falkenhayn had switched from the west. Although Italy had joined the Entente in April, she did little, if anything, to draw additional divisions from the effort of the Central Powers on either the Western or Eastern fronts. Joffre regarded it as urgent to keep up the pressure to prevent von Falkenhayn from transferring yet more divisions eastward. If Russia were to give up the struggle, the whole might of the German army could be concentrated against France. Another offensive was called for in which the British must play their part, and he wished them to do so on

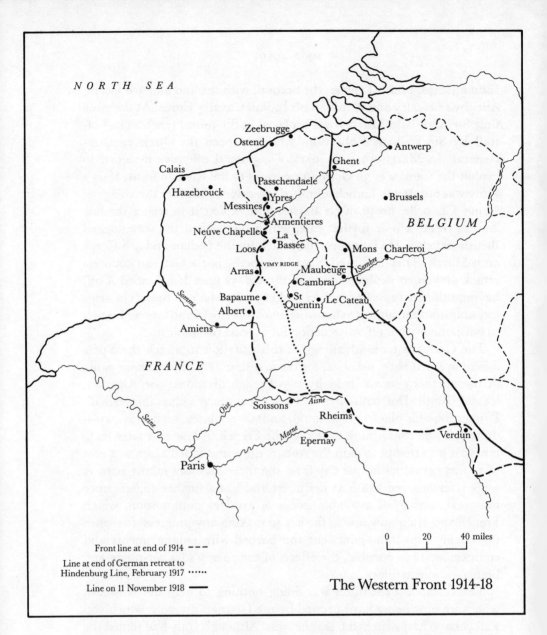

NORTH SEA

Zeebrugge
Ostend
Antwerp
Calais
Ghent
Hazebrouck
Passchendaele
Ypres
Brussels
Messines
Armentieres
BELGIUM
Neuve Chapelle
La
Bassée
Loos
Mons
Charleroi
VIMY RIDGE
Arras
Maubeuge
Cambrai
Bapaume
St
Quentin
Le Cateau
Albert
Amiens

FRANCE

Somme
Seine
Oise
Aisne
Soissons
Rheims
Marne
Epernay
Verdun
Paris

0	20	40 miles

Front line at end of 1914 `- - -`
Line at end of German retreat to
Hindenburg Line, February 1917 `· · · · · ·`
Line on 11 November 1918 `———`

The Western Front 1914-18

the immediate left of the French between La Bassée and Loos, on the
right of First Army's sector. Haig was opposed to this and suggested, as
an alternative, as he was to do on many subsequent occasions, a thrust
from the Ypres salient, aimed to cut the German rail links with the
Belgian coast and turn their flank. In order to release French troops for
his own planned offensive, Joffre also demanded that the British take
over part of the French line, the BEF having now been expanded by a

further 16 divisions, formed into 14 corps in three armies, Monro's Third Army taking over from the French on Haig's right. The latter's First Army was to attack on a front of five miles with six divisions, supported by 110 heavy and 841 field-guns and howitzers, three infantry and five cavalry divisions being held in reserve to exploit success. This force of 75,000 men faced only two German divisions totalling not more than 11,000 men.

The attack was to be launched on 25 September 1915, preceded by four days of artillery bombardment and supported by gas. The first day's attack was successful, but the French Tenth Army on Haig's right had failed to capture the vital Vimy ridge, which overlooked the area over which further advance by his troops to Loos must take place. Two new divisions, the 21st and 24th, were in GHQ reserve, but allotted to him. French had refused to place them under his command beforehand. They arrived late and exhausted, to be flung into battle on the 26th in the face of German reinforcement. They were mown down, losing 8,229 men. Further attempts to gain ground proved fruitless, and the battle was brought to an end in the heavy rain of mid-October, Haig's army having suffered a total of 50, 380 casualties in this battle, known as that of Loos.

Haig had never had confidence in French, and regarded the latter's failure to provide him with reserves under his own control, which could have exploited the success of the first day of the battle, and his attempt to lay the blame on Haig himself, as the last straw. He made his views known to King George V, who elicited them on a visit to France on 24 October. A month later, when he was on leave in England, Asquith invited him to lunch to seek his view about the higher command. Haig recommended that Robertson should be appointed CIGS in place of Sir Archibald Murray, who had recently replaced his namesake, Sir James Wolfe Murray. Assisted by the Directors of Military Operations and Military Intelligence, he – and not Kitchener, the Secretary of State – should be responsible for giving military advice to the Cabinet and for giving orders to Commanders-in-Chief, the Secretary of State confining himself to administrative matters. Kitchener was visiting Gallipoli at the time, and on his return visited Haig and told him that he had recommended to Asquith that he should take over as C-in-C in France from French. This he did on 16 December, his suggestion about Robertson being adopted at the same time.

General dissatisfaction about the performance of French applied also to that of Kitchener. The Government was itself under criticism, not least for failure to provide sufficient artillery ammunition, which French publicly declared to have been primarily responsible for the failure of all his attacks. Total British army casualties since the beginning of the war amounted to 21,747 officers and 490,673 soldiers, of whom about 200,000 were dead or missing. This compared with French losses of 50,355 officers and 1,911,332 soldiers. There was little to show for it, but the Government dared not get rid of so prestigious a figure as Kitchener, although they were deeply dissatisfied at the way he tried to run the army almost single-handed, while keeping his colleagues completely in the dark as to his intentions or thoughts about events.

Two major errors, linked to each other, had been made from the beginning. The first was that most of the general staff in the War Office had gone to form General Headquarters of the BEF. The second was for Kitchener to act both as Secretary of State and also, in effect, as CIGS, the actual holder of that post in August 1914 being Sir Charles Douglas, a stop-gap who succeeded French when the latter was forced to resign over the Curragh incident. Douglas died a few weeks after the war started, and was succeeded by Wolfe Murray, a soldier of no great distinction. Kitchener knew little and cared less about how the War Office or the army in Britain was meant to work. He took no notice of other people's views and never moved from his initial intention to form a large new army totalling 70 divisions, based on cadres drawn from the regular army and its reservists. The Territorial Army was to be used partly for home defence, partly to relieve regular units overseas so that they might return to Britain to form the basis for the creation of 'Kitchener's Army'. To fill the ranks, volunteers were called for, summoned to the colours by the famous poster showing Kitchener's grim face and accusing finger, supported by the words: 'Your country needs you!'. The response was embarrassingly prompt. By September 1914 half a million had volunteered, and by the end of February 1915 the number had doubled, far more than could be equipped and trained in the time. Meanwhile the reinforcement of Gallipoli and the successive offensives on the Western Front forced him to send formations, units and individuals across the Channel and into action before they had been properly trained, the Territorial Army included. The so-called shell scandal revealed the failure of the War Office to provide for the needs of the battlefield, and Lloyd George's appointment as Minister of Munitions was seen as a reflection on Kitchener's inability to carry out his responsibilities effectively. Failure at Gallipoli was also laid by some at his door, although he had never been enthusiastic about the army's participation in the expedition. But he was not a convinced 'Westerner' either. He seemed to take a fatalistic view and had no firm strategy of his own to propose. It was in the hope that he would assume command in the Near East himself that Asquith sent him off to Gallipoli in November 1915 to report on whether or not the recommendation of General Monro (who had succeeded Hamilton) to withdraw totally should be agreed. Typically, he returned with no firm recommendation.

By the time of Kitchener's return, however, Robertson had taken post as CIGS, insisting very firmly on having the responsibilities which Haig had outlined to Asquith. He also insisted on total evacuation from Gallipoli, and this was successfully completed on 9 January 1916, 118,000 men, 5,000 horses and mules and over 300 guns being embarked without loss and transferred to Egypt. The total British Empire casualties of the campaign amounted to 250,000, of whom 43,000 British, Australian and New Zealand soldiers were killed, died of wounds or disease or were taken prisoner. One division had already been moved to join the French at Salonika, in the malarial climate of which 300,000 allied troops were stuck until the end of the war, facing the Bulgarians who had joined the Central Powers in October.

Another eastern venture had fared little better: the expedition sent from India primarily to secure the oilfield terminal at Abadan at the head of the Persian Gulf. A subsidiary aim was to show the Arab sheikhs of the Gulf, who had treaties of protection with the Government of India, and their fellows in Mesopotamia (as Iraq was then called) that they would be assured of British support in throwing off the Turkish yoke of the Ottoman Empire. In 1914 the Indian army numbered 160,000 and the British army in India 75,000. The despatch of a division from India in the first few months of the war to occupy the port of Basra was accompanied by no preparations to make it a base for an advance inland, and the general administrative arrangements for the maintenance of the force in one of the hottest and unhealthiest ports in the world were reminiscent of the early months of the Crimean War. Once Basra had been occupied and a Turkish attempt to recapture it defeated, it was decided to advance up the Tigris and Euphrates in the vague hope of rallying the Arabs against the Turks and eventually occupying Baghdad. But instead of waiting, as Kitchener had done on the Nile, until the logistic arrangements to support such an advance had been made, a force under Sir John Nixon began to move up the river by steamer at the hottest time of the year in 1915. Having reached Amara on 4 June, over 100 miles upstream from Basra, Nixon was all for continuing on to Kut, a further 150 miles, and to Baghdad itself, another 100 miles on. The Viceroy, Lord Hardinge, although initially doubtful, was carried away by the idea of the influence it would have on Moslem opinion, counter-acting the failure to achieve anything at Gallipoli. Townshend, whose division was chosen to execute the advance, was enthusiastic, and by the end of September had occupied Kut after inflicting severe losses on the Turks. From then on everything began to go wrong. Shortage of transport of all kinds delayed any further advance and limited the force that could be supported beyond Kut to 12,000. Meanwhile the Turks had strengthened their force at Ctesiphon, another 80 miles on and only 20 from Baghdad. Townshend attacked them there on 22 November, lost over a third of his men, and had to return to Kut, where he decided to stay, although Nixon gave him the choice of withdrawing further. Misjudging the time that his food supplies would last, he allowed himself to be besieged by the Turks. Three ill-organized attempts at relief by General Aylmer were all defeated, and lack of food forced Townshend to surrender with 12,000 men on 29 April 1916.

With Haig as C-in-C in France and Robertson firmly in control in Whitehall, there was no doubt that the Western Front would receive priority. Yet, out of a total British Empire strength of 89 divisions, Haig had only 38, and these were 75,000 men under strength. The French, with 95 in France, were continually pressing for Britain to assume a greater share of the burden of attacking the German army, thus contributing to keeping Russia in the war, even if the hopes of driving the Germans from France were slender. 'Sideshows' in the Middle East held out little hope of contributing much, nor did Italy. However, a tactical innovation to overcome the formidable combination of machine-guns and barbed-wire showed promise. It was the 'tank', a codename adopted to maintain secrecy about the development of an armed and armoured tracked vehicle, which could crush wire and straddle trenches, while its crew were protected against small arms, shrapnel and shell splinters. It originated in two minds at the same time. One was that of Major Ernest Swinton, sent from Hankey's secretariat of the Committee of Imperial Defence to take charge of public relations at GHQ in France; the other, that of Admiral Bacon, responding to the

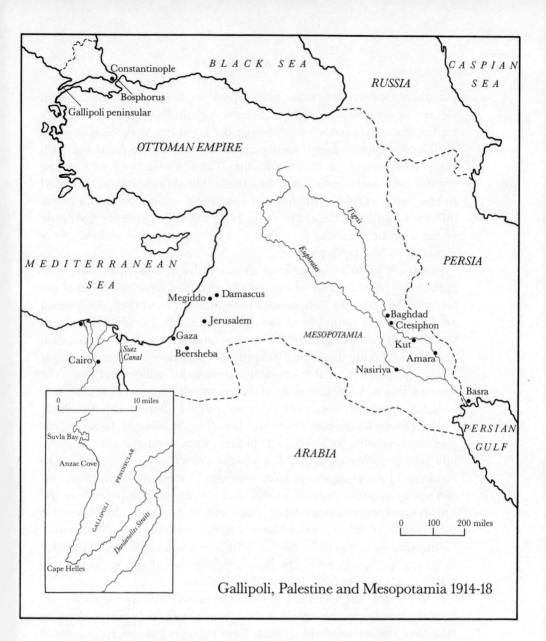

BLACK SEA

RUSSIA

CASPIAN SEA

Constantinople

Bosphorus

Gallipoli peninsular

OTTOMAN EMPIRE

PERSIA

MEDITERRANEAN SEA

Megiddo • Damascus

• Jerusalem

Baghdad
Ctesiphon

MESOPOTAMIA

Gaza

Kut

Cairo • Suez Canal Beersheba

Amara

Nasiriya •

Basra

PERSIAN GULF

ARABIA

Tigris

Euphrates

0   10 miles

Suvla Bay

Anzac Cove

GALLIPOLI PENINSULAR

Dardanelles Straits

Cape Helles

0   100   200 miles

Gallipoli, Palestine and Mesopotamia 1914-18

needs of the Royal Naval Division and the Royal Naval Air Service in Belgium in 1914, both to move naval guns on land and to provide mobile bridges for the armoured cars of the RNAS. On 22 June 1915 Sir John French had forwarded Swinton's detailed proposal for such a vehicle to the War Office, commenting that 'it appeared to have considerable tactical value'. Swinton's return to Whitehall to replace Hankey as Secretary of the Dardanelles Committee gave him the opportunity to urge action on his proposal at the highest level. Lloyd George at the Ministry of Munitions was enthusiastic; but at the successful demonstration of a prototype on 2 February 1916, Kitchener remained sceptical. Lloyd George took the decision to go ahead with the production of 50 tanks, and the War Office agreed to form an organization under Swinton to man them. The order was later increased to 150, but there was little hope of producing enough to have a major influence on the battlefield in 1916. Haig asked for some for the Battle of the Somme and was promised 150 by 31 July, but only 49 were available to him by September.

Although an allied conference at Chantilly in December 1915 had agreed that 'decisive results will only be obtained if the offensives of the armies of the coalition are made simultaneously' and that 'the general action should be launched as soon as possible', the British Cabinet was reluctant to give Haig its authority to commit himself to a firm plan, and did not finally do so until 7 April. He had grave reservations about a third paragraph of the Chantilly agreement, which said that 'the wearing down [French, 'usure'] of the enemy will henceforward be pursued intensively by means of local and partial offensives, particularly by the Powers which still have abundant reserves of men'. In an important meeting with Joffre on 14 February, he resisted attempts to make him take the offensive in April, when the French were not intending to do so until July. Haig would have preferred to make his main effort east of Ypres, but Joffre pressed for the area astride the Somme, where the British and French sectors joined. Although there was no clear objective there which, if gained, would have a significant effect on the German position, as there was in Flanders; Joffre seems to have chosen it in order to tie the British so firmly to the French action that they could not delay, evade or otherwise restrict their action.

A week later the Germans launched a major offensive against Verdun, the first impact of which on Haig was to persuade him to agree to take over the sector of the French Tenth Army. However, he resisted attempts to make him take the offensive before the agreed date. Nevertheless, 'minor operations' between 19 December 1915 and 30 June 1916 cost him the loss of 5,845 officers and 119,296 soldiers, many of them resulting from reaction to German initiatives.

Although called the Battle of the Somme, the British sector of the attack all lay to the north of the river, where the German Second Army's positions lay along the low ridge in open chalk-down country astride the small River Ancre and the main road from Albert to Bapaume. Haig's plan was to use Rawlinson's Fourth Army of eight infantry and three cavalry divisions in five corps (with two divisions also of Allenby's neighbouring Third Army) to assault the ridge after a prolonged and intense artillery bombardment by 1,500 guns firing 200,000 rounds a day for five days. When Rawlinson had broken through the three successive lines of German defences, Haig would launch Hubert Gough's Reserve Army of three cavalry and two infantry divisions through to the open country near Bapaume to swing north behind the German lines as far as Arras, 14 miles away.

Rawlinson's original plan, favoured by Foch, had been for an assault before dawn, so that his infantry could approach the German defences under cover of darkness, and a short intense bombardment to achieve surprise. He would then try and carry all three successive German lines in one attack. Joffre opposed this. Having plenty of ammunition, he wished to rely principally on prolonged observed artillery fire and a daylight attack. In order to conform to the French plan, Haig forced Rawlinson to change his. The result was disastrous. When the artillery barrage lifted at 7.30 am on the clear sunny morning of 1 July 1916, the German machine-gunners came up out of their deep dug-outs and mowed the advancing infantry down. In the first day Rawlinson lost 57,470 men, of whom 19,240 were killed. A fortnight later only a very short section of the German line had been breached and they had doubled the strength of their forces in the area. Kitchener's new army had received a bloody baptism of fire. One of the divisions which suffered most was the 36th (Ulster), formed from the illegal Ulster Volunteers.

Urged to maintain pressure on the Germans to relieve that which they were exerting to great effect on the French at Verdun, Haig battled on until 18 November, by which time the firm chalky ground had been reduced, in the words of the *Official History*, to a place where 'in a wilderness of mud, holding water-logged trenches or shell-hole posts, accessible only by night, the infantry abode in conditions which they might be likened to those of earth-worms, rather than of humankind'. Four-and-a-half months of this grim struggle had advanced the allied lines by an average of 5 miles on a front of 14, two-thirds of it within the British sector, at a cost of 419,654 British and 204,253 French casualties. The British *Official History*[2] originally assessed the German casualties at

²*France and Belgium 1916*, Vol. II, Preface, p. xv.

465,000 (280,000 against the British, 185,000 against the French), but the editor, Sir James Edmonds, later revised the figure upwards to 680,000. Another source[3] interprets the official German account to indicate that, if the lightly wounded are included, as they are in the allied figures, provided that they were evacuated from their units, the total German casualties on the Western Front in the whole of 1916 amounted to 1,820,000, of which 1,240,000 were incurred between 1 July and 30 October. Yet another source[4] puts the Somme casualties at about 560,000 on each side.

1916 had been a bad year at sea also. Although the Battle of Jutland on 31 May was hailed as a victory, it did nothing to compensate for the continuing loss of ships at sea from submarine attack.[5] This led Jellicoe, who became First Sea Lord in November, to attach great importance to the capture of the German-occupied Belgian ports from which he believed, erroneously, that the submarines operated. Pressure for this fitted in with Haig's own preference for Flanders as the scene of any offensive in 1917. Another conference was held at Chantilly in November, which could think of nothing better than to repeat the formula for 1916. Haig said he would be prepared to renew the offensive in February, but would prefer May. Joffre favoured the earlier date, fearing that the Germans would strike first, as they had in 1916. Haig sensed two things. First, that no major effort could be expected from the French army, which had suffered 1,675,000 casualties since the start of the war; and, secondly, that the French Government had lost confidence in Joffre. He was right on both counts, Joffre being replaced on 26 December by the 61-year-old General Robert Nivelle, the day before Haig received a letter from King George v promoting him Field-Marshal.

At Verdun in October and December, Nivelle's Second French Army had carried out two remarkably successful limited offensives, which had impressed the French Prime Minister, Briand. Nivelle seemed to hold the secret which eluded Joffre and Haig, limited as the objectives of his attacks had been. He was also persuasive, with the advantage that he was fluent in English, the language of his mother. Lloyd George, who

---

[3]Terraine, *Douglas Haig*, p. 233.

[4]Sir Charles Oman, 1927, quoted Terraine, p. 236.

[5]141,193 tons of merchant shipping were sunk in April, after which there was a lull: then 43,534 in August; 104,572 in September; 176,248 in October; 168,809 in November and 182,292 in December.

had become Secretary of State for War when Kitchener was drowned on 5 June on the way to Russia[6], having firmly resisted Haig's intention of renewing the offensive in 1917 in conformity with Joffre's plan, was won over by Nivelle. Haig's first impressions were also favourable, but were dispelled as soon as Nivelle explained his plan. The French army would form a '*masse de manoeuvre*' of 27 divisions to effect a breakthrough, which could immediately be exploited. To make it possible both to create this force and to produce the conditions on the French front which would favour success, the British should not only take over part of the French line, but would carry out a series of attacks which would pin the enemy down in the Arras-Bapaume sector, while other French forces would do the same between the Somme and the Oise. His plan 'did not exclude the possibility, if the need arises, of an operation for the conquest of Ostend and Zeebrugge', but assumed that his offensive would force the German armies in the north to withdraw, making it unnecessary. 'If our attack fails', he wrote, 'it will always be possible to carry out the projected Flanders operations in the good weather [French, '*a la belle saison*'].' Haig did not like this. In reply, he pointed out that, although he nominally had 56 divisions, for one reason or another they were really only the equivalent of 50. He would need 36 to carry out a significant offensive, which limited his ability to take over more of the front from the French.

These plans to repeat in 1917 what had been attempted in 1916 were made against a background of general disillusionment with the war. The patriotic enthusiasm with which volunteers had flocked to the colours in the first year of the war, echoing Rupert Brooke's 'Now, God be thanked Who has matched us with His hour', had died, as had so many of the volunteers themselves on the battlefield of the Somme. The politicians blamed the generals for lack of imagination, and the 'brass hats' blamed the 'frocks' for failing to provide the human and material sinews of war. Peace was mooted, the most significant mediator being the American President Woodrow Wilson, who asked both sides to define their war aims. The Entente had great difficulty in agreeing them, apart from insistence on the restoration of Alsace and Lorraine to France and guarantees of the independence of Belgium and Serbia. To provide an idealistic motive to please Wilson, the principle of national

[6]HMS *Hampshire*, in which he was travelling, struck a mine only two hours out from Scapa Flow. Lloyd George would have been on board also, but cried off at the last minute, as he was engaged in political negotiations concerning Ireland, arising out of the Easter Rebellion.

self-determination was proposed, implying the break-up of the Ottoman and Austro-Hungarian Empires.

The difficulty was that the military situation of the Central Powers was not such that Germany felt any need to concede such demands. The Russian effort was weakening, the submarine campaign showed promise, and apart from her casualties and the inconvenience of the naval blockade, Germany saw no reason to lower her demands, which included the occupation of Belgium and Luxemburg, as well as the retention of Alsace and Lorraine and some of the fortresses on the soil of France itself. General dissatisfaction with Asquith's dilatory and indecisive methods of conducting business, in particular his handling of conscription – it had been introduced for bachelors only in January 1916 and he had given rash promises to married men – erupted into a political crisis, the outcome of which was that Lloyd George replaced him as Prime Minister on 7 December, with the support of the Unionists, Labour and a section of the Liberal party: the rest followed Asquith into opposition. Lord Derby took Lloyd George's place as Secretary of State for War.

Lloyd George's accession to power was viewed with concern by Robertson and Haig, who had experienced his opposition to giving priority to the Western Front. At a conference in Rome in January 1917, he surprised everyone by suggesting a major allied offensive from Italy to knock the Austrians out of the war. To the relief of Robertson, the Italian C-in-C Cadorna turned it down. On his way back Lloyd George met Nivelle and was completely won over to the latter's ambitious plan, about which Haig was in the process of establishing a number of pre-conditions. He was principally concerned to ensure that the British were not committed to another Somme, which could drag on until Nivelle's offensive had either broken through or failed, and that the operations which the British did undertake as part of his plan should not prejudice Haig's ability to launch an offensive to clear the Belgian coast in the summer. Nivelle evaded the issue. He wrote:

One cannot be too literal about particular phases because, quite obviously, it could not enter your mind that, once engaged in a joint battle by our two armies, you could, on your own appreciation of the situation, abandon the battle and leave me alone at grips with the enemy. If we embark on this battle, it is with the avowed intention of following through to the end, and engaging all our forces in it. It would be disastrous to deliver battle under other conditions.

Haig's doubts and his reluctance to take over more of the French line, unless he was reinforced from Britain, where a large force was still kept for home defence, antagonized Lloyd George. The latter took the opportunity of the need to do something about the failure of the French railways to meet Haig's requirements, to arrange a conference with Briand and their military advisers at Calais on 28 February. Under its cover a proposal was made by the French, which Lloyd George supported, that the British armies should come under Nivelle's command and Haig's responsibility be reduced to that of administration and logistic support. Robertson exploded, while Haig's reaction, although naturally adverse, was more phlegmatic. Hankey saved the day with a formula which left Haig firmly in command, but subordinated him to Nivelle for the duration of the planned offensive, while retaining the right of appeal to the British Government, if he thought that Nivelle's orders imperilled his armies. From that day forward any feelings of confidence or trust there may have been between the Prime Minister on the one hand and Robertson and Haig on the other were dispelled. Haig's suspicions were not removed by the appointment of the Francophile intriguer, Henry Wilson, as his representative at Nivelle's head quarters. In the event Wilson was totally loyal to Haig and the interests of the BEF. Argument between Haig and Nivelle continued, until the procedure for Nivelle's exercise of command was settled at a conference in London on 12 March.

While the allied generals had been arguing, Ludendorff, who had succeeded von Falkenhayn on 28 August 1916,[7] took the initiative, not by attacking, but by withdrawing from the salient astride the Somme and Oise to a shorter line, known by the allies as the Hindenburg Line and by the Germans as the Siegfried Line. It ran from just south-east of Arras, west of St Quentin, to the Aisne east of Soissons. Haig's reaction was that this would free German reserves for a major offensive; that Nivelle's plan should be scrapped and that he should keep his army in hand, prepared to deal with whatever surprise Ludendorff might have up his sleeve. Nivelle's was to maintain that the German withdrawal called for no change. Their new line would be outflanked, the French attacking at its southern end on the Aisne and the British at the northern end near Arras. While attempts to reconcile these differing views were being made, the Russian Revolution began and the French Government changed hands, the aged Ribot replacing Briand, and

[7]The day after Romania joined the Entente.

Painlevé, who was not favourably disposed towards Nivelle, becoming Minister for War. Nivelle had his way, and in April Haig's forces were launched into the Battle of Arras, three days after the United States of America, incensed at German attempts to subvert Mexico to her cause and her resumption of unrestricted submarine warfare, joined the Entente.

Haig's plan was for Horne's First Army with 13 divisions to capture Vimy Ridge north of Arras and Allenby's Third Army with 18 to advance astride the Arras–Cambrai road to high ground five miles beyond Arras, while Gough's Fifth Army with 6 divisions carried out a subsidiary attack near Bullecourt on the right. The Cavalry Corps was to exploit any success. Sixty tanks were available, more or less equally split up among the attacking corps. Haig, with nearly 5,000 guns, had a four to one superiority in artillery over the Germans facing him, and insisted on a preliminary bombardment lasting five days, although Allenby wished to restrict it to two. Initial results were encouraging. By 14 April the infantry of the First and Third Armies had reached their objectives and captured over 11,000 prisoners. The Canadians were on Vimy Ridge, but the cavalry had not been able to move forward, and Gough on the right had made no progress against the northern end of the Hindenburg Line. Nivelle's offensive on the Aisne, although leading to the capture of 20,000 prisoners and 175 guns, gained hardly any ground, incurred 96,125 casualties and sparked off widespread mutinies in the French army. This failure, combined with the gloomy news from Russia and prospects of future American participation, made the French Government reluctant to continue the offensive, although Nivelle assured Haig that he would do so. Haig felt the the results of Arras had been promising and that, if he did not make a further effort there, 'the enemy would be left free to recover and reorganize and to seize the initiative in this theatre or another'. At the beginning of May he resumed the attack, intending to secure a 'good, defensive line' east of Arras. Two further weeks of fighting resulted in nothing but more casualties, bringing the total since 9 April to 158,660, of whom 29,505 were killed. By that time, Nivelle had been replaced by Pétain, who was determined to put a stop to further French offensive action.

Haig's principal interest all along had been his plan for an offensive in Flanders, aimed at the rail-junction of Roulers 12 miles north-east of Ypres, the capture of which he believed would force the Germans to withdraw from the Belgian coast. As a preliminary to his main offensive, he had ordered the 60-year-old Plumer's Second Army to capture the Messines–Wytschaete ridge at the southern end of the Ypres salient, under which 21 mines had been tunnelled. After a bombardment by 2,266 guns, 756 of which were 'heavies', lasting two weeks, in the second of which $3\frac{1}{2}$ million shells were fired, 90 tons of explosives were set off and 19 of the 21 mines erupted beneath the German defences, which were assaulted by nine divisions in three corps (one ANZAC), supported by 72 tanks, 48 of which were bogged down and 11 knocked out. The ridge was captured in 35 minutes and over 7,000 prisoners captured for a loss of 21,000 men.

This success did not, however, persuade Lloyd George, nor even Robertson, that Haig should go ahead with his plans for a major offensive to clear the whole ridge from Wytschaete ten miles north-east to Passchendaele. They considered that his chief intelligence officer, Charteris, was painting too optimistic a picture of the difficulties facing the Germans. Lloyd George had his eyes on Italy again and wanted to send some of Haig's artillery to support an offensive there. Precious summer weather was lost in argument and, still without formal approval, Haig, who gave the principal task to Gough's Fifth Army, ordered the preliminary bombardment to start on 16 July. He received formal approval on the 25th, the day the assault was planned; but, as the First French Army on Gough's left was not ready, it was postponed until the 31st, by which time heavy rain, lasting for four days, had started to fall. Gough's army of four corps had ten infantry divisions with two cavalry divisions in reserve west of Ypres. They were supported by 2,174 guns (752 heavy or medium) and 136 tanks, most of which became bogged down. St Antoine's First French Army of six divisions and Plumer's Second Army, using five, attacked on Gough's left and right respectively. In the first four days little progress was made at a cost of 31,850 British casualties. By the end of the month that total had risen to 68,010, of whom 10,266 had been killed. On 20 September the offensive was resumed, Plumer's army taking over the main task of trying to clear the ridge from south-west to north-east. Haig plodded doggedly on, his troops sinking deeper and deeper into the mud, partly because Gough's army would be in a very awkward situation if it stayed where it was stuck. He persevered until the ridge up to Passchendaele had been captured, and on 10 November, when the whole area had been reduced to a sea of mud, he called it off, British casualties since 31 July in this Third Battle of Ypres, according to the *Official History*, having reached a total of 244,897. The same source puts German casualties at 400,000, but even Terraine[8] thought that figure high.

The tank enthusiasts had viewed with dismay the prolonged effort in Flanders, where most of their vehicles became bogged down before they could even reach the front line. They sought an area for the employment of tanks *en masse* which had not already been ploughed into a morass by the prolonged artillery bombardments of both sides. Brigadier-General Hugh Elles, commander of the Tank Corps, finally selected the area between Bapaume and Cambrai in Byng's Third Army sector as a suitable one in which to propose a 'raid' by six battalions of tanks, supported by two infantry or cavalry divisions. It was originally seen as an operation lasting only 12 hours, which would destroy enemy guns, sow confusion and then withdraw. By the time that Haig, seeing his Flanders offensive petering out in October, authorized it, Byng had developed it into a more ambitious plan, expecting it to lead to a major breakthrough and allotting to it six infantry and five cavalry divisions, supported by 1,000 guns. There were 375 tanks available, of which 54 were in reserve. The Battle of Cambrai, as it became known, was launched on 20 November and initial success was dramatic. By noon of the first day the German first and second defence lines had been captured, and church bells in Britain were rung to celebrate the victory. On that first day, 179 tanks had fallen out, 65 from direct hits, 71 from mechanical troubles and 43 by ditching or other causes. Such swift success had not been catered for, and Byng's reserves, especially the cavalry, could not be moved forward quickly enough to support it, so that momentum was lost. Haig had said that he would call off the operation if it did not succeed after the first 48 hours, but for various reasons he did not. By the end of the month all progress had come to an end and Byng's army was thinly spread and vulnerable to counter-attacks on its flanks. The Germans launched these on 30 November and soon regained all that they had lost. But the victory of Cambrai lay in the proof of what the tank could do, if properly used, and from then on it was established as a major weapon on the battlefield.

If 1916 had been a bad year for the Entente, 1917 had been worse. The French Army was recuperating, the Russian had ceased to exist, the Italian had suffered a severe defeat at Caporetto in May, the British

[8]*Douglas Haig*, p. 372.

was running out of manpower. The introduction of full-scale conscription in May 1916 had made little difference, the addition of men between 18 and 41, who had not already volunteered, being balanced by the increase in registration of reserved occupations. The allies had not been able to do anything to help Romania, whose forces were totally defeated and her capital, Bucharest, occupied by the Germans in December. These setbacks were only partially offset by the turn of the tide in the submarine war, brought about by Lloyd George's insistence on the introduction of the convoy system against Jellicoe's advice, the capture of Baghdad by General Maude in March, and Allenby's rejuvenation of the campaign against the Turks in Palestine with the Third Battle of Gaza in November. Two previous attempts to dislodge the Turks from the Gaza–Beersheba line in March and April had failed, as a result of which Sir Archibald Murray was replaced as C.-in-C. in Egypt by Allenby in June. He put new life into the command, and with three infantry divisions and the Desert Mounted Corps turned the Turks out on 6 November, drove them back and entered Jerusalem on 9 December.

Lloyd George was determined to prevent men being swallowed up in further offensives in France and Belgium, but Haig's problem was not that of planning a new series of attacks, but of having enough men to hold his front, which had been extended by taking over a further 28 miles from the French in September, against the likelihood of a German offensive, now that they no longer had to worry about the Eastern front. He had been forced to send Plumer with five divisions to support the Italians, reducing his strength to 47 British, ten Dominion and two Portuguese divisions. Lloyd George's strategy, which also appealed to the French, even to the pugnacious 76-year-old Clemenceau who had succeeded Painlevé in November, was to remain on the defensive on the Western Front while trying to eliminate Germany's allies – Austria-Hungary, Bulgaria and Turkey – from the war by operations in Italy and further east. An offensive on the Western Front would have to wait until the Americans had deployed enough divisions to counteract the transfer of German divisions from the east. This could not be until 1919, by which time a major programme of tank production should have produced several thousand of them.

Haig and Robertson were opposed to this, seeing that it handed the initiative to the Germans, particularly as they were continually being pressed to send troops to Italy and take over more front from the French, while Haig's actual fighting strength was falling. Lloyd George would have liked to get rid of them both, and found one way of clipping their wings in the establishment of a Supreme War Council in November; the French military representative appointed to the Council was Foch and the British Wilson. The Council recommended the formation of a general reserve for the Western and Italian fronts, a proposal Lloyd George welcomed as effectively preventing Haig from carrying out any attacks. A further recommendation that an executive committee of the Council should be formed to determine the employment of the reserve was hotly opposed by Robertson and less strongly by Haig. Lloyd George saw this as his opportunity to be rid of them both, and sent Smuts and Hankey on a tour of France to detect a potential successor to Haig. They could not find one. In any case Haig's position was a strong one. He had a stalwart supporter in his friend King George V with whom he kept in close touch, and, in spite of all the casualties suffered under his command, his subordinates and the troops they commanded had confidence in him. His very taciturnity and inability to project any other image than that of an immovable rock made of him a symbol of determination and reliability. To sack Haig would cause a major row. To get rid of Robertson was easier, and he played into the Prime Minister's hand. He took the line that he had pursued over Lloyd George's previous proposal to restrict Haig's powers: that to hand over responsibility for British troops in France to a committee presided over by a French general was unconstitutional and undermined his own position. Haig was more subtle. He had no objection to the formation of a general reserve, not even to its control by an allied committee, provided that he did not have to contribute to it; and he assessed that he had a cast-iron case for not doing so. If Robertson distrusted the Executive Committee so much, Lloyd George would trump his hand by making him change places with Wilson and himself become the British military representative. Robertson refused the appointment, but Wilson took his place as CIGS and Rawlinson replaced him at Versailles. Robertson was relegated to Britain's Eastern Command, and in June 1918 took over from Sir John French as C-in-C Great Britain when the latter went to Ireland as Viceroy.

Haig did nothing to help Robertson in this crisis, relations between the two having cooled as Haig considered that Robertson did not fight hard enough for his cause in Whitehall. The major battle at that time was over manpower. Haig's divisions were all seriously under strength in infantry. Instead of stripping the United Kingdom, which could no longer realistically be thought to require troops for home defence, and filling the gaps in Haig's ranks, the Government decided to reduce the number of battalions in each brigade from four to three and to maintain a general reserve of 120,000 men in Britain. Haig viewed this with dismay, as his intelligence staff noted the progressive increase in the number of German divisions. In mid-February 81 German divisions faced Haig's 59 on a front of 126 miles, while 71 faced 99 French and one American division on their 324-mile front. In addition, the Germans had 25 divisions in reserve. This figure of 177 increased steadily over the following four weeks, reaching a total of 201. For the first time since 1914 the British army had to think in terms of defence. Haig could not afford to yield ground in the northern sector of his front, nearest to the Channel coast. Further south, down to the junction with the French Sixth Army at Barisis, the actual line held was less critical. His allotment of divisions to armies reflected this. Plumer's Second, round Ypres, had 14 Divisions for 23 miles of front; Horne's First, between Armentières and Arras, 16 for 33; Byng's Third, from Arras to the Cambrai battlefield, 16 for 28; and Gough's Fifth, for the 42 miles from there to Barisis, 14 with three cavalry divisions in reserve behind him. Gough was understandably concerned, particularly as a significant stretch of his line had recently been taken over from the French and was in a poor state. Labour to construct new defences in depth was hard to come by.

At 4.40 am on 21 March an intense bombardment, incorporating large quantities of gas shell, opened up on the whole front of Byng's and Gough's armies. Five hours later, in a thick mist, the infantry of three German armies (65 divisions supported by 6,608 guns) attacked, using new tactics of infiltration, by-passing any posts which held out, and overran the whole of Gough's defensive system. By the evening of the 23rd Gough's army had been driven back 12 miles. Byng's left held, but his right swung back in line with Gough. Ludendorff's plan was for this first blow to break through at the junction of the British and French and swing north behind the former: a second blow in Flanders would then turn Haig's left flank, and the whole British army would be cut off from the sea. While his only reserve of eight infantry and three cavalry divisions was thrown into the battle to hold the Germans off Amiens, Haig appealed to Pétain for help in seeing that their two armies were not separated. Pétain expressed sympathy, but was more concerned with fears that the next blow would fall on his front in Champagne.

On 26 March the Supreme War Council was convened at Doullens. Haig realized that, alone among the French generals, Foch had the determination, backed by Clemenceau, to grip the situation. He willingly accepted the agreement that 'General Foch is charged by the British and French Governments with coordinating the action of the Allied Armies on the Western Front'. Ludendorff's southern thrust ran out of steam by 5 April, when his forward troops were ten miles from Amiens. By that time Haig's casualties amounted to 177,739, of whom 14,823 were killed, and Fifth Army had lost 500 guns. German casualties were over 250,000 and, as a result, Ludendorff had to reduce the strength of his northern thrust. This was delivered on 9 April by eight divisions with six in reserve on a front of 12 miles, held by Horne's First Army north of the La Bassee Canál with three British and one Portuguese division, extended next day by an attack on the Messines ridge in Second Army's sector. Both armies were driven back, but the Messines ridge on the left was held. The important rail junction of Hazebrouck was threatened and Haig called on his troops for a supreme effort in his famous 'Backs to the Wall' message on 11 April. Foch sent reinforcements, and the position was held until the German attacks ceased at the end of the month. Haig's casualties between 9 and 30 April amounted to 82,040, of whom 7,918 were killed, and the Germans suffered another 98,300.

Foch and Haig were now united in their resolve to exploit the situation created by these German losses and the existence of two large German salients on ground not previously reduced to a quagmire; but they had to battle against the politicians and generals in both countries, who shrank from a return to the offensive until the full strength of the Americans could be deployed in 1919. However, they won the argument. On 18 July Pétain and the Americans under Pershing launched attacks all round the major salient which extended from Villers Cotterets south of the Aisne to west of Epernay on the Marne, and on 8 August Rawlinson, who had returned from Versailles to relieve Gough, who had been made the scapegoat for the withdrawal in March, his army renamed the Fourth, launched an attack east of Amiens with Monash's Australian Corps of five and Currie's Canadian of four divisions, supported by 324 Mark V tanks. On his right Debeney's First French Army, under Haig's command, attacked simultaneously. Rawlinson also had Kavanagh's Cavalry Corps of three cavalry divisions and 96 14-ton Whippet tanks to exploit.

Rawlinson attacked at dawn, and by mid-day all objectives had been captured: the Germans suffered heavy losses and Ludendorff described it as 'The black day of the German army'. On 14 August Haig halted this thrust and ordered Byng to attack near Arras on 21 August, when he advanced two miles and took 5,000 prisoners. Three days later, Rawlinson resumed his attacks, and by the end of the month Haig was approaching the formidable defences of the Hindenburg Line. Wilson sent him a warning that the Government would not view favourably an attack with heavy losses which did not succeed in breaching it. Haig was furious. He pointed out that he had captured 77,000 prisoners and 800 guns in the last month, and insisted that the pressure had to be maintained. Foch was of the same mind, and planned coordinated attacks over the whole allied front at the end of September. They brought the war to an end, by which time Haig's armies had suffered a further 180,000 casualties. Bulgaria surrendered on 30 September, and Turkey on 31 October after Allenby had defeated Liman von Sanders's Eighth Turkish Army in an attack with four divisions on 19 September, known as the Battle of Megiddo, and occupied Damascus on 1 October. Austria-Hungary sued for peace on 4 November. Kaiser Wilhelm dismissed Ludendorff on 26 October and himself abdicated and sought refuge in Holland on 9 November. Two days before that, German plenipotentiaries had crossed the lines to seek an armistice, which became effective on 11 November. In a letter to his wife on 1 November Haig had written: 'I am afraid the Allied Statesmen mean to exact humiliating terms from Germany. I think this is a mistake, because it is merely laying up trouble for the future, and may encourage the wish for revenge.' It did.

Haig's army was unlike any British army that had preceded it. It was the nation in arms. Eight million men had been called up, the great majority into the army. Almost a million (950,000) had died and two million had been wounded, most of them on the Western Front. After the war, Haig had to bear most of the odium for that grim list, Lloyd George, in his *War Memoirs*, doing his best to pin the blame on him. Assembling, maintaining and operating this huge military machine turned the army into a vast industrial complex, employing all the skills of civilian life; and the need to create and sustain it wrought profound changes in the life of the nation, especially in expanding the field of government activity. It was a railwayman's war. The huge volume of supplies was transported by rail almost to the front line, and major troop movements were executed by the same method, although the use of motor vehicles increased steadily as the war progressed.

The machine-gun, combined with barbed-wire entanglements, was the chief enemy of the infantry and rendered cavalry useless. The hand grenade and the mortar were the principal close-quarter weapons. The trench and its 'dug-out' shelters enabled infantrymen to survive the intensity of the artillery fire, which was deadly to men, and even more so to horses, in the open. The tank was the answer to the combination of obstacles and fire-power, but had not been developed to a sufficient degree of reliability nor produced in adequate numbers by the end of the war to prove its real potential. Artillery remained dominant up to that time.

The principal innovation was the aeroplane. Its effect as an offensive weapon was slight, even by 1918, but its main value was to make it possible to see 'the other side of the hill', both to provide information and to direct artillery fire. In 1914 a total of 63 out of the Royal Flying Corps's 150 aircraft were sent to France. For the final battles in September 1918 1,058 aircraft supported Haig's armies. By that time the RFC had been removed from the army and a separate Royal Air Force formed; the navy, however, retained its own Fleet Air Arm. A further innovation, which could have had a significant effect, if it had been more fully developed, was that of wireless (or radio). Even when reserves were available to exploit success in attack, and had sufficient mobility to do so, they were seldom used in time, because the higher commanders had no idea what the situation was. Communication relied either on field telephone or on a man on his feet, carrying a written message. The enemy's artillery fire invariably cut all telephone lines and killed many of the 'runners'. Plans had to be rigid, both because the information on which to change them could not be obtained and because the orders to effect the changes could not be transmitted. The one traditional arm which had proved almost useless was horsed cavalry; but its success in Allenby's campaign in Palestine, both at the Third Battle of Gaza and, notably, at Megiddo, obscured the reality that its day was done.

In the light of history, the war appears to have been a terrible waste of life and effort. On the allied side, 5,200,000 men died, of whom

2,300,000 were Russians, while Central Powers' deaths were 3,450,000. European civilization and the balance of power were fundamentally affected, and the seeds sown of the totalitarian régimes that developed in Russia and, later, in Germany. One of the most undesirable aspects of the war was the way in which hatred of the enemy was instigated on both sides as a means of whipping up enthusiasm for the war effort. If it was meant to be 'The War to end War', and if ensuring that democracy should replace autocracy was one of the means of achieving that, it was certainly fought in vain. 'Never again' was the intention of all – people, politicians and soldiers alike; but to the soldiers that meant many different things. To some it meant a return to the old ways, believing that a major European war and static trench warfare was an aberration in which the British army should never get involved again. The tank enthusiasts saw their fighting vehicles as the key to restoration of mobility to the battlefield. Some airmen thought that their ability to fly over the enemy and attack his headquarters and cities directly made armies superfluous. Others thought the answer lay in seeing that all the techniques which had succeeded from the Battle of Amiens up to the Armistice should be preserved and improved upon. Lieutenant-Colonel Bernard Montgomery, chief-of-staff of the 47th (London) Division in those battles, was one of those.

Haig was justifiably given a large share of the credit for victory. He was loaded with honours and served on in command of the army in Great Britain until 31 January 1920. Thereafter, he devoted himself to the affairs of the British Legion, which he founded in 1921, both to care for the ex-serviceman, especially those disabled by wounds, and also, through its local branches, to provide a meeting place to preserve the comradeship of the ranks which all who had experienced it recognized as the feature of army life that helped to mitigate its dangers, hardships and miseries. He could never have been called a popular figure. His taciturnity, inarticulateness and aloofness, his immaculately turned-out figure, the undemonstrativeness of his nature, all militated against that. But, while the war lasted, he was highly respected. None doubted his mastery of the details of his profession. They might understandably accuse him of lack of imagination, but the solid Scottish granite of his character, like Edinburgh Castle on its rock, was a source of assurance in difficult times, providing hope that, in spite of all the tragic disappointments, his determination would win through and inspire others to persevere to the end.

By the time he died in 1928 this wartime faith in his leadership had faded, and, largely thanks to Lloyd George, he was regarded by many as a callous butcher, caring nothing for the men of his huge army. To judge him fairly, one has to realize that he sincerely believed that, unless the German army were defeated, the existence of Britain as a free nation was at stake, and that his men went willingly to almost certain death in that cause. It was the great tragedy of that war that, although the second of those beliefs was true of most of the army at the time he expressed it – as a comment on the Battle of the Somme – the former was almost certainly an exaggeration.

6

THE AGE OF MONTGOMERY

1919–1945

Bernard Montgomery was born on 17 November 1887 in London, third son of the Vicar of Kennington, who two years later was to become Bishop of Tasmania, where Bernard spent 12 years of his boyhood. On his parents' return to London in 1901, he entered St Paul's School, where he showed no greater academic inclination than Wellington had at Eton. To the dismay of his parents, he chose to join the army and entered Sandhurst in 1907. Narrowly avoiding expulsion for setting fire to the shirt-tails of a fellow 'gentleman cadet', he was commissioned into the Royal Warwickshire Regiment in 1908. In the retreat from Mons in 1914 he took part in the Battle of Le Cateau and was severely wounded in the First Battle of Ypres, gaining the Distinguished Service Order for his courage, a remarkable award for a 27-year-old subaltern. He returned to duty in February 1915 as a brigade-major, and served on the staff on the Western Front for the rest of the war, in the final stages of which he was GSOI, or chief-of-staff, of the 47th (London) Division. He was serving in that capacity in the army of occupation at Cologne, and had hoped that his name would be among those selected to attend the staff college course due to start in January 1920, but he was disappointed. However, an invitation to tennis from the Commander-in-Chief, Field-Marshal Robertson, brought him to the latter's notice, and his name was added to the list.

The army was running down from its wartime to its peacetime establishment on a scale far beyond that of previous ages. On the Western Front alone, at the time of the Armistice there were 1,794,000 men, serving in or supporting 61 infantry and 3 cavalry divisions. The plan for demobilization, which gave priority to the needs of industry for skilled men or former employees, soon led to trouble, which was remedied by a switch to one based on a combination of age and length of service. One and all wished to throw off uniform and put behind them the years dominated by war. With Britain's potential rivals – Russia, Germany and France – all prostrated, there seemed to be no need to maintain the size of forces which the developments of the late-nineteenth century and the first decade of the twentieth had rendered necessary. The fact that Britain had significantly extended its imperial responsibilities was at first overlooked. It had come about by the assumption of responsibility for many of the countries of the Ottoman Empire and, to a lesser extent, for former German colonies. In addition, forces were maintained to support anti-Bolshevik movements in Russia and to occupy the Rhineland in order to ensure German compliance, first with the terms of the armistice, and later with those of the Versailles Treaty. In 1919, 45,000 men were stationed on the Rhine, and the occupation force remained there until 1930. Trouble also immediately raised its head in two traditional areas – Ireland and India.

In the former, resentment at the repression of the 1916 Easter rebellion and the failure of Lloyd George's Government to implement the plans for Home Rule, which had been put on ice in 1914, led to the declaration of a republic in Dublin in January 1919 and the eruption of a rebellion, organized by the Irish Republican Army. In May of that year the English garrison totalled 53,000 and rose to 80,000 by July 1921. The Government had no clear policy, either political or military. Neither the police nor the army were in any respect trained or prepared to use force to suppress the rebellion, and the Government was ambivalent about its use. While the army carried out ineffectual 'sweeps' of the countryside, the Government, fearful of criticism of the excessive use of military force, unofficially condoned – even encouraged – the indiscriminate use of force by the police and their hastily raised reserve of ex-soldiers, the notorious Black and Tans. Montgomery was involved as Brigade-Major of 17th Infantry Brigade at Cork, his first appointment after leaving the staff college. In his memoirs[1] he wrote: 'In many ways this was far worse than the Great War ... such a war is thoroughly bad for officers and men; it tends to lower their standards of decency and chivalry, and I was glad when it was over.'

The campaign against the IRA came to an end with the signing of the treaty creating the Irish Free State in December 1921, and a year later the last British troops left. The army had not, however, seen the last of the Irish problem, nor did it cease to recruit significant numbers

[1] Montgomery of Alamein, *Memoirs*, p. 39.

of men from south of the newly created border. Five Irish infantry regiments were disbanded, but the Irish Guards, only formed in 1900, and those regiments which had links with Ulster were retained.

If the Irish problem appeared at last to have been settled, that of India had not. The old running sores reappeared – the North-West Frontier and internal security, the latter arising partly from the familiar cause of Muslim–Hindu clashes and partly from agitation for greater participation by the Indians themselves in the government of the country. 1919 saw an attempted invasion of the North-West Frontier Province by Afghanistan, events in Russia having for the moment relieved her of any threat from that direction. This was accompanied by a rising in the Punjab, to deal with which 40,000 men, three-quarters of them Indian, were deployed. As Indian Army troops were gradually withdrawn from Istanbul in 1922 (where the Chanak incident nearly led to war with Turkey, Ataturk having flung the Greeks out of the country), from Egypt in 1923 and from Iraq in 1928, the British army in India was reduced to 60,000 (45 infantry battalions, 5 cavalry regiments, 8 armoured car companies and 69 artillery batteries) and the Indian Army to 190,000 (100 infantry battalions, 21 cavalry regiments and 18 mountain artillery batteries). The need to maintain the British establishment through the Cardwell system was to have a significant effect in preserving the conservative pattern of the army based in Britain. India was not the only overseas commitment that had to be balanced by units on home service. In 1923 there were six infantry battalions in Egypt, two in Iraq and three in other colonies. The five battalions in Northern Ireland and eight in the Rhineland were included in the nine cavalry regiments and 53 infantry battalions balancing those deployed overseas. The assumption by the Royal Air Force, at the instigation of Winston Churchill, then Secretary of State for the Colonies, on the advice of T.E. Lawrence, of responsibility for Iraq, Palestine and Aden, to the irrational annoyance of the General Staff, had made the balance possible; but successive crises, notably in Palestine and China, upset it.

Faced with this confused amalgam of imperial responsibilities, the army struggled, as it always had and has ever since, with the attempt to establish a rational justification of its organization. A committee set up for this purpose in 1919 had recommended a field army of 20 divisions, each of which would throw off another division on mobilization, the Brigade of Guards being expanded also into a division. This would entail either compulsory home service in peacetime or an annual intake of 150,000 volunteer recruits. Even if either of those had been practicable, an end was put to any possibility of an organization on that scale by the drastic reductions in defence expenditure called for in 1919 by the Treasury: from £502 million to £135 million, of which £75 million was to be shared between the army and the RAF. This was accompanied by the famous 'Ten Year Rule', which stated that:

It should be assumed that the British Empire will not be engaged in any great war during the next ten years, and that no Expeditionary Force is required for this purpose ... The principal function of the Military and Air Forces is to provide garrisons for India, Egypt, the new mandated territory and all territories (other than self-governing) under British control, as well as to provide the necessary support to the civil power at home ...

The 'rule' was to be renewed annually until 1932, when Hitler came to power in Germany. It was to have a significant effect on the principal factor affecting the modernization of the army between the wars, that of the replacement of the horse by the automobile machine, the most controversial aspect of which was the replacement of horsed cavalry by the tank. The fact that, although the value of the armoured car for internal security was accepted, the tank did not seem suitable for operations in India and similar undeveloped countries, was used as an argument for the retention of horsed cavalry, and later for devoting a large proportion of such money as was allotted to tank production to the provision of very light tanks, which were suitable for such areas.

Colonel Fuller, who had been the principal staff officer of the Tank Corps on the Western Front, had been transferred to the War Office, where, after the Armistice, he had to fight fiercely for the retention of tanks in the army at all. Their opponents regarded them as a specialized siege-weapon for trench warfare, which was thought to have been an aberration which would not recur. Their potential in a more mobile role was brushed aside. Unfortunately, in advocating the latter, Fuller let his imagination run riot, especially while he was an instructor at the staff college. The obvious impracticability of many of his highly theoretical ideas discredited concepts that were basically sound, and were proved so, principally by the Germans in 1940. His mantle was assumed by Captain Liddell Hart, whose initial interest has been the modernization of infantry tactics on the lines of those used by the Germans in their offensive in March 1918. From that offensive both Fuller and Liddell Hart, in different ways, had drawn the lesson that one should devise both tactics and strategy to avoid the areas of the enemy's main strength and aim, indirectly or directly, for his weak points, especially his headquarters and communications. This led them both to support direct air attacks on cities, in which they assumed that gas would be used, which they expected would have a devastating effect on the enemy's will to continue fighting. Like most of their contemporaries, military and civilian, they sought to avoid the prolonged direct frontal attacks which had involved such slaughter for so little gain in what was still known as the Great War.

In spite of opposition, the Tank Corps, with the prefix Royal, became a permanent part of the army in 1923, but its acceptance and development as a principal element of the combat troops still had to overcome many obstacles. Some saw it only as a subsidiary supporting arm, both in its original role of providing support to an infantry attack and as replacing cavalry in the latter's reconnaissance and screening task. There was great reluctance to accept that tank formations could operate on their own as the principal arm in mobile operations. The tendency of the tank enthusiasts to claim that the tank could be entirely independent, and replace other arms, naturally aroused strong opposition from the latter. Although Fuller was in that category, Liddell Hart was not. He argued for a mobile force of all arms, equipped with armoured tracked vehicles. Even among those who supported the development of tank formations, there were strong differences of opinion about the characteristics that should govern design. There was a tendency to suggest several different types, the light, small tank being regarded by some as suitable for infantry support as well as for other roles.

In a period of shrinking defence budgets – the army estimates were reduced every year from 1923 to 1932, as its strength fell from 231,000 to 207,000 – finance was a dominant factor, and an average of only £2 million a year was spent on new army equipment. When, in the 1930s, money was made available for 'mechanization', the Royal Tank Corps competed for funds with the mechanization of the cavalry in a reconnaissance role and with the replacement of the horse as a means of traction and of transport throughout the army. Even when the National Government woke up to the threat from Germany and decided upon a degree of rearmament in 1934, there was little to spare for tanks. The army's needs were subordinated to those of the RAF and the navy, and a high proportion of its allocation of £20 million, to remedy its deficiencies up to 1939, had to be given to anti-aircraft defence of the United

Kingdom. The only function of a small expeditionary force of four infantry divisions and one mobile division was seen as that of securing airfields in the Low Countries to prevent their use by the Germans, and, possibly, for use by the RAF to enable them to reach targets in Germany. The War Office did not like the idea of that rôle, and insisted that the expeditionary force must be designed so that it could be deployed further afield, for instance in the Middle East. Even that enthusiast for tank formations, Liddell Hart, supported this policy of giving priority to home and imperial defence, opposing the provision of an expeditionary force on the Continent. In that climate, it is not surprising that development was slow.

The 1st Tank Brigade had been provisionally formed from three of the four battalions of the Royal Tank Corps in 1933, and it was given permanent status in 1935, when it was decided to form another battalion, entirely of light tanks, as its reconnaissance unit. However, the Italian invasion of Abyssinia in that year caused the 1st (Light) battalion to be sent to Egypt, where the garrison was still, in spite of the deserts, almost entirely horsed. Realization of the vulnerability of Egypt to a mechanized invasion from Libya, as well as the growing threat from Hitler's Germany, lent greater urgency to the mechanization and modernization of the army; but, when war came in 1939, while the German army, which had been forbidden tanks by the Versailles Treaty, deployed ten panzer divisions in France (the majority of their tanks admittedly light ones), the one British armoured division, the 1st, was not fit to take the field. It had been formed from the original Tank Brigade and a mechanized cavalry brigade. It began to arrive in France just as the Germans attacked in May 1940. In September 1939 the only tanks to cross the Channel with the BEF were one battalion of infantry support tanks and four regular and three yeomanry divisional cavalry regiments, equipped with light tanks. A second infantry support battalion arrived in May 1940. In Egypt another armoured division, the 7th, was being formed, but most of its tanks were light ones.

Finance had not been the army's only anxiety during this period. In spite of a reduction in numbers and the incidence of high unemployment in the country, it was not easy to attract recruits. Pay, as it had always been, was at the heart of the problem. Army pay had remained virtually static from the eighteenth century to 1914. In that year a captain received 12s 6d a day, a lieutenant 8s 6d and a private soldier still 1s, with a free issue of food up to the value of 5s a week. A married soldier over the age of 30 also received a marriage allowance of 1s a day. By 1919, largely owing to discontent within the Royal Navy, this rate of pay had been almost doubled. Comparison with wages paid in civil life was complicated by the fact that soldiers, living in barracks or married quarters, paid nothing for their accommodation nor for the principal items of their military uniform, although its upkeep cost them a certain amount. In 1914 the average wage of adult men in industry was 31s 4d a week, while that of the private soldier, adding 5s to represent the value of his rations, was 13s 9d. By 1923 the former had risen to 66s 6d and the latter to 37s 3d. In 1925 the latter was reduced by 5s 3d a week. Making allowance for inflation, the soldier's 2s a day was almost half the real value of the 1s a day he received in 1797.

The Anderson Committee, in 1925, assessed the value of the soldier's 'emoluments', that is the benefits he received in kind, as 23s a week on top of his pay of 19s 3d. They compared this with the average wage of an agricultural labourer of 27s 11d, an engineering labourer's 40s 4d and a building labourer's 53s 4d and concluded that the soldier was paid too much. The cost of living actually fell thereafter until the mid-1930s, and the soldier's pay remained at the Anderson Committee's 1925 level until Hore-Belisha became Secretary of State for War in 1937. In an effort to stimulate recruitment, he raised the rate of pay of the private soldier from 2s a day in his first year to 3s a day after three years' service. He also increased the daily pay of a 2nd Lieutenant (which the author then was) from 9s 10d to 10s a day. At that time the weekly cost of feeding a soldier was 9s, and the average weekly earnings of equivalent civilians had risen: the agricultural labourer to 34s, the postman to 42s 6d, the general labourer to 60s, the bricklayer to 77s and the bus driver to between 82s and 90s.

The small sum that a soldier would actually receive in cash on joining was not the only factor discouraging men from enlisting in the army either as officers or in the ranks. The 1920s saw a general revulsion against the experiences of 1914–18. In many cases this took the form of anti-militarism, pacifism and a belief that war could be prevented by international organizations and disarmament. The army, driven in upon itself and not entirely unhappy in the cozy seclusion of its regimental life, appeared to be, as in many respects it was, antiquated, philistine and set in its old ways, more appropriate to the eighteenth than to the twentieth century. The cartoonist David Low's caricature of Colonel Blimp epitomized the popular view. The Great War had effected radical changes in society, from which the Royal Navy and the army seemed immune. Only the Royal Air Force, the Royal Tank Corps and Royal Army Service Corps in the army, and the Fleet Air Arm and the submariners in the navy seemed to have moved with the times. An army that in 1933 still had 136 infantry battalions and 18 horsed cavalry regiments, but only four tank battalions and two regiments of armoured cars, certainly gave that impression. Even by 1938 little had changed. At that time there were 47 infantry battalions in a British garrison of 55,498 in India, 18 battalions in one of 21,187 in the Middle East and Mediterranean, one in a garrison of 1,800 in the West Indies, and eight in one of 12,143 in the Far East: a total of 90,634 men overseas, balanced by 106,704, including 64 infantry battalions, in the United Kingdom.

The garrison in the Middle East had been increased partly as a result of the threat to Egypt from the Italians in Libya and Abyssinia, and partly to deal with the growing trouble from the Arabs in Palestine, who opposed the increase in Jewish immigration resulting from persecution of the Jews in Germany and Austria, as well as in other countries of eastern Europe, including the Soviet Union. Between 1933 and 1936 the Jewish population of Palestine had increased from 230,000 to 400,000 – a third of the Arab population. Widespread rioting and attacks on Jewish settlements initiated a full-scale rebellion. In the 1920s the RAF had assumed responsibility for military support to the police, as they had in Iraq and Aden. One squadron of aircraft and two of armoured cars were supposed to look after the external and internal security of both Palestine and Jordan. But bombing villages to keep the people in order could clearly not be applied to Palestine, and the army had to take over. By 1938 two divisions were deployed there, O'Connor commanding the 7th and Montgomery taking over command of the 8th in December of that year.

He set about his command in his usual forthright and uncompromising manner. 'What has been lacking out here', he wrote to a friend, 'has been any clear-cut statement defining the situation and saying what was to be done about it. I decided that I must issue such a statement of policy at once in my division.'[2] The situation had already improved when, in May 1939, he fell ill with what appeared to be pleurisy or possibly tuberculosis. He had already been selected to command the 3rd Division in England and was sent home on sick leave in July to face

[2] Hamilton, *Monty – the Making of a General*, p. 293.

a medical board in August which would decide whether or not he was fit to do so. His journey home by sea effected a miraculous cure, and he unofficially assumed command a month before war broke out. He nearly lost it when mobilization was ordered, as the rules laid down that it should revert to his predecessor, who was still the official commander. Fortunately for all concerned Alan Brooke, his senior at Southern Command, persuaded the War Office to ignore the rules.

It is impossible to understand why the British army was so much less well prepared to fight the German army on the Continent in 1939 than it had been in 1914, unless one realizes that the Government's policy, up until almost the last moment, had been that it should not do so. After Hitler had defied the verdict of Versailles and marched into the Rhineland in March 1936, while Britain and France did nothing, there was talk of providing an expeditionary force of two infantry divisions, which would be sent to Belgium as a reserve to bolster the resolution of its army and thereby prevent the Germans from occupying Belgian airfields. But Belgium's subsequent declaration of neutrality in that year put paid to the plan. The Francophile Duff Cooper[3], then Secretary of State for War, pressed his colleagues in Baldwin's Cabinet to agree to the provision of full war equipment for five regular (four infantry and one mobile) and 12 Territorial Army divisions; but this was hotly contested by Neville Chamberlain, Chancellor of the Exchequer, who, supported by the Cabinet, would not even consider a modified proposal to equip five regular and four Territorial divisions, the remaining eight of the latter to be equipped after mobilization.

In May 1937 Chamberlain succeeded Baldwin as Prime Minister and appointed the 44-year-old dynamic Liberal Jew, Leslie Hore-Belisha, as Secretary of State for War. Duff Cooper's appreciation of the politico-military realities of the European scene had been sounder and more realistic than that of his colleagues, as befitted a historian; but he was by nature indolent and indecisive. Hore-Belisha was his opposite in almost every respect: full of energy, brash and determined to bring the army up to date. In a short period he did an immense amount for it. He built new and much better barracks; he improved conditions of service, at last introducing professionalism into the army's cooking and feeding arrangements; he improved pay; introduced clothing more appropriate

[3] Later Viscount Norwich.

both to the daily and the fighting tasks of the soldier; and, generally, created an impression that the dead hand of tradition was being swept away and the army brought into the twentieth century. Recruitment improved dramatically, but it was too much to expect that such a radical new look would not meet opposition. By the conservative, Hore-Belisha was regarded as a bounder, and he antagonized the top brass of the War Office, not so much by promoting younger and promising generals, like Gort and Wavell, to replace the Old Guard, but by introducing Liddell Hart into the War Office as his personal adviser.

The combination of Hore-Belisha and Liddell Hart did nothing to clarify the army's task, as Liddell Hart was a firm opponent of a major Continental commitment. His suggestion was the formation of an Imperial Strategic Reserve of four regular and two Territorial armoured divisions and eight regular and eight Territorial slimmed-down infantry divisions. Nor was there any support for a Continental commitment from Inskip, who had been appointed Minister for Coordination of Defence in 1936. A Cabinet meeting in December 1937 nearly abolished consideration of such a commitment on the grounds that the French had completed the Maginot Line and it would not therefore be needed. The priorities laid down for defence were, first, the security of the United Kingdom, especially from air attack; second, the protection of imperial communications; third, defence of British imperial possessions; and, finally, 'cooperation in defence of territories of any allies Britain might have in war'. Money was not to be spent on providing for the last, if it prejudiced the other three. Liddell Hart, in common with almost all the politicians and many of the military, was obsessed by the fear that an army commitment to cooperate with France would mean that Britain would be dragged by them into an offensive similar to those of 1915-18. If anything was to be sent, Liddell Hart suggested that two armoured divisions would be the best contribution Britain could make, as the French had plenty of infantry divisions. The immediate effect of the Cabinet's priorities was to establish a large demand on the army to man anti-aircraft guns and searchlights for the air defence of Great Britain.

In spite of the Cabinet's decision, talks with the French began in May 1938 and continued up to and beyond the Munich crisis in September. The army's representatives were rigidly restricted to discussing the embarkation and installation of up to two divisions within 16 days of the outbreak of war, but with no promise that they would actually be sent. Not surprisingly, this did not impress the French. Although the result of Munich was to remove the threat of 35 Czechoslovak divisions from Germany's eastern flank, the conclusion was not drawn that France would now need a larger British army contribution. At the time of the crisis the Chiefs-of-Staff had emphasized that the first priority for the army was to secure 'the home base'; it was thought that the army, as well as manning anti-aircraft defences, would be needed to maintain order in the aftermath of heavy German air attacks, while the next priority would be to ensure the security of Egypt and the Middle East against possible threats from Italy and Japan.

Returning from a visit to Paris in November, Chamberlain is said to have remarked that, as the British army was so small, it was hardly worth worrying about whether it was ready to go to war or not. Discussions were still based on the provision of two divisions within 16 days. The General Staff, now headed by Gort, took the more realistic view that, once the army was committed to the support of France, the liability could not remain limited, and began to press for authority and finance to equip four regular infantry and one mobile division, and as many of the 12 Territorial divisions as possible, for war on the Continent. The Chief of the Air Staff, Newall, strongly opposed it. He did not believe that, even with a British contribution, the Low Countries could be held, and thought that equipping the Territorial Army divisions for war would lead to 'the unlimited expansion of land warfare'. But the First Sea Lord, Backhouse, swung to the support of the army, concerned at the possibility of German occupation of the Channel ports. The French continued to press for a concrete demonstration of British support (conscription being the only one that they recognized as meaningful), and the Foreign Office became anxious that, unless something were done to meet her demands, France might opt for a settlement with Germany at British expense. The whole weight of the German armed forces, particularly that of the dreaded Luftwaffe, the capability of which was grossly exaggerated – by Winston Churchill among others – could then be directed at Britain.

Early in 1939 the Chiefs-of-Staff supported the army's demand, Hore-Belisha's fall-back position being that, of the Territorial divisions, other than the five anti-aircraft, four should be fully equipped for war and the remainder provided with full training equipment at a cost of £82 million. Chamberlain and his Chancellor of the Exchequer, Simon, opposed it; but on 22 February the Cabinet agreed to full equipment and reserves for the five regular divisions and war equipment for four Territorial, but stipulated that the second contingent of the Field Force (one mobile and two infantry divisions) need not arrive in France until 40 to 60 days after mobilization and the four Territorial not until four to six months after it. Conscription was rejected, as was Hore-Belisha's request for the establishment of a Ministry of Supply to organize procurement.

Three weeks later Hitler occupied Prague and absorbed Slovakia. This had a dramatic effect on Chamberlain's attitude. Suddenly he went from one extreme to the other. At the end of March, without consultation with the Chiefs-of-Staff, he announced a hundred per cent increase in the Territorial Army and, three days later, 31 March, a guarantee of the defence of Poland, followed a week later by further guarantees to Romania and Greece. Both announcements were meaningless. Nothing effective could be done about either, and they certainly did not have the desired politico-military effect of deterring Hitler. On 3 April the latter told his generals to start planning to attack Poland in September. The Chiefs-of-Staff had opposed the guarantees. As in the case of Czechoslovakia, there was nothing effective that Britain could do, unless France was prepared to launch an offensive, which she had not the slightest intention of doing. The guarantees left the decision as to peace or war in the hands of governments over whom Britain had no control and little influence. Only if Russia could be associated with them, would they make military sense, and the Conservative Chamberlain and Halifax, his Foreign Secretary, were firmly opposed to that. Inskip's successor, Chatfield, in reporting the views of the Chiefs-of-Staff to the Cabinet, significantly distorted them. He reported that they were in favour of fighting with Poland as an ally, rather than seeing her defeated without a fight.

The French continued to press for conscription, to which the Trades Union Congress was strongly opposed. However, it was introduced on 20 April, largely because it was impossible to provide an effective anti-aircraft defence without it, and staff talks with the French were resumed. They were still based on only two infantry divisions being despatched to reach their assembly areas within a month of mobilization, the third to embark after three months, the fourth, the mobile division and the Territorial divisions even later. It was assumed that the neutrality of Belgium and Holland would be respected, and, as the French had no intention of launching an offensive against the German Siegfried Line, reliance was placed on forming an eastern front, based on Poland, Romania, Greece and Turkey, and the possibility considered of an offensive against Italy and her colony of Libya. It was made clear to the Poles that they could expect no direct help – even air attacks on Germany were ruled out for fear of retaliation. Ironside, C.-in-C. at Gibraltar, assuming that he would command what was known as the Field Force, urged that it should not be sent to France, but to the Middle East. A further bone of contention was its air support. Newall was reluctant to provide any, classing direct air support of land forces as a 'gross misuse of air power'. Gort requested that seven bomber and five fighter squadrons should be provided, but the actual 'Air Component' that accompanied the force to France in September 1939 consisted of two bomber-reconnaissance, six army cooperation and four fighter squadrons, with two flights of light communication aircraft.

On 21 August, 11 days after Montgomery had unofficially assumed command of the 3rd Division and a week before he was confirmed in it, the bombshell exploded in the form of the Soviet-German non-aggression pact, which Ribbentrop signed in Moscow on the 23rd. Two days later, the Anglo-Polish treaty of mutual assistance was signed. On 31 August Hitler gave the order for his troops to cross the Polish frontier next day. Two days after that, Britain and France were at war with Germany.

The British army was in no state to fight the German, and fortunately did not have to do so for some months. In spite of all the hesitations and changes of plan, four infantry divisions, with 160,000 men and 22,000 vehicles, crossed to France without a hitch, and within a month took their place on the left of the French behind the Belgian frontier round Lille. Ironside was disappointed in his hopes of command. He had returned to England confidently expecting it, but Hore-Belisha, no longer on speaking terms with Gort and hardly so with Ironside, wanted above all to get Gort out of the War Office. Dill, commanding the 1st Corps, was the obvious choice for CIGS, but the problem of what to do with Ironside led to the highly inappropriate decision to appoint him CIGS, while Gort took command of the BEF. In that capacity, it was assumed that, with the usual reservations about ultimate responsibility to his own Government, he would be subordinate to General Georges, Commander-in-Chief of the North-East Theatre of Operations. General

Gamelin, the overall Chief-of-Staff, however, insisted that Gort should be directly subordinate to him. In the event, when the Germans attacked in May 1940, Gort received his orders from General Billotte, commanding the First French Army Group under Georges.

Before that onslaught, the army was involved in a short campaign reminiscent of some of Pitt's follies. It originated partly from the desire to help Finland, which had been invaded by Russia in November 1939, partly in an attempt to interfere with the supply of iron ore from Sweden to Germany, and principally from the pressure for Britain and France to do something, in the absence of any operational activity in France. However, Finnish resistance collapsed before help was provided, other than the supply of some aircraft and the despatch of volunteers who could ski. A plan to capture Narvik, the Norwegian terminal of the railway from the Swedish ore mines, and to mine the 'Leads', Norwegian territorial waters between the coast and the string of islands offshore, was forestalled by the German invasion of Denmark and Norway on 9 April 1940. The original plan had been to land troops also at Stavanger, Bergen and Trondheim. In view of the German occupation of southern Norway, it was out of the question to go for the first two. The force to seize Trondheim was enlarged, but operations to capture it and Narvik, both of which had been occupied by the Germans, failed in the face of German air superiority and the general professionalism of her land forces. The attempt to seize Trondheim was abandoned on 2 May, and that to hold Narvik on 7 June, four weeks after the German offensive had been launched in France. The heaviest casualties had been at sea, losses on both sides having been severe, the Royal Navy's aircraft-carrier HMS *Glorious* among them.

On 10 May the 'phoney war' came to an end with Germany's invasion of Holland, Belgium and Luxemburg. Their attitude of strict neutrality had posed grave difficulties for Anglo-French planning. Initially it had been assumed that defence would be based on a prolongation of defences from the northern end of the Maginot Line, which ended west of Longwy, the southern tip of the Ardennes. But a realization that if, in spite of their neutral stance, Belgium and Holland appealed for help, it would be difficult to refuse it, and that, if their cooperation were offered in time, a move forward to align Franco-British forces with theirs would not only make use of their forces but also shorten the line to be defended, led to Gamelin's decision that, if the Germans attacked, his left wing would swing forward into Belgium.

In the best case, it would move forward to the River Dyle; if the situation did not favour this, it would only swing up to the River Scheldt to join with a mythical Belgian redoubt, based on holding that river between Ghent and Antwerp. As part of this plan, General Georges's only reserve, Giraud's Seventh Army, was to move along the coast to support the Dutch and hold the mouth of the Scheldt. Alan Brooke, commanding the 2nd Corps, in which Montgomery commanded the 3rd Division, was not alone in having misgivings about the plan to abandon prepared positions and launch into the unknown at the critical moment. Gort now had nine infantry divisions, a tenth, 51st Highland, having for some curious reason been placed under French command in the Saar sector.

The original German plan had been a repetition of Schlieffen's, the main effort to be by von Bock's Army Group B, driving through Belgium to the Channel ports and then enveloping the Anglo-French left wing; but Hitler was persuaded by von Rundstedt and Manstein to switch priority to Army Group A, which, with seven out of the ten panzer divisions, would gain surprise by penetrating the Ardennes and, by a bold dash for the Channel along the Somme, cut off the British and Belgian armies and the cream of the French, which had been allotted to the northern sector. They would then swing south and isolate the rest. The spearhead of this plan, Guderian's 19th Corps of three panzer divisions, totalling 828 tanks, struck the inferior troops of Corap's Ninth French Army at Sedan on 13 May, and crossed the Meuse without difficulty. Four days later, brushing aside an attempted counter-attack by de Gaulle's light armoured division, he came up against British troops near Peronne on the Somme. On the 19th he swept past Amiens and next day was at Abbeville, near the river's mouth.

While this astounding out-flanking movement had been in train, the BEF had advanced almost without incident to the Dyle, east of Brussels, but had then been forced to withdraw, as the French on their right and the Belgians on their left retreated, the former in an attempt to maintain a continuous front, the latter under attack not only from von Bock's Army Group B, but significantly from the Stukas of the Luftwaffe. Alan Brooke's 2nd Corps, and notably Montgomery's 3rd Division within it, never lost cohesion or control, which was more than could be said for their allies, or even some of the British divisions in Barker's 1st Corps (Dill had returned to Britain as VCIGS, Ironside obviously needing the help of a clearer brain). For fear of air attack, the British line of communications ran back to the ports of north-west France, and Guderian's swift advance had severed the BEF's lifeline. Supplies began to dry up and the general situation was clearly precarious. On 19 May Gort proposed a contingency plan for withdrawal of his force through Dunkirk. He received a rap over the knuckles from Churchill, who had succeeded Chamberlain on 10 May, and was told to cooperate with Gamelin in an attack from north to south to sever Guderian's arteries.

At Arras on 21 May Martel's 50th (Tyne and Tees) Division, with all the available tanks (74), caused Rommel's 7th Panzer Division to pause for a time; but next day Guderian attacked and captured Boulogne, adding Calais on the 23rd. The 73-year-old Weygand had by this time replaced Gamelin, and paused to take stock. French counter-strokes had throughout been ponderous both in preparation and in execution, so that, if they resulted in anything at all, they were too late to affect the situation. Weygand now called for another simultaneous pincer movement from north and south, but Gort had to use what troops he could lay his hands on to plug the gaps in his left flank caused by the collapse of Belgian resistance. In any case the French blow from the south never materialized, and late on 26 May Gort was told by Eden, Churchill's Secretary of State for War, that his first priority was to evacuate to England as much of his force as he could, while Admiral Ramsay organized a vast flotilla of every available craft to transport his men, and Dowding concentrated the effort of the RAF's Fighter Command overhead. Miraculously 200,000 British, 130,000 French and 10,000 other allied soldiers were evacuated, but they left all their equipment behind.

The only British formations then left in France were the unfortunate 51st Highland Division, which, struggling back from the Saar, was surrounded by Rommel at St Valéry near Dieppe on 12 June, and 1st Armoured Division, which had been sent over to Cherbourg at the end of May without its infantry, which had been used to defend Calais and Boulogne. When it was clear, on 14 June, that the French had given up hope, the division, with all remaining British troops in north-western France - 150,000 with 20,000 Poles - was evacuated through Cherbourg. Only three divisions with 500 guns and 200 tanks, most of them light, were available in Britain to face an invasion which, without regard to the practical problems facing the Germans in launching it, Britain anticipated daily. Total British army casualties in the campaign had been 68,111 (4,438 killed, 14,127 wounded and 39,251 taken prisoner). RAF casualties totalled 1,526. French were estimated at 90,000 dead 200,000 wounded and 1,900,000 taken prisoner, while German casualties were 27,000 dead, 111,000 wounded and 18,000 missing.

Hitler's 'junior partner', Benito Mussolini, had waited until he could be sure of the outcome before he decided to jump on the bandwagon, and declared war on 10 June. Plans for the defence of the Mediterranean and Middle East had relied on cooperation with the French. With the collapse of France the security of the area appeared precarious. Wavell, the army Commander-in-Chief in the Middle East, had only 36,000 soldiers in Egypt and Palestine to face vastly superior numbers. The RAF Commander-in-Chief, Longmore, was no better off, and their naval colleague, the redoubtable A.B. Cunningham, also faced very unfavourable numerical and geographical odds, especially in the air. Nevertheless the exiguous force deployed in Egypt's Western Desert, half of an extremely ill-equipped 7th Armoured Division and an infantry brigade, immediately took the offensive and thereafter maintained a moral superiority over the numerically superior opponents under Marshal Graziani in Libya, in spite of having soon to adopt a defensive posture in order to conserve the very limited supplies of every sinew of war – ammunition, spare parts and equipment of all kinds.

The reinforcement of the theatre by Indian, Australian and New Zealand troops aggravated the logistic problem, as they had no reserves of their own. The exhilaration of these early forays across the Libyan border was tempered by the loss of British Somaliland, for which Wavell received from Churchill an ill-tempered comment on the small number of casualties – 260. His reply, saying that 'A big butcher's bill is not necessarily evidence of good tactics', may have laid the seeds of Churchill's later lack of confidence in him. Another cause may have been Wavell's concealment of his plan to take the offensive against the Italian General Berti's Tenth Army, which, with nine divisions, two of them Libyan, had advanced ponderously as far as Sidi-Barrani, 60 miles inside Egypt, in September and settled down there. Wavell had planned the attack, to be carried out by O'Connor's Western Desert Force of two divisions, 7th Armoured and 4th Indian, as a raid to clear the Italians out of Egypt, after which 4th Indian would be switched to the Sudan to strike at the Italian forces under the Duke of Aosta, which were threatening the Sudan from Eritrea. At the same time he planned an advance from Kenya into Italian Somaliland and southern Abyssinia by a force composed of East and West African troops and the 1st South African Division. Churchill did not approve of that either, and would have preferred to let the 250,000 Italians in Abyssinia wither on the vine, while the South Africans joined the Australians and New Zealanders in Egypt. Before any of these operations had started, Mussolini, without consulting Hitler, decided to attack Greece from Albania, which he had occupied in April 1939, thereby introducing another complication into Middle Eastern strategy.

O'Connor's attack at Sidi Barrani on 8 December 1941 was brilliantly successful. In the course of three days, at a cost of only 624 casualties, his forces had captured 38,300 prisoners, 237 guns and 73 tanks, and had driven what was left of the Italian force back behind the Libyan frontier. The victory had to be exploited, but O'Connor was forced to wait while the 6th Australian Division relieved the 4th Indian. The capture of Bardia followed on 2 January (40,000 Italians killed or captured, over 400 guns and 130 tanks taken at a cost of 456 casualties), and that of Tobruk on the 22nd (25,000 prisoners, 208 guns and 87 tanks for 400 casualties). In each case, as at Sidi-Barrani, 7th Armoured Division had moved swiftly forward to isolate the Italian garrison, after which the Australian infantry, supported by the Matilda tanks of the 7th Royal Tank Regiment, attacked the greatly superior Italian force in its fixed defences.

Having reached Tobruk, the logistic support of O'Connor's force was stretched to the limit and the armoured division's tank strength reduced by wear and tear to 40 medium and 80 light tanks. A pause had been decided upon before tackling the more difficult terrain of the Cyrenaican Jebel. A fresh armoured division, the 2nd, was expected to be available in the forward area by 9 February, and O'Connor hoped that, soon after its arrival, he would be able to resume the advance with the aim of capturing Benghazi by the end of the month. But, when signs of Italian withdrawal from the Jebel were detected, the 7th Armoured Division, with such forces as it could muster and support, was despatched 150 miles across the desert to cut the road leading south from Benghazi to Tripolitania. It set off on 4 February, and, by the afternoon of the following day, its leading troops were astride the road west of Antelat, just in time to block the head of the retreating Italian army under General Tellera, to whom Graziani had handed over command,

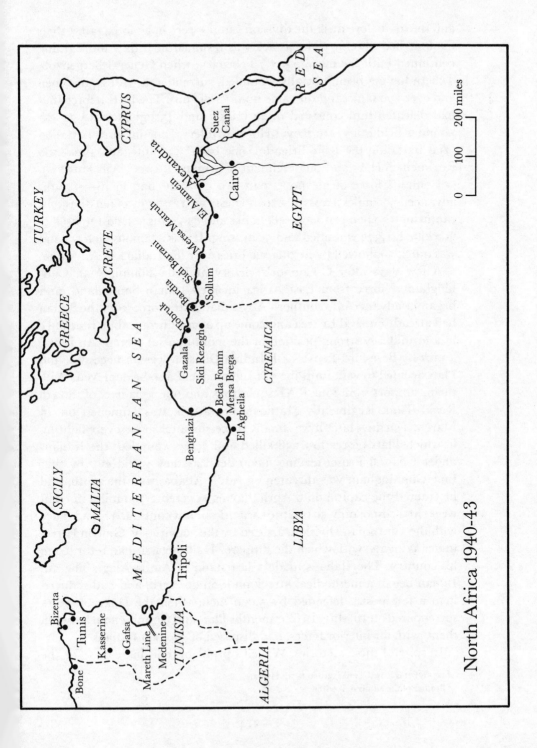

North Africa 1940-43

and shortly before dusk the division's tanks were in action against their flank at Beda Fomm. The attack was resumed next day and fighting continued until the morning of 7 February, when General Bergenzoli, Tellera having been mortally wounded, surrendered with 25,000 men and over 100 tanks and the same number of guns. The British force that had defeated him consisted of 22 cruiser and 45 light tanks,[4] 24 25-pounder field guns (4th Royal Horse Artillery), one infantry battalion (2nd Battalion the Rifle Brigade), one battery of anti-tank guns (106 Regiment RHA) and one regiment of armoured cars (11th Hussars). O'Connor's force of no more than two divisions had in two months advanced 500 miles across desert and destroyed an army of ten divisions, capturing 130,000 prisoners, 380 tanks and 845 guns at a cost to itself of 500 killed, 1,373 wounded and 55 missing. It was a famous victory, and was quickly followed by further victories over the Italians in Abyssinia.

A few days after O'Connor's victory at Beda Fomm, Alan Cunningham's[5] force from East Africa invaded Italian Somaliland, and began its advance into southern Abyssinia. Platt's force from the Sudan had already entered Eritrea and come up against firm Italian resistance in a formidably strong position in the mountains at Keren. An initial attack by Beresford-Peirse's 4th Indian Division was unsuccessful, and Platt decided to wait until the 5th Indian could also be deployed. With them, support from four RAF squadrons and one squadron of the 4th Royal Tank Regiment's Matildas, the attack was launched on 15 March. Ten days later it was finally successful after some severe fighting in which Platt's force lost 536 killed and 3,229 wounded, the Italians under General Frusci leaving 3,000 dead as they withdrew. By that time Cunningham was threatening Addis Ababa from the south, and he entered the capital on 6 April, having covered 1,700 miles in eight weeks at a cost of only 501 battle casualties. Platt continued his advance with the 5th Indian Division, assisted by the activities of 'Gideon Force' under Wingate, with which the Emperor Haile Selassie had returned to his country. The Italians made a last stand at Amba Alagi. The 5th Indian began a methodical attack on it on 20 April, and had reduced it to a few posts, defended by 5,000 men, when the Duke of Aosta surrendered on 16 May. In four months Platt and Cunningham between them, with far inferior forces, had disposed of 350,000 Italians.

In spite of these victories, Wavell's problems had increased, for the

[4] 1st and 2nd Royal Tanks, 3rd and 7th Hussars.
[5] Brother of the admiral, Andrew.

Germans had come to the rescue of their allies. On 12 February Rommel had landed at Tripoli with the 5th Light Panzer Division, and it appeared likely that Hitler also intended to pull Mussolini's chestnuts out of the fire in Greece, where his forces were being no more successful than they had been elsewhere. Churchill's eyes were now on Greece and Turkey. With the victory in Cyrenaica, priority was now to be given to help to Greece, although the latter was not too anxious to receive it for fear that it would provoke a German attack. Dill, who had taken over from Ironside as CIGS after the fall of France, and Eden, now Foreign Secretary, visited Wavell and with him flew to Athens to discuss the matter on 22 February, offering active participation in the defence of Greece. Agreement was complicated by uncertainty over the attitude both of Yugoslavia and of Turkey. It was assumed that the Germans would enter Bulgaria without opposition. Agreement was reached that, unless Yugoslavia resisted German aggression, Salonika could not be held, and that the Greek forces in Macedonia and Thrace would be withdrawn to the line of the Aliakmon River, halfway between Salonika and Mount Olympus, where British (in fact mostly Australian and New Zealand) forces would join them. The Regent of Yugoslavia's reply to an inquiry from Eden as to his intentions was equivocal, and Turkey was clearly determined to remain neutral.

On 2 March German forces crossed the Danube, and Bulgaria declared its adherence to the Axis. Eden and Dill arrived in Athens again that afternoon and were horrified to find not only that General Papagos had made no move to adjust the deployment of his forces, but was proposing to hold a more northerly and extensive position. They were faced with the difficult decision of accepting a fundamentally unsound plan or abandoning their new-found ally. By this time Churchill and the Chiefs-of-Staff at home were getting cold feet, and did not put pressure on Eden and Dill. After Papagos had agreed to a compromise proposal, Wavell and Dill accepted that it had a chance of success, and the fateful order was given on 4 March in the full realization that the air situation would be critical and the naval one dependent on it. Planning provided for the arrival of one armoured brigade from 2nd Armoured Division and one New Zealand brigade to reach the Aliakmon Line by the third week of March, and Freyberg's New Zealand Division and one brigade from 6th Australian to be there by the end of the month. The rest of that division and the 7th Australian would follow in the succeeding weeks. It was estimated that two German divisions might reach the line by mid-March and five before the end. Maitland Wilson would be in command of the forces in the Aliakmon Line under Papagos's overall direction. It was a decision that was subsequently severely criticized, as it was by some involved at the time. The easy victories over the Italians against great numerical odds, on land, in the air and at sea, no doubt influenced the Commanders-in-Chief to accept the considerable risks involved, of which the greatest was the near certainty that the force would have to move and operate by sea and land in a situation of severe inferiority in the air, in terrain and waters which accentuated vulnerability to air attack.

On 6 April Germany declared war on Yugoslavia and Greece and delivered a devastating air raid on Belgrade. The Yugoslav army was quickly defeated, opening the route through Monastir into Greece. Wilson's force was not fully concentrated, and he judged that he could not hold the Aliakmon Line. With Papagos's approval, he withdrew to a shorter line north of Mount Olympus. However, just as his troops were beginning to occupy it, news came that the Germans had penetrated the mountains further west, between Wilson's force and the Greek troops facing the Italians in Albania, threatening to turn his left flank. The decision was taken on 14 April to withdraw 100 miles to Thermopylae, just as the New Zealanders were being attacked near Mount Olympus.

Before the withdrawal was complete, Papagos had come to the conclusion that it would be better for Greece if she did not become a battleground between Germany and Britain. Wavell flew to Athens on 19 April and, having been told by the Australian General Blamey that he could not hold Thermopylae for long without greater Greek help, which was clearly not going to be forthcoming, he decided on 21 April to evacuate the whole force, a formidable task for the navy in the face of overwhelming air superiority, the RAF by that time having lost its airfields in Greece. Hard-pressed by German troops, constantly attacked from the air and bewildered at the turn of events, having seen very little fighting, 50,732 men were taken off from various points in the following eight days. Some 10,000 men and 8,000 vehicles were left behind, and two destroyers and four transports were sunk. Half of those evacuated, including the whole of the New Zealand Division, were taken to Crete, which the War Cabinet in London had decided must be held. Wilson had grave doubts about the wisdom of the decision, given the lack of air support, and Freyberg accepted the task with misgiving.

Almost nothing had been done to prepare the island for defence, although arrangements to provide a defended forward base for the navy at Suda Bay had been put in hand in January, but other activities in Wavell's busy command had taken priority.

While greatly concerned with the critical situation in Greece, Wavell had had to face a crisis in Cyrenaica. On 24 March 1941 Rommel had moved his 5th Light (later renamed 21st) Panzer Division up to El Agheila, the border between Tripolitania and Cyrenaica, where he was in contact with the forward patrols of Gambier-Parry's 2nd Armoured Division, which had relieved O'Moore Creagh's 7th. O'Connor, who was not in good health, had taken Wilson's place in command of British Troops in Egypt and had been replaced in Cyrenaica by Neame. Wavell had told him that he did not expect that Rommel would be in a position to take the offensive before May. Meanwhile the Australian divisions, which had originally been earmarked for Cyrenaica, were sent to Greece. However, contrary to the orders of his Italian superior, Gariboldi, Rommel developed an operation intended as a reconnaissance in force into a brilliant combination of Liddell Hart's indirect approach and expanding torrent. Neame lost control and, together with O'Connor, whom Wavell had sent up to hold his hand, was captured by the Germans, as his disorganized force struggled back to Tobruk.

There the rot stopped, but by 11 April Rommel had surrounded the troops of the 9th Australian Division, who stoutly defended it, while a scratch force, found from the 7th Armoured Division, then re-equipping in the Nile delta, was sent up to the frontier at Sollum under Gott. Rommel was reinforced by another panzer division, the 15th, prompting Churchill to take the risk of sending a convoy carrying 295 tanks and 53 Hurricane fighter aircraft through the Mediterranean to reinforce Wavell, 57 tanks and 10 aircraft being lost when the ship carrying them was sunk on passage. Rommel's attacks on the tough Australians in Tobruk made no headway, and he turned his attention to the frontier, where he drove Gott off the escarpment on 26 May, in retaliation for an attack by the latter eleven days previously.

Six days before that, Student's Fliegerkorps XI of 13,000 men, reinforced by 9,000 men from the 5th Mountain Division, had launched an assault by air and sea against Crete. The seaborne forces did not make it, but, after fierce fighting, particularly round Maleme airfield by the 5th New Zealand Brigade, the airborne landings were successful. The Germans enjoyed almost total air superiority, greatly restricting the ability of Freyberg to redeploy his forces, stretched all along the 160-mile north coast of the island, and limiting the possibility of re-inforcement by sea from Egypt. After a week of bitter fighting, in the course of which the Germans suffered heavy casualties, Wavell agreed with Freyberg that a successful outcome was impossible, and gave the order for evacuation. Admiral Cunningham faced a daunting task. The only hope was to try and get most of the 32,000-strong garrison away from the minute port of Sphakia on the precipitous south coast. The result was that 18,000 were rescued, leaving 11,835 behind as prisoners (5,315 British, 3,079 Australians and 2,180 New Zealanders); 1,742 had been killed (797 British, 274 Australians and 671 New Zealanders) and 1,737 wounded (263 British, 507 Australians and 967 New Zealanders) of whom 1,500 were evacuated, some of the remainder avoiding capture and being cared for by British medical personnel, hidden by the Cretans. The cost to the navy was heavy: one aircraft-carrier and three battle-ships damaged, three cruisers and six destroyers sunk, six cruisers and seven destroyers damaged, 1,828 men killed and 183 wounded. The Germans lost 1,990 killed, 2,131 wounded and 1,995 missing.

Problems landed thick and fast on Wavell's plate at this time. Trouble brewed in Iraq, and it appeared that the Vichy French régime in Syria was preparing to grant facilities to the Germans, while Cyprus, although garrisoned by the 50th Division, looked very vulnerable. Wavell was reluctant to get involved either in Iraq or in Syria, but was pushed into it against his will by Churchill, only to find that success was gained at small cost. The arrival of one battalion and six guns from Palestine to reinforce the garrison of the RAF station at Habbaniya, west of Baghdad, which had put up a stout defence against an Iraqi siege, was enough to persuade Rashid Ali, who had seized power, to flee to Iran. Operations against the French in Syria, carried out by the 7th Austral-ian Division with two brigades of its own and one from 4th Indian, under Wilson's overall command, started on 8 June and were success-fully concluded on 12 July with the surrender of General Dentz's force, when Wilson's troops were in the outskirts of Beirut. Casualties on both sides had been light.

By that time attention had swung back to the Libyan front. Churchill expected his bold move of sending tanks through the Mediterranean to have immediate effect. Against his own inclination and the technical advice of his staff, Wavell ordered Beresford-Peirse, now commanding 13 Corps, as Western Desert Force had been renamed, to launch an attack to relieve Tobruk on 15 June with the 4th Indian and 7th Armoured Divisions. The latter had 100 cruiser tanks and the former was supported by 100 Matildas. It failed, heavy losses being inflicted on the tanks by Rommel's anti-tank guns, notably the 88 mm anti-aircraft gun used in that role. Human casualties on both sides were light. This was the final straw for Churchill, who, on 21 June, ordered Wavell to change places with Auchinleck, Commander-in-Chief India, whose eagerness to send troops to Iraq had contrasted favourably, in Churchill's eyes, with Wavell's hesitation. On the following day Hitler launched his offensive against the Soviet Union, thereby totally transforming the strategic picture.

If Churchill thought that in Auchinleck he would have a commander who would bend more easily to pressure for an offensive to relieve Tobruk, he was much mistaken. Summoned to England at the end of July, he stood firm on the view, shared by his fellow Commanders-in-Chief, that it should not be attempted until mid-November at the earliest, by which time he would have been reinforced by two additional brigades of tanks, one of cruisers, the 22nd, and one of Matildas, the 1st. Churchill feared that the delay would merely give the enemy time to build up his strength also, and, perhaps, subdue the fortress of Tobruk before it could be relieved. He was under pressure from the Australian Government, whose troops were shut up there, and Auchinleck was forced to relieve them with Scobie's 70th (late 6th) British Division by sea in September, at a heavy cost to naval and transport shipping. In the same month, Rommel made a sortie across the frontier, hoping, in vain as it proved, to disrupt the preparations of the Eighth Army, which had now been formed and was commanded by Cunningham, whom Auchinleck had preferred to Churchill's choice, Wilson.

Cunningham was to have two corps under his command. One was the 13th, headed by Godwin-Austen, who had commanded the 12th African Division under him after having conducted the withdrawal from British Somaliland. It included Freyberg's New Zealand and Messervy's 4th Indian Divisions, supported by Watkins's 1st Army Tank Brigade. The other was a newly-formed 30th Armoured Corps, to command which Vyvyan Pope was flown from England. He would have Gott's 7th Armoured Division, with three armoured brigades, and Brink's 1st South African Division of two motorized infantry brigades,

22nd Guards Brigade providing a third. Unfortunately Pope and his two principal staff officers were killed when the aircraft in which they were flying to a conference with Cunningham crashed on 5 October. His place was taken by Willoughby Norrie, who was on his way out in command of the 1st Armoured Division.

Excluding light tanks on both sides, Cunningham had 710 – 477 with Norrie, 132 with Watkins and 101 inside Tobruk. Rommel had 174 German tanks and his Italian allies 146. Cunningham's plan was for Norrie to cross the frontier 40 miles south of and outflanking the Italian frontier defences, engage and defeat Rommel's armour and then join hands with Scobie's forces thrusting out of Tobruk. Meanwhile Godwin-Austen would surround the frontier defences, mop them up, and, when Norrie had defeated Rommel's armour, move west to join him and Scobie. Godwin-Austen, and notably Freyberg, did not relish the idea of having only Watkins's slow Matildas with them, fearing that Rommel might deploy all his tanks against them, before he had been defeated by Norrie. The upshot was a compromise, which tied Norrie's strongest brigade to Freyberg's flank and prevented him from moving straight for Tobruk.

In spite of warnings from his Italian allies, Rommel had eyes only for his preparations to attack Tobruk from the east. When Norrie's tanks crossed the frontier at dawn on 18 November, he was taken totally by surprise. Soon both sides were moving their tanks about on the basis of a misleading interpretation of the other's moves; but Rommel's armour, once the Afrika Korps had concentrated, had the better of the argument, notably at Sidi Rezegh on 22 November, at the end of which two of Norrie's brigades had been badly battered and the other thrown into confusion. None of them therefore intervened effectively next day, while Cruewell's Afrika Korps ran rings round them and overran the unfortunate 5th South African Brigade, losing nearly half of his remaining tanks in the process. Rommel was out of touch and, assuming that Norrie had hardly any tanks left, set off next day on a wild dash back to the frontier through the area in which Norrie's forces were dispersed. Cunningham, alarmed at the severe reduction in Norrie's tank strength (which was not in fact as bad as he had been told) had already concluded that he should temporarily abandon the attempt to relieve Tobruk, and reorganize Norrie's corps back on the frontier before trying again. Rommel's 'dash to the wire' confirmed him in this view, but Auchinleck thought differently, as did both Godwin-Austen and Norrie, and he decided to replace Cunningham with Ritchie from his own staff. Ritchie renewed the attempt, using the New Zealand Division to advance west from the frontier defences, which were left to 4th Indian to deal with, while Norrie pulled his tanks together (now reduced to 122 tanks in two brigades) and tried to get the reluctant Pienaar's 1st South African Brigade to join Freyberg. The latter had actually joined hands on 27 November with a thrust by Scobie towards Sidi Rezegh, when Rommel brought his Afrika Korps back into the fray, Norrie's tanks having intercepted them, but then pulled away and let them through. Nor did they succeed, in the following three days, in preventing Rommel from dealing Freyberg such heavy blows that, separated once more from Tobruk, his division withdrew right out of the battlefield area on 1 December.

Undeterred, Ritchie renewed the offensive a week later, using Norrie's corps, reinforced by the 4th Indian Division, on a wide out-flanking move well south of Tobruk. Rommel had suffered heavy losses in infantry and had only 107 tanks left. More significantly, he was running short of both fuel and ammunition, the Royal Navy having sunk 14 and the RAF, operating from Malta, three of the supply ships crossing from Italy. On 7 December he drew his forces away from the Tobruk perimeter and, after a heated meeting two days later with the Italian Generals Bastico and Cavallero, they withdrew from Cyrenaica altogether. By the end of the year he was back at Mersa Brega, from which he had set off in February, abandoning the garrisons on the Egyptian frontier, which were soon forced to surrender. Of the 119,000 men of the Italian and German forces in Cyrenaica on 18 November, 2,300 had been killed (half German, half Italian), 6,100 wounded (mostly German) and 29,900 were missing (two-thirds Italian). British (including Indian, South African and New Zealand) forces had numbered 118,000, of whom 2,900 had been killed, 7,500 wounded and 7,500 were missing. The great majority of the missing on both sides were prisoners of war. It was a victory, but a muddled and messy one.

One of the reasons why the North African victory could not be exploited was that the overall strategic situation had once more been totally changed – by Japan's decision to launch an offensive against the British and Dutch imperial territories in the Far East, combined with one against American naval bases in the Pacific. The series of disastrous defeats which they rapidly inflicted on all three were more than out-balanced in the longer run by bringing the United States immediately and actively into the alliance against the Axis, as Churchill was quick to recognize. There was never any hope of holding Hong Kong with its garrison of five battalions, two British, two Canadian and one Indian, supported by five aircraft. One Japanese division attacked the brigade in the New Territories early on 8 December at the same time as they attacked the American naval base at Pearl Harbor. By the morning of 12 December the mainland had been abandoned. On the night of the 18th the Japanese crossed to the island, and on the afternoon of Christmas Day all was over, the garrison having put up a stiff fight against hopeless odds, suffering 4,500 casualties and inflicting 2,754. Ten thousand were taken prisoner. This humiliation was inevitable, but the total loss of Malaya and Singapore was not. Warnings of Japanese concentrations in southern French Indo-China and the South China Sea had been received in November by Air Chief-Marshal Sir Robert Brooke-Popham, who had been appointed Commander-in-Chief in November 1940, his command embracing land and air forces in Burma, Malaya, Singapore and Hong Kong. His main concern was the defence of the large and valuable naval base at Singapore.

General Percival, Brooke-Popham's army subordinate for Malaya and Singapore, had two Indian divisions, the 9th and 11th, and one Australian, the 8th, of only two brigades, commanded by Major-General Gordon Bennett. His task was greatly complicated not only by the need to provide protection for RAF airfields, widely dispersed over northern Malaya, but also by the plan to advance on the outbreak of hostilities into southern Thailand to pre-empt Japanese capture of the Kra Isthmus.

The first landings of Yamashita's Twenty-Fifth Japanese Army took place on 8 December, the day before the *Prince of Wales* and *Repulse* were sunk. Heath's 3rd Corps, responsible for the defence of Malaya, had Murray-Lyon's 11th Indian Division on the west coast and Barstow's 9th, with only two brigades, on the east. Their brigades were widely separated and dependent for supply on two railway lines and one road, vulnerable to attack by the Japanese air force, which immediately established total air superiority as the RAF's few and obsolete aircraft abandoned their forward airfields. Bennett's 8th Australian Division, directly under Percival, was responsible for Johore. Within a week Penang had been abandoned and the threat of being outflanked led to the withdrawal of the already weakened 11th Indian Division to the Perak River near Ipoh by Christmas, two days after which Brooke-Popham was replaced by General Pownall. Both of Heath's divisions withdrew from one position to another, as each was in danger of being out-flanked, the physical and moral state of their ill-trained troops deteriorating with every step back. On 29 December Wavell was appointed Commander-in-Chief of an American, British, Dutch, Australian (ABDA) Command, embracing Burma, South-East Asia as far south as the north coast of Australia, the eastern boundary including Dutch New Guinea and extending as far north as Okinawa. It therefore included the Philippines, where General MacArthur was besieged on the Bataan peninsula in Manila Bay. Wavell had precious little means of influencing events or even of exercising command. He was told that his first priority was to gain general air superiority as early as possible; that Burma and Australia were to be the principal bases from which an eventual counter-offensive would be launched; that he was to hold the Malayan peninsula, Sumatra, Java and North Australia as 'the basic defensive position', and that he was to re-establish communications with and support MacArthur.

On a visit to Malaya on 8 January he decided to withdraw Percival's forces to Johore and, as a precaution against failure, told Percival to prepare the defences of Singapore island, to which the British 18th Division, on its way to the Middle East, was diverted. In spite of a successful action by his Australian troops on 16 January, Bennett was forced to withdraw again, as his flanks were turned, and on the last day of the month his troops were pulled back into Singapore and the causeway demolished. Percival had 85,000 men on the island, a large proportion of whom were administrative troops. Its defence was complicated by the existence of a large number of creeks which prevented lateral movement, so that transfer of men or vehicles from one sector to another involved a journey to the centre of the island. The first problem was to decide whether to hold the perimeter, with troops strung out along the coast, or to occupy lines further back with flanks resting on the creeks. The presence of important installations and reservoirs forward of such a line influenced Percival in deciding to try and defend the perimeter.

On 8 February the Japanese attacked the north-western corner of the island, held by the Australians, and it was not long before they had infiltrated behind the forward positions. Withdrawal to lines linking the heads of creeks meant abandoning the reservoirs on which depended the water supply of the town, which was subject to continuous air attack, and, as the Japanese advanced, to artillery bombardment also. By 13 February the 18th Division had been pushed back from the only remaining reservoir to the edge of the built-up area, water was only expected to last for 24 hours and civil defence, including fire-fighting, had broken down. Having previously demanded that Percival should resist to the last man and round, regardless of the effect on the population, in the hope of gaining time to build up an effective defence based on Sumatra and Java, Churchill relented and Percival was told that, when he was satisfied that his troops were no longer physically capable of inflicting losses on the enemy, he had discretion to cease resistance. He did so on 15 February, by which time the garrison had been reduced to 50,000, of whom 15,000 were Australian, their number bringing the total of men captured by the Japanese since 8 December to 130,000, the prisoners out-numbering their captors. 8,708 men had been killed or wounded and evacuated; the distribution of the total casualty figure was: British 38,496, Indian 67,340, Australian 18,490, local Volunteer forces 14,382. Japanese casualties had numbered 9,824.

Even before Singapore fell, the Japanese Fifteenth Army had invaded southern Burma from Thailand with two divisions. To face them Lieutenant-General Hutton had·four brigades, three Indian and one Burmese, under Major-General Smyth's 17th Indian Division, ordered to defend the Salween River east of Rangoon. In central Burma he had 1st Burma Division with two more Burmese brigades.

The Chinese, under the American General Stilwell, were covering the approaches to the Burma Road, which led from Mandalay into the Chinese province of Yunnan. The Japanese crossed the Burmese frontier on 20 January, and the process which had led to successive withdrawals in Malaya was now repeated in Burma, until Smyth's division, reduced to 4,000 infantry with only 1,400 rifles, was forced back to Rangoon, where it was reinforced by the British 7th Armoured Brigade, sent from the Middle East with two regiments of Stuart tanks. Hutton proposed to withdraw up the Irawaddy, where he had prudently prepared supply depots, but Wavell, who had by then returned to India as Commander-in-Chief on the disbandment of ABDA Command, refused to agree, pinning his hopes on the arrival at Rangoon of the 63rd Brigade from India and Lieutenant-General Sir Harold Alexander to replace Hutton. By the time both had arrived in the first few days of

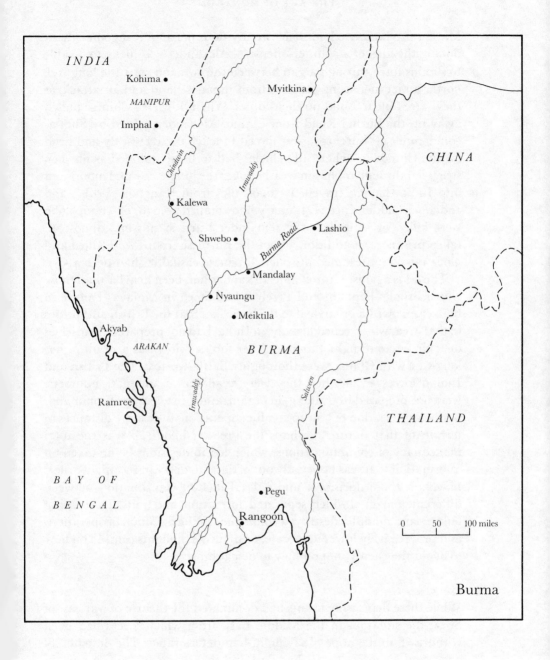

INDIA

Kohima ●

MANIPUR

Myitkina ●

Imphal ●

CHINA

Chindwin

Irrawaddy

Kalewa ●

Burma Road

Shwebo ●

● Lashio

● Mandalay

Nyaungu ●

● Meiktila

Akyab ●

ARAKAN

BURMA

Irrawaddy

Salween

THAILAND

Ramree

BAY OF

BENGAL

● Pegu

Rangoon ●

0   50   100 miles

Burma

March, the Japanese had their two divisions north of Rangoon. Abandoning the idea of a counter-offensive, Alexander was lucky to be able to slip his force through a gap between the two and start the long trek north, under increasing pressure from Japanese land and air attack, as they were able to build up their forces. When Stilwell's Chinese pulled away up the Burma Road from Lashio, Alexander, joined by Slim as commander of 'Burcorps', was forced to leave the Irawaddy and head for the Chindwin, where all vehicles had to be abandoned as his men struggled through monsoon weather over the jungle-covered mountains into India, having travelled 1,000 miles from Rangoon. British and Indian casualties since 20 January had totalled 10,036, of whom 3,670 were killed or wounded, the remainder listed as missing, almost all taken prisoner. In addition 363 of the Burmese troops were killed and 3,064 missing, presumed prisoner. Japanese casualties had been 4,597.

The odds against Hutton and Alexander had been heavier than those which Brooke-Popham and Percival had faced in Malaya. Failure in both cases owed a great deal to the basic fact that the British authorities in that area, which relied heavily on India, had not prepared themselves or their forces to fight Japan and her forces, which, as a result of her long war with China, were thoroughly battle-worthy. The British and Indian forces, even when they were available in adequate numbers, were not prepared in training, in organization, in exercise of command, nor in appreciation of how to conduct operations over large distances in terrain of that nature. Perhaps the greatest handicap was the total inadequacy of communications, which led to decisions being taken on information that was hopelessly out of date; to delay in receipt of orders based on those decisions; and a fatal lack of coordination between different, and often widely separated, formations and units. The ensuing failures and muddles destroyed confidence in the direction of operations and progressively lowered morale, until men's thoughts centred on how to avoid the enemy, not on how to defeat him.

While these depressing events had dominated the theatre of war east of Suez, the situation in the Middle East, from which forces had been withdrawn in the hope of saving it, had deteriorated. The despatch of army and air forces to the Far East and the success of the Germans in Russia persuaded Auchinleck that there was no hope of exploiting Ritchie's victory at the end of 1941. The naval situation in the Mediterranean had deteriorated and Malta was hard pressed, due in no small measure to the transfer of German air forces from the Russian front, where air operations were severely limited in winter. In January 1942, Rommel repeated against the newly-arrived, inexperienced and logistically starved 1st Armoured Division, in the area south of Benghazi, the act he had performed a year earlier in the same area. The play followed the same pattern: only the actors on the British side had changed. The result was a hasty and ill-coordinated withdrawal to a line running south from the south-east corner of the Cyrenaican 'bulge' at Gazala, 40 miles west of Tobruk. There the Eighth Army stayed, while both sides built up their forces with the intention of resuming the offensive against the defences which both were developing, the anti-tank mine taking the place of the barbed-wire of the First World War.

Auchinleck was under strong pressure from Churchill to recapture the Cyrenaican 'bulge' so that air forces, operating from it, could cover ships sailing from Alexandria to beleaguered Malta. Under constant air attack, the island was running short of essential supplies and contributing less and less to the naval and air war against the German and Italian supply-line to Libya. Auchinleck had reservations. He was greatly concerned with the potential German threat to Iraq and Iran from the Caucasus, and with the Japanese threat to India and Australasia, from which so many of his troops came. He would have preferred to remain on the defensive in the desert; but, if forced to take the offensive, did not wish to do so until he had three complete armoured divisions to give him an advantage in tank strength of three to two over Rommel. He gave way to pressure just as it became clear, in May 1942, that Rommel himself was preparing to attack. Offensive plans were cancelled, and, with fewer qualms, Ritchie girded the Eighth Army's loins to meet him.

He had good reasons for confidence. He had 843 tanks, including 167 American Grants with 75 mm guns, to oppose Rommel's 560, 228 of which were Italian. Unfortunately, the layout of Ritchie's army was primarily determined by its suitability as a launching pad for the intended offensive, and was too widely dispersed to be suitable for defence. Rommel's plan of attack was based on poor intelligence and was foolishly over-optimistic. Thanks to ULTRA,[6] there was no surprise about its timing, when he moved forward on 26 May; but his wide turning movement round Ritchie's southern flank during the night,

[6] The codename given to information derived from the interception and decipherment of German radio communications, using the ENIGMA cipher.

although reported, was not accepted as his major thrust until too late, partly because Auchinleck had forecast a breakthrough in the centre. Caught on the wrong foot and never certain where Rommel's forces were, the Eighth Army's reactions were belated and ineffective. After the first 48 hours Rommel's Afrika Korps had lost a third of its tanks, was surrounded and had almost exhausted its fuel and ammunition. However, by pulling in his horns, concentrating his mobile force and driving a way for his supplies through undefended minefields, Rommel regained the initiative. He was still almost surrounded, but all the Eighth Army's attempts to attack him failed. Ritchie's army had just not developed effective tactics of attack, whether by tanks alone, by infantry, or by both in combination. In the desert, infantry were hopelessly vulnerable, whether they were on foot or moving in lorries. The tanks failed to appreciate that the enemy's anti-tank gun was a greater threat than the enemy tanks and that only a carefully orchestrated attack with artillery support could succeed.

The crisis came on 12 and 13 June when, in two days of fighting round the Guards Brigade's position at 'Knightsbridge', the Eighth Army's tank strength, all concentrated under Lumsden (commander of the 1st Armoured Division), fell from 269 to 70, while Rommel was left with about double that number. Two of Ritchie's infantry divisions, 1st South African and 50th, were still sitting in the Gazala Line in imminent danger of isolation. Of the other two, 2nd South African was in Tobruk, which was not well prepared for defence, and 5th Indian's brigades were scattered about the desert in widely separate posts, forming, it was hoped, *points d'appui* around which the armour could manoeuvre to protect the huge supply base at the railhead at Belhamed and the airfields to the east of it.

When the Gazala Line had first been occupied in February, the Middle East Commanders-in-Chief had insisted that Tobruk must not again be invested: the navy could not face the losses involved in supplying it, as they had in 1941. Ritchie had decided to withdraw to the frontier at Capuzzo, and referred to Auchinleck the problem as to whether or not Tobruk should be held, with the risk that it might become invested. Auchinleck was not prepared to face the awkward choice, and told Ritchie to hold a line, based on the western perimeter of Tobruk and El Adem, with the remaining armour on the southern flank. By the time he received this order Ritchie felt it impracticable to counter-order the withdrawal of 1st South African and 50th Divisions to the frontier. He tried to compromise by saying that he was doing his best to hold Auchinleck's line; but he had no confidence that he could do so, and did not exert himself greatly to try. He rested his hopes on the ability of the Tobruk garrison to hold out until he had reorganized on the frontier and resumed the offensive. Both he and Auchinleck under-estimated Rommel's ability to continue attacking. On 17 June Tobruk was invested, and three days later Rommel carried out the attack from the south-east which he had planned eight months before. It was immediately successful, and, after only 24 hours, General Klopper surrendered with 32,220 men, of whom 19,000 were British, 10,720 South African and 2,500 Indian, handing over 2,000 vehicles and 5,000 tons of food. German casualties since 26 May had been 3,360.

When Rommel had started his offensive, it had been intended that, after capturing Tobruk, the Italo–German effort should be switched to attack Malta, before any attempt was made to advance into Egypt; but Rommel's startling success persuaded his superiors to let him drive on. Crossing the frontier on 23 June with only 44 tanks, as Ritchie withdrew to Mersa Matruh, 150 miles inside Egypt, Rommel caught up with him two days later. Auchinleck had ordered Ritchie to hold the small port and, for that purpose, sent Freyberg's New Zealand Division to join 50th and 10th Indian Divisions there, under command of Holmes's 10th Corps Headquarters. Gott's 13th Corps was to operate on the desert flank with all the remaining armour – 159 tanks – under 1st Armoured Division. However, on taking over direct command of Eighth Army from Ritchie on 25 June, Auchinleck decided not to hold a firm position, but to fight a mobile battle between Matruh and El Alamein, reorganizing the infantry divisions into mobile brigade groups in order to do so. The result was to add to the doubt and confusion in the minds of his subordinates. A misunderstanding between Gott and Freyberg was a major factor in contributing to the ease with which Rommel, with only 60 tanks, sent the Eighth Army scurrying back in a state of disorganization to the El Alamein line, which Norrie's 30th Corps had been organizing, based on the position held by the 1st South African Division astride the coast road at El Alamein itself.

Rommel drove his men on and launched his first attack on the position on 1 July. He was held, and, as reinforcements were brought into play, Auchinleck carried out a series of attacks to try and drive Rommel back. On several occasions he nearly succeeded, but the operations were hastily prepared and ill-coordinated, and at the end of the month he reluctantly accepted that a pause was needed to reorganize the Eighth Army and prepare methodically for a resumption of the offensive in a more ordered fashion, even though it meant giving Rommel the opportunity to do the same. Since November 1941 army casualties in battle had totalled 102,600;[7] the Eighth Army's strength averaged 100,000, which rose to 126,000 at its peak in May.

By this time Churchill and Alan Brooke, CIGS since he had relieved Dill on Christmas Day 1941, had decided that drastic action was called for, and that the first need was to find a new commander for the Eighth Army. Their first choice, after their arrival in Cairo on 3 August, was Gott. When he was killed, when the aircraft flying him down from the desert was shot down, Brooke had no doubt that Montgomery was the right man. Churchill was persuaded. He had already decided that Alexander should take over as Commander-in-Chief, Auchinleck having been offered and having refused a command formed out of those parts of the Middle East Command east of Suez.

Since returning from Dunkirk with his 3rd Division, Montgomery had commanded two corps in England, the 5th and the 12th, and had then been promoted to South-East Command, which included both of them. His vigorous and uncompromising methods of command, injecting a rigorous degree of realism into training, had made him enemies, as had his habit of disregarding the orders of his superiors, while refusing to tolerate any deviation from his own. But Alan Brooke realized that his virtues as a commander outweighed his faults. On 7 August, when Alexander had been chosen to succeed Auchinleck, Montgomery had been told to take his place in command of the British army to take part in the planned Anglo-American invasion of French North Africa. This was cancelled 24 hours later. On 12 August he reached Cairo, and next day took over command of the Eighth Army. Reviewing the situation with Brigadier de Guingand, an old friend whom he had taken on from Auchinleck as chief-of-staff, he quickly realized that, with one additional division, the 44th, which he knew was available in the Nile delta, the position could be firmly held, and he immediately cancelled contingency plans based on the possibility of failure.

While the Eighth Army had been building up its strength, Rommel's Panzerarmee Afrika had been doing the same, and all the signs pointed to his resuming the offensive in the full moon period at the end of

[7] British 49,000; Australian 2,700; New Zealand 9,500; South African 20,400; Indian 17,300; Free French 1,360; Colonial 540; Polish 480; Czech 100.

August. It was assumed, correctly, that he would attempt a turning movement round the southern flank, which, although covered by mine-fields, was only thinly held. Montgomery's plan was to refuse his left flank and employ what tanks he had (450) in defensive positions, avoiding as far as possible a fluid mobile action. On the night of 30 August Rommel's 203 German and 279 Italian tanks moved forward, and were heavily bombed by the RAF. They were delayed by 7th Armoured Division's defence of the minefields, and two of their best commanders, Nehring of the Afrika Korps and von Bismarck of 21st Panzer Division, were casualties, the former wounded, the latter killed. Rommel's hopes of a swift encirclement of the Eighth Army's left flank were dashed, and his tanks did not come up against the main position at Alam Halfa until late in the day. There they were held in a skilful hour-long battle by Roberts's 22nd Armoured Brigade, detached from Renton's 7th Armoured Division to the command of the recently formed 10th. Next day, 1 September, Rommel tried again, but his troops, having been bombed and shelled all night, seem to have lost heart. Their supplies of fuel were now running low, thanks to successful air and naval action at sea, and Rommel decided to withdraw. Montgomery ordered Horrocks, commanding the 13th Corps in the south, to use Freyberg's New Zealanders, with a brigade from Hughes's 44th Division, to cut off Rommel's retreat by an attack from the north, while 7th Armoured Division, which had few tanks and none of them Grants, harried his southern flank. The attack failed with heavy loss, and Montgomery did not press it, leaving Rommel in possession of the forward minefields and the dominating height of Himeimat. In spite of the failure in exploitation, it was a decisive victory. Rommel's hopes of reaching the Nile had been forever denied. The Eighth Army had been given confidence in itself and its new commander. All doubts were cast aside, and the spirits of even the most cynical of sand-encrusted veterans were raised to new heights.

Montgomery now set about reorganizing and training his army for the tough battle which lay ahead. A major outflanking move was ruled out by the sea at the northern and the Qattara depression at the southern end of the 30-mile stretch of desert that formed the El Alamein Line. It had to be a set-piece battle, reminiscent of those of 1918 in which he had played a prominent part. The new factor was the anti-tank minefield, sown also with anti-personnel mines, and it was the dominating one. Montgomery's first plan envisaged an infantry attack by Leese's 30th Corps, the principal parts played, from right to left, by Morshead's 9th Australian, Wimberley's 51st Highland and Freyberg's 2nd New Zealand Division, which would capture the enemy minefields in one night. Lumsden's 10th Corps, with Briggs's 1st and Gatehouse's 10th Armoured Divisions, the latter with two armoured brigades, would then pass through gaps made in the minefields and, swinging round in an arc southwards, hinged on the New Zealanders, who would return to Lumsden's command, cut Rommel's supply routes and destroy his encircled armour, while the infantry 'crumbled' his static defences. Neither the armoured nor the infantry commanders thought this plan practicable, and Montgomery changed it on 6 October to a less ambitious one. The 30th Corps would destroy the enemy infantry, while the 10th, having passed through the minefields, would hold off the enemy armour, which Rommel would have to commit to attack in order to save his infantry. In the south, the 13th Corps with Harding's 7th Armoured and Hughes's 44th Infantry Division, would attempt to break through the minefields north of Himeimat and, if possible, thrust round Rommel's southern flank. Horrocks was not to incur heavy losses, his principal task being to keep 21st Panzer Division tied down to the south, which an extensive deception plan had been designed to convince the enemy was to be the area of the main attack.

Rommel himself had gone on sick leave on 19 September, handing over command to Stumme, who could see few reasons for optimism in the situation. The build-up of his German and Italian forces had been slight in comparison with that of the Eighth Army; his logistic position was precarious, and the British were masters of the skies. He had 220 German and 318 Italian tanks to face Montgomery's 1,351, of which 631 were Shermans or Grants with the 75 mm gun. The latter's artillery had also been greatly increased. He had 52 medium and 832 field guns, and anti-tank guns totalled 550 2-pounders and 850 of the new, very effective, 6-pounders. His army had 164,000 men to Stumme's little more than 100,000.

Montgomery's artillery bombardment opened at 9.40 pm on 23 October, the infantry and engineers following closely behind it to enter the minefields. All seemed to be going well, but in the later stages, particularly in the Highland Division's sector, which widened as it advanced, some enemy defences held out and caused delays and confusion. The Australians had reached almost all their objectives, but their sector was not one through which the 10th Corps was to move its

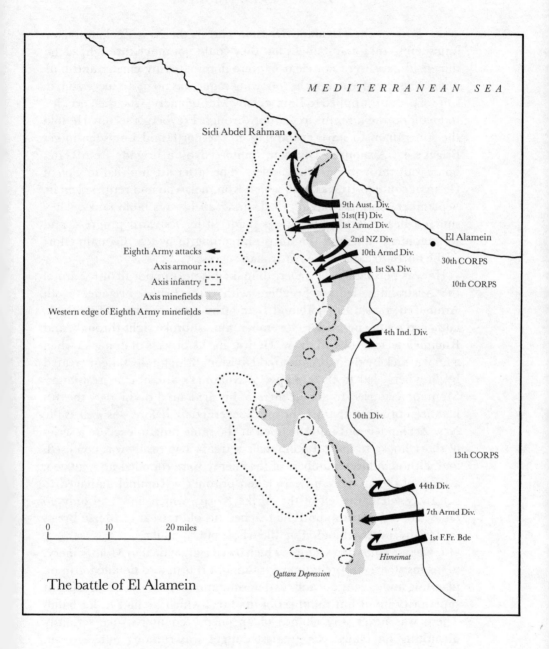

MEDITERRANEAN SEA

Sidi Abdel Rahman •

9th Aust. Div.
51st(H) Div.
1st Armd Div.
2nd NZ Div.
El Alamein
10th Armd Div.
30th CORPS
1st SA Div.

Eighth Army attacks
Axis armour
Axis infantry
Axis minefields
Western edge of Eighth Army minefields

10th CORPS

4th Ind. Div.

50th Div.

13th CORPS

44th Div.

7th Armd Div.

0   10   20 miles

1st F.Fr. Bde

Himeimat

Qattara Depression

The battle of El Alamein

tanks. Both in the Highland Division and in the New Zealand sector Lumsden's tanks maintained that they could not move through, as the minefield gaps were not clear or were dominated by enemy anti-tank guns. A renewed attempt the following night was no more successful, in spite of pressure applied to Lumsden by Montgomery, who then decided to abandon the attempt to get out through Freyberg's sector. He told the Australians to start 'crumbling' in the north and Lumsden to get Briggs's 1st Armoured Division, reinforced by a brigade from Gate-house, out through the Highlanders. The latter attempt led to violent German counter-attacks, into which Rommel, who had returned on 25 September, Stumme having died, flung all his available tanks. They suffered heavy losses, but Briggs made little westward progress, and Montgomery called off the thrust, intending to switch the main effort to the north to exploit the Australian success.

He was persuaded, however, to make his next major thrust south of the Australians, led by Freyberg with three British brigades – 9th Armoured, 151st from 50th and 152nd from 51st Division. This attack, launched on the night of 1 November, almost broke right through, and Rommel decided to withdraw. He was in the process of doing so when a final attack by the 1st Armoured Division, through the salient created by Freyberg, led to the collapse of Rommel's attempts at resistance. Montgomery tried to get all three of his armoured divisions – the 7th had been brought up from the south several days before – as well as the New Zealanders out into the open at the same time to execute a series of short hooks to cut off Rommel's retreat. The result was confused, and, although large numbers of the enemy were rounded up – 30,000, a third of them German, were taken prisoner – Rommel managed to get away what was left of the Afrika Korps, which now had only 20 tanks. He did not stop until he reached his old retreat of Mersa Brega on 15 November, abandoning the whole of Cyrenaica.

It was a resounding victory, which owed a great deal to Montgomery: to his insistence on preliminary training; his firm and detailed grip on planning and execution; and his determination. He enjoyed a significant superiority in all but numbers of infantry, which he had to husband. There was never any chance of an enemy counter-stroke seriously disrupting his plans. His greatest danger was running out of steam before Rommel's forces were finally broken, and he was consistently disappointed in the ability of Lumsden's armoured brigades to exploit the success of Leese's infantry divisions. Although 500 tanks were put out of action in the battle (only 150 destroyed beyond repair), he was still left with more than Rommel had at the start. Rommel lost 450 out of 600; his losses in men killed and wounded were officially listed as 7,800, but were probably considerably higher. Montgomery lost 13,500, 58 per cent of whom were British.

Just as the battle ended, another campaign was launched at the opposite end of the Mediterranean. The Americans had been reluctant to undertake any operation which might divert resources from a landing in France, which would not only be the first step in its liberation, but would also take pressure off the Soviet Union. They feared that, if Russia's allies did not do something active to help her, she might give up the struggle. Britain and America alone would not then be able to liberate Europe. However, rather than do nothing until the summer of 1943, the earliest time that a cross-Channel operation could possibly be launched, President Roosevelt agreed to an Anglo-American invasion of French North Africa, commanded by General Eisenhower.

On 8 November 1942 American forces landed at Casablanca and Oran and an Anglo-American force of three brigades, one from the British 78th and two from the American 34th Division, under command of the British Lieutenant-General Anderson, landed at Algiers, a second brigade from the 78th landing unopposed two days later at Bougie, 100 miles further east. On 12 November the British 1st Parachute Battalion captured the airfield at Bone, another 150 miles nearer Tunis, which, with Bizerta, was Anderson's objective. There was some sporadic resistance from the French, which ceased on 10 November on the orders of Admiral Darlan, who happened to be in Algiers. But the Germans reacted swiftly, their first troops arriving by air at the Vichy French airfields near Tunis on 9 November. Nehring, recovered from his Alam Halfa wounds, took command the day before the first contact was made with British soldiers of Anderson's First Army at Djebel Abiod, 50 miles west of Tunis. For the rest of the month it was a race between the two sides to build up their strength against each other and neither side gained much ground.

A major effort to break through to Tunis was made in torrential rain on 22 December by Allfrey's 5th Corps (6th Armoured and 78th Infantry Divisions) round Tebourba. It was initially successful, but the ground gained was lost to a strong German counter-attack, and Eisenhower's forces, as the Americans from Oran and Casablanca arrived, extended the front southwards over 200 miles to Gafsa near the Libyan frontier. By early February 1943 they had been organized into three corps: Allfrey's 5th in the north, to which 46th Division, 1st Guards Brigade and 25th Army Tank Brigade, with the new Churchill infantry support tank, had been added; a French 19th Corps, formed from French troops that had been under Vichy command in Algeria and Morocco, in the centre; and Fredendall's 2nd US Corps in the south. The situation was changed for both sides in February, as Montgomery drove Rommel back until the latter's forces joined those which von Arnim was now commanding, known as the Fifth Panzerarmee, in Tunisia.

Montgomery had taken no chances on the long pursuit from El Alamein. Rommel's first stop had been at Mersa Brega. Montgomery attacked him there on 13 December with the Highland and New Zealand Divisions and 7th Armoured. When threatened with encirclement, Rommel withdrew 200 miles to Buerat. Montgomery planned a major build-up against him there, but, when a storm at Benghazi early in January upset that plan, he launched the same three divisions against the Buerat position on 14 January. 7th Armoured and New Zealand Divisions' outflanking move over rocky and hilly desert forced a further withdrawal, Rommel abandoning Tripoli, which the Eighth Army entered on 23 January, 7th Armoured following Rommel up to the Tunisian frontier.

There was now a clear need to coordinate the actions of the First and Eighth Armies. Anderson's relations with his American and French subordinates were strained. As a solution to both problems, Alexander was transferred from Cairo to form 18th Army Group and command all Eisenhower's land forces. Before he arrived on 18 February, Rommel and von Arnim launched strong attacks on Fredendall's corps, capturing Gafsa and throwing the Americans back in confusion from the Kasserine Pass on the 19th. Rommel could not exploit his success, as the 7th Armoured Division had that day reached Medenine, 50 miles inside Tunisia and 20 from the Mareth Line, which the French had built to face the Italians in Libya. He planned to give Montgomery a bloody nose, which would keep the Eighth Army away until von Arnim, who was placed under his command on 23 February, had dealt with Anderson. Von Arnim started first at the end of the month with a strong thrust south-west of Tunis against 46th and 78th Divisions, the fiercest battle round Beja seeing the first use of the huge Tiger tank in North

Africa. But the Germans suffered heavily, and made no progress. ULTRA gave Montgomery warning of Rommel's intention to attack Medenine, and he took advantage of it to move Freyberg's New Zealanders up to join Erskine's[8] 7th Armoured in Leese's 30th Corps. When Rommel attacked with 141 tanks in three panzer divisions on 6 March against Leese's 300, supported by 460 anti-tank guns, including a few of the powerful 17-pounders, and 350 field and medium guns, he lost 52 tanks and did not gain a yard. It was Rommel's nose that was left bloody, and, while he left Africa for good, handing over to von Arnim, Montgomery proceeded with his plan to attack the Mareth Line.

It was not an imaginative one. The main thrust was to be a frontal assault near the coast by the 50th Division, supported by the 4th Indian. This was preceded by an expensive and unsuccessful attack by the 200th Guards Brigade in the centre. Freyberg meanwhile was to be slipped through the hills round the southern flank, in the hope of cutting off the enemy as they withdrew to the strong natural position behind Wadi Akarit. Two armoured divisions, 1st and 7th, were given no major part to play. The main attack was launched on 21 March and soon ran into severe difficulties. Montgomery saw that nothing was to be gained by reinforcing 50th Division's failure by flinging the Indians in, and switched his effort to reinforce Freyberg with Briggs's 1st Armoured Division, for which no previous preparation had been made. Assisted by an imaginative air support plan, devised jointly by de Guingand and Broadhurst, commander of the Desert Air Force, this succeeded in forcing the enemy's withdrawal, but did not cut them off.

Montgomery was then faced with another set-piece battle to force them off the Akarit position, which could not be outflanked, with the sea on one side and a salt marsh on the other. There was no alternative to a direct frontal assault on this naturally strong position by three infantry divisions under Leese's 30th Corps – 4th Indian, 50th and 51st – after which Horrocks would pass the 1st Armoured and New Zealand Divisions through. A brilliant attack by Tuker's 4th Indian on the moonless night of 5 April against the hills dominating the centre of the position was the forerunner of tough infantry fighting by all three divisions. On 6 April it appeared to have created a gap through which the tanks could be passed, but attempts to do so were brought to a halt by a handful of 88 mm guns. A massive concentration of air and artillery bombardment to destroy these next day was found to have been un-

[8] He had succeeded Harding, when the latter had been wounded in the approach to Tripoli.

necessary, as the enemy had slipped away during the night, over 5,000 Italians having surrendered. Alexander had already planned a stroke to cut the enemy off further north by a thrust eastwards from the hills west of Fondouk by Crocker's 9th Corps with the British 6th Armoured and 34th US Infantry Divisions, starting on 7 April. It made slow progress, and von Arnim had little difficulty in getting his force back to its final position covering Tunis. To deal with this, Alexander re-organized his forces, transferring the 7th Armoured and 4th Indian Divisions to Anderson, leaving Montgomery with only a holding role on his right flank, and taking Bradley's 2nd US Corps, directed on Bizerta, under his direct command on the left.

A series of toughly fought actions between 22 and 30 April laid the foundations for the final attack on 6 May by 9th Corps, commanded by Horrocks, Crocker having been injured. An assault by the 4th British and 4th Indian Divisions astride the Medjez-el-Bab–Tunis road, preceded by an intense air and artillery bombardment, broke through to release 6th and 7th Armoured Divisions, whose armoured cars entered Tunis next day. Five days later von Arnim surrendered with 100,000 Germans and 90,000 Italian soldiers, bringing the total of prisoners taken in the Tunisian Campaign to 238,000, at a cost of 38,000 British casualties, of whom 6,000 had been killed. The veterans like 7th Armoured and 4th Indian Divisions, who had started from the Nile in 1940, were justified in feeling a great sense of achievement and relief; but for them, as for others, many tough battles lay ahead.

Neither of these divisions took part in the first step in the invasion of what Churchill called 'the soft under-belly of Europe' – the landings in Sicily on 10 July 1943, the largest amphibious operation ever undertaken hitherto. For this, Alexander's 15th Army Group consisted of Patton's Seventh US and Montgomery's Eighth Armies, the latter with four infantry divisions, 5th, 50th, 51st British and 1st Canadian, followed up by 46th and 78th, all supported by three British and one Canadian brigade of tanks. A large number of 1st Airborne Division's glider-borne brigade were dropped into the sea, and others were too dispersed to be effective. The landings on 26 beaches met little opposition. That came later, as the Germans withdrew methodically into the north-east corner of the island, pressed by Montgomery from the south and Patton, who had captured Palermo on 22 July, with greater urgency from the west, while Alexander attempted to settle the competing claims of the two for the few roads available. When Patton entered Messina on 16 August, General Hube had successfully evacuated all his 70,000 German troops to the Italian mainland. Montgomery had lost 9,000 men and over 11,000 had been struck down by malaria, in spite of preventive pills. On 3 September the Eighth Army crossed the straits to the mainland, and began a slow crawl through the mountains of Calabria, demolitions rather than active opposition causing most delay.

Montgomery had not got far when, on 9 September, as Italy announced its withdrawal from the war and 1st Airborne Division, transported by the navy, landed unopposed at Taranto, General Mark Clark's Fifth US Army, one of its corps being McCreery's British 10th, landed at Salerno. McCreery's assaulting troops were 46th and 56th Divisions, and they, as well as their American comrades, soon found themselves in difficulties as General von Vietinghoff rapidly concentrated against them. Intense naval and air bombardment helped to save the day, and the crisis had passed by the time that 7th Armoured Division began to come ashore on 15 September, the day before Montgomery's troops joined hands with Clark's. Von Vietinghoff gradually withdrew, abandoning Naples, to the River Volturno, and, pressed there at the beginning of October, back to the Gustav Line on the Garigliano, exploiting every suitable delaying position and sowing the land liberally with anti-tank and anti-personnel mines and booby-traps. Alexander hoped that the Eighth Army, advancing up the east coast, would break through the Gustav Line on the Sangro, capture Pescara and thus lever von Vietinghoff out of his defences, making a direct assault by the Fifth Army across the Garigliano unnecessary. But a combination of the terrain, the deteriorating weather, and the skill and tenacity of the Germans in defence and delaying operations, made Montgomery's progress slow and costly. By the time he attacked across the Sangro on 22 November, he had eight divisions, of which three were British – 1st, 5th and 78th; but the six German divisions that faced him fought toughly for every hill and river, and he had still not reached Pescara at the end of the year, when Alexander called off further attacks in that area until the spring, transferring several divisions to the Fifth Army. Montgomery handed over to Leese on 30 December and went back to England to plan the invasion of France.

Meanwhile Clark's Fifth Army had been making equally slow progress in forcing the Germans back to the Garigliano, Hawkesworth's

46th and Templer's 56th Divisions having a tough fight in their second and successful attempt to capture Monte Camino. It was not until the middle of January 1944 that the enemy was finally driven back behind the Garigliano and Rapido Rivers. Clark was not going to rest there, but planned to combine a crossing of the rivers on 17 January by McCreery's 10th and Keyes's 2nd US Corps with an amphibious landing at Anzio, 60 miles behind the Gustav Line, by Lucas's 6th US Corps with the 3rd US and 1st British Divisions. These operations were designed to capture Cassino and open up the route to Rome through the Liri valley. McCreery's two divisions, 5th and 56th, got across the Garigliano, but Keyes's attempts to cross the Rapido, including that of the British 46th Division on his left, failed. Casualties on both corps had been heavy, and Clark switched his effort to Juin's French Corps in the mountains on his right. Tough and skilful fighting by the latter, reinfoced by 2nd US Corps, drove the Germans back to the hills immediately overlooking Cassino by 11 February.

By that time a crisis had arisen at Anzio. The initial landing had met no opposition, but the German reaction was swift and effective. Without affecting the defence of the Gustav Line, reinforcements were sent to seal off Lucas's bridgehead, which had been extended to a depth of 17 miles from Anzio. Attacks increased in intensity from 3 February onwards, two more American divisions and Templer's 56th having been brought in. They continued until the end of the month, when von Mackensen's Fourteenth Army gave up, and the gallant bridgehead garrison settled down to static trench warfare until May. While these attacks had been in progress, a further unsuccessful attempt to capture Cassino had been made. It had been carried out on 15 February by the New Zealanders and Tuker's 4th Indian Division, both under Freyberg's command, after a massive aerial bombardment of the town and the historic monastery which overlooked it, both of which were reduced to rubble. They tried a month later and failed again, after which Alexander decided to bring Leese's Eighth Army headquarters over to the west of the watershed, leaving only Allfrey's 5th Corps to the east.

It was therefore with two armies that Alexander resumed the offensive to clear the Liri valley on 11 May, the main effort, centred on Cassino, to be made by Leese, with New Zealand, Canadian, Indian, Polish and three British divisions (6th Armoured, 4th and 78th). It was, however, Juin's French Moroccans, operating under Clark through the Aurunci mountains south of the Liri valley, who first persuaded Kesselring that

The Italian campaign 1943-45

he must withdraw from the Gustav Line on 18 May. Juin opened the
way for Truscott's 6th Corps to break out from Anzio, and, as he in
turn advanced, resistance in front of Leese weakened. The race for
Rome was on. Clark was determined that the Americans should get
there first. By disregarding Alexander's orders for Truscott to thrust to
Valmontone behind the Germans withdrawing in front of Leese, he

achieved his aim, and his troops entered the city on 4 June, two days before Montogomery's landed in Normandy, while Kesselring withdrew to the Gothic Line in the mountains north of Florence.

The tide which had turned at El Alamein turned later farther east. Operations on the borders of India and Burma were limited to the dry months from November to May, and even then the limitations of overland supply restricted the forces which could be deployed and the effort they could exert. In the winter of 1942 these limitations restricted Wavell to an experiment with one brigade of Wingate's Chindits in long-range penetration in the north of Burma and an attempt to clear the coast of Arakan, culminating in the capture of Akyab island, used as a forward airfield by the Japanese. A remarkable feat of endurance by the Chindits paid no operational dividends, but persuaded Wavell and Wingate that, if repeated on a larger scale in combination with a major offensive, it would. The Arakan offensive failed miserably, following the pattern of previous operations against the Japanese. 1943 saw a transformation. Auchinleck had succeeded Wavell as Commander-in-Chief India in June, and he did much to stimulate improvements of every kind in the Indian army, on which the campaign relied so heavily. American operations in the Pacific were hitting the Japanese, and their army in Burma was almost as much a forgotten one as Slim's Fourteenth Army liked to regard itself. The United States was prepared to devote considerable airlift to operations which would maintain a link with Chiang Kai-shek in southern China, and the appointment of Mountbatten to head a South-East Asia Command, relieving Auchinleck of operational responsibility, was a condition of American cooperation. His appointment and a major emphasis on Wingate's proposals resulted from the Quebec conference in August.

In February 1944, both sides were planning offensives, the Japanese limited ones as a form of defence in Arakan and Manipur. At first it looked as if the previous pattern might be repeated in Arakan, but Slim gave Christison, commanding the 15th Corps, firm orders that Messervy's 7th Indian Division, although its supply-line was cut, must hold out until counter-attacks by other divisions could relieve it. His calm and rugged determination reached down through every level of command. The crisis passed; the Japanese were driven back, and attention switched to Manipur. There Scoones's 4th Corps held forward positions on the Chindwin, supplied by a single road through the mountains from the railhead at Dimapur. Kohima to the west and Imphal to the east were the key points on the road. Mutagudi's Fifteenth Japanese Army launched attacks against these positions on a wide front on 10 March, five days after Wingate's division-sized force had been flown into the area south of Myitkina, 120 miles beyond the Chindwin, where it was expected to force the withdrawal of the Japanese facing Stilwell's Chinese forces. Scoones withdrew his three forward divisions into the plain of Imphal, where, with a month's supplies and a daily airlift of 500 tons, he was prepared to fight indefinitely, as Slim rapidly reinforced Kohima, bringing Christison up from Arakan to take over command of three divisions – 2nd British, 5th and 7th Indian – which he had concentrated there. The Japanese, at the very limits of their supply capability, beat their heads in vain against the stubborn resistance of these two fortresses, nurtured by air supply, and fell back exhausted at the beginning of July, two weeks after the monsoon had broken.

Slim's immediate concern was for the fate of the Chindits. Wingate had been killed in an aircrash, and Stilwell's Chinese were making slow progress southwards. They captured Myitkina in August, and in that month Slim flew the Chindits back to India. Many of them were utterly exhausted and suffering severely from disease. These battles in the summer of 1944 had restored the morale of the Indian army, unaffected by a serious anti-British movement in India itself, and given Slim's soldiers of all races confidence that, once the monsoon rains were over, they could drive the Japanese out of Burma and avenge the earlier humiliations at their hands.

The summer of 1944 was also to see the day of action come at last for all those soldiers in Britain, who had begun to wonder if the repeated training in handling their weapons, in digging holes, acting as sentry, marching up and down dale, would ever be put into practice. Frustration of this kind had been a major impetus to many of the best of them to join the airborne forces: at least there was the danger and excitement of parachute training. On his return to England at the turn of the year, Montgomery had demanded changes in the plan for the invasion of France, prepared by the staff headed by General Morgan for whoever was chosen as Supreme Commander, the post to which Eisenhower was appointed in January. Montgomery's demands were for a widening of the area of assault, a clear separation of American and British sectors, a simplification of command so that one corps did not pass through the beaches and sector of another, and the allocation of all available landing craft to the initial assault. Eisenhower accepted these, and it was on Montgomery's plan that the invasion took place on 6 June 1944 between the south-eastern corner of the Cotentin peninsula, where Bradley's First US Army landed two divisions from the sea and dropped two from the air, and the 25-mile stretch of coast between Bayeux and Caen on which Dempsey's Second British Army landed the 50th British, 3rd Canadian and 3rd British Divisions, and on the left flank of which Gale's 6th Airborne Division was dropped. Each assault division was immediately followed up by a second one, so that each corps had two divisions ashore within 48 hours. In the case of 50th Division, it was their fellow desert veteran, 7th Armoured, the first armoured division ashore. The assault was preceded by massive air and naval bombardment and supported by a variety of amphibious craft, both to give fire support and to clear mines and obstacles on the beaches. These specialist forms of armoured vehicle had been developed and trained by 79th Armoured Division, commanded by Montgomery's brother-in-law, Hobart, resurrected by Churchill from retirement in the ranks of the Home Guard.

In spite of the overwhelming air superiority of the allies Rommel, who, under von Rundstedt's overall command, was responsible for the defence of northern France, moved his panzer divisions rapidly to try and fling Montgomery's troops back to the beaches. They came too slowly to effect that, but they succeeded in giving the 7th Armoured Division a bloody nose at Villers Bocage on 13 June, when Erskine's tanks spearheaded what seemed to be a breakthrough. From then on, it became a slogging match as Montgomery built up his forces inside the bridgehead and gradually extended it by attacking first in one corps sector, then in another. His general plan was to draw Rommel's armour into counter-attacks on his eastern flank, while the Americans, having captured Cherbourg, built up their strength to effect a break-out, which would release Patton's armoured divisions to strike west to Brittany and swing round to envelop Rommel's southern flank. It all took much longer and cost more in terms of casualties than had been anticipated. Montgomery had not expected that the close-in fighting in the restricted terrain of Normandy's bocage country would last so long, and had

A patrol of 9th Hodson's Horse in Mametz village, the Somme, 1916. The machine-gun and barbed wire had now severely restricted the use of cavalry.

Carrier pigeon being released from a tank porthole near Albert, 1918 – the only dependable way of getting information back.

The first official photograph of a tank going into action, the Somme, September 1916. It is armed only with machine-guns; the wire-mesh screen and trailing wheels were soon abandoned.

General (later Field Marshal) Sir Claude
Auchinleck in 1940, by R.G. Eves.

General Sir Archibald (later Field Marshal Earl)
Wavell at Middle East Command, 1940.

A Grant tank moving up before the battle of El Alamein, October 1942. Note 75mm
gun in sponson and 37mm gun in turret. The tank had a crew of six.

After a heavy artillery duel, British troops enter the Italian village of Sparanise, October 1943. The British soldier faced severe problems, military and psychological, in the Italian campaign.

In Italy, December 1943: General Sir Harold (later Field Marshal Earl) Alexander and, in the back seat, General Sir Bernard (later Field Marshal Viscount) Montgomery and General Sir Alan Brooke (later Field Marshal Lord Alanbrooke). Montgomery was the popular hero but Alanbrooke was the real architect of victory.

Lieutenant-General Sir William (later Field Marshal Viscount) Slim in Burma, 1944. The outstanding British commander in the Far East.

Northern Burma, November 1944. The monsoon rains over, Slim begins his advance to drive the Japanese out of Burma. British infantry firing rifle grenade, probably smoke, while a sergeant talks on radio.

6 June 1944. British troops make their first landings on the beaches of Normandy.

Palestine: cars and buses being searched by Royal Irish Fusiliers outside Jerusalem, December 1946.

Field Marshal Sir Gerald Templer, CIGS
1955-8.

Malaya: British infantry on jungle patrol.
Note the variety of weapons carried.

Aden, 1964. A patrol of the Royal Tank Regiment in the mountainous Radfan area, supported by a Beaver of the Army Air Corps.

Northern Ireland: Royal Fusiliers on patrol in Strabane, on the border.

The Falkland Islands 1982: a Gurkha soldier acting as anti-aircraft sentry.

The Falkland Islands 1982: troops were required to carry heavy loads long distances over rough, wet, roadless terrain, the helicopters being reserved for priority loads such as artillery ammunition.

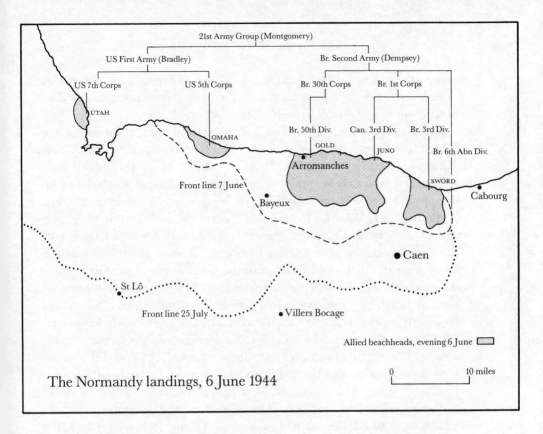

The Normandy landings, 6 June 1944

21st Army Group (Montgomery)

US First Army (Bradley) — Br. Second Army (Dempsey)

US 7th Corps — US 5th Corps — Br. 30th Corps — Br. 1st Corps

Br. 50th Div. — Can. 3rd Div. — Br. 3rd Div. — Br. 6th Abn Div.

UTAH

OMAHA

GOLD

JUNO

SWORD

Arromanches

Front line 7 June

Bayeux

Caen

Cabourg

St Lô

Front line 25 July

Villers Bocage

Allied beachheads, evening 6 June

0   10 miles

envisaged that his armoured divisions would be racing for the Seine and then the Somme at an earlier stage. Casualties mounted, especially among the infantry. The airmen, led by Tedder, had expected more space in which to build airfields, and got tired of being asked to provide massive air support, which did not seem to produce results on the ground. The Americans became critical, although Bradley's troops were no more successful than Dempsey's in breaking through the German crust. Montgomery's attempt to thrust his three British armoured divisions out through a narrow funnel east of Caen on 17 July failed with a loss of 270 tanks, and was a major source of disappointment to him, reinforcing the arguments of his critics.

It was not long, however, before his strategy bore fruit. On 26 July, preceded by yet another massive air bombardment, Bradley's breakout from the Cotentin peninsula began. Four days later his leading troops reached Avranches, and Patton's Third Army broke out into the open, as Bradley handed over the First Army to Collins, assuming command of the 12th Army Group. He remained subject to Montgomery's overall direction until 1 September when Eisenhower assumed overall com-

245

mand of the land forces in addition to being Supreme Commander. A week before, Crerar's First Canadian Army had assumed command of Montgomery's Canadian divisions, grouped in Simonds's 2nd Canadian Corps, and Crocker's 1st British Corps – all the troops east of Caen. Von Kluge, who had succeeded von Rundstedt at the end of June – Rommel had been wounded in an air attack on 17 July, three days before the plot on Hitler's life – now played into Eisenhower's hands by launching a major counter-attack with his Seventh Army to try and cut off Patton. It failed, and Crerar and Patton became the pincers which were to close behind him, Simonds thrusting south towards Falaise and Patton swinging up to Argentan, the outskirts of which he had reached on 13 August. Patton wished to continue north in the hope of delivering the *coup de grâce* without British help, and was furious at being stopped by Bradley north of Argentan, while Simonds, 25 miles away, fought his way south to close the gap finally with Maczek's 1st Polish Armoured Division on 19 August. In those five days many of the German troops managed to escape: estimates vary from 20,000 to 50,000. Fifty thousand surrendered, and the fields and roads were littered with dead – 10,000 at least. The Battle of Normandy was over. Total German casualties were over 300,000. The allies had lost 209,672, of whom 36,976 were killed, the share of these totals falling on British, Canadian and Polish troops being 83,000 and 16,000. Three British armoured divisions (7th, 11th and Guards), eight infantry (3rd, 15th, 43rd, 49th, 50th, 51st, 53rd and 59th) and one airborne (6th) had been involved.

While Dempsey's Second Army swept forward into Belgium, Crerar's had the less exhilarating task of dealing with the Germans left on the coast, principally the Fifteenth Army, which had been held east of the Seine to meet the successful deception of another landing in the Pas de Calais. Montgomery now let success go to his head. He thought that, if he were given priority in fuel supplies, he could thrust across the Rhine and envelop the Ruhr, bringing the war to an end. Although Eisenhower was not prepared to hold Bradley and Patton back to give overall priority to the 21st Army Group, he acquiesced in Montgomery's plan, which made use of the frustrated First Allied Airborne Army. Its two American airborne divisions, 82nd and 101st, had taken part in the initial landings, as had the British 6th. Browning's 1st British Airborne Corps and Urquhart's 1st Division had planned a series of operations between Normandy and Belgium, and seen them cancelled as Dempsey's troops got there first. If they were not employed now, they foresaw disbandment and the use of their troops as normal infantry, if the war went on much longer.

Montgomery's over-optimism and Browning's pressure were important factors leading to Operation *Market Garden*, launched on 17 September to drive a deep, narrow thrust to cross the Maas at Grave, the Waal at Nijmegen and the Rhine at Arnhem. It succeeded in the case of the first two, but a combination of factors led to failure in the third: the presence of stronger German forces there than expected – two panzer divisions recuperating; delay in clearing Nijmegen and joining up from the south; and a plan for 1st Airborne Division's assault which broke all the rules for such an operation by dropping the troops too far away from their objectives. Of Urquhart's 10,000 men, little over 3,000 returned, 1,200 being killed. They had fought gallantly and inflicted 3,000 casualties on the enemy. In spite of the failure at Arnhem itself, the operation had resulted in a major advance; but it was clear that the war was not going to be over in 1944. Arduous fighting on a wide front was in prospect, and logistics was the main problem, with Cherbourg still the only major port in use. Clearance of the Scheldt estuary, so that Antwerp could be used, was essential, and Montgomery had to concentrate Crerar's and Dempsey's efforts on that. It proved a slow process, and was not completed until the end of November, by which time the enemy had been cleared from southern Holland, south of the Maas.

While Montgomery was planning the next stage which would bring him up to the Rhine, the Germans launched a major counter-offensive on 13 December in the Ardennes, which took everybody by surprise, under the command of Model's Army Group B. Its ambitious aim was to split the British from the Americans and cut both off from their base at Antwerp. Sixteen divisions of the Fifth and Sixth Panzer Armies struck the four divisions of 5th and 7th US Corps. Model made good progress towards the Meuse, leaving isolated American garrisons, such as that of Bastogne, behind him. On Christmas Day he was only five miles from the river, but that was as far as he got. Eisenhower had given Montgomery responsibility for the northern flank of the salient, with Hodges's First and Simpson's Ninth US Armies under his command, while Bradley brought Patton's Third up from the south and Dempsey placed Horrocks's 30th Corps as a backstop. These moves, and the action of the air forces as the weather cleared after Christmas, turned the tide, and on 23 January 1945, when the Americans recaptured St Vith, the

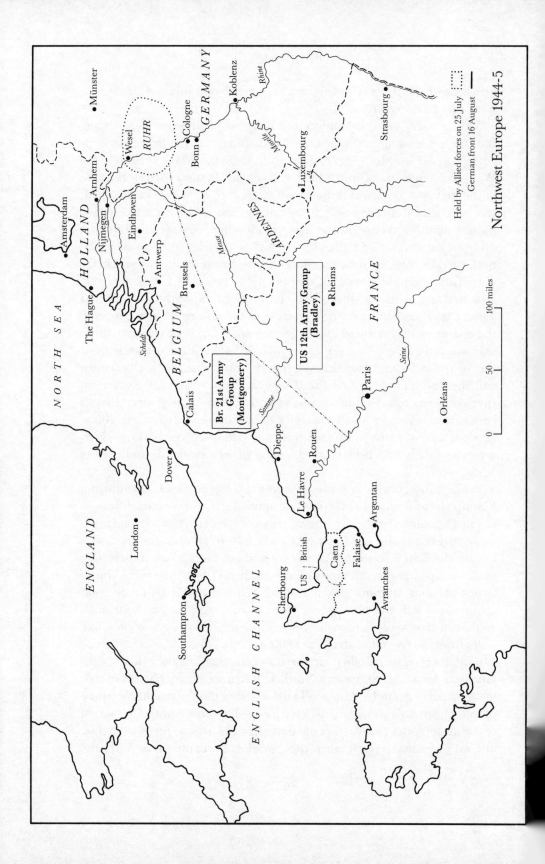

Northwest Europe 1944-5

Held by Allied forces on 25 July
German front 16 August

salient had been eliminated.

Montgomery, whose tactless claim to have been the architect of victory nearly forced Eisenhower to demand his dismissal, was now free to proceed with clearing the area between the Meuse and the Rhine. He planned to do this with an advance by Crerar's First Canadian Army south-east from Nijmegen, between the rivers, while Simpson's Ninth US Army attacked north-eastwards from his position on the Roer. While these operations were in train, Dempsey was planning the crossing of the Rhine which would follow. The first phase of Crerar's attack was carried out by Horrocks's 30th Corps of four British (15th, 43rd, 51st and 53rd) divisions and two Canadian, supported by 1,000 guns, through the Reichswald forest. The weather was foul, the fighting tougher than any since Normandy, and casualties were high. It was not until 23 February that Horrocks was through the forest and the second phase could begin with Simonds's 2nd Canadian Corps taking over the Canadian divisions from Horrocks and adding the British 11th Ar-moured and 43rd Infantry, coming up on the left, while Simpson started his attack from the south. German resistance was stubborn, but they were forced back, and on 10 March blew the Rhine bridge at Wesel. Crerar's operation had incurred 10,000 British and 5,000 Canadian casualties and had inflicted heavy losses on the Germans – 22,000 had been taken prisoner, and it is estimated that the same number had been killed or wounded. The allies were now in Germany, and on 7 March the Americans seized intact a bridge over the Rhine at Remagen, between Bonn and Koblenz. On 23 March Dempsey launched his assault over the river on a 12-mile front north of Wesel, Ritchie's 12th Corps on the right crossing with the 1st Commando Brigade and 15th (Scottish) Division, Horrocks's 30th Corps on the left with the 51st (Highland). Ritchie had one armoured and two infantry divisions, Horrocks one armoured and three infantry to follow up. 6th Airborne Division was dropped on the far side on the morning after the assault crossing. Fighting was initially fierce, but by the time that bridges for heavy vehicles were complete on 26 March, the German withdrawal had started.

The end was clearly in sight: the Russians were only 50 miles east of Berlin and the allied advance north and south of the Ruhr, with com-plete superiority in the air, removed all hope from von Rundstedt of forming a cohesive defence facing west. Delaying actions, at which they were expert, were all that the Germans could achieve. To

Montgomery's intense annoyance, Simpson's Ninth Army was removed from him and he was left with Dempsey's three British corps, Barker's 8th joining the other two, while Crerar liberated Holland. On 16 April the Russians began their long awaited offensive from the Oder, by which time Montgomery's forward troops were over the Weser and driving the remaining German forces north to the coast. Bremen was captured on the 26th, and three days later the first troops were over the Elbe. On 1 May the tanks of the Royal Scots Greys, supporting the 6th Airborne Division, met the Russians at Wismar on the Baltic coast. All fighting ceased at 8 am on 5 May; Montgomery, on behalf of Eisenhower, had received the surrender, at 6.30 pm on 4 May on Luneburg Heath, of all German forces in Holland, north-west Germany and Denmark. He had good reason to be proud of his contribution, as had the soldiers under his command, some having fought all the way from the Nile.

Total British (excluding Canadian and Polish) casualties between the landings in Normandy on 6 June 1944 and VE Day on 8 May 1945 totalled 141,646, of whom 30,276 were killed, 96,672 wounded and 14,698 were missing or taken prisoner – both in total and in each category approximately 5 per cent of all allied casualties in the campaign.

The war had finished three days earlier in Italy, by which time Freyberg's New Zealanders, egged on by Harding, commanding the 13th Corps, had entered Trieste. The armies in Italy had been through a difficult time. Alexander had planned to break through the centre of the Gothic Line to Bologna, hoping to clear Kesselring's forces from the Po valley before the winter of 1944-5. He would then develop a thrust north-eastwards through Llubjana in northern Yugoslavia, heading for Vienna. Whether or not that would have been possible, it was ruled out by the removal of three American and two French divisions to take part in a landing in southern France in August 1944. Close cooperation between Clark and Leese had never been easy, and had been made less so by Clark's behaviour over the capture of Rome. This influenced Alexander to agree to Leese's suggestion that the Eighth Army should be switched back to the Adriatic coast, and make its major effort from there, aimed at Rimini, while Clark advanced astride the main road over the Apennines from Florence to Bologna.

Leese started his attack on 25 August with Foulkes's 1st Canadian, Keightley's 5th British and Anders's 2nd Polish Corps. Keightley had one armoured (1st) and four infantry divisions (4th, 46th, 56th and 4th Indian). Von Vietinghoff's Tenth Army was pushed back from the Gothic Line, but Leese did not break through. Rimini was taken on 20 September, but progress became slower and slower over a seemingly endless series of streams and rivers. Clark's progress through the mountains was also slow, and casualties to both armies were high. Alexander kept up the pressure until the first few days of 1945, by which time Ravenna had been taken and the forward troops of the Eighth Army, now commanded by McCreery,[9] had reached the Senio River, more than halfway from Rimini to Bologna, and the Fifth Army, which included Kirkman's 13th British Corps, was only nine miles south of the city. Both were out of steam, and Alexander called off his offensive until the weather improved. Morale in both armies was wavering. The war was clearly not going to last a great deal longer, but it was not in Italy that it would be won. The motive for sacrifice – that greater effort could bring the end of the war nearer – was not obvious to soldiers in Italy. The fact that pressure there could divert German effort from opposing Eisenhower did not greatly appeal to them. Desertions were running at a high level in both armies, and Alexander had to consider carefully how much he asked of his men. On 12 December he had replaced Wilson[10] as Supreme Commander, Clark taking over 'Allied Armies Italy', as the 15th Army Group had been renamed, and Truscott the Fifth Army.

Alexander resumed his offensive in April, McCreery launching his troops across the Santerno River and Lake Commachio on 8 April, Clark postponing Truscott's attack south of Bologna until the 14th. By then von Vietinghoff's reserves had been drawn to meet the threat posed by the Eighth Army, which at that time incorporated only three British divisions, 56th, 78th and 6th Armoured – the New Zealanders, 8th and 10th Indian and two Polish divisions making up a total of eight. 4th and 46th Divisions had been sent to deal with the critical situation in Greece. On 20 April Truscott cut the main route west of Bologna,

---

[9] Leese had replaced Giffard as Commander Land Forces South-East Asia.

[10] Wilson had replaced Eisenhower in that post in the Mediterranean, and now went to Washington as the British representative on the Combined Chiefs-of-Staff instead of Dill, who had died.

which Anders's Poles entered the next day. Thereafter German resistance quickly collapsed, and a week later, on the day that Mussolini was shot by partisans near Lake Como, von Vietinghoff's delegates came to Alexander's headquarters at Caserta to sue for an armistice.

From start to finish the fighting in Italy, and the conditions under which it took place, were the toughest of any faced by British troops in the Second World War and the nearest to those experienced in the First. The campaign had been fought under constant doubt as to whether it served a useful purpose and the knowledge that it was regarded, even by the British who favoured it most, as a subsidiary theatre of war. But there is little doubt that it served an essential purpose – to draw German effort away from opposition first to a landing in France and, later, to its exploitation. Those who fought there had every reason to be proud of the Italy Star. The casualties of the allies in the Sicilian and Italian campaigns totalled 312,000, of which the British share was 98,907: of them, 20,772 were killed and 64,247 wounded.

In all the rejoicings over Victory in Europe, the sober thought remained that Japan had still to be dealt with. As far as Burma was concerned, however, that had already been accomplished with the occupation of Rangoon on 4 May. Slim had begun his advance as soon as the monsoon period ended in November 1944, Stopford's 33rd Corps closing up to the west bank of the Chindwin at Kalewa, and the 4th Corps, now commanded by Messervy, further north at Sittaung. Slim had originally intended to combine an advance from Kalewa to Mandalay with a major airlifted operation direct to Shwebo, 50 miles to its north-west and nearly 100 miles beyond Kalewa, but the fact that the parachute brigade would not be available to seize airfields until February and the threat of withdrawal of Chinese divisions from the command of Sultan, who had taken Stilwell's place in October, were factors persuading him to move earlier. He directed Messervy to cross the Chindwin and link up with Festing's 36th Division at Pinlebu, 50 miles east of Sittaung, which he did on 15 December. By that time Stopford had built a bridge at Kalewa, and all was set for both corps to head for Mandalay. Resistance was slight, and Slim sensed that the Japanese General Kimura was withdrawing east of the Irawaddy. Ordering Stopford to take command of all the forces making for Mandalay, he switched Messervy, with the 7th and 17th Indian Divisions, southwards, west of the Chindwin to cross the Irawaddy at Nyaungu and head for Meiktila, 60 miles south of Mandalay. Evans's 7th Division crossed the river on 14 February, two days after the 20th Indian, in Stopford's corps, had done the same a short distance west of Mandalay; his 19th was threatening the city from the north. At the same time the 2nd British Division was moving to complete its encirclement. Meiktila fell to Cowan's 17th on 5 March and the assault on Mandalay opened three days later. Its massive Fort Dufferin held out until 20 March. By then the Japanese were counter-attacking at Meiktila, but gave up when the rest of Messervy's corps began to join Cowan and Stopford's leading troops were approaching. Kimura's armies were now only capable of withdrawal, and, when the monsoon broke on 2 May, Slim's leading troops were at Pegu, 50 miles from Rangoon. On that day 26th Division landed south of the city, preceded by a parachute drop by one battalion. This direct assault from sea and air had been made possible by the advance in Arakan by Christison's 15th Corps, which had captured the islands of Akyab on 4 January and Ramree on the 21st. The airfields on both had become fully operational by 20 March and 15 April respectively.

The efforts of Mountbatten's South-East Asia Command were not to cease with the liberation of Burma. His next task was to recapture Singapore and Malaya, and thereafter Churchill intended that Britain should provide five divisions for the invasion of Japan itself. The explosion of the atomic bombs on 6 and 9 August, however, put paid to those ideas, to the great relief of all those soldiers who had been earmarked to take part in those expeditions. The Japanese surrendered to Mountbatten in Singapore on 12 September and to Admiral Harcourt in Hong Kong on the 16th. The Second World War was over.

3,463,000 men and 300,000 women from the United Kingdom had been enlisted into the army, and, at their peaks the numbers serving were 2,766,000 men in 1944 and 207,500 women in 1943. Total casualties numbered 569,501, of whom 144,079 were killed, 239,575 wounded and 152,076 taken prisoner; 33,771 were reported as missing, and all but some 6,000 were later accounted for, mostly as prisoners. Eleven per cent of the casualties and 12 per cent of the prisoners were attributable to the war against Japan.

Compared to the First World War, the number of fighting formations which the British army – that is, excluding Dominion and colonial formations – put into the field was small. Although a total of 48 divisions was raised – 11 armoured, 35 infantry and 2 airborne – a large proportion of these were disbanded, most of them without having left the shores of Britain. At their peak the major campaigns involved the following number of British divisions: France and Belgium 1940 – one armoured and ten infantry; Middle East and Mediterranean – four armoured, eight infantry and one airborne; North-west Europe – three armoured, eight infantry and two airborne; Far East – three infantry. On VE Day, Montgomery's 21st Army Group also included five Canadian and a Polish division, while the American divisions in Bradley's 12th and Devers's 6th Army Groups totalled 72. In the Middle East infantry divisions from the Dominions had always outnumbered the British, and in the Far East the overwhelming majority were Indian. But the British army everywhere provided the essential framework of command, communications, logistics and a high proportion of the supporting arms – tanks, artillery and engineers. There was one British for every three Indian soldiers that served in Burma.

The air war also made great demands on manpower. At its maximum strength Anti-Aircraft Command in Britain absorbed the equivalent of 12 divisions, and the Royal Air Force far more. Even if the manpower could have been found to provide more divisions in the field, the limiting factor would have been the production and maintenance of weapons, vehicles and equipment of every kind for them. As it was, it was only the fact that, until quite a late stage of the war, a large part of the army remained in Britain, not involved in active operations, that it was possible to keep those formations that were active – in the Middle and Far East – supplied and equipped; and for a great deal of its equipment the army depended on supply from across the Atlantic.

Montgomery was the popular hero of the hour, although Alanbrooke was the real architect of victory. He had borne the double burden of directing all the affairs of the army and, as Chairman of the Chiefs-of-Staff Committee, of handling the impetuous and demanding Prime Minister. Slim, although ranking only as an army commander, had been the outstanding soldier in the Far East. Alexander was not of their calibre, but he had managed with skill an awkward multinational team, given the thankless task of drawing the enemy's fire in order to allow others to deliver the *coup de grâce* and gain the laurels. The army could justifiably be proud of its recovery from a bad start to breast the finishing tape after a long and gruelling cross-country race.

If the First World War had been the war of the steam-engine, the Second was that of the internal combustion engine. In the armies of Britain and her allies it had totally replaced horse-power, and in aircraft it had introduced a major new factor in operations. In the early stages of the war, except in the Far East, the tank had appeared to dominate land operations. As the war progressed, however, the anti-tank mine, combined with anti-tank guns effective at considerable ranges, began to play the same sort of part in restricting mobility as barbed-wire entanglements, covered by machine-guns, had in 1914-18, and light, short-range weapons, using hollow-charge warheads, provided another hazard to the armoured vehicle in the later stages. But this combination was only effective when natural features or the strength of the enemy or a combination of both made it possible to form a continuous static defence. Where that was not possible, the tank dominated operations.

By the end of the war the idea that different types of tank were needed for different roles was discredited. The American Sherman tank had satisfactorily fulfilled all of them, except that of reconnaissance, and the British distinction between 'cruiser' and 'infantry support' tanks was to disappear. Also to disappear was the concept that cavalry regiments should perform the 'cruiser' as well as the reconnaissance role, while the Royal Tank Regiment should specialize in infantry support, as well as being employed in the 'cruiser' role, as it had been since the Royal Tank Corps and the mechanized cavalry had been brought together in 1939 in the loose association of the Royal Armoured Corps.

A highly significant development, which had only been in its infancy in the First World War, was that of radio communication. Although it made it easier for the enemy to divine one's intentions, organization and location, it alone made possible the control of mobile operations. Lack of effective radio communication on a wide scale was a major factor in contributing to the army's failures in the early stages.

The application of airpower to the battlefield had been a major factor, more effective against the enemy's rear areas than his forward troops, protected by being dug in or behind armour. It was particularly important in restricting road and rail movement, especially where that was limited to a few routes, and even more effective against shipping.

Airborne forces were another innovation, but one which had much less general effect on the conduct of operations. Occasions suited to their employment occurred only rarely, and their use did not prove as decisive as had been hoped, although it can be argued that the Germans could not have captured Crete without them, and that the employment of the 6th British and 82nd and 101st US Airborne Divisions was essential to the success of the Normandy landing. The potential of air transport for supply, both by landing and by paradrop, and for the movement of infantry and casualties had been amply demonstrated by Slim's campaign in Burma.

The intensity of fire-power that could be produced on the battlefield made infantry attack in daylight, even with the support of the fire-power of tanks, artillery and its own mortars and machine-guns, almost as hazardous as it had been in Haig's day, the anti-personnel mine joining the bullet and the shell-fragment as a killer and maimer of men. Attacks, particularly in open country, tended increasingly to be delivered under the cover of darkness, although that increased the hazard of the mine, and it was not until the closing stages of the war in north-west Europe that the British infantry were sometimes protected in the attack by being carried to their objectives in armoured personnel-carriers, although small numbers, in motorized battalions, had done so in thinly-armoured Bren-gun carriers or scout-cars. German *Panzergrenadiers* had advanced into the attack in them from 1940.

From El Alamein onwards artillery came back into its own. Not only was it available in greater quantity, but battlefields were more concentrated, making it possible for the gunners, in turn, to concentrate their fire. British weakness in numbers of artillery of all kinds, including its new forms, anti-tank and anti-aircraft, had been a severe handicap to the army's forces in the field until then. The varied skills of the Royal Engineers had been in as great a demand as ever, for demolition and construction, the latter including airfields. A new challenge to their skill and courage was the detection and lifting of mines and the disposal of unexploded bombs.

One clear lesson of the war was that, although men could be enlisted or conscripted quickly, particularly with all the Commonwealth to draw on, weapons, vehicles and radio sets could not be produced at the drop of a hat. They had to be ordered, designed, proved, produced, delivered to the battlefield and maintained there in working order. A modern army could not be raised at the last moment by the methods of previous centuries, and, without the support of adequate numbers of modern equipment of all kinds, infantry, however numerous and brave they might be, could achieve little against an enemy who enjoyed that support.

7
THE AGE OF TEMPLER
1945-1982

Gerald Templer was born on 11 September 1898 at Colchester, where his father, a captain in the Royal Irish Fusiliers, was then stationed. The First World War had started when he left Wellington College to enter Sandhurst in December 1915, being commissioned into his father's regiment in the following year. As he was under the age of 19, he had to spend a year in Ireland before he joined their 1st Battalion in France in November 1917, with which he served as a platoon commander for the rest of the war, and later in Persia, Iraq and Egypt. His service in the Middle East then, and as a company commander in Palestine in 1935, gave him an abiding interest in Britain's imperial role. Reluctantly, he was to be much concerned in its dissolution. Chance did not allow him to play as active a part in the Second World War as he had wished.

In 1940 he was on Gort's intelligence staff as a lieutenant-colonel. On return from Dunkirk he commanded in succession a brigade, a division and a corps district in Britain, until frustrated at not seeing active service, he volunteered a reduction in rank to command a division overseas. His chance came when the commander of 56th Division was injured near Capua in October 1943, and he took his place. He led the division in the approach to and the crossing of the Garigliano, and at Anzio. He had just been transferred to the command of the 6th Armoured Division, approaching Florence in July 1944, when he was severely injured by débris from a truck which exploded a mine by the roadside. In the closing stages of the war he joined Montgomery to head the staff at 21st Army Group, concerned with civil affairs in Germany. He imagined that he was in his last appointment at Britain's Eastern Command in 1951, when he was chosen to be High Commissioner and Commander-in-Chief in Malaya, where operations to defeat the Communist rebellion were making little headway.

The struggle, first to re-establish British authority over its empire;

then to deal with challenges to it; and, finally to ensure that its withdrawal took place in an orderly fashion, as far as possible in accordance with the wishes and interests of its inhabitants, was to be the principal activity of the British army in this era. As in previous ages, this imperial role competed with the need to preserve a favourable balance of power in Europe, threatened by the power and presence of Britain's wartime ally, the Soviet Union.

The first challenge had come in Palestine, not, as before the war, from its Arab inhabitants, but from the Jews. Their persecution by Hitler, as well as in countries of Eastern Europe, had inflated the immigrant flow to a level which was hotly opposed by the Arabs of Palestine and surrounding countries. Britain's attempt to limit immigration to a level acceptable to the latter provoked armed Jewish resistance, uniting those Jewish organizations which looked to Britain to help them establish their national homeland and those who wished to drive the British out by terrorist action and leave the Jews to fight the Arabs by themselves. Ben Gurion's Haganah was the army of the former, Begin's Irgun Zvai Leumi of the latter. The British Government could find no compromise solution acceptable to both sides. Anti-terrorist operations were the primary responsibility of the Palestine Police, the army, brought up to a strength of 100,000 in Palestine in 1947, supporting them by cordoning villages or sectors of towns, and helping the police to search them. It was a frustrating task, and there were no regrets among the soldiers when Britain decided to wash its hands of the affair and transfer responsibility for establishing the state of Israel in three different and limited regions of the country to the United Nations. On 15 May 1948 the British army departed, leaving the Jews and Arabs to fight it out, which they had already started to do.

A withdrawal from empire on a much larger scale, fundamentally affecting the British army, had already taken place in India in August 1947. As the last British soldiers left on 28 February 1948, lowering the curtain on so much of the army's history, the Indian army, containing so many of their faithful, loyal and courageous comrades-in-arms, was split in two, Auchinleck presiding over that distasteful task, which Mountbatten, who had succeeded Wavell as Viceroy, had hastened forward.

Attlee's Labour administration, which had brought about these withdrawals, had expected, when it came to power in 1945, that the army would soon be able to return to its traditional basis of voluntary service.

But the burden of imperial responsibility, in spite of the abandonment of Palestine and India, did not significantly diminish, and to it was added concern for the security of Western Europe and, partly in order to ensure the continued participation of the United States in that, a commitment to take part with the Americans, under the banner of the newly created United Nations Organization, in the defence of southern Korea. Attlee's Foreign Secretary, Bevin, was the prime mover in the foundation of the North Atlantic Treaty Organization (NATO) in 1949, following the breakdown of negotiations over the future of Germany, the Soviet Union's attempt to blockade West Berlin, and their instigation of a forceful communist seizure of power in Czechoslovakia. Attlee found himself committed both to the conversion of the British Army of the Rhine (BAOR) from a non-operational occupation force of a strength equivalent to two divisions to an operational army of five, supported by the logistics required for war; and also to the provision of a contribution, which grew to the strength of two brigades, at the other end of the world in Korea, where the withdrawal of the American occupation force in 1949 had encouraged the North Korean Communists, encouraged by Mao Tse-tung's victory over Chiang Kai-shek in China, to invade the South.

The wartime conscription act could not be prolonged indefinitely. In July 1947, therefore, Parliament passed the National Service Act, establishing one year's compulsory service for all fit males aged 18, to be followed by a liability to call-up in emergency for another six years. This would produce a serving army of 305,000. Staff officers in the War Office were busy drawing up plans, under the direction of Montgomery as CIGS, to produce an army on mobilization which resembled in almost every detail that which had stood ready in Britain before the return to France in 1944, relying on this large reserve of men, who had finished their National Service, to fill the ranks. Before Montgomery handed over to Slim in 1948, the period of National Service had been increased to 18 months, the reserve liability being reduced to three and a half years, during which time the reservist would be on the books of a unit in the Territorial Army. This increase did not provide enough men to meet all the army's commitments, and in 1950 it was extended to two years. By 1952 this had produced an army of 442,000, most of the increase going to the infantry, raising the number of battalions to 77, excluding the eight battalions of Gurkhas which had joined the British army when India became independent.

The Korean War was one of the factors affecting the army's manpower needs. When the war broke out in June 1950, Britain's initial contribution was two battalions from Hong Kong, but this was soon raised to a complete infantry brigade with supporting arms, the 27th. It was later expanded to form the major part of the Commonwealth Division, composed of one wholly British brigade, a second which included two Australian battalions and a New Zealand artillery regiment, and a Canadian brigade. Its most notable action was on the Imjin River, where the Gloucestershire Regiment fought a gallant action when surrounded, justifying the cap badge, back and front, which, as the 28th Foot, they had earned at the Battle of Alexandria in 1801. After his brilliant landing at Inchon in September, MacArthur drove the North Koreans back to the Yalu River, provoking the entry of China into the war in October. At the end of November the Chinese attacked and drove MacArthur's forces back to the 38th Parallel. It was in the course of this withdrawal that the action on the Imjin River took place. From January to July 1951, Ridgway, who had succeeded Mac-Arthur in command, tried to force the Chinese back, but made only slight gains at considerable expense. Thereafter the front line was stabilized and remained so, while negotiations continued until the final armistice was signed in July 1953. British casualties were 793 killed and 2,878 wounded and missing. One of the features of the war was the intense interrogation of prisoners by the Chinese and the attempts they made to brainwash them.

The Korean War, however, was not the major demand on army manpower in the Far East. That came from Malaya. In June 1948 a state of emergency had been declared in the Federation of Malay States, where the Malayan Communist Party (MCP)'s Malayan Peoples Anti-Japanese Army, led by Chin Peng, had been clandestinely supported by the British during the Second World War. Its members were almost exclusively Chinese, and exploited the disappointment of their compatriots at seeing their hopes of obtaining equal rights with the Malays dashed. They had been led to believe that Britain would obtain these rights for them. Their disappointment arose from the abandonment by Attlee's Government of its plan for a Malayan Union in the face of Malay opposition. By June 1948 the MCP was causing grave disruption to the economy and had initiated a campaign of terrorism.

The British administration of the Federation had faced serious difficulties in re-establishing its authority. The débâcle of 1941–2 had seriously undermined its prestige. It was totally unprepared to deal with a ruthless terrorist campaign, and its police were inadequate for the task in quantity and quality. When the British army was appealed to, Ritchie, the army Commander-in-Chief in Singapore, was none too keen to help. He saw his principal task as planning to defend the Far East against a major threat of the Second World War type, originating from an alliance between the Soviet Union and China. The French in Indo-China would be in the front line and his meagre forces were in reserve, to be supplemented, when the challenge came, by American, Australian and New Zealand troops. The security of the joint service base at Singapore took priority over the internal security of Malaya. Malcolm MacDonald, Commissioner-General for South-East Asia, took a wider view, persuading Ritchie to give full support to Boucher, commanding the troops in Malaya, which consisted of six Gurkha, two Malay and three British battalions, supported by one British field artillery regiment. By the end of the year he had been reinforced by six more British battalions, three in the 2nd Guards Brigade. It was a break with tradition that, in times of peace, the Guards should serve so far afield.

With this force Boucher proposed to break up the major concentrations of Chin Peng's Malayan Races Liberation Army (MRLA), keep them constantly on the move, and drive them into the jungle, where, he hoped, they would be deprived of material and physical support. His troops would pursue them there and gradually eliminate them, while the police and administration restored order and authority in the settled and cultivated areas. His soldiers were neither sufficiently numerous nor adequately trained and equipped to achieve more than partial success. The police were in an even worse position, and the administration, under the High Commissioner, Gurney, failed to provide a firm and determined grip of the deteriorating situation.

Harding, who replaced Ritchie in July 1949, put new life into the army's support of Boucher. In March 1950 an additional Gurkha brigade was transferred from Hong Kong, followed in July by the 3rd Commando Brigade Royal Marines, Urquhart replacing Boucher at that time. Pressure from MacDonald and Harding led to the appointment in April 1950 of the retired Indian Army Lieutenant-General Briggs as Director of Operations. A distinguished Second World War divisional commander in North Africa and Italy, he had finished his service commanding the troops in Burma before it became independent in 1947. He quickly sized up the situation and produced the Briggs Plan, the basis of which was a methodical campaign to clean up the country, sector by sector, from south to north. Intense activity by the army, combined with severe restrictions on the civil population, would be followed by equally intense efforts by the police and administration to clean up the area and restore life to normal. This demanded a high degree of central control, coordinating all the agencies involved, which the administration failed to provide. Harding, before he handed over to Keightley in May 1951, had recommended that, in order to achieve it, the High Commissioner should be replaced by a general, who would have full powers over the armed forces, the police and the administration. In October two events brought this suggestion to fruition: the death of Gurney in a terrorist ambush and the coming to power in Britain of a Conservative Government, headed by Churchill. Templer was chosen for the post.

Briggs had left two months before Templer arrived in February 1952, but it was his plan that Templer adopted and pursued with a vigour and determination that had hitherto been lacking. He applied it as much to the political and civil field as he did to the operational one. Strongly supported by MacDonald, he set as his political target a multi-racial society, confident in its own ability to run its own affairs, including that of ensuring its security. Operational detail was delegated to Lockhart, who now had 45,000 men in 24 battalions, of whom 25,000 came from Britain. There were 15,000 Gurkhas, and the remainder were Malay, Australian, New Zealand, Fijian and African, one battalion each coming from Nyasaland and Kenya. One of the British battalions was the Special Air Service, resuscitated at Harding's request and incorporating a Rhodesian squadron commanded by its wartime leader, Stirling. By the end of the year the security situation had clearly begun to improve, and significantly so a year later. 1953 had seen the number of incidents drop from 3,727 in the previous year to 1,170, those classified as major from 1,389 to 258. This compared with 2,333 major and 3,749 minor incidents in 1951. The number of terrorists killed remained at the 1000 mark and surrenders had risen to 372, while security force and civilian casualties had fallen to 209 and 143 respectively, from 1951 totals of 1,195 and 1,024 and, in 1952, 664 and 632.

This improvement in the situation led Templer to recommend a return to civil administration, which came about when his deputy,

McGillivray, became High Commissioner in October 1954 and he returned to England. The army continued to keep up the pressure on the terrorists, who by then had been driven into the jungle, while rapid political advances towards independence were made; this was granted on 31 August 1957. By then the number of active terrorists had fallen to some 1,500. In that year they had lost 540, of whom 209 had surrendered, in addition to those who had died unrecorded in the jungle. There were only 40 major and 150 minor incidents, the security forces, which included the police, suffering 44 casualties, of whom only 11 were killed, and civilian casualties attributable to terrorist activity amounting only to 31. Operations continued at a low level for a further three years, by which time Chin Peng and his depleted band had fled over the border into Thailand.

The methods which Briggs had devised, based on close cooperation between armed forces, police and administration, working to a single plan under a Director of Operations, rather than as independent bodies attempting to coordinate their actions with each other, was to be a model for similar situations elsewhere. The first to which it was to be applied was Kenya. There a state of emergency had been declared in October 1952 to deal with the serious situation among the Kikuyu. Jomo Kenyatta's Kenya African Union, agitating for a return of what they claimed to be expropriated tribal land, was gaining increasing support from the Kikuyu, aided and abetted by an atavistic terrorist movement known as Mau Mau, which had recently been responsible for the murder of a distinguished loyal Kikuyu chief. The only troops normally in Kenya were three battalions of the King's African Rifles (KAR), and one of them was serving in Malaya. The colony police did not normally operate in tribal areas, where the maintenance of law and order was left to the tribal police under the authority of the district officers and provincial commissioners. One British battalion was flown to Nairobi to 'show the flag' as the emergency was proclaimed and 183 Mau Mau leaders, including Kenyatta, were arrested and detained.

Lieutenant-General Cameron headed East Africa Command. His responsibilities included Uganda and Tanganyika, from each of which one battalion of the KAR was raised. He was engaged in transferring responsibility for military matters, including command of the KAR battalions, in Nyasaland and Northern Rhodesia to the newly formed Central African Federation. He took the line that military support to the police in Kenya was a local affair which a subordinate could handle.

This was unsatisfactory, and the recently arrived Governor, Baring, pleaded for and obtained the services of a major-general as Director of Operations, to which Hinde was appointed. He arrived in February 1953, just after a body of European settlers, dissatisfied with the ineffectiveness of measures to counter Mau Mau activities, had marched on Government House. Shortly afterwards he was reinforced with a British infantry brigade, the 39th, the five KAR battalions, including one each from Uganda and Tanganyika, forming the 70th Brigade. In June General Erskine arrived as Commander-in-Chief with authority over the RAF as well as the army, and over the police when they were engaged in anti-terrorist operations. At that time the number of active Mau Mau, organized in gangs, based in the forests but operating both in the tribal area and in the adjacent European settled areas, was about 12,000, of whom only 1,200 had firearms, many of them very primitive. Erskine's plan was to clean up the Kikuyu tribal area, extending operations into the adjacent forests as he did so, dealing with the worst affected districts first, and leaving the others largely to the care of the Kikuyu Home Guard, which had reached a strength of 25,000 by the end of the year. Police numbers had also greatly increased – to 21,000 – and the army had been reinforced by another British brigade, the 49th, bringing the total army strength, including the KAR, to 10,000.

Operations were slow to show results. Murders of loyal Kikuyu ran at a high level – 613 killed and 359 wounded by the end of 1953 – while 16 European civilians had been killed and five wounded by the Mau Mau, who themselves had lost 3,064 killed and 1,000 captured. 156,459 suspects had been arrested, of whom 64,000 had been brought to trial. 1954 was to see the turn of the tide. Three events contributed to this. One was the establishment of an effective, small War Cabinet, presided over by the Governor and served by an able civil servant, Mallaby, on loan from the Cabinet Office in London, and a joint civil-military staff. The second was the integration of police and military intelligence staffs under a single head, Prendergast, who had served with the Palestine police. The third was a major operation in April to clean up Nairobi, which was the main source of supplies and information to the Mau Mau. In 1955 Erskine turned his attention to the large forest areas, the Aberdares and Mount Kenya; major operations, involving all available troops, concentrated on one area at a time, new tactics and organizations taking the place of unsophisticated 'sweeps', from which the Mau Mau gangs had little difficulty in escaping.

When Erskine handed over to Lathbury in April 1955, the back of the rebellion had been broken and the Kikuyu population was held under tight control. Most able-bodied males were either in the Kikuyu Home Guard or in detention. The Mau Mau gangs had been reduced to a strength of 5,000, the same number having been accounted for in the previous 12 months. By the end of the year their strength had been reduced to 2,000, 24 out of the 51 principal gang leaders having been killed. Lathbury realized that the pursuit of smaller numbers of hard-core terrorists required more sophisticated methods, and he gave emphasis to the employment of special forces, guided by or consisting of ex-terrorists, who had been persuaded to change sides. In 1956 these methods proved increasingly successful, and the climax came when one of the principal Mau Mau leaders, Dedan Kimathi, was killed on 17 October. In the following month the army was withdrawn from operations, although the emergency was not finally declared at an end until 1960. Casualties in the security forces had been 63 Europeans, 3 Asians and 534 Africans killed, 102 Europeans, 12 Asians and 465 Africans wounded. Civilian casualties at the hands of the Mau Mau had been: Europeans, 32 killed, 26 wounded; Asians, 26 killed, 36 wounded; Africans 1,826 killed, 918 wounded. The Mau Mau themselves had lost 10,527 killed; 2,633 had been captured, 26,625 arrested and 2,714 had surrendered. In addition 50,000 of their supporters had been detained. It had taken 10,000 British and African soldiers, 21,000 police and 25,000 Kikuyu Home Guard four years to defeat a rebellion limited to one tribe, which had no support of any kind from outside and a very limited supply of firearms.

Just as the tide had turned in Kenya, another challenge to Britain's colonial authority broke out in Cyprus, where, on 31 March 1955, Grivas's EOKA[1], agitating for *Enosis* – union with Greece – set off a series of explosions in Nicosia. As in Malaya and Kenya, the colonial administration and the police were not geared to deal with a well-organized terrorist threat, and the army on the island – two infantry battalions, an artillery and an engineer regiment – were only concerned with preparations for the transfer to the island of headquarters and communications from the Suez Canal zone and a garrison to protect them. The garrison was increased in September by two infantry batta-

[1] *Ethniki Organosis Kuprion Agoniston* – National Organization of Cypriot Fighters.

lions from the Suez Canal and two Royal Marine Commandos from Malta. Throughout the summer the situation deteriorated, and Eden's Government – he had succeeded Churchill as Prime Minister on 6 April – decided to apply the solution that had brought success in Malaya: to appoint a senior soldier as Governor with full powers over civil and military alike. Harding, about to hand over to Templer as CIGS, was persuaded to accept the appointment, to which he brought great gifts of energy and enthusiasm, as well as clarity of mind and integrity of character. On arrival in October, he immediately instituted the equivalent of a Briggs Plan, appointing Baker as his chief-of-staff and director of operations, assisted on the civil side by Sinclair of the Colonial Service. Attempts to find a solution by negotiation with Archbishop Makarios met with deadlock, and Harding was reinforced with a British infantry brigade, bringing the army strength on the island up to 12,000.

While EOKA stepped up its activity, adding murders of servicemen off duty to explosions, Harding instituted a series of major operations in the hills from which EOKA gangs operated, one of which involved the search of Kykko monastery, high up on the slopes of Mount Troodos. Grivas himself narrowly escaped capture. January 1956 saw further increases in the garrison, bringing the number of units engaged in operations to 14, organized in four brigades, 50th, 51st, 16th Parachute and 3rd Commando Brigade Royal Marines – a total of 17,000 men. At this stage Harding was concentrating on cleaning up the towns and ensuring that communications between them were secure. When that was done, he would switch effort to the countryside. A further deterioration in the security situation took place when EOKA initiated attacks on Turkish Cypriots serving the administration. Meanwhile Harding continued to negotiate with Makarios, but was given little freedom of action. As soon as agreement on some proposed advance towards self-government seemed near, the Archbishop would introduce a new demand. Suspecting that, if he was not the instigator of trouble, he was at least under the influence of EOKA, the decision was taken to remove him from the island. On 9 March he was arrested and flown with three others to Mombasa, whence he was taken to exile in the Seychelles.

EOKA's reaction was less violent than had been expected, perhaps because the forces available to Grivas consisted only of seven groups, totalling 53 men, in the mountains, and 75 groups of part-time terrorists, totalling 750, armed only with shotguns, in villages. One of the reactions was an attempt on Harding's life by placing a bomb in his bed. (It failed, the time fuze having depended on the maintenance of a more or less constant temperature. EOKA had not bargained on the puritan English opening their bedroom windows at night.) Major operations were restricted by the preparations for operations against Egypt, which culminated in the Suez affair in November. The Royal Marines returned to Malta and the Parachute Brigade was taken off anti-EOKA operations to prepare for it. After Suez, Harding was able to step up operations, and in January 1957 two major EOKA leaders, Drakos and Afxentiou, were killed, their gangs broken up and others, including Georgadjis and Sampson, captured.

Macmillan, who had succeeded Eden as Prime Minister in that month, now put forward constitutional proposals, recommended after an inquiry by Lord Radcliffe, which had been agreed with Turkey. Karamanlis's Greek Government was not prepared to give any undertaking in the absence of Makarios and put pressure on Grivas to announce that EOKA was ready to suspend operations, if the Archbishop were released. Macmillan authorized this, provided that he did not return to Cyprus until agreement on the constitutional proposals had been reached. An offer to EOKA of safe conduct out of the island to men who surrendered met with no response, and Harding continued to hunt them down, although EOKA incidents had ceased and no further operations were undertaken by the army. In the two years since the campaign had started, EOKA had killed 203 people, of whom 78 were British servicemen, 9 British police, 16 British civilians, 12 Cypriot policemen and 4 Turkish civilians. They had set off 1,382 bomb explosions: 51 of their members had been killed, 27 imprisoned and 1,500 detained. Harding left in November, handing over the Governorship to Sir Hugh Foot.[2]

In April 1958 Grivas renewed his activity and a major modification was made in the British Government's proposals. It reduced the requirement for British military facilities after independence to two Sovereign Base Areas and a small number of 'retained sites' outside them, as well as giving greater power to the Greek Cypriots. This was opposed by Turkey and led to inter-communal rioting. Grivas accused Britain of having instigated Turkish opposition and stepped up his activity; but, in August, Menderes, the Turkish Prime Minister, accepted the plan. In September Makarios, supported by Karamanlis, announced that he would accept an independent republic as a substitute for *Enosis*.

[2] Later Lord Caradon.

When his proposals for the former were rejected by Britain and Turkey, Grivas lashed out again, killing two British soldiers' wives in Famagusta. Macmillan decided to go ahead with a conference in London, whatever the views of the Archbishop. In February 1959 the latter reluctantly gave his agreement and returned to Cyprus, received by widely enthusiastic crowds, on 1 March. He and Grivas met eight days later. On 13 March Grivas was flown to Athens by the Greek Air Force, but the troubles of Cyprus were not at an end.

While these colonial campaigns had been in progress, decisions had been taken by the Conservative administrations under, successively, Churchill, Eden and Macmillan, which had far-reaching effects on the army. The first was the promise made by Eden, as Foreign Secretary, that Britain would maintain on the Continent the effective strength of forces then assigned to NATO, that is four divisions and a tactical air force, or whatever the Supreme Allied Commander Europe regarded as having equivalent fighting capacity; and that she would not withdraw these forces against the wishes of a majority of the Brussels Treaty powers. At that time the British Army of the Rhine numbered 80,000. Eden gave this undertaking in order to persuade the French, Dutch and Belgians to accept German rearmament and her membership of NATO. While making this important commitment, the Government was nevertheless greatly concerned at the economic effects of maintaining such large armed forces all over the world and at the prospect of the increasing cost of equipping them, as Second World War stocks evaporated. When Eden succeeded Churchill in 1955, he addressed himself to the problem of how to reduce the burden. As Foreign Secretary he had played a major part in laying the foundation both of the Central Treaty Organization (CENTO), which had its origins in the Baghdad Pact in January 1955 between Iraq and Turkey, and of the South-East Asia Treaty Organization (SEATO), founded in July 1954. Although both could be regarded as adding to Britain's military commitments, Eden saw them in the opposite light – as taking the place of the large purely British military bases and establishments maintained in the Middle and Far East.

The continuance of the former, which housed 85,000 soldiers, was the subject of negotiations with Nasser, who had come to power in Egypt in 1954. The 1936 Anglo-Egyptian Treaty, under which Britain stationed troops in the Suez Canal zone, terminated in 1956. In any case it imposed limits which were far exceeded by the current garrison. The negotiations became entangled both with Nasser's demand for a loan to heighten the Aswan dam on the Nile and with restrictions imposed by Britain, France and the USA on sales of arms to Arab countries, neighbours of Israel, and to Israel herself, with whom the Arabs were technically at war. Agreement had been reached in October 1954 that British troops would be withdrawn within 20 months and that the installations of the base would be preserved as British property by a British civilian organization. Eden had failed to persuade Egypt to join a Middle Eastern alliance, which would, he hoped, have guaranteed Britain's use of the base in emergency. The large army and air force headquarters of Middle East Command would be transferred to Cyprus.

The last troops left at the end of March 1956. Six weeks later Eden told the Chiefs-of-Staff to prepare plans to return. This *volte-face* had been brought about by Nasser's proclamation that he had nationalized the Suez Canal as a means of funding the Aswan dam project, after the USA, followed by Britain, had withdrawn offers to contribute to the project. While various ways of countering Nasser's move were bandied about, including the formation of a Suez Canal Users Association, France and Britain agreed that, if no progress was made in negotiations, they would use military force to occupy the Canal, and even go further and topple Nasser from power. Not surprisingly, there was no contingency plan prepared for such an operation, and it was soon discovered that means of transport and assault by both sea and air were sadly lacking, as was the army's ability to provide the necessary logistic support. It was largely to operate the latter that 23,000 reservists were called up. With the recent withdrawal of 1st and 3rd Divisions from Egypt, there was no shortage of infantry; but the 10th Armoured Division, based in Libya, could not be used, owing to the objections of the country's ruler, King Idris. Shipping to move the few tanks available in England was hard to find. Stockwell's 2nd Corps headquarters was withdrawn from Germany to command the assault, in cooperation with the French General Beaufre, both being subordinate to Keightley, Commander-in-Chief Middle East, in Cyprus.

The original plan had been to land at Alexandria, and thrust an armoured column up the desert road to Cairo, from which columns would make for the Canal at Port Said, Ismailia and Suez. The assault was to be made on 15 September, if Nasser had not by then accepted the Canal Users' Association proposal, and Stockwell assumed that the whole operation would last only eight days. For a number of reasons, partly realization of the limitations imposed by the paucity of amphibious craft, the plan was changed to an assault on Port Said, followed by a swift dash down the length of the Canal. Britain and France had found little support for their idea of the use of force, to which Eisenhower, with a Presidential election looming, was opposed. The French and Israelis were in collusion over the possibility of joint action, and the former drew in the British also. A plan was concocted by which the Israelis would invade Sinai, while Britain and France would pose as peacemakers between Israel and Egypt and occupy the Canal in that guise. 31 October was agreed as D-Day. The Israelis began the operation with a parachute drop on the Mitla Pass, and by the time that the 668 British and 487 French parachutists dropped behind Port Said at dawn on 5 November, Israel had completed the conquest of Sinai. Twenty-four hours later the first Buffalo-tracked amphibians landed with men of 40th and 42nd Royal Marine Commandos. The 45th came ashore by helicopter, the first occasion on which this form of assault had been employed. Next to land – from the sea – were the rest of Butler's 16th Parachute Brigade. Fighting in Port Said was sporadic, and Stockwell planned that Massu's French parachutists should launch a combined air- and canal-borne attack on Ismailia, while Butler broke out of Port Said to join him. But international pressure, principally from the USA, intervened, and a cease-fire was ordered from midnight. It came as a frustrating anti-climax to the 3rd Commando and 16th Parachute Brigades, as it did to the large number of troops earmarked for the operation, who had not even been landed. British casualties were 11 killed and 92 wounded; French, 10 and 33.

The Suez fiasco reinforced the determination of Macmillan, who succeeded Eden as Prime Minister in January 1957, having been in succession Minister for Defence and Chancellor of the Exchequer, to reduce the size and expense of the armed forces and abolish National Service. Major overseas bases were to be done away with and reliance placed on a central strategic reserve, transported by air. The introduction of tactical atomic weapons would make a reduction in other forms of fire-power possible and made it unnecessary to plan for protracted campaigns. Forces raised in the colonies, then numbering 60,000, would be increased. The 1957 Defence White Paper stated that the National Service call-up would end in 1960 and set a target for reduction of all three services from 690,000, of whom 300,000 were national servicemen, to 375,000 (all regular) by the end of 1962. The army's share of this was a subject of fierce argument. Its strength at that time, excluding 6,000 women and 4,000 boys, stood at 373,000, of whom 164,000 were regular, although half of them only on a three-year engagement. Anticipating the eventual abolition of National Service, the War Office had set up a committee to examine the strength that a wholly regular army should have. The answer given was 220,000, but the Army Council decided to lower their sights to 200,000. Macmillan's Defence Minister, Duncan Sandys, did not believe that the army could recruit that number and insisted that it plan on the basis of 165,000 only, a figure which Templer, as CIGS, continued to argue was insufficient to meet the army's worldwide commitments, as was proved to be the case.

Reliance on a central reserve, to be deployed and supplied by air, soon proved an illusion. Commitments in southern Arabia increased, as Nasser fomented Arab opposition to British influence in the Middle East, and air transport proved pitifully inadequate. The few transport aircraft which the RAF possessed had insufficient range and load-carrying capacity. Transport Command's fleet was to improve year by year, but always had to face the difficulty of finding a route to the Indian Ocean which was not subject to diplomatic clearance. The need to have troops immediately available, with the ability to support them in operations, led in practice to the creation of new bases east of Suez, in Kenya, Aden and the Persian Gulf, in the development of a new one in Malaya, and the dispersion of the intended central reserve. This was explained away by referring to troops stationed there as forming part of the overall strategic reserve. The demands on manpower, and the difficulties of regular recruiting as long as conscripts were still serving, led to a further reduction of the BAOR to 55,000 in 1959. There were also financial reasons for this. The government had tried to reduce it to 45,000, but the German Chancellor, Adenauer, backed by the Americans, protested at such a drastic reduction. At the same time the army was allowed 180,000 as the target at which to aim its recruiting. It was not to reach that figure for a long time. By 1965 it had risen to 176,000.

This severe shrinkage in the army forced a major reorganization. In 1951 British infantry battalions had numbered 85. By 1957 they had come down to 77, and were now reduced to 60. The Royal Armoured Corps lost 7 of its 30 regiments, and the Royal Artillery, which had already lost 14 regiments as a result of the disbandment of Anti-Aircraft

Command, lost another 20: the Royal Engineers only four. Wholesale amalgamations took place, involving the disappearance of many famous regimental titles. The Army Council , faced with intense lobbying by regimental colonels and retired officers, stuck to a policy of seniority, determined by the date at which a regiment was raised, amalgamations being influenced by historical links, similar historic roles – e.g. Fusiliers, Light Infantry, Hussars, Lancers – or territorial proximity. Infantry regimental depots were abolished, regiments being 'brigaded' and sharing a depot. The reorganization took five years to complete, and, while it was going on, the army was almost as heavily involved as it had been before Suez.

The political defeat in the Suez operation of the old imperial powers with links in the Middle East had encouraged Arab nationalists, opposed to the sheikly régimes which Britain and France supported. 1957 saw British troops from Aden in action in support of the Sultan of Muscat and Oman to suppress a rebellion, aided by Saudi Arabia, which maintained a claim to the Buraimi Oasis. The rebels occupied a mountain stronghold in a remote desert area, and were defeated in January 1958 in a skilful operation in which the 22nd Special Air Service (SAS) Regiment played a major part, the army having to revert to animal transport with 200 donkeys hastily bought in Somaliland.

July 1958 was a crisis month in the Middle East. The young King Hussein of Jordan faced a rebellion, and his cousin, King Feisal of Iraq, and the latter's pro-British elder statesman, Nuri-es-Said, were murdered. At Hussein's request, the 16th Parachute Brigade was flown into Amman, Israel agreeing to the use of its airspace, while US Marines landed in the Lebanon to pre-empt trouble there. Calm was restored without the need for action by the parachutists, and they were withdrawn in October.

The next threat came from the new régime in Iraq. In June 1961 its President, Kassem, announced that Kuwait formed part of his country and that he proposed to take it over. The ruler of that tiny oil-rich territory appealed to Britain to implement the newly signed defence agreement. Within three days a brigade had been deployed, one Royal Marine Commando from its carrier, which happened to be carrying out hot weather trials off Karachi, one flown from Aden and the 2nd Coldstream Guards, who happened to be in Bahrain on detachment from 24th Brigade in Kenya. A squadron of tanks, kept permanently in landing-craft in the Gulf, was put ashore, and four days later the rest of

24th Brigade was flown in from Kenya. The nearest aircraft-carrier was at Hong Kong and arrived three days later. A formidable force had been assembled in a remarkably short time, and the operation was quoted for many years to come as proof of the success of the new strategy of maintaining an air-portable reserve, combined with an amphibious one. The only enemy it had to face was the heat, to which many of the troops were not acclimatized. In October it was withdrawn, replaced in part by a force drawn from the Arab League.

In 1963 Cyprus was once more the scene of action. At the end of December, Greek Cypriot fighters attacked Turkish Cypriot areas, the origin of the fighting being the different interpretations both placed on the constitution under which the island had become independent in 1960. The Turkish Cypriots, egged on by Ankara, resisted attempts by the Greek Cypriots to regard the island as a unitary state. Makarios had tried to introduce some constitutional amendments to overcome Turkish obstruction and insistence on separation. The fighting was a threat to the security of British service families living outside the sovereign base areas of Episkopi and Dhekelia. There was a large number of families in Limassol and Larnaca, as well as in Nicosia, where the airfield was still an RAF station. Duncan Sandys, then Commonwealth Secretary, brought pressure to bear on Makarios and the Turkish Vice-President, Kutchuk, to accept the intervention of a peace-keeping force from the garrison of the base areas.

Although the force succeeded in restricting the fighting in Nicosia, it was unable to prevent serious attacks by organized bodies of Greek Cypriots on the Turkish areas of Limassol, Larnaca, Ktima and Polis, as well as in villages all over the island. The 3rd Division, the strategic reserve in Britain, was despatched by air in February 1964 to relieve the overstretched garrison and try and suppress the fighting. In March the United Nations Organization assumed responsibility for peace-keeping, and the division put on its light blue beret and came under its control, gradually reducing its strength as contingents from other nations arrived over the following two months, until the British contribution stabilized at the level of one brigade. The original Security Council mandate was for three months. At the time of writing, 19 years later, the force is still there, although both its total size and that of the British contribution have been considerably reduced.

In the same year trouble was brewing in Aden and its hinterland, the sheikly rulers of which had recently been brought together in a rather precarious Federation, into which, in January 1963, was merged the colony of Aden itself. Four months before, Imam Ahmed, the ruler of the Yemen, which maintained a long-standing claim to the area, had died. His son was overthrown by Colonel Sallal, who was supported by Egypt, and his rebellion was welcomed by Abdullah al Asnag, leader of the People's Socialist Party in Aden, which favoured integration of Aden and its hinterland with the Yemen. Nasser sent troops to the Yemen to support Sallal against the Royalists, who were helped by Saudi Arabia and were concentrated north of the capital Sana'a. Rioting, agitation and terrorist acts in Aden were combined with incidents up-country, notably in the mountainous Radfan area astride the road to Dhala, by which posts guarding the Yemen frontier were maintained. In January 1964 General Harington, the newly-appointed joint service Commander-in-Chief, despatched a punitive expedition, the core of which was three battalions of the Federal army, which occupied the area while a new road was built. The force was then withdrawn in March. No sooner had it left than trouble broke out again. Operations were resumed at the end of April with 45th Royal Marine Commando, 3rd Parachute Regiment and 1st East Anglian, supported by the RAF and by naval helicopters, Blacker's 39th Brigade headquarters from Northern Ireland being flown out to assume command of 'Radforce'. At the end of May, Blacker had seven battalions, two more British and two from the Federal Army having been added. In operations lasting from 19 May to 11 June the rebels were defeated, and, although troops were kept in the Radfan thereafter, it was not again the scene of major operations. Casualties had been five killed and 13 wounded.

Meanwhile Aden itself had been quiet since December, when a serious bomb incident had taken place at the airport, from which the British High Commissioner, Trevaskis, narrowly escaped. Following it, a state of emergency had been declared throughout the Federation, 57 members of Asnag's party had been arrested and 280 Yemeni subjects deported. Two events in 1964 precipitated the outbreak of further trouble. The first was the announcement by Douglas-Home's Conservative Government that Britain intended to grant independence to the Federation not later than 1968, but would maintain her base in Aden, to the extension of which, in Little Aden, 24th Brigade was to be transferred by the end of 1964 from Kenya, which would then become independent. The second was the advent to power in October of Wilson's Labour Government, which was expected to be less keen to keep the base and to support the traditional rulers. From then on a struggle was waged between the various factions which hoped to inherit power. Prominent among them was the National Liberation Front (NLF) which aimed at the removal of the British, the break-up of the Federation and the establishment of a Marxist-orientated state in league with Egypt and the Yemen. It had no inhibitions about the use of force to achieve its aim. November saw a serious outbreak of violence, which continued throughout 1965, in which there were 286 terrorist incidents, causing 237 casualties, one of the most unpleasant on 17 September, when a grenade was thrown at a party of 73 British school-children about to fly back to Britain after the holidays, five of them being injured. Operations continued up-country, in which 10 British soldiers were killed and 61 wounded.

1966 was the decisive year. In February Wilson's Government announced that it no longer intended to maintain defence facilities in the Federation after independence in 1968. Not surprisingly this intensified the internal struggle and undermined the authority and confidence of the Federation's rulers, who knew that Egypt had 60,000 troops in the Yemen at that time. There were 480 terrorist incidents in the year, causing a total of 573 casualties, of whom five dead and 218 wounded were British servicemen. 1967 was even worse, exacerbated by the Six Day War between Israel and Egypt, in which accusations were made that Britain had helped the former. The hopes of the Foreign Secretary, George Brown, of finding a peaceful solution to the Federation's future by improving relations with Egypt were dashed, and trouble brewed in the Federal army, as its officers began to be concerned about their future. The rulers' choice of the Arab officer to replace the British commander, Brigadier Dye, sparked off a mutiny, which spread to the police. Rumours that the British were shooting Arab mutineers led to an ambush in Aden's Crater town of British soldiers by police mutineers, in which four of the soldiers were killed. The High Commissioner, Trevelyan, and the Commander-in-Chief, Admiral Le Fanu, faced a difficult decision. If they ordered more troops into the city to rescue the bodies and deal with the police, they would put the lives of at least 100 Britons all over the Federation at risk. To the anger of the commanding officer of the Argyll and Sutherland Highlanders, to which three of the dead men belonged, they stayed their hand. Two weeks later, after the affair had simmered down, the Highlanders re-entered the Crater in a skilful operation, in which hardly a shot was fired. From then until the last of them left at the end of November, British troops stood aside while the rival factions, the NLF, no longer supported by Egypt, and FLOSY, the Federation for the Liberation of Southern Yemen, which was, fought it out between them, the NLF gaining the upper hand.

Supported by a strong naval task force from the Far East, including an aircraft-carrier, a commando-carrier with one Royal Marine Commando deployed ashore, and an assault landing ship, the remaining garrison of 3,500 men was evacuated between 24 and 29 November, feeling a guilty conscience at abandoning the rulers and the Federation Army soldiers, with whom they had fought side by side up-country, and resentment at the political decisions which had made their efforts all in vain. In the 11 months of 1967 there had been over 3,000 incidents, in which the casualty list totalled 1,248, the British forces having suffered 44 killed and 325 wounded. The Aden garrison was replaced by a smaller body of troops stationed at Sharjah and Bahrain in the Persian Gulf, the army element of which numbered 900.

While Aden's troubles had been brewing, the army was engaged in a more satisfactory campaign farther east. This started in December 1962 with a rebellion against the Sultan of Brunei in northern Borneo, supported from across the border by Indonesia, whose pro-Communist dictator, Sukarno, objected to the incorporation of the territories of northern Borneo, Sarawak and Sabah, into the Federation of Malaysia, due to come into existence in September 1963. It had been hoped that Brunei would also accede to it. Sukarno wished to add all these territories to the rest of Kalimantan – the Indonesian name for their four-fifths of the huge island. The prompt despatch of two battalions, one Gurkha and one Highland, from Singapore, followed by a third and two Royal Marine Commandos, snuffed out the rebellion in 11 days, 40 rebels being killed and nearly 2,000 detained. The only British casualties were five Royal Marines killed and several more wounded in an amphibious assault on Limbang.

Although the rebellion within Brunei was thus rapidly and effectively quelled, proving the value of having forces available near at hand, rather than dependent on deployment half across the world, there were signs that the Indonesians were intent upon subverting all three territories by infiltrating their own men across the 1,000-mile-long frontier, which ran through jungle-covered mountains up to 8,000 feet high. By this time, Major-General Walker, commander of the 17th Gurkha Division, had assumed command of all forces in the three territories. When Malaysia came into being in September 1963, he became technically subordinate to the Malaysian National Operations Committee, of which the Joint Service Commander-in-Chief Far East, Admiral Begg, was a member. He had succeeded the first occupant of the post, Admiral Luce, in April. There were a number of incidents in the rest of the year before a ceasefire in January 1964, following an appeal by the Secretary-General of the United Nations; but when the talks broke down in February, the Indonesian army openly assumed responsibility for operations across the border, abandoning the pretence that the soldiers and marines in its special units were volunteers, helping local insurgents. Its tactics were to send bodies of 100 or 200 men over the border to establish jungle bases, from which they would intimidate the local inhabitants, mostly Dyak tribesmen, and gradually bring about a *de facto* extension of Indonesian authority.

Hitherto, Walker had held his troops well away from the frontier, relying for information on small patrols, many from the SAS, in contact with the tribesmen. To counter the Indonesian tactic, he had to set up bases of his own near the frontier, strong enough to resist attack by Indonesian forces of 100 or more. These were established at company strength, dependent for their supply and reinforcement on helicopters, of which there were never enough. The majority of the heavier-lift ones were the naval Wessex, detached from the commando-carrier. Further talks in Tokyo in June 1964 between Tunku Abdul Rahman for Malaysia and Sukarno, under the chairmanship of President Macapagal of the Philippines, proved fruitless, and were soon followed by further Indonesian incursions into Sarawak, of which there were 13 in July, and in August an unsuccessful attempt to land 100 men from the sea and 200 from the air in southern Malaya. Walker viewed with concern the growing Indonesian activity, combined with the internal security problem posed by communist penetration of the Chinese community in Sarawak, and asked for reinforcements, which he received. By the end of the year he had 14,000 men in three Malay and 18 British battalions, of which eight were Gurkha and two Royal Marine Commandos, supported by five batteries of light artillery, two squadrons of armoured cars, 60 RAF and Royal Navy helicopters and 40 army ones, the Army Air Corps by then being seven years old. Neither Britain nor Malaysia

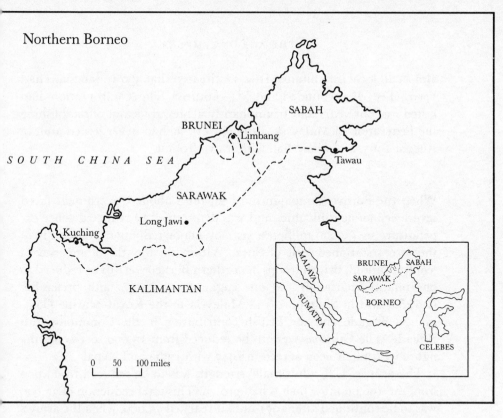

Northern Borneo

was technically at war with Indonesia and the conflict was referred to by both sides as 'confrontation'. It did not suit either side to extend hostilities to the sea nor to air attacks against targets on the territory of the other. Walker, however, obtained authority to operate across the border into Kalimantan, provided that the fact that he did so was kept strictly secret. Acting on interception of Indonesian radio communications, these operations proved highly effective. By the time Walker handed over command to Lea in March 1965, the tide had turned clearly in favour of Britain and Malaysia, although Indonesian attacks across the border continued. Their effort virtually ceased after the internal coup in Indonesia in October, which led to a struggle between pro- and anti-communist factions. The victor was the anti-communist General Suharto, who ousted Sukarno in March 1966.

Five months later 'confrontation' came to an end. It had been a satisfactory and successful campaign, skilfully and economically conducted. At its peak, 17,000 servicemen, including Australians and New Zealanders from the Commonwealth Brigade in Malaya, had taken part. There had been 114 killed and 181 wounded, a high proportion Gurkha; 36 civilians had been killed, 53 wounded and 4 captured, almost all local inhabitants. It was estimated that 590 Indonesians had been killed, 222 wounded and 771 captured. The 'confrontation' had lasted for four years and triumphantly achieved its aim of establishing the Federation of Malaysia, although Brunei had never joined and, in August 1965, Singapore had withdrawn from it.

When the Borneo campaign finished, the Labour Government faced severe economic difficulties and was determined to reduce defence expenditure to £2,000 million a year by major reductions, especially in the forces stationed east of Suez. Within six months of the end of 'confrontation', British troops in northern Borneo were to be reduced to one infantry battalion and one engineer squadron, both preferably Gurkha, and in Singapore and Malaysia to the Royal Marine Commando Brigade and the British contribution to the Commonwealth Brigade. The Gurkhas were to be reduced from 15,000 to 10,000, the figure which had been agreed in 1947 with India and Nepal.

The army's 'UK adult male' strength was to be reduced by 11,000 from the 196,000 to which it had grown. This total reduction of 37,000 was to be continued after 1971 until it reached 75,000, when the army's strength would be reduced to only 1,100 above Duncan Sandys's 1957 target figure of 165,000. For the army, the initial reduction meant the loss of four regiments each in the Royal Armoured Corps and Royal Artillery, and three squadrons in the Royal Engineers. The infantry was reduced by eight battalions, some preferring disbandment to amalgamation. The Fusiliers, Light Infantry and the remaining Irish regiments each formed a 'large regiment', Templer's own regiment, the Royal Irish Fusiliers, being absorbed into the two battalions of the new Royal Irish Rangers. Fierce arguments had raged behind the scenes before these decisions had been arrived at. The principle followed by the Army Council had been that each infantry 'brigade' (in its organizational, not its operational sense) should lose one battalion, normally the junior in terms of age.

Less than six months later, the deepening economic crisis led the Government to decide on more drastic measures. Withdrawal both from Malaysia and Singapore and also from the Persian Gulf was to be total and completed by 1971, the Gurkhas being further reduced to 6,000, most of them in Hong Kong. Britain's defence effort was to be 'concentrated mainly in Europe and the North Atlantic area' and 'No special capability for use outside Europe' would be maintained when withdrawal from the Far East and the Gulf was completed. The navy's aircraft-carrier fleet was then to be phased out. The total reduction of 75,000 in service manpower was to be accelerated. The result of this was that, when Heath's Conservative Government came to power in 1970, the Household Division had been reduced to two cavalry regiments, each of which contributed one mounted ceremonial squadron, and seven battalions of Foot Guards, the Scots Guards having lost their 2nd battalion, which was soon restored; the Royal Armoured Corps was reduced to 13 regiments of cavalry and four of the Royal Tank Regiment; the Royal Artillery to 21 regiments, and the infantry, including the SAS and the Parachute Regiment, to 41 battalions. Two regiments, reduced to company strength, were restored as full battalions shortly after, raising the total to 43, while the Gurkhas had been reduced to five.

Earlier in its term of office, Wilson's Government, with Healey as Defence Secretary, had effected a major reorganization of the Territorial Army, merging it with the army's other volunteer reserve, the Army Emergency Reserve. The latter was generally a reserve of individuals, rather than of units with a local territorial connection. In their 1957 reorganization, Macmillan's Conservative administration had recognized that, as Territorial Army formations could not be made ready for operations in less than at least three months, they were only suited to home defence, which was generally taken to mean assistance to civil defence in dealing with the aftermath of nuclear attack. The Territorial Army had relied heavily on using stocks of equipment left over from the Second World War, which by then were worn out and obsolete. It was clearly impossible to provide modern equipment, even for training purposes, for a force which, in theory, was organized to provide 11 divisions. It was in any case becoming difficult to recruit enough men for each unit to give them any sort of interesting or meaningful training. That in itself discouraged volunteers. These inescapable realities persuaded the Army Council to approve a major reduction in the size of the two reserves combined, and to alter the emphasis of the new reserve, given the clumsy title of the Territorial Auxiliary and Volunteer Reserve, to that of filling the gaps in the regular army's organization required for war. Such a smaller reserve could be adequately provided with modern equipment and uniform, and be given realistic training. The plan was fought tooth and nail by the county Territorial Associations and the hierarchy of the Territorial Army, led by the Duke of

Norfolk, as they saw their local units disappearing. Reductions in those arms which required expensive equipment were especially heavy, the Yeomanry being cut to one armoured car regiment, although a second was formed some years later. Some Yeomanry maintained their existence in name by conversion to infantry. The latter were reduced to 37 battalions.

1968 was a unique year, being the only one since 1660, it is believed, in which the British army was not actively engaged in some form of operation, unless its presence in the United Nations Force in Cyprus is counted as such. But 1969 was to see an old sore re-opened – that of the Irish troubles. In August of that year the inability of the Royal Ulster Constabulary (RUC) to cope with the disorders arising from the activities of the Catholic-based Northern Ireland Civil Rights Association (NICRA) and the reaction to them of the hard-line Protestants, led by the Reverend Ian Paisley, and the hostility of the Catholic population to the intervention of the RUC, led Wilson's Government to order the intervention of troops in Belfast and Londonderry as a form of peace-keeping force, more acceptable to the Catholics than the RUC. The normal garrison consisted of the 39th Brigade with two infantry battalions and an armoured car regiment. This garrison did not suffice to deal with the rioting crowds, especially in Belfast, and it was soon reinforced by six more. By the end of the year the garrison had increased to ten, by which time its task had changed. It was no longer just one of keeping the Protestants and Catholics apart, nor of replacing the police in Catholic areas, for the Irish Republican Army (IRA), which had had a hand in instigating the agitation of NICRA, had exploited the situation to turn the Catholic population against the army and had themselves entered the fray. Whatever may have been their original intention, they were not prepared to tolerate a situation in which the British army, their traditional target, could be accepted as the protectors of the Catholic population, a role they claimed for themselves.

1970 was a year of major rioting on both sides of the sectarian fence, combined with the occasional armed attack on police stations, individual members of the RUC, particularly of the Special Branch, and on army patrols. The RUC had ceased to operate in the predominantly Catholic areas of Belfast and Londonderry, and the army operated out of company and platoon bases that more and more resembled fortresses, as did police stations in adjacent areas. To cover the sensitive period of traditional Protestant marches, commemorating the· Battles of the Boyne and of the Somme in July in Belfast, and the resistance, in James II's siege of Londonderry, of the Apprentice Boys from London, who added the name of England's capital to the town of Derry, the garrison was increased to 15 units, and reduced again by the end of the year to eight. In June Heath's Conservative administration had replaced Wilson's, Carrington taking Healey's place as Defence Secretary and Maudling, as Home Secretary, assuming responsibility for Northern Ireland from Callaghan. In 1970 also an addition was made to the army's organization in the form of the Ulster Defence Regiment, a part-time volunteer body, intended to replace the RUC's 'B Special' Reserve, which had been accused of being a purely Protestant force, oppressing the Catholics.

The situation did not improve in the new year. The IRA increased its activity, armed attacks on the security forces becoming more frequent. In March a particularly callous incident struck the headlines, when three young soldiers of the Royal Highland Fusiliers were brutally murdered. Pressure from the Protestant right wing, indignant at what they saw as the weakness of the Stormont Government, which they attributed to its deference to Westminster, ousted Chichester-Clark[3] as Prime Minister and replaced him with Faulkner, a tough, realistic and pragmatic businessman, the most effective politician the province ever produced. He exploited Heath's reluctance to involve the Westminster Government in direct responsibility for the affairs of the province. Tuzo, who had taken over command after the death of Erskine-Crum immediately after he had replaced Freeland, was in a difficult position. Faulkner's Northern Ireland Government was responsible for the affairs of the province, including the RUC, although, like other police forces in the United Kingdom, they maintained that they were responsible only to the law. Tuzo and the armed forces in the province were responsible to the Secretary of State for Defence in London. He therefore had to walk like Agag between Stormont and Westminster. Trouble escalated in June when two men in Londonderry were shot dead by the army when seen to be about to fire weapons. Tuzo had been persuaded to let the local Catholic community attempt to convince the inhabitants of the Bogside and Creggan to bring things back to normal, but after this incident it was clear that that policy was not effective. By mid-July

[3] Later Lord Moyola.

the situation both there and in Belfast had deteriorated; rioting was frequent, petrol- and nail-bombs often being thrown at the troops. Pressure on Faulkner from Paisley and other hard-line Protestants to introduce internment increased, and the annual Apprentice Boys' march in August became a test case. Paisley insisted that it must take place, demanding internment as a *quid pro quo* if it were cancelled or restricted. The possibility of introducing it had been under considera-tion in Whitehall for some time and preparations put in hand in case it were decided upon, but they would not be complete before November. A week before the march was due, Faulkner faced Heath with the challenge of either agreeing to internment or assuming responsibility from Stormont. The decision was for the former.

Tuzo was reinforced with three battalions to assist in the operation, which picked up 326 out of a list of 520 names provided by the RUC Special Branch, the accuracy of which was open to considerable doubt. It had always been hoped that a by-product of the pick-up would be the information obtained from interrogating a select few of the more important IRA personalities, and the army's intelligence experts had given instruction and administrative help to the RUC Special Branch to implement it. Procedures were based on those which had been used in Aden and had been developed as a result of the experience of British troops taken prisoner in the Korean War, in order to train men to resist such interrogation. Their use in this case caused the Government con-siderable embarrassment.

In spite of the introduction of internment, violence and terrorism increased, incidents escalating from an average of 60 a month to over 100. The predominantly Catholic housing areas of Londonderry and Belfast became IRA strongholds, in which the authority of both the Stormont and Westminster Governments was flouted. In Londonderry gangs of rioting youths were gradually reducing the streets on the borders of the Bogside to rubble. NICRA planned a protest march there on Sunday 30 January 1972, and it was decided that, if it resulted in further rioting, an attempt would be made to 'snatch' a number of the rioters and bring them to court. Two additional battalions were sent to Londonderry to man 26 roadblocks in order to prevent the marchers from penetrating into the Protestant area of the city. When the 'snatch' operation was ordered, the troops involved, from 1st Battalion the Parachute Regiment, came under fire, or at least thought they had, and returned it, killing 13 and injuring the same number. The IRA quickly named it 'Bloody Sunday', and, although Lord Widgery's tribunal, which investigated the affair, concluded that 'The soldiers acted as they did because they thought their orders required it', he described the action of some of them as 'bordering on the reckless' and stated that the brigade commander might have under-estimated the hazard to civilians in employing an arrest force in circumstances under which the troops were liable to come under fire. Whatever the rights or wrongs, it set back current hopes of a possible political solution.

One clear result was Heath's decision no longer to carry the can for decisions and policies made at Stormont. On 24 March Faulkner and his Government resigned rather than accept that full responsibility for security should pass to Westminster, with the result that the latter acquired it for all the affairs of the province. Direct rule became the order of the day. The Home Secretary's rather vague responsibility for it was transferred to a Secretary of State for Northern Ireland, to which post Whitelaw was appointed. This eased Tuzo's problems, although there remained the one of dual responsibility to Whitelaw and, through the CGS, to Carrington.

The new régime, hoping to be more popular with the Catholic community than the Protestant dominated Stormont, ushered in a policy of low profile in the hope that the 'hearts and minds' of the Catholic population could be weaned away from the IRA. One of the difficulties of implementing it was that both the IRA and the Protestant hardliners had a vested interest in trying to ensure that it did not work. Any concession to Catholic sensitivities roused Protestant anger and suspicion, while failure to deal with acts of violence or defiance of authority by Protestant organizations brought Catholic accusations that the authorities were in league with them. One example of this was attempts by the Ulster Defence Association (UDA) to establish 'no-go' areas, equivalent to those established in the Catholic areas, such as the Bogside and Creggan in Londonderry and Andersonstown in Belfast. Because the latter were both a challenge to the Government's authority and a provocation to the Protestants, planning started for a major operation in which the army would clear away the barricades and establish its presence and authority within them. Any hesitation over the possibility of something bloodier than Bloody Sunday was dispelled by a serious bomb outrage in a bus depot in Belfast on 21 July. Tuzo was reinforced to a strength of 27 battalions, giving him 21,000 men. Nine thousand UDR were also called up for Operation 'Motorman', as it was called, which took place on 31 July. It was not resisted by the IRA and was entirely successful in its aim. By the end of the year the garrison had been reduced again to 18 battalions.

During this time an attempt to find a political solution was made at the Darlington Conference in September, the outcome of which was a proposal that, after a plebiscite to obtain the views of the population of the province as to whether the border with the Republic should be maintained or not, a Northern Ireland Government would be reinstated at Stormont on a 'power-sharing' basis. At the same time the possibility of some form of link with the Republic would be pursued. The plebiscite was postponed until March 1973, by which time King had replaced Tuzo. It passed off without incident and gave the answer expected. The elections to the new Northern Ireland Assembly also passed off quietly at the end of June, Faulkner's Official Unionists gaining the highest number of seats – 23 out of 78; but other Unionists, West's 10 and Paisley and Craig's 17, came close. Without their cooperation, Faulkner formed an Executive with five of his own supporters, four of Fitt's Catholic SDLP and one, Cooper, from the middle-of-the-road Alliance Party. Violent incidents of all kinds continued, but at a reduced level. In 1972 there had been 10,628 shooting and 1,853 bomb incidents; 239 civilians, 103 regular army, 20 UDR soldiers and 17 RUC men had been killed. In 1973 the figures fell to 5,018 shooting and 1,520 bomb incidents; 127 civilians, 58 regular army, 8 UDR and 12 RUC killed.

The hopes raised by these constitutional changes were dashed in 1974. The first General Election in Britain in that year came at a critical time for Faulkner's delicately poised Executive. The Sunningdale Conference in December 1973 about methods of pursuing the 'Irish Dimension' had aroused Protestant suspicions, giving a handle to Paisley and Faulkner's other critics. The election result showed that Faulkner did not have the support of the majority of the Protestant electorate, and a general strike brought him, and Whitelaw's constitutional experiment, down. Wilson accepted that direct rule was, at least for the present, the only solution. Although attempts have been made to escape from it, it has continued to the time of writing (1983), as has the operational presence of the British army in the province, although this has been progressively reduced in strength, from 15 battalions in 1976 to nine in 1983, and it has handed over responsibility to the RUC for most aspects of security.

1979 saw a setback in the process. On 27 August of that year two serious incidents took place. One was the murder of Lord Mountbatten when on holiday at his estate in the Republic. He, his grandson Nicholas Knatchbull and his daughter's mother-in-law, the Dowager Lady Brabourne, were killed, and his daughter Lady Brabourne, her husband and their other son Timothy were seriously injured, when a bomb exploded in their fishing boat. The other was at Warren Point, near the border south of Newry. A remotely detonated bomb killed six men of 2nd Battalion the Parachute Regiment, and another one 12 men, including the commanding officer, Lieutenant-Colonel Blair, of the Queen's Own Highlanders, who came to their assistance. The death of 48 British soldiers in Northern Ireland in that year brought the total in the ten years since August 1969 to 373.

While almost every unit of the army had served in Northern Ireland, most of them on four-month tours, temporarily detached from Britain or Germany, a small number had been involved in two significant operations. One was the reinforcement of the United Nations Force in Cyprus in July 1974 when Turkey invaded the island after the coup against Makarios, instigated by the Government of Colonels in Greece. Rapid reinforcement of the UN Force from the base at Dhekelia helped the former to deter Turkish forces from seizing Nicosia airfield. More publicity was given to the rescue by the Royal Navy of British and other non-Cypriot citizens from the north of the island.

The other was a much longer drawn-out affair, the war in the Dhofar, the southern area of Oman. There the authority of the young Sultan Qaboos, who replaced his obscurantist old father in 1970, was threatened by a rebellion among the wild inhabitants of the rugged Jebel north of Salalah, where the RAF had the use of an airfield. The rebellion was actively supported by the Peoples' Republic of South Yemen, the Marxist Government of which now ruled over what had been both the Western and the Eastern Aden Protectorates. British officers and non-commissioned officers served in the Sultan's forces and commanded them, and some British army units, notably the SAS and Royal Engineers, served with them. The campaign resembled those fought in days gone by on the North-West Frontier, aircraft, helicopters, rocket-propelled projectiles and mines adding new features to a form of warfare in which the skill, courage and endurance of the man on his feet remained the decisive factor. The campaign was successfully concluded in 1975.

* * *

Templer died two months after Mountbatten. They had enjoyed a friendly rivalry as colonels of the two regiments of Household Cavalry, Mountbatten of the Life Guards and Templer of the Blues and Royals, formed in 1969 by amalgamation of the Royal Horse Guards (known colloquially as the Blues from the colour of their tunics) and the Royal Dragoons, originally raised as the Tangier Horse, both of which dated from the Restoration. Templer's love of tradition and sense of history delighted in this, as did the successful completion of the project to which he had devoted his retirement – the establishment of the National Army Museum.

The army's origins, in a fusion of the Cromwellian and Royalist armies at the Restoration, were to have a far-fetched parallel in an activity in which the army was involved in December 1980. As a result of the Lancaster House Conference in that month, the former territory of Rhodesia (which had unilaterally declared its independence from Britain in 1965 under Ian Smith's Government of white settlers) was to become independent as Zimbabwe after elections to be held on a universal franchise. A force of 1,300 men, mostly from Britain, but including soldiers also from Australia, Fiji, Kenya and New Zealand, was despatched to keep the fighting men of Mugabe's ZANLA[4] and Nkomo's ZIPRA[5] apart from the Rhodesian armed forces and police in the run up to and during the election, in which the polling booths were supervised by British police, under the eyes of a body of observers, drawn from the Commonwealth. Forty-five two-man teams were attached to the Rhodesian armed forces, and 16-strong teams manned 16 assembly points and 24 rendezvous, into which marched peaceably 20,860 African fighters, of whom 15,240 were from ZANLA and the rest from ZIPRA. All the arrangements passed off peacefully, and when he had been announced victor after the election, Mugabe requested that a British army training mission should set about the delicate task of welding together into one army the former soldiers of the Rhodesian army and the two rival armies of the Patriotic Front. This unprecedented task was achieved to the surprise of many with the skill, tact and good humour which everyone had come to expect of the British soldier of Templer's age. It remains to be seen how durable that shotgun marriage will prove to be.

It was sad that Templer did not live to see the brilliant success of an

[4] Zimbabwe Army of National Liberation.
[5] Zimbabwe Independent Peoples' Republican Army.

operation which savoured of the Age of Wolseley and Roberts – the liberation of the Falkland Islands after the Argentine invasion in April 1982. As a dedicated lover of the old British Empire, he would have relished it. When Mrs Thatcher's Government ordered an expedition to sail to recover the islands, it appeared that the Royal Navy thought that they would be able to complete the task with 3rd Royal Marine Commando Brigade, embarked on the passenger liner *Canberra*, to which a squadron of 22nd SAS and 3rd Battalion the Parachute Regiment had been added, to be joined later by the 2nd Battalion. A further reinforcement was provided by 5th Infantry Brigade, with 2nd Battalion the Scots Guards, the Welsh Guards and 1/7th Gurkhas, which sailed on the liner *Queen Elizabeth* on 12 May. Before the initial assault at San Carlos Bay took place on 21 May, it was clear that 5th Brigade would need to add its strength to that of 3rd Commando Brigade in order to deal with the 6,000-strong Argentine force in defensive positions in the hills round Port Stanley. On 28 May, 2nd Parachute Regiment attacked the Argentine garrison covering the airfield at Goose Green, 15 miles south of San Carlos Bay. In a brilliant action, in which the infantry had little fire support, they forced the surrender of the 1,400-strong garrison, after killing 250 of them. The battalion's casualties were 17 killed and 36 wounded, the dead including the adjutant and the commanding officer, Lieutenant-Colonel Jones, who was posthumously awarded the Victoria Cross.

A number of factors, including the deteriorating weather, made it necessary to hasten the day when the assault on the hills surrounding Port Stanley should begin. The loss of heavy-lift helicopters, when the *Atlantic Conveyor* was hit by Argentine aircraft, was a limiting factor and 5th Brigade was, therefore, moved round from Goose Green to Bluff Cove, to the south of those hills, by sea. Two of the Landing Ships Logistic (LSLs) were hit by Argentine aircraft and set on fire on 8 June. One of them was carrying half of the Welsh Guards, who lost 38 men killed and 85 wounded. The final battle for Stanley started on 11 June, 3rd Parachute Regiment successfully assaulting Mount Longdon while 42nd and 45th Royal Marine commandos captured Two Sisters and Mount Harriet to the south of them. 5th Brigade then took over, 2nd Parachute Regiment passing through their sister battalion to capture Wireless Ridge on the night of the 13th, while the Scots Guards attacked Tumbledown Mountain, the Gurkhas Mount William and the Welsh Guards Sapper Hill, to which they were lifted by helicopter.

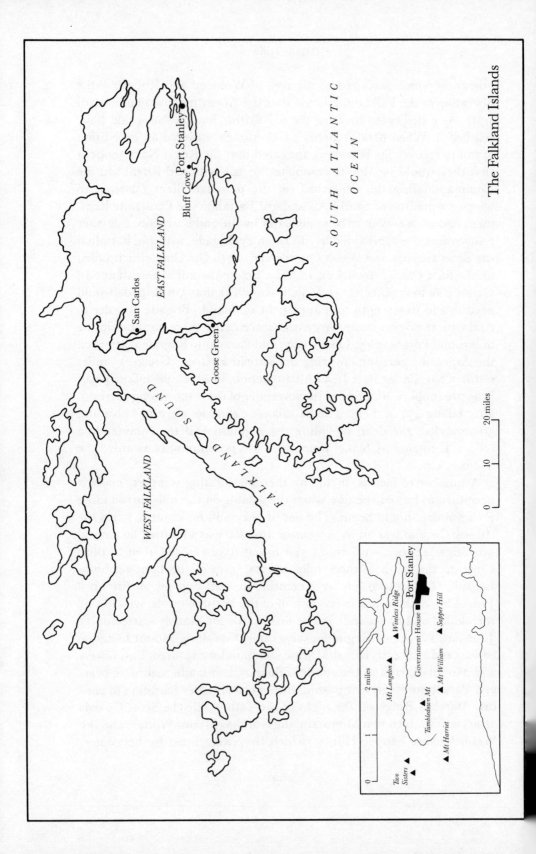

The Falkland Islands

SOUTH ATLANTIC

OCEAN

Port Stanley
Bluff Cove

EAST FALKLAND

San Carlos

Goose Green

FALKLAND SOUND

WEST FALKLAND

0   10   20 miles

Two
Sisters

Mt Longdon

Wireless Ridge

Port Stanley

Tumbledown Mt

Government House

Mt William

Sapper Hill

Mt Harriet

0   1   2 miles

Fighting was fiercest at Tumbledown, and in the afternoon of 14 June the enemy surrendered. Twenty-eight thousand men of all three services had taken part in the expedition, of whom 10,000 army and Royal Marines had landed. Casualties had been 255 dead (86 Royal Navy, 27 Royal Marines, 123 Army, 1 RAF, 18 Merchant Navy) and 777 wounded, of whom 464 were army. Argentine prisoners totalled 11,400 and they reported their dead as 672, of whom 386 were lost when their cruiser, the *General Belgrano*, was sunk. The landing force, under the Royal Marine Major-General Moore, had not only been outnumbered, but had had to operate in increasingly severe weather, marching long distances, carrying heavy loads, over rough, wet terrain which offered no shelter from the permanently fierce wind and no concealment. The performance of the British soldier in 1982 in the Falkland Islands was fully worthy of the feats of arms of his predecessors, emblazoned on his regimental colours.

There were many things about this army which had not changed since the day in 1916 on which Templer had been commissioned into the Royal Irish Fusiliers. One, to which he was passionately attached, was devotion to the regiment as a family, although, as he did, one might change regiments or the latter might itself change by amalgamation or in some other way. The men of the Parachute Regiment and the Special Air Service, which were created in the Second World War, and the Welsh Guards in the First, were just as fiercely proud of their regiments as the Blues and Royals and Scots Guards serving alongside them in the Falklands, who could claim continuous service since the Restoration.

But much had changed. The proportion of the army providing its logistic support in peacetime .had greatly increased. The scale of its equipment, in vehicles, radios, and all that went together to form a weapon system, led to the formation in 1939, from the Royal Army Ordnance Corps, of the Corps of Royal Electrical and Mechanical Engineers. By the 1970s it had overtaken the Royal Artillery as the largest corps in the army, providing a high proportion of men in every combat unit, as well as the repair units behind them. Its original parent had absorbed the supply function of the Royal Army Service Corps, which had become the Royal Corps of Transport. One change that would have surprised Templer's soldier father was the presence of

6,000 women in uniform in the peacetime regular army. That army was still shrinking, not because it could not recruit the men and women it needed, but because the cost of keeping them, and their comrades in the Royal Navy and Royal Air Force, in the service, and of providing modern equipment for them, escalated at a rate even beyond that of the inflation which raged in Templer's later years.

Soldiers were needed to man, and to maintain, new weapons and vehicles, including armoured personnel carriers for the infantry in Germany and helicopters. The latter was the most important innovation in Templer's age, as far as effect on the operations which the army actually carried out was concerned; both those manned by the Royal Navy and RAF, which transported troops, equipment, including guns, and supplies, and those manned by the army itself, for reconnaissance and liaison duties, and also as anti-armour weapons. The period also saw important developments in other anti-armour weapons. The gun, relying on kinetic energy to penetrate armour, had grown too large to be mounted in anything but a tracked vehicle. The anomaly of calling such weapons 'self-propelled anti-tank guns' and others 'tanks' led to the latter assuming the long-range anti-armour task from the artillery, adding the wire-guided missile to its armoury. Shorter-range systems, based on chemical energy warheads, propelled by rockets, developed from the Second World War 'bazooka' and *'panzerfaust'*, greatly increased the anti-armour capability of infantry. The Falklands operation showed that they could also be used for other purposes. The army in Germany was 'heavy', its artillery armoured and tracked, including the guns and missiles designed to fire nuclear warheads: that based in the United Kingdom and elsewhere was 'light', its normal method of movement by aircraft, by the ubiquitous Land Rover or on foot. The greatest revolution was in the electronics field, the transistor and then the silicon-chip affecting communications, weapons and their delivery systems, detection and vision devices, and, using the computer and its adjuncts, all aspects of command, control and staff work. All these innovations posed serious problems of recruiting, training, retaining in service and distribution of manpower (including womanpower) within the army.

The constant demand was for more men, but, in the Defence Review carried out by Wilson's Government in 1974, the results of which were announced in 1975, the army's 'UK adult male' manpower target was set at 155,000, and it had slimmed down to that by 1982, when

Thatcher's Government, going through the same process, but reluctant to describe it as a Defence Review, lowered it yet further to 135,000. These reductions forced the army into a number of contortions, one of which was to abolish brigade headquarters, a step from which it had the good sense to recover a few years later. Somehow or other the agony of further regimental disbandments and amalgamations was avoided, but it was a close-run thing. The slimming process had one advantage. It made it possible to be more selective in accepting recruits, a large proportion, at times as much as a half, of whom enlisted as 'juniors', that is before the age of 17. They tended to opt for longer service, the terms of which had been made more flexible than in the past. The soldier of the 1980s was a better educated and better behaved man than his predecessors of previous ages, often marrying young and expecting a standard of living far higher than would have been dreamed of by the 'old codgers' of earlier generations. Thanks to the introduction of the Armed Forces Pay Review Body, his pay was related to that of his civilian counterpart. In 1982 the majority of private soldiers earned £4,811 a year, corporals £7,125, sergeants £7,917, warrant officers class I £10,129; while 2nd lieutenants earned £6,000, captains £9,700, majors £13,000, brigadiers £21,000 and generals £34,000. Improvements in the method by which these amounts were paid were made by the attachment, in 1955, of teams from the Royal Army Pay Corps to every battalion-sized unit and, later, by the introduction of a computer to hold all soldiers' pay accounts.

Relations between all ranks were much easier, less dependent on formal discipline; but in action and emergency there was no letting up of standards, that of physical fitness being exceptionally high. In Northern Ireland the soldier had learned the need for all the soldierly qualities which his forbears had found necessary on the battlefield and in tight corners all over the world. Wherever the army was called to its duty, his officers would echo the remark Wellington made to Creevey a few weeks before Waterloo in a park in Brussels. Creevey was sounding him out about the chances of defeating Napoleon. Pointing to a British soldier, who was peering at a statue, the Duke replied: 'There, it all depends upon that article whether we do business or not. Give me enough of it, and I am sure.'

Appendix A
The Regiments of Foot

Showing nomenclature after the Cardwell reforms

Pre-1881	**Post-1881**
1st Foot Guards	The Grenadier Guards (The First Regiment of Guards)
2nd Foot Guards	The Coldstream Guards (The Coldstream Regiment of Foot Guards)
3rd Foot Guards	The Scots Guards (The Scots Fusilier Guards)
—	The Irish Guards
—	The Welsh Guards
1st Foot	The Royal Scots (Lothian Regiment)
2nd Foot	The Queen's (Royal West Surrey Regiment)
3rd Foot	The Buffs (East Kent Regiment)
4th Foot	The King's Own (Royal Lancaster Regiment)
5th Foot	The Northumberland Fusiliers
6th Foot	The Royal Warwickshire Regiment
7th Foot	The Royal Fusiliers (The City of London Regiment)
8th Foot	The King's (Liverpool Regiment)
9th Foot	The Norfolk Regiment
10th Foot	The Lincolnshire Regiment
11th Foot	The Devonshire Regiment
12th Foot	The Suffolk Regiment
13th Foot	Prince Albert's (Somerset Light Infantry)
14th Foot	The Prince of Wales's Own (West Yorkshire Regiment)
15th Foot	The East Yorkshire Regiment
16th Foot	The Bedfordshire Regiment
17th Foot	The Leicestershire Regiment
18th Foot	The Royal Irish Regiment (Disbanded 1922)
19th Foot	Alexandra, Princess of Wales's Own (Yorkshire Regiment) (Green Howards)
20th Foot	The Lancashire Fusiliers

21st Foot	The Royal Scots Fusiliers
22nd Foot	The Cheshire Regiment
23rd Foot	The Royal Welsh Fusiliers
24th Foot	The South Wales Borderers
25th Foot	The King's Own Scottish Borderers
26th Foot	The Cameronians (Scottish Rifles)
27th Foot	The Royal Inniskilling Fusiliers
28th Foot	The Gloucestershire Regiment
29th Foot	The Worcestershire Regiment
30th Foot	The East Lancashire Regiment
31st Foot	The East Surrey Regiment
32nd Foot	The Duke of Cornwall's Light Infantry
33rd Foot	The Duke of Wellington's (West Riding Regiment)
34th Foot	The Border Regiment
35th Foot	The Royal Sussex Regiment
36th Foot	The Worcestershire Regiment (2nd Battalion)
37th Foot	The Hampshire Regiment
38th Foot	The South Staffordshire Regiment
39th Foot	The Dorsetshire Regiment
40th Foot	The Prince of Wales's Volunteers (South Lancashire Regiment)
41st Foot	The Welch Regiment
42nd Foot	The Black Watch (Royal Highlanders)
43rd Foot	The Oxfordshire and Buckinghamshire Light Infantry
44th Foot	The Essex Regiment
45th Foot	The Sherwood Foresters (Nottinghamshire and Derbyshire Regiment)
46th Foot	The Duke of Cornwall's Light Infantry (2nd Battalion)
47th Foot	The Loyal North Lancashire Regiment
48th Foot	The Northamptonshire Regiment
49th Foot	Princess Charlotte of Wales's (Royal Berkshire Regiment)
50th Foot	The Queen's Own (Royal West Kent Regiment)
51st Foot	The King's Own (Yorkshire Light Infantry)
52nd Foot	The Oxfordshire and Buckinghamshire Light Infantry (2nd Battalion)
53rd Foot	The King's Shropshire Light Infantry
54th Foot	The Dorsetshire Regiment (2nd Battalion)
55th Foot	The Border Regiment (2nd Battalion)
56th Foot	The Essex Regiment (2nd Battalion)
57th Foot	The Duke of Cambridge's Own (Middlesex Regiment)
58th Foot	The Northamptonshire Regiment (2nd Battalion)

59th Foot	The East Lancashire Regiment (2nd Battalion)
60th Foot	The King's Royal Rifle Corps
61st Foot	The Gloucestershire Regiment (2nd Battalion)
62nd Foot	The Duke of Edinburgh's (Wiltshire Regiment)
63rd Foot	The Manchester Regiment
64th Foot	The Prince of Wales's (North Staffordshire Regiment)
65th Foot	The York and Lancaster Regiment
66th Foot	The Royal Berkshire Regiment (2nd Battalion)
67th Foot	The Hampshire Regiment (2nd Battalion)
68th Foot	The Durham Light Infantry
69th Foot	The Welch Regiment (2nd Battalion)
70th Foot	The East Surrey Regiment (2nd Battalion)
71st Foot	The Highland Light Infantry
72nd Foot	The Seaforth Highlanders (Ross-shire Buffs, The Duke of Albany)
73rd Foot	The Black Watch (The Royal Highlanders, 2nd Battalion)
74th Foot	The Highland Light Infantry (2nd Battalion)
75th Foot	The Gordon Highlanders
76th Foot	The Duke of Wellington's (West Riding Regiment) (2nd Battalion)
77th Foot	The Middlesex Regiment (2nd Battalion)
78th Foot	The Seaforth Highlanders (2nd Battalion)
79th Foot	The Queen's Own Cameron Highlanders
80th Foot	The South Staffordshire Regiment (2nd Battalion)
81st Foot	The Loyal North Lancashire Regiment (2nd Battalion)
82nd Foot	The Prince of Wales's Volunteers (South Lancashire Regiment) (2nd Battalion)
83rd Foot	The Royal Irish Rifles (1st Battalion Ulster Rifles)
84th Foot	The York and Lancaster Regiment (2nd Battalion)
85th Foot	The King's Shropshire Light Infantry (2nd Battalion)
86th Foot	The Royal Irish Rifles (2nd Battalion Royal Ulster Rifles)
87th Foot	Princess Victoria's (Royal Irish Fusiliers)
88th Foot	The Connaught Rangers (Disbanded 1922)
89th Foot	Princess Victoria's (Royal Irish Fusiliers) (2nd Battalion)
90th Foot	The Cameronians (Scottish Rifles) (2nd Battalion)
91st Foot	Princess Louise's (Argyll and Sutherland Highlanders)
92nd Foot	The Gordon Highlanders (2nd Battalion)
93rd Foot	Princess Louise's (Argyll and Sutherland Highlanders) (2nd Battalion)
94th Foot	The Connaught Rangers (2nd Battalion) (disbanded 1922)

95th Foot	The Sherwood Foresters (2nd Battalion)
96th Foot	The Manchester Regiment (2nd Battalion)
97th Foot	The Queen's Own (Royal West Kent) (2nd Battalion)
98th Foot	The Prince of Wales's (North Staffordshire Regiment) (2nd Battalion)
99th Foot	The Duke of Edinburgh's (Wiltshire Regiment) (2nd Battalion)
100th Foot	The Prince of Wales's Leinster Regiment (Royal Canadians) (disbanded 1922)
101st Foot	The Royal Munster Fusiliers (Royal Bengal Fusiliers) (disbanded 1922)
102nd Foot	The Royal Dublin Fusiliers (Royal Madras Fusiliers) (disbanded 1922)
103rd Foot	The Royal Dublin Fusiliers (The Royal Bombay Fusiliers) (disbanded 1922)
104th Foot	The Royal Munster Fusiliers (Bengal Fusiliers) (disbanded 1922)
105th Foot	The Kings Own (Yorkshire Light Infantry) (2nd Battalion) (The Madras Light Infantry)
106th Foot	The Durham Light Infantry (2nd Battalion) (Bombay Light Infantry)
107th Foot	The Royal Sussex Regiment (2nd Battalion) (Bengal Infantry)
108th Foot	The Royal Inniskilling Fusiliers (2nd Battalion) (Madras Infantry)
109th Foot	The Prince of Wales's Leinster Regiment (Royal Canadians) (2nd Battalion) (Bombay Infantry) (disbanded 1922)
—	1st, 2nd, 3rd and 4th Battalion The Rifle Brigade (The Prince Consort's Own)

Appendix B

Regiments and Corps of the British army in 1979 and Their Chief Forbears[1]

For reasons of space regiments' main titles only are given, e.g. The 9th Queen's Royal Lancers are shown as 9th Lancers, The Middlesex Regiment (Duke of Cambridge's Own) as Middlesex Regt. The dates in brackets are those of regiments' formation, amalgamation or major change of title.

HOUSEHOLD CAVALRY
Each one regiment plus one mounted regiment of two squadrons.

Life Guards (1922) .... {
1st Life Guards (1788) .... {
1st Troop, Horse Guards (1660)
1st Troop Horse Grenadier Guards (1678)
2nd Life Guards (1788) .... {
2nd (3rd) Troop, Horse Guards (1660)
2nd (3rd) Troop, Horse Grenadier Guards (1702)

Blues and Royals (1969) .... {
Royal Horse Guards (Blue) (1750) .... Royal Regiment of Horse (1661)
Tangier Horse (1661)
1st Royal Dragoons (1751) .... Royal Regt of Dragoons (1683)

ROYAL ARMOURED CORPS
All one regiment unless otherwise stated.

Queen's Dragoon Guards (1959) .... {
1st King's Dragoon Guards (1746) .... 2nd Horse (1685)
Queen's Bays (2nd Dragoon Guards) (1746) .... 3rd Horse (1685)

Royal Scots Dragoon Guards (1971) .... {
3rd Carabiniers (DG) (1922) .... {
3rd Dragoon Guards (1746) .... 4th Horse (1685)
6th Dragoon Guards (Carabiniers) (1788) .... 9th Horse (1685)
Royal Scots Greys (2nd Dragoons) (1877) .... Royal North British Dragoons (1707) .... Royal Scots Dragoons (1678)

4th/7th Dragoon Guards (1922) .... {
4th Dragoon Guards (1788) .... 1st Irish Horse (1746) .... 6th (5th) Horse (1685)
7th Dragoon Guards (1788) .... 4th Irish Horse (1747) .... 10th (8th) Horse (1688)

5th R. Inniskilling Dragoon Guards (1922) .... {
5th Dragoon Guards (1788) .... 2nd Irish Horse (1747) .... 7th (6th) Horse (1685)
6th Inniskilling Dragoons (1751) .... Inniskilling Dragoons (1689)

[1] From Barthorp, *The Armies of Britain 1485-1980* (see Bibliography).

Current regiment	Antecedents	Earliest antecedents
Queen's Own Hussars (1959)	3rd Hussars (1861) (Light Dragoons 1818)	3rd Dragoons (1685)
	7th Hussars (1807) (Light Dragoons 1784)	7th Dragoons (1690)
Queen's Royal Irish Hussars (1958)	4th Hussars (1861) (Light Dragoons 1818)	4th Dragoons (1685)
	8th Hussars (1822) (Light Dragoons 1775)	8th Dragoons (1693)
9th/12th Lancers (1960)	9th Lancers (1816) (Light Dragoons 1783)	9th Dragoons (1715)
	12th Lancers (1816) (Light Dragoons 1768)	12th Dragoons (1715)
Royal Hussars (1969)	10th Hussars (1806) (Light Dragoons 1783)	10th Dragoons (1715)
	11th Hussars (1840) (Light Dragoons 1783)	11th Dragoons (1715)
13th/18th Hussars (1922)	13th Hussars (1861) (Light Dragoons 1783)	13th Dragoons (1715)
	18th Hussars (1858)	
14th/20th Hussars (1922)	14th Hussars (1861) (Light Dragoons 1776)	14th Dragoons (1715) ... HEIC 2nd Bengal European Light Cavalry (1858)
	20th Hussars (1861)	
15th/19th Hussars (1922)	15th Hussars (1807)	15th Light Dragoons (1759) ... HEIC 1st Bengal European Light Cavalry (1858)
	19th Hussars (1861)	
16th/5th Lancers (1922)	16th Lancers (1816)	16th Light Dragoons (1759)
	5th Lancers (1861) ... 5th Dragoons (1751–99)	Royal Irish Dragoons (1689)
17th/21st Lancers (1922)	17th Lancers (1822) ... 17th Light Dragoons (1763)	18th Light Dragoons (1759)
	21st Lancers (1897) ... 21st Hussars (1861)	HEIC 3rd Bengal European Light Cavalry (1858)
Royal Tank Regiment (1939) (Four regts.)	Royal Tank Corps (1917)	Heavy Section, Machine-Gun Corps (1916)
Royal Yeomanry (TA) (1965)	Royal Wiltshire Yeomanry (1794)	
	Sherwood Rangers (1794)	
	Kent & County of London Yeomanry (1961)	Royal East Kent Yeomanry (1830)
		West Kent Yeomanry (1831)
		3rd County of London Yeo. (1902)
		4th County of London Yeo. (1939)
	North Irish Horse (1902)	
	Berkshire & Westminster Dragoons (1961)	Berkshire Yeomanry (1831)
		Westminster Dragoons (1901)
Queen's Own Yeomanry (TA) (1971)	Queen's Own Yorkshire Yeomanry (1956)	Yorkshire Hussars (1794)
		Yorkshire Dragoons (1803)
		East Riding Yeo. (1903)
	Ayrshire Yeomanry (1803)	
	Cheshire Yeomanry (1794)	
	Northumberland Hussars (1819)	

Wessex Yeomanry (TA) (1971) ....
{ Royal Wiltshire Yeomanry (1794)
Royal Gloucestershire Hussars (1830)
Royal Devon Yeomanry/1st Rifle Volunteers (T)
{ Royal 1st Devon Yeo. (1831)
Royal North Devon Yeo. (1831) .... 1st Devon Rifle Volunteers (1852)
4th Devons (TA) (1881)

Queen's Own Mercian Yeomanry (TA) (1971) ....
{ Warwick & Worcester Yeomanry (1956) .... { Warwickshire Yeomanry (1794)
Worcestershire Hussars (1831)
Staffordshire Yeomanry (1794)
Shropshire Yeomanry (1795)

Duke of Lancaster's Yeomanry (TA) (1971) .... { Duke of Lancaster's Yeomanry (1819)
40th/41st Royal Tank Regiment (1956)

ROYAL REGIMENT OF ARTILLERY
Regiments: 21 Regular, 6 TA. Batteries: 4 Regular, 3 TA.

Royal Horse Artillery (1862) .... { Royal Horse Artillery (1793)
HEIC Bengal, Madras, Bombay Horse Artillery (1800)

Royal Artillery (1862) .... { Royal Artillery (1801) .... { Royal Artillery (1716)
Royal Irish Artillery (1756)
HEIC Bengal, Madras and Bombay Foot Artillery (1748)

Honourable Artillery Company (TA) (1668) .... Guild of St George (1537)

CORPS OF ROYAL ENGINEERS

Royal Engineers (1862) .... { Royal Engineers (1855) .... { Royal Engineers (Officers) (1787) .... Engineer Officers (1757)
Royal Sappers & Miners (1813) .... Royal Military Artificers (1772)
HEIC Bengal, Madras and Bombay Engineers (1764)

Royal Monmouthshire Royal Engineers (TA) (1872) .... Monmouthshire Trained Bands (1577)

ROYAL CORPS OF SIGNALS

Royal Corps of Signals (1920) .... Corps of Royal Engineers (see above)

INFANTRY
All regiments one battalion except where stated.

Guards Division
Grenadier Guards (1815) (2 Regular battalions) .... 1st Foot Guards (1685) .... King's Royal Regiment of Guards (1660)

Coldstream Guards (1670) (2 Regular battalions) .... Lord General's Foot Guards (1660) .... Colonel Monck's Regiment (1650)

Scots Guards (1877) (2 Regular battalions) .... Scots Fusilier Guards (1831) .... 3rd Foot Guards (1713) .... Scots Regiment of Guards (1660)

Irish Guards (1900)

Welsh Guards (1915)

Scottish Division
Royal Scots (1881) .... 1st Foot (1633)

Royal Highland Fusiliers (1959) .... { Royal Scots Fusiliers (1881) — 21st Foot (1678) / Highland Light Infantry (1881) — 71st Foot (1777) / 74th Foot (1787)

King's Own Scottish Borderers (1881) .... 25th Foot (1689)

Black Watch (1881) .... { 42nd Foot (1739) / 73rd Foot (1786)

Queen's Own Highlanders (1961) .... { Seaforth Highlanders (1881) — 72nd Foot (1778) / 78th Foot (1793) / Cameron Highlanders (1881) — 79th Foot (1793)

Gordon Highlanders (1881) .... 75th Foot (1787) / 92nd Foot (1794)

Argyll & Sutherland Highlanders (1881) .... 91st Foot (1793) / 93rd Foot (1800)

51st Highland Volunteers (1967) (3 TA battalions) .... Territorial (1908) and Volunteer (1881) battalions of Highland regiments

52nd Lowland Volunteers (1967 & 1971) (2 TA battalions) .... Territorial (1908) and Volunteer (1881) battalions of Lowland regiments

302

Queen's Division

Queen's Regiment (1966) (3 Regular, 2 TA battalions)

- Queen's Royal Surrey Regt. (1959)
  - Queen's Royal Regt. (1881) — 2nd Foot (1661); 31st Foot (1713); 70th Foot (1758)
  - East Surrey Regt. (1881)
- Queen's Own Buffs (1961)
  - Buffs (1881) — 3rd Foot (1572); 50th Foot (1755); 97th Foot (1824); 35th Foot (1702)
  - Royal West Kent Regt. (1881) — 107th Foot (1862) ... HEIC 3rd Bengal Europeans (1854); 57th Foot (1755); 77th Foot (1787)
- Royal Sussex Regt. (1881) — 5th Foot (1674); 6th Foot (1673); 7th Foot (1685); 20th Foot (1688)
- Middlesex Regt. (1881)

Royal Regiment of Fusiliers (1968) (3 Regular, 2 TA battalions)

- Royal Northumberland Fusiliers (1881)
- Royal Warwickshire Fusiliers (1963) (Regiment 1881)
- Royal Fusiliers (1881)
- Lancashire Fusiliers (1881)

Royal Anglian Regiment (1964) (3 Regular, 3 TA battalions)

- 1st East Anglian Regt. (1959)
  - Royal Norfolk Regt. (1881) — 9th Foot (1685); 12th Foot (1685)
  - Suffolk Regt. (1881)
  - Royal Lincolnshire Regt. (1881) — 10th Foot (1685); 48th Foot (1741); 58th Foot (1755)
- 2nd East Anglian Regt. (1960)
  - Northamptonshire Regt. (1881) — 16th Foot (1688); 44th Foot (1741); 56th Foot (1755)
  - Bedfordshire & Hertfordshire Regt. (1881)
- 3rd East Anglian Regt. (1958)
  - Essex Regt. (1881) — 17th Foot (1688)
- Royal Leicestershire Regt. (1881)

King's Division

King's Own Royal Border Regt. (1959) (1 Regular, 1 TA battalions)

- King's Own Royal Regt. (1881) — 4th Foot (1680); 34th Foot (1702); 55th Foot (1755)
- Border Regt. (1881)

King's Regiment (1958) (1 Regular, 1 TA bn)

- King's Liverpool Regt. (1881) — 8th Foot (1685); 63rd Foot (1756); 96th Foot (1824)
- Manchester Regt. (1881)

Prince of Wales's Own Regt. of Yorkshire (1958)

- West Yorkshire Regt. (1881) — 14th Foot (1685)
- East Yorkshire Regt. (1881) — 15th Foot (1685)

Green Howards (1881) — 19th Foot (1688)

Royal Irish Rangers (1968) (2 Regular, 2 TA bns)

- Royal Inniskilling Fusiliers (1881) — 27th Foot (1689); 108th Foot (1862) ... HEIC 3rd Madras Europeans (1854)
- Royal Ulster Rifles (1922) — Royal Irish Rifles (1881); 83rd Foot (1793); 86th Foot (1793)
- Royal Irish Fusiliers (1881) — 87th Foot (1793); 89th Foot (1793)

Queen's Lancashire Regt. (1970)
(1 Regular, 1 TA btn)
 ├ Lancashire Regt. (1958)
 │   ├ East Lancashire Regt (1881) ⎰ 30th Foot (1714), 59th Foot (1755)
 │   └ South Lancashire Regt (1881) ⎱ 40th Foot (1717), 82nd Foot (1741)
 └ Loyal North Lancashire Regt. (1881) ⎰ 47th Foot (1741), 81st Foot (1793)

Duke of Wellington's Regiment (1881) { 33rd Foot (1702), 76th Foot (1787) }

Yorkshire Volunteers (1967) (3 TA bns) — Territorial (1908) and Volunteer (1881) battalions of West and East Yorkshire Regts, Green Howards, Duke of Wellington's

Prince of Wales's Division

Devon & Dorset Regt. (1958)
 ├ Devonshire Regt. (1881) ... 11th Foot (1685)
 └ Dorset Regt. (1881) ... 39th Foot (1702), 54th Foot (1755)

Cheshire Regt. (1881) ... 22nd Foot (1689)

Royal Welch Fusiliers (1881) (1 Regular, 1 TA bn) ... 23rd Foot (1688)

Royal Regiment of Wales (1969)
(1 Regular, 2 TA bns)
 ├ South Wales Borderers (1881) ... 24th Foot (1689)
 └ Welch Regiment (1881) ... 41st Foot (1719), 69th Foot (1756)

Gloucestershire Regt. (1881) ... { 28th Foot (1694), 61st Foot (1756) }

Worcestershire & Sherwood Foresters Regt. (1970)
(1 Regular, 1 TAVR, bn)
 ├ Worcestershire Regt. (1881) ... 29th Foot (1694), 36th Foot (1702)
 └ Sherwood Foresters (1881) ... 45th Foot (1741), 95th Foot (1823)

Royal Hampshire Regiment (1881) { 37th Foot (1702), 67th Foot (1758) }

Staffordshire Regt. (1959)
 ├ South Staffordshire Regt. (1881) ... 38th Foot (1705), 80th Foot (1793)
 └ North Staffordshire Regt. (1881) ... 64th Foot (1756), 98th Foot (1824)

Duke of Edinburgh's Royal Regt. (1959)
 ├ Royal Berkshire Regt. (1881) ... 49th Foot (1743), 66th Foot (1746)
 └ Wiltshire Regt. (1881) ... 62nd Foot (1755), 99th Foot (1824)

Wessex Regiment (1967) (2 TA bns) .... Territorial (1908) and Volunteer (1881) battalions of Devons, Dorsets, Gloucesters, Royal Hampshires, Royal Berkshires, Wiltshires

Mercian Volunteers (1967) (2 TA bns) .... Territorial (1908) and Volunteer (1881) battalions of Cheshires, South and North Staffords

Light Division

Somerset & Cornwall Light Infantry (1959) .... { Somerset Light Infantry (1881) .... 13th Foot (1685)
Duke of Cornwall's Light Infantry (1881) ... { 32nd Foot (1702) / 46th Foot (1741) / 51st Foot (1754)

Light Infantry (1968) (3 Regular, 3 TA bns) ....
King's Own Yorkshire Light Infantry (1881) .... {105th Foot (1861) .... HEIC 2nd Madras Europeans (1839) / 53rd Foot (1755) / 85th Foot (1793)
King's Shropshire Light Infantry (1881) .... 68th Foot (1756)
Durham Light Infantry (1881) .... 106th Foot (1861) .... HEIC 2nd Bombay Europeans (1826)

1st Green Jackets (43rd & 52nd) (1958) ...... Oxfordshire & Buckinghamshire Light Infantry (1881) ..... { 43rd Foot (1741) / 52nd Foot (1755)
Royal Green Jackets (1966) (3 Regular, 1 TA bns) ...... 2nd Green Jackets (KRRC) (1958) .... King's Royal Rifle Corps (1881) .... 60th Foot (1756)
3rd Green Jackets (RB) (1958) .... Rifle Brigade (1816) .... 95th Rifles (1800)

AIRBORNE FORCES
Parachute Regiment (1942) (3 Regular, 3 TA bns)

Special Air Service Regiment (1941) (1 Regular, 2 TA regts.)

Army Air Corps (1942) (Reconstituted 1957)

BRIGADE OF GURKHAS
2nd Gurkha Rifles (1906) (2 Regular bns) .... 2nd Gurkha Regt. (1861) .... HEIC Sirmoor Battalion (1815)

6th Gurkha Rifles (1903) .... 42nd Bengal Native Infantry (1861) .... HEIC Cuttack Legion (1817)

7th Gurkha Rifles (1907) .... 2/10th Gurkha Rifles (1903) .... 8th Gurkha Rifles (1902)

10th Gurkha Rifles (1901) .... 10th Madras Infantry (1st Burma Gurkha Rifles) (1895) .... 1st Burma Infantry (1891)

Queen's Gurkha Engineers (1960) .... 50th Field Engineer Regt. RE (1951) .... 67th Field Squadron RE (1948)

Queen's Gurkha Signals (1954) .... Gurkha Brigade Signal Squadron (1948)

Gurkha Transport Regiment (1965) .... Gurkha Army Service Corps (1958)

Ulster Defence Regiment (1970) (11 battalions)

DISBANDED INFANTRY REGIMENTS
In 1922 (each 2 Regular bns)

Royal Irish Regiment (1881) .... 18th Foot (1689)

Connaught Rangers (1881) .... { 88th Foot (1793) / 94th Foot (1823)

Leinster Regiment (1881) .... 109th Foot (1862) .... HEIC 3rd Bombay Europeans (1853) / 100th Foot (1858)

Royal Munster Fusiliers (1881) .... 101st Foot (1861) / 104th Foot (1861) .... { HEIC 1st Bengal Europeans (1756) / HEIC 2nd Bengal Europeans (1839)

Royal Dublin Fusiliers (1881) .... 102nd Foot (1861) / 103rd Foot (1861) .... { HEIC 1st Madras Europeans (1748) / HEIC 1st Bombay Europeans (1661)

In 1968 (each 1 Regular bn)

Cameronians (Scottish Rifles) (1881) .... { 26th Foot (1689) / 90th Foot (1794)

York & Lancaster Regiment (1881) .... { 65th Foot (1758) / 84th Foot (1793)

SERVICES

Royal Army Chaplains Department (1858) .... Army Chaplains (1796) .... Regimental Chaplains (1662)

Royal Corps of Transport (1935) .... Royal Army Service Corps (1888) .... Military Train (1857–69) / Land Transport Corps (1855–56) .... Royal Waggon Train (1802–23) .... Royal Waggon Corps (1799)

Royal Army Medical Corps (1898) .... { Army Medical Staff (Officers) (1873) / Medical Staff Corps (1884) } .... Army Hospital Corps (1856) .... Regimental Surgeons (18th Cent.–1872) / Medical Staff Corps (1855)

Royal Army Ordnance Corps (1922) .... { Army Ordnance Department (1894) / Army Ordnance Corps (1896) } .... { Ordnance Store Branch (1877) / Ordnance Store Corps (1881) } .... Board of Ordnance (1418)

Royal Electrical & Mechanical Engineers (1942) ....

Royal Military Police (1926) .... { Military Mounted Police (1877)
Military Foot Police (1885)

Royal Army Pay Corps (1893) .... Army Pay Department (Officers) (1878) .... Regimental Paymasters .... Army Agents (17th Cent.)

Royal Army Veterinary Corps (1903) .... Army Veterinary Department (Officers) (1881) .... Regimental Veterinary Surgeons (1796)

Royal Military Academy Band Corps

Small Arms School Corps (1929) .... { Small Arms School (1919) .... School of Musketry (1902) ...... Royal Corps of Musketry Instructors (1853)
Machine-Gun School

Military Provost Staff Corps (1906) .... Military Prison Staff Corps (1901)

Royal Army Education Corps (1920) .... Corps of Army Schoolmasters (1846) .... Regimental Schools (1812)

Royal Army Dental Corps (1921) .... Royal Army Medical Corps

Royal Pioneer Corps (1940) .... Auxiliary Military Pioneer Corps (1939)

Intelligence Corps (1940)

Army Physical Training Corps (1940)

Army Catering Corps (1941)

Army Legal Corps (1978) .... Army Legal Services Staff List (1948)

General Service Corps (1942) (in abeyance)

Queen Alexandra's Royal Army Nursing Corps (1949) .... Queen Alexandra's Imperial Military Nursing Service (1902) .... Army Nursing Service (1881)

Women's Royal Army Corps (1949) .... Auxiliary Territorial Service (1938) .... Women's Auxiliary Army Corps (1917-18)

Royal Engineers
Royal Army Service Corps
Royal Army Ordnance Corps

Bibliography

General

Barnett, Correlli, *Britain and Her Army 1509–1970*, Allen Lane, London, 1970.

Barthorp, Michael, *The Armies of Britain 1485–1980*, National Army Museum, London, 1981.

Clode, S, *The Military Forces of the Crown*, 2 Vols., Murray, London, 1869.

Cole, D.H. and Priestley, E.C., *An Outline of British Military History*, Sifton Praed, London, 1936.

Fisher, H.A.L., *A History of Europe*, Eyre and Spottiswoode, London, 1935.

Fortescue, Hon. J.W., *A History of the British Army*, 13 Vols., Macmillan, London, 1879–1930.

Haswell, Jock, *The British Army*, Thames and Hudson, London, 1975.

King, C. Cooper, *The Story of the British Army*, Methuen, London, 1897.

Macaulay, Lord, *History of England*, Penguin, London, 1979.

Montgomery of Alamein, Viscount, *A History of Warfare*, Collins, London, 1968.

Myatt, Frederick, *The Soldier's Trade*, Macdonald and Janes, London, 1974.

Roe, F.P., *The Soldier and the Empire*, Gale and Polden, Aldershot, 1932.

Sheppard, E.W., *A Short History of the British Army to 1914*, Constable, London, 1926.

Wood, Sir Evelyn, *Our Fighting Services*, Cassell, London, 1916.

Young, Peter, *The British Army*, Kimber, London, 1967.

The Age of Cromwell

Childs, J., *The Army of Charles II*, Routledge and Kegan Paul, London, 1976.

Clark, Sir George, *The Later Stuarts*, Oxford University Press, Oxford, 1934.

Davies, J.D.G., *Honest George Monck*, Lane–Bodley Head, London, 1936.

Firth, Sir Charles, *Cromwell's Army*, Methuen, London, 1902.

Fraser, Antonia, *Cromwell, Our Chief of Men*, Weidenfeld and Nicolson, London, 1973.

Gillingham, John, *Cromwell*, Weidenfeld and Nicolson, London, 1976.

Woolrych, Austin, *Battles of the English Civil War*, Batsford, London, 1961.

Young, P. and Burne A.H., *The Great Civil War*, Eyre and Spottiswoode, London, 1959.

The Age of Marlborough

Atkinson, C.T., *Marlborough and the Rise of the British Army*, Putnam, London, 1921.

Barnett, Correlli, *Marlborough*, Eyre Methuen, London, 1974.

Rogers, H.C.B., *The British Army of the 18th Century*, Allen and Unwin, London, 1977.

Scouller, R.E., *The Armies of Queen Anne*, Oxford University Press, Oxford, 1966.

Williams, Basil, *The Whig Supremacy*, Oxford University Press, Oxford, 1962.

The Age of Wellington

Aldington, Richard, *Wellington*, Heinemann, London, 1946.

Davies, Geoffrey, *Wellington and His Army*, Oxford University Press, Oxford, 1964.

Fortescue, Sir John, *Wellington*, Williams and Norgate, London, 1925.

Glover, Michael, *Wellington as Military Commander*, Batsford, London, 1968.

Glover, Michael, *Wellington's Army*, David and Charles, London, 1977.

Glover, Richard, *Peninsular Preparation*, Cambridge University Press, Cambridge, 1963.

Guedalla, Philip, *The Duke*, Hodder and Stoughton, London, 1931.

Longford, Elizabeth, *Wellington – The Years of the Sword*, Weidenfeld and Nicolson, London, 1969.

Naylor, John, *Waterloo*, Batsford, London, 1960.

Oman, Carola, *Sir John Moore*, Hodder and Stoughton, London, 1953.

Oman, Sir Charles, *Studies in the Napoleonic Wars*, Methuen, London, 1929.

Oman, Sir Charles, *Wellington's Army*, Edward Arnold, London, 1912.

Ward, S.P.G., *Wellington*, Batsford, London, 1963.

Watson, J. Steven, *The Reign of George III*, Oxford University Press, Oxford, 1960.

The Age of Wolseley and Roberts

Barclay, Glen St J., *The Empire Is Marching*, Weidenfeld and Nicolson, London, 1976.

Fredericks, P.G., *The Sepoy and the Cossack*, Allen, London, 1972.

Harries-Jenkins, Gwyn, *The Army in Victorian Society*, Routledge and Kegan Paul, London, 1977.

James, David, *Lord Roberts*, Hollis and Carter, London, 1954.

Lehmann, Joseph, *All Sir Garnet*, Cape, London, 1964.

Pakenham, Thomas, *The Boer War*, Weidenfeld and Nicolson, London, 1979.

Skelley, A.R., *The Victorian Army at Home*, Croom Helm, London, 1977.

Vulliamy, C.E., *Crimea*, Jonathan Cape, London, 1939.

Woodham-Smith, Cecil, *The Reason Why*, Constable, London, 1953.

Woodward, Sir Llewellyn, *The Age of Reform*, Oxford University Press, Oxford, 1962.

The Age of Haig

Official Histories of the Great War, HMSO, London, various dates.
Cooper, Duff, *Haig*, Faber, London, 1936.
Ensor, R.C.K., *England 1870–1914*, Oxford University Press, Oxford, 1936.
Ferro, Marc, *The Great War 1914–1918*, Routledge and Kegan Paul, London, 1973.
Marshall-Cornwall, James, *Haig as Military Commander*, Batsford, London, 1973.
Robertson, Sir W., *From Private to Field Marshal*, Constable, London, 1921.
Taylor, A.J.P., *English History 1914–1945*, Oxford University Press, Oxford, 1965.
Taylor, A.J.P., *The Struggle for Mastery in Europe*, Oxford University Press, Oxford, 1954.
Terraine, John, *Douglas Haig*, Hutchinson, London, 1963.
Woodward, Sir Llewellyn, *Great Britain and the War of 1914–18*, Methuen, London, 1967.

The Age of Montgomery

Official Histories of the Second World War, HMSO, London, various dates.
Agar-Hamilton, J.A.I. and Turner, L.C.F., *Crisis in the Desert*, Oxford University Press, Oxford, 1952.
Belchem, David, *Victory in Normandy*, Chatto and Windus, London, 1981.
Belfield, Eversley and Essame, H., *The Battle for Normandy*, Batsford, London, 1965.
Bond, Brian, *British Military Policy Between the Two World Wars*, Clarendon, Oxford, 1980.
Carver, Michael, *El Alamein*, Batsford, London, 1962.
Carver, Michael, *The Apostles of Mobility*, Weidenfeld and Nicolson, London, 1979.
Carver, Michael, *Tobruk*, Batsford, London, 1964.
Central Office of Information, *The Campaign in Burma*, H.M.S.O. London, 1946.
Connell, John, *Wavell*, Collins, London, 1964.
Eisenhower, Dwight D., *Crusade in Europe*, Heinemann, London, 1948.
Essame, H., *The Battle for Germany*, Batsford, London, 1969.
Fraser, David, *Alanbrooke*, Collins, London, 1982.
Fraser, David, *And We Shall Shock Them*, Hodder and Stoughton, London, 1983.
Grenfell, Russell, *The Men Who Defend Us*, Eyre and Spottiswoode, London, 1938.
de Guingand, F.W., *Operation Victory*, Hodder and Stoughton, London, 1947.
Hamilton, Nigel, *Monty – The Making of a General*, Hamish Hamilton, London, 1981.
Hart, Liddell, *History of the Second World War*, Cassell, London, 1970.

Hart, Liddell (ed.), *The Rommel Papers*, Collins, London, 1953.

Horne, Alistair, *To Lose a Battle*, Macmillan, London, 1964.

Jackson, W.G.F., *The Battle for Italy*, Batsford, London, 1967.

Jackson, W.G.F., *The North African Campaign*, Batsford, London, 1975.

Lewin, Ronald, *The Chief*, Hutchinson, London, 1980.

Lewin, Ronald, *Slim*, Cooper, London, 1976.

Montgomery of Alamein, Viscount, *Memoirs*, Collins, London, 1958.

Moulton, J.L., *The Norwegian Campaign of 1940*, Eyre and Spottiswoode, London, 1966.

Wigmore, Lionel, *The Japanese Thrust*, Australian War Memorial, Canberra, 1957.

The Age of Templer

Statements on Defence and Army Estimates, Command Papers, H.M.S.O., London, various dates.

Blaxland, Gregory, *The Regiments Depart*, Kimber, London, 1971.

Byford-Jones, W., *Grivas and the story of EOKA*, Hale, London, 1959.

Carver, Michael, *Harding of Petherton*, Weidenfeld and Nicolson, London, 1978.

Carver, Michael, *War Since 1945*, Weidenfeld and Nicolson, London, 1980.

Clutterbuck, Richard, *The Long, Long War*, Cassel, London, 1960.

Darby, Phillip, *British Defence Policy East of Suez 1947-68*, Oxford University Press, London, 1973.

James, Harold and Sheil-Small, David, *The Undeclared War: Confrontation with Indonesia*, Cooper, London, 1971.

Leckie, Robert, *The Korean War*, Barrie and Rockliffe, London, 1962.

Majdalany, Fred, *State of Emergency*, Longmans, London, 1962.

O'Ballance, Edgar, *Korea 1950-1953*, Faber, London, 1969.

O'Ballance, Edgar, *Malaya: The Communist Insurrection*, Faber, London, 1966.

Paget, Julian, *Last Post*, Faber, London, 1969.

Short, Anthony, *The Communist Insurrection in Malaya*, Muller, London, 1975.

Thomas, Hugh, *The Suez Affair*, Weidenfeld and Nicolson, London, 1966.

Wilson, R.D., *Cordon and Search*, Gale and Polden, Aldershot, 1949.

INDEX